Artificial Intelligence and Smart Agriculture Applications

An essential resource work for understanding how to design and develop smart applications for present and future problems in the field of agriculture. – Dr. Deepak Gupta, Maharaja Agrasen Institute of Technology, Delhi, India.

As a result of the advances in Artificial Intelligence (AI), many aspects of daily life have been transformed by smart digital technology. Advanced intelligent algorithms can provide powerful solutions to real-world problems. Smart applications have become commonplace. All areas of life are being changed by smart tools developed to deal with complex issues challenging both humanity and the earth.

Artificial Intelligence and Smart Agriculture Applications presents the latest smart agriculture applications developed across the globe. It covers a broad array of solutions using data science and AI to attack problems faced by agriculture worldwide.

Features:

- Application of drones and sensors in advanced farming
- A cloud-computing model for implementing smart agriculture
- Conversational AI for farmer's advisory communications
- Intelligent fuzzy logic to predict global warming's effect on agriculture
- Machine learning algorithms for mapping soil macronutrient elements variability
- A smart IoT framework for soil fertility enhancement
- AI applications in pest management
- A model using Python for predicting rainfall

The book examines not only present solutions but also potential future outcomes. It looks at the role of AI-based algorithms and the almost infinite combinations of variables for agricultural applications. Researchers, public and private sector representatives, agriculture scientists, and students can use this book to develop sustainable solutions for smart agriculture. This book's findings are especially important as the planet is facing unprecedented environmental challenges from over-farming and climate change due to global warming.

Artificial Intelligence and Smart Agriculture Applications

Edited by
Utku Kose, V.B. Surya Prasath,
M. Rubaiyat Hossain Mondal,
Prajoy Podder, and Subrato Bharati

CRC Press
Taylor & Francis Group
Boca Raton London New York

CRC Press is an imprint of the
Taylor & Francis Group, an **informa** business
AN AUERBACH BOOK

First edition published 2023
by CRC Press
6000 Broken Sound Parkway NW, Suite 300, Boca Raton, FL 33487-2742

and by CRC Press
4 Park Square, Milton Park, Abingdon, Oxon, OX14 4RN

CRC Press is an imprint of Taylor & Francis Group, LLC

ISBN: 9781032223575 (hbk)
ISBN: 9781032318653 (pbk)
ISBN: 9781003311782 (ebk)

DOI: 10.1201/9781003311782

Typeset in Adobe Garamond
by KnowledgeWorks Global Ltd.

Contents

Foreword

As a result of innovative movements by the Artificial Intelligence, the field of agriculture has been open for many smart applications enabling the humankind to find effective solutions for the faced problems. As it is too critical to derive careful combinations of Artificial Intelligence techniques, both software and hardware components have been started to be used actively after the start of the 21st century. That is also a cause of the high momentum of hardware resources, which resulted in the speedy advances in software technology. Now, the 2000s is the era of smart technologies, triggering rise of physical technologies in the context of wearables, Internet of Things, and many other alternative technological components of practical life. Among all fields of life, agriculture has a unique role as it touches both human and the earth.

Although it is not a new trend to use technology in agricultural applications, developing smart tools is a very recent research way to find out new solutions or derive improved solutions against the known findings. So, smart applications have been an active scientific focus to combine foundations of both Artificial Intelligence and agricultural research. As the target components are often physical objects in agricultural fields, there has been a great interest to design smart hardware-oriented applications but the background of all applications employs an active use of analytic data processing steps and Artificial Intelligence models to give necessary predictive or descriptive outputs. Use of Artificial Intelligence models often includes Machine/Deep Learning, rule-based inferencing roads, or intelligent optimization functions. Out of all these efforts, the target outcomes have been in the context of sustainable, effective, and efficient agriculture for the well-being of humankind and the earth.

Connected with the mentioned points, this edited book project, *Artificial Intelligence and Smart Agriculture Applications*, provides the most recent research outcomes for meeting with the aims on well-being. I found that book as a comprehensive view for different problem sides of smart applications. In detail, the book combines a total of fifteen chapters with a unique use of control models and Machine/Deep Learning techniques, by also covering important supportive data processing methods such as image processing. Some hot topics like plant diseases, global warming, agricultural monitoring, and sustainability are among target research interests in the related chapters.

I believe that the readers will find that book as an essential resource work for understanding how to design and develop smart applications for present and future problems in the field of agriculture. In order to have an enjoyable mixture of knowledge and practice, I would like to suggest the readers to have a look to another book, *Artificial Intelligence and Smart Agriculture Technology* (CRC Press), by the same editors. While this book considers more about application side with findings and experiences, the technology-focused book gives detailed information about the literature and the background knowledge. The best way to have better advantages of both books may be choosing the starting point: theoretical or practical side. But the most important thing is to gather both sides somehow for a better knowledge-ability status for smart agricultural research.

I would like to send my warm congratulations and thanks to the editors: Dr. Kose, Dr. Prasath, Dr. Mondal, Dr. Podder, and Dr. Bharati for their timely book contribution to the associated literature. While reading more about the theoretical side, it may be often possible to miss to learn about application experiences. So, this book will be a good supportive work for a wide audience, including researchers, experts, professionals, and even degree students. In order to leave a better, green world for the new generations, it is important to use smart technology. So, I invite all readers to spend their time to turn the pages and gain the necessary practical knowledge for smart agriculture applications. For a green future!

Assist. Prof. Dr. Deepak Gupta
Maharaja Agrasen Institute of Technology (MAIT),
Dept. of Computer Science and Engineering,
Delhi, India

Preface

Current technological era has caused the word of 'smart' to be a generic adjective for defining use of Artificial Intelligence algorithms in technological solutions. As a result of the unstoppable wind of the Artificial Intelligence, technological aspects of the daily life were transformed into an innovative version where digital outcomes of different human actions have been started to be used by advanced algorithms, which are capable of giving accurate solutions for real-world problems. So, rise of the smart applications has been a common thing for especially last decade. Eventually, all fields are currently highly enrolled in the use of smart tools for their problems and agriculture takes its place within first priorities, as it affects the way of both earth and humanity.

This edited book employs the latest reports regarding international outcomes of smart agriculture applications. Titled as *Artificial Intelligence and Smart Agriculture Applications*, it provides a mixture of smart applications, considering different aspects of using Data Science and Artificial Intelligence combination for different problems of agriculture. As it is known, current developments in smart technology area require an optimum use of software and hardware components, as the Data Science and the latest formations of Artificial Intelligence and additional technologies (i.e. use of Deep Learning and image processing or running optimum predictive Machine Learning through Internet of Things – IoT – ecosystem) find their best performances in that near relation. So, we have done our best to gather the most competitive research in a total of fifteen chapters. In detail, the first chapter focuses on the future of smart agriculture, by discussing about drone technology. The second chapter provides information about design and development of a greenhouse monitoring solution. Next, the third chapter is based on a critical component: cloud computing to build up smart agriculture applications. The fourth chapter ensures research for the farmers and considers the use of Artificial Intelligence for advisory and communication purposes. The fifth chapter follows a very critical topic: global warming and ensures design of fuzzy controller to predict the effects of global warming. After that, the sixth chapter focuses on using Machine Learning for mapping of the soil macronutrient elements variability. The seventh chapter is based more on IoT use as building a framework for soil fertility enhancement through Deep Learning. The eighth and the ninth chapters give their interest to plants and focus on using Artificial Intelligence for, respectively, disease detection and phenomics in high-throughput stress phenotyping. The tenth chapter focuses on the plant disease detection again but provides information regarding the use of hybrid Artificial Intelligence model this time. The eleventh chapter calls for the use of image processing and Artificial Intelligence synergy for coffee leaf disease detection. The twelfth chapter informs the readers about Artificial Intelligence-based modeling of oil extraction yields from seeds and nuts. Next, the thirteenth chapter provides information about using Artificial Intelligence for pest management. Finally, the last two chapters consider the use of different models for rainfall clustering and predictions.

As it can be seen from the chapters, the book gives a look at not only present outcomes but also future states with an intense role of Artificial Intelligence algorithms taking place in almost infinite combinations of variables in agricultural applications. We believe that all findings from the chapters will encourage researchers, public and private sector representatives, farmers, and even degree students who are all taking important roles in sustainable, efficient technological agricultural applications. Especially in the last five years, the earth has faced many environmental side-effects due to false use of agricultural fields; unresponsible use of technology (causing climate change/global warming), and a lack of practical, up-to-date information in the literature. We believe that it is urgent to act responsibly for a sustainable future with better agricultural applications for all living organisms around the world. So, we hope that the book will be a timely contribution for the associated literature.

We would like to thank all authors for their valuable contributions. Also, special thanks go to the CRC Press team for all their efforts, and dear Dr. Deepak Gupta for his kind, valuable foreword. As the editors, we always want to hear from readers around to world. All contributive ideas, suggestions for new editions, and book projects are welcome. Enjoy the stay in next pages!

Acknowledgments

The editors would like to express their gratitude and congratulations to everyone who contributed in the publishing of this book. We would also like to convey our deepest appreciation to each chapter contributor for their efforts, which made this book possible. Our deepest appreciation and gratitude also go to the subject matter experts who took the time to review the chapters and ensured their timely delivery, so enhancing the book's quality, prominence, and consistency of organization. Additionally, we would like to express our gratitude to the CRC Press Publication team for their constant support and help with the publication of this edited book. Finally, we would like to thank the Institute of Information and Communication Technology (IICT) of Bangladesh University of Engineering and Technology (BUET) for providing a computing facility and other technical assistance to three of the editors of this book.

Editors

Utku Kose received BS degree in 2008 in Computer Education from Gazi University, Turkey as a faculty valedictorian. He received the MS degree in 2010 in the field of Computer from Afyon Kocatepe University, Turkey and the DS/PhD degree in 2017 in the field of Computer Engineering from Selcuk University, Turkey. Between 2009 and 2011, he had worked as a research assistant in Afyon Kocatepe University. Following this, he had also worked as a lecturer and vocational school – vice director in Afyon Kocatepe University between 2011 and 2012, as a lecturer and Research Center director in Usak University between 2012 and 2017, and as an assistant professor in Suleyman Demirel University between 2017 and 2019. Currently, he is an associate professor in Suleyman Demirel University, Turkey. He has more than 100 publications, including articles, authored and edited books, proceedings, and reports. He is also in editorial boards of many scientific journals and serves as one of the editors of the Biomedical and Robotics Healthcare book series by CRC Press. His research interests include artificial intelligence, machine ethics, artificial intelligence safety, optimization, the chaos theory, distance education, e-learning, computer education, and computer science.

V.B. Surya Prasath graduated from the Indian Institute of Technology Madras, India in 2009 with a PhD in Mathematics. He is currently an assistant professor in the Division of Biomedical Informatics at the Cincinnati Children's Hospital Medical Center, and at the Departments of Biomedical Informatics, Electrical Engineering and Computer Science, University of Cincinnati since 2018. He has been a postdoctoral fellow at the Department of Mathematics, University of Coimbra, Portugal, for two years from 2010 to 2011. From 2012 to 2015, he was with the Computational Imaging and VisAnalysis (CIVA) Lab at the University of Missouri, USA as a postdoctoral fellow, and from 2016 to 2017 as an assistant research professor. He had summer fellowships/visits at Kitware Inc. NY, USA, The Fields Institute, Canada, and IPAM, University of California Los Angeles (UCLA), USA. His main research interests include nonlinear PDEs, regularization methods, inverse and ill-posed problems, variational, PDE-based image processing, and computer vision with applications in remote sensing and biomedical imaging domains. His current research focuses are in data science and bioimage informatics with machine learning techniques.

 **M. Rubaiyat Hossain Mondal** received BSc and MSc degrees in electrical and electronic engineering from Bangladesh University of Engineering and Technology (BUET), Dhaka, Bangladesh. He obtained the PhD degree in 2014 from the Department of Electrical and Computer Systems Engineering, Monash University, Melbourne, Australia. From 2005 to 2010, and from 2014 to date, he has been working as a faculty member at the Institute of Information and Communication Technology (IICT) in BUET, Bangladesh. He has published a number of papers in journals of IEEE, IET, Elsevier, Springer, Wiley, De Gruyter, PLOS, MDPI, etc. He has also published several conference papers and book chapters, and edited a book published by De Gruyter in 2021. He has so far successfully supervised 10 students to complete Master's Thesis in the field of Information and Communication Technology at BUET, Bangladesh. His research interests include artificial intelligence, image processing, bioinformatics, wireless communications, and cryptography.

 **Prajoy Podder** is currently a researcher at the Institute of Information and Communication Technology, Bangladesh University of Engineering and Technology. He worked as a lecturer in the Department of Electrical and Electronic Engineering, Ranada Prasad Shaha University, Narayanganj, Bangladesh. He received a BSc (Engg.) degree in Electronics and Communication Engineering from Khulna University of Engineering and Technology, Khulna, Bangladesh in 2014. He has also recently completed a MSc program in Information and Communication Technology from Bangladesh University of Engineering and Technology, Dhaka, Bangladesh. He authored/co-authored over 45 Journal articles, conference proceedings, and book chapters published by IEEE, Elsevier, Springer, Wiley, De Gruyter, and others. His research interests include wireless sensor networks, digital image processing, data mining, smart-cities, Internet of Things, machine learning, big data, digital signal processing, wireless communication, and VLSI.

 **Subrato Bharati** received his BS degree in Electrical and Electronic Engineering from Ranada Prasad Shaha University, Narayanganj 1400, Bangladesh. He is currently working as a researcher in the Institute of Information and Communication Technology, Bangladesh University of Engineering and Technology, Dhaka, Bangladesh. He is a regular reviewer for a number of reputed international journals, including Elsevier, Springer, and Wiley. He is an associate editor of *Journal of the International Academy for Case Studies* and a guest editor of a special issue in *Journal of Internet Technology* (SCI Index Journal). He is a member of scientific and technical program committee in some conferences such as CECNet 2021, ICONCS, ICCRDA-2020, ICICCR 2021, and CECIT 2021. His research interests include bioinformatics, medical image processing, pattern recognition, deep learning, wireless communications, data analytics, machine learning, neural networks, and feature selection. He has published a number of papers in journals of Elsevier, Springer, PLOS, IOS Press, etc., and also published several conference papers for reputed publishers such as IEEE and Springer. He published book chapters in Springer, Elsevier, De Gruyter, CRC Press, and Wiley.

Contributors

Chinedu M. Agu
Chemical Engineering
  Department
Michael Okpara University
  of Agriculture
Umudike, Nigeria

Albert C. Agulanna
Materials and Energy Technology
  Department
Projects Development Institute
  (PRODA)
Enugu, Nigeria

Raina Bajpai
Department of Mycology and Plant
  Pathology
Institute of Agricultural
  Sciences
Banaras Hindu University
Varanasi, India

Sudeepa Keregadde Balakrishna
NMAM Institute of Technology
Karnataka, India

Levent Başayiğit
Department of Soil Science and Plant
  Nutrition
Isparta University of Applied
  Sciences
Isparta, Türkiye

Maria Bibi
Department of Computer Science
Government College University Faisalabad
Faisalabad, Pakistan

H. Chekenbah
Laboratory of Sciences and Advanced
  Technologies FPL
Abdelmalek Essaadi University
Larache, Morocco

Annadurai Chinnamuthu
Department of ECE
Sri Sivasubramaniya Nadar College
  of Engineering
Kalavakkam, Chennai, Tamil Nadu, India

Kumar Chiranjeeb
Department of Soil Science, SoAg
GIET University
Gunupur, India

S. El Fatehi
Laboratory of Applied Botany
Department of Life Sciences, FPL
Abdelmalek Essaadi University
Larache, Morocco

Imane El Hassani
Laboratory of Applied Botany
Department of Life Sciences, FPL
Abdelmalek Essaadi University
Larache, Morocco

Ömer Can Eskicioglu
Department of Computer
 Engineering
Burdur Mehmet Akif Ersoy
 University
Burdur, Türkiye

Den Whilrex Garcia
Department of Engineering
Lyceum of the Philippines University –
 Cavite Campus
Cavite, Philippines

Muhammad Kashif Hanif
Department of Computer Science
Government College University
 Faisalabad
Faisalabad, Pakistan

Y. Hmimsa
Laboratory of Applied Botany
Department of Life Sciences, FPL
Abdelmalek Essaadi University
Larache, Morocco

Nelson Iruthayanathan
Department of ECE
Sri Sivasubramaniya Nadar
 College of Engineering
Kalavakkam, Chennai,
 Tamil Nadu, India

Ali Hakan Işik
Department of Computer
 Engineering
Burdur Mehmet Akif Ersoy
 University
Burdur, Türkiye

Nirmala Devi Kathamuthu
Department of CSE
Kongu Engineering College
Perundurai, Erode, Tamil Nadu, India

Fuat Kaya
Department of Soil Science and Plant
 Nutrition
Isparta University of Applied
 Sciences
Isparta, Türkiye

M. L. Kerkeb
Research Group, Information Systems
 Engineering
Abdelmalek Essaâdi
 University
Tétouan, Morocco

Shouket Zaman Khan
Department of Entomology
University of Agriculture
 Faisalabad Sub-Campus
 Burewala-Vehari
Burewala-Vehari, Pakistan

Ambeshwar Kumar
School of Computing
SASTRA Deemed University
Tamil Nadu, India

Gagan Kumar
Krishi Vigyan Kendra
 Narkatiaganj
Dr. Rajendra Prasad Central
 Agricultural University
Pusa, Samastipur, Bihar, India

M. Kumar
Department of Genetics and Plant
 Breeding
CPBG, Tamil Nadu Agricultural
 University
Coimbatore, Tamil Nadu, India

Murat Kunelbayev
Al-Farabi Kazakh National
 University
Almaty, Kazakhstan

R. Lasri
Laboratory of Sciences and Advanced
Technologies FPL
Abdelmalek Essaadi University
Larache, Morocco

L. Mahalingam
Department of Genetics and Plant
Breeding
CPBG, Tamil Nadu Agricultural
University
Coimbatore, Tamil Nadu, India

Jason Elroy Martis
NMAM Institute of
Technology
Karnataka, India

C. Matsika
Midlands State University
Gweru, Zimbabwe

Charles C. Orakwue
Chemical Engineering
Department
Nnamdi Azikiwe University
Awka, Nigeria

Debadatta Panda
Department of Genetics and Plant
Breeding
CPBG, Tamil Nadu Agricultural
University
Coimbatore, Tamil Nadu, India

Manikandan Ramachandran
School of Computing
SASTRA Deemed University
Tamil Nadu, India

Md. Mahtab Rashid
Department of Plant Pathology
Bihar Agricultural University
Sabour, Bhagalpur, Bihar, India

Kali Charan Rath
Department of M.E
GIET University
Gunupur, India

M. Raveendran
Department of Plant Biotechnology
CPMB, Tamil Nadu Agricultural
University
Coimbatore, Tamil Nadu, India

Rajani Shandilya
Department of PBG, SoAg
GIET University
Gunupur, India

Sannidhan Manjaya Shetty
NMAM Institute of Technology
Karnataka, India

Shivam Singh
Department of Plant Pathology
School of Agriculture Lovely
Professional University
Punjab, India

Anurag Sinha
Department of Information
Technology
Amity University Jharkhand
Ranchi, India

Murugan Subramanian
Department of Computer Science
and Engineering
Sri Aravindar Engineering College
Tamil Nadu, India

Basavaraj Teli
Department of Mycology and Plant
Pathology
Institute of Agricultural Sciences
Banaras Hindu University
Varanasi, India

Amantur Umarov
Al-Farabi Kazakh National University
Almaty, Kazakhstan

Nitin Jaglal Untwal
Department of Management
Maharashtra Institute of Technology
Aurangabad, Maharashtra, India

M. Zhou
Midlands State University
Gweru, Zimbabwe

Chapter 1

Application of Drones and Sensors in Advanced Farming: The Future Smart Farming Technology

Kumar Chiranjeeb[1], Rajani Shandilya[2], and Kali Charan Rath[3]

[1]*Department of Soil Science, SoAg, GIET University, Gunupur, India*
[2]*Department of PBG, SoAg, GIET University, Gunupur, India*
[3]*Department of M.E, GIET University, Gunupur, India*

Contents

DOI: 10.1201/9781003311782-1

1

1.1 Introduction to Advanced Farming, Scope and Importance of Agriculture in Indian Economy

The word agriculture dates back to older civilizations nearly thousands of years ago. The old farmers' community started planting wild-collected grains about 11,500 years ago. The agricultural sector is the most important and promising sector in India and the whole world in terms of economy, production, processing and livelihood prospects. In India, around 70% of the rural population is engaged in the agricultural sector and fulfills the emerging growing food scarcity due to population explosion all over the world. The agricultural sector faces a lot of challenges; however, still, it is the chief contributor of development and plays a key role in boosting the economy of any country. Agriculture along with its allied sectors like fishery and forestry contributes to about one-third of the country's GDP which accounts for about 13–16% in particular; this sector not only provides food and raw materials but also employs majority of labor forces. Farming defines the concept of growing crops and raising livestock on a large-scale basis to orient it toward business or to raise money for it.

Wang et al. (2014) published a review paper on the realistic literature in the area of contract farming for emerging countries. This paper helps to examine the roles and challenges of smallholding agriculture in India's further development.

Indian government with public-private partnerships is researching the technological development to help farmers with innovative ideas (IT-based solutions) through the Digital India initiative. Different challenges related to agriculture crop production get solved through a strong foundation, mutual interests in physical, human and institutional resources, and farmer-friendly e-stages as presented in the worked-out paper by Lele and Goswami (2017).

Advanced farming is the new, innovative farming method that uses highly advanced, efficient machines or equipment such as drones and sensors in agricultural fields. The central concept of advanced farming synchronizes with precision farming which itself devotes more and more focus on the use of highly productive, advanced techniques of farming with the help of smart agricultural machinery, thus ensuring efficient work along with high productivity and fulfilling the gaps in the sector of agriculture starting from raising of crops to getting maximum profit. There are multiple factors responsible for the growth of agriculture as well as activities like organic farming concept practices, increase in private participation and the use of latest information technologies with augmentations of recent advanced machines and techniques, i.e. drones, sensors and satellites, which change the overall concept of agriculture, thus giving it a new dimension for the future. There are certain advancements that can be seen in the field of precision agriculture or advanced farming.

1.1.1 Autopiloted Tractors

Tractors are now connected with GPS so that it can track the different lines of work in agricultural fields. The trackers have trackers attached to their steering systems, and tractors can also move in curved lines. The controlled mechanism keeps a track of the balance of machines and their working efficiencies.

1.1.1.1 Smart Irrigation by Mobiles and Sensors in Agriculture

Vaishali et al. (2017) attempted to use an automation system for checking the moisture contents in soil. The crop was monitored through sensors and it was controlled through the irrigation system. Their idea focused on a few parameters like temperature and soil moisture. The worked-out plan was completely based on monitoring the plants through a smartphone and focusing to control the water supply only. Mobile phones are fitted with smart sensors that are connected with irrigation machine sensors, thus giving a window to regulate the irrigation to the crops whenever needed. It saves energy, cost and timing of operations. Scheduling of irrigations is now monitored for different crops through mobiles. Agricultural crops require different amounts of irrigation water at different time periods to save crops from water imbalances or deficiencies which are now being monitored by mobiles. All these are possible with the use of sensors.

Keswani et al. (2019) worked out their research work on precision agriculture that controls the land throughput and optimizes the impact on surroundings through agriculture automation processes. Various sensors are used having the mechanism to detect any problematic situations such as irrigation requirements, crop disease and pest control with early detection and fertilizer scheduling with smart ways of applications to mitigate the nutrient imbalance conditions developed in crop plants during their growth time period.

1.1.1.2 Advanced Genetics in the Field of Agriculture

Population growth is increasing day by day, so does the food demand. To mitigate this problem, high amount of pesticides and fertilizers is being used in agriculture which not only declines the production but also disturbs the soil ecology. Thus, high genetic yielding and demand for pesticide and herbicide tolerance varieties of different crops have emerged, and scientists are now able to develop such promising varieties to tackle the current scenario.

1.1.1.3 Drone-Based Farming

Fanigliulo et al.'s (2020) light robot application had the option to reproduce the outcomes acquired by the customary techniques, presenting benefits as far as time, repeatability and dissected surface are concerned while lessening the human mistakes during the information assortment from one viewpoint and permitting a work-concentrated field observing answers for computerized farming automation system. This is one of the most advanced techniques which surveys the crops standing on the field and gives details about crop growth status, detection of pests and diseases, prediction of weather-based parameters, etc., by providing spectral images.

1.1.1.4 Precision Farming as an Important Component of Advanced Farming

In the agricultural sector, yield loss is the major setback that affects farming economy and also losses of carbon footprint. The loss of yields also there before crop harvesting is due to a lack of improved mechanisms in the field of agriculture and near about 15–20% losses are seen after harvesting due to lack of storage. The emerging population growth depletes the soil health even more to grow a large amount of crops from the field. Therefore, advanced and improved cropping systems with innovative machinery are required to mitigate this problem.

Precision farming is the integrated or holistic approach to utilize resources and advanced techniques-based machines with the aim of achieving maximum output and conservation of environment that shows the positive response in every possible way for agriculture, thus ensuring sustainability in agricultural future production. Precision farming is highly influenced by all the latest technologies which are described in the following sections.

1.1.1.4.1 GPS (Global Positioning System)

This is the most important component of precision farming. The operation of whole precision farming is impossible without GPS which has been used extensively in machines such as tractors, drones, other running machines and also in remote sensing sensors. GPS is a navigational system that helps map the whole farm of a particular area. It has pinpoint accuracy over the place and timing of each element or components present in the farm. No errors are found when it is used in mapping the resources, estimating the distance between components present in the farms, locating resources, and detecting good quality soil present in farm which can be used in any adverse conditions such as heavy rain, fog and mist conditions. GPS systems fitted in machines control the speed and distance to be traveled, influence the mode of operations of some machines, etc.

1.1.1.4.2 Advanced Farm Machines

High-standard equipment such as wireless sensors, farm machinery, production machines and various mobile devices are the most important components that make precision farming a great success in achieving the desired target of maximum output without hampering the environment. For all functions, machines are used in agriculture such as weeders with sensors that can control the weeds in the farm field remotely as it is attached to GPS systems. The hoes are also attached with GPS-fitted tractors for their smooth operation. Irrigation equipment is also attached with GPS and placed at an equal desired distance to regulate the irrigation in plants when there is a requirement. Equipment fitted with sensors and GPS can also be tracked via different mobile software. It is easy, cost-effective and the most reliable technology in the field of agriculture.

1.1.1.4.3 Variable Rate Technology (VRT)

VRT focuses on on-time and precise applications, rate of application and positions of application of inputs. The sole purpose is to reduce the wastage of inputs by utilizing it efficiently so that maximum output can be achieved from the same piece of land. It is associated with different farm operations such as seeding, irrigation, fertilizer application and weed control in association with technologies like GPS, electronic processor, virtual reality software and advanced farm machinery. The machines are programmed in a way that the rate of sowing seed per plot per hole and the rate of seed application can be performed efficiently by this technology so that there can be no loss of seed input and proper depth of planting and timing can be managed. During fertilizer application, the machines are acquainted with precise dose and place of application so as to minimize the losses of fertilizer and to enhance the nutrient use efficiency for getting maximum output. Späti et al. (2021) developed a bio-monetary displaying structure to assess the utility of different detecting modalities in factor rate treatment to distinguish natural inconstancy at the firm level, going from satellite photography to drones and handheld N-sensors. Their work shows the significance of ecological field factors, for example, soil heterogeneity and spatial grouping of soil types, in deciding the financial advantages of VRT.

1.1.1.4.4 Remote Sensing

The remote sensing method collects various useful data from the field without making any sort of physical contact. Owing to its multiple functions, remote sensing is very important for precision farming. Special spectral imaging methods of crop analysis and identifications are used in remote sensing. The healthy and infected or unhealthy crops release different energy signatures in terms of light energy which is reflected from crop canopies and are detected by sensors used in remote sensing. The soil and animals also release different energy levels which are captured and analyzed in remote sensing with the help of an imaging spectrometer so that healthy and unhealthy elements can be detected in farms and can be managed properly. Other functions such as moisture measurement, detection of weather phenomena, farm resource management and mapping are performed by remote sensing.

1.1.1.4.5 Database Management

The data collected from drones, sensors, machines and remote sensing are raw in nature and they should be processed properly by an expert before recommending it to the farmers. That's why a proper and advanced database management system is required to store, process and disseminate the useful data among the farmers and other growers for getting maximum benefit; also, it checks the data losses and improves its management. With a proper management system, farms can be monitored and resources can be efficiently utilized.

1.1.1.5 Scope of Agriculture in Economic and Other Sectors

Following are some important scopes of agriculture in economic and other sectors:

a. Employment opportunity
b. Contribution to economy
c. Supply of food and raw materials
d. Importance of international trade

1.2 Description of Drones in Agricultural Application

The work starts with a verifiable assessment of the use of flying vehicles in farming, as precursors of their application in present-day accuracy horticulture strategies, which are currently focused on the use of various applications in the agricultural field. This is the motivation of the chapter to work out the application of drones with sensors in the agricultural field. The survey on literature has been carried out from different sources of published reputed journals by providing a classification of technological applications in the agricultural field. Few journals get selected as references and are summarized below.

Smartphones are outfitted with keen sensors that speak with water system machine sensors, giving a window to controlling harvest water system depending on the situation [Ahirwar et al. (2019); Farooq et al. (2016)]. It rations energy, diminishes costs and works on the proficiency of activities [Garcia et al. (2018); Ježová and Lambot (2019); Kale et al. (2015)]. These sensors can distinguish any risky situations, for example, water system needs, crop sickness and irritation on the board with early location, compost planning with keen application techniques and supplement unevenness conditions in crop plants during their development cycle [Kabra et al. (2017); Kumar and Ilango (2018); Klotzsche et al. (2018); Kattenborn et al. (2019)].

In agribusiness, a lot of herbicides and manures are used, which lessens usefulness as well as disturbs the dirt biology. Thus, high hereditary yielding and pesticide and herbicide opposition variations of numerous harvests are in incredible interest, and researchers are presently in a situation to create such encouraging assortments to address the momentum circumstance [Mone et al. (2017); Morey et al. (2017); Mattupalli et al. (2018); Nair et al. (2014)].

Exactness cultivating is an incorporated or comprehensive way to deal with utilizing assets and progressed methods-based machines fully intent on accomplishing the most extreme yield while likewise rationing the climate, bringing about a positive reaction in all parts of agribusiness and guaranteeing agrarian future creation manageability [Pederi and Cheporniuk (2015); Reinecke & Prinsloo (2017); Spoorthi et al. (2017); Shivaji et al. (2017)].

The present-day approach for looking over crops on the field and giving otherworldly pictures provides data on crop development status, illness location and climate-based boundary expectation, in addition to other things [Shilin et al. (2017); Vardhan et al. (2014); Wani and Shish (2015)].

Drones are generally the unmanned aerial vehicles (UAVs) used in agriculture (Figure 1.1) and other sectors for monitoring, surveying, data image collection, etc. Drones are also used in precision farming, livestock farming, smart greenhouse, and horticulture and forestry sectors. These are advanced, low-cost, aerial-camera equipped with GPS systems and have various sensors for all types of data collection in agriculture [Watanabe et al. (2017); Wu et al. (2019); Yallappa et al. (2017); Yanliang et al. (2017)]. The multispectral sensors can capture various images of both healthy and diseased/unhealthy crops and detect other problems which cannot be seen in the visible spectrum; soil and nutrient mapping is also possible by drones [Zhang et al. (2018)].

Unmanned aerial motors (UAVs) for plant protection have advanced swiftly in recent years in some international locations, as well as India [Chung and Sah (2020); García-Berná et al. (2021); Habibi et al. (2021)].

The progress of digitalization and estimating advancements has empowered computerized gadgets and sensors to create monstrous measures of information. Image-based total information amassing and evaluation has quite a few promises to help with those targets. Visual facts obtained from agricultural fields can be used to automate evaluation operations and provide real-time crop and leaf health information. Drones (Figure 1.1 (a) and (b)) with sensors are used to monitor the health condition of crops in the agricultural field through image processing which is the interesting part of this chapter.

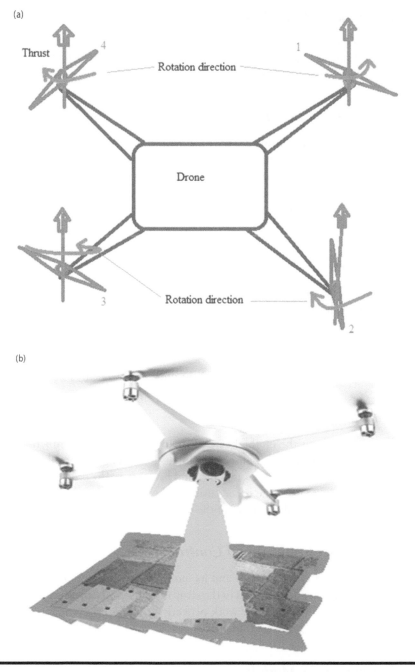

Figure 1.1   (a) Drones flying mechanism. (b) Drone taking image from the agricultural field.

1.2.1 Standard Propellers

Propellers are situated at the front of the drones and these are made up of either plastic material for lower quality purpose uses or carbon fiber materials of high standards. These propellers are used to maintain the body balance of the drones while in air.

1.2.2 Pusher Propellers

Pusher propellers are responsible for the forward and reverse push of drones during their flight. The pusher propellers decide the course of the drone, either it will move in a forward or reverse direction, and are placed at the back of the drones. They counterbalance the engine torques during the stationary mode of flight prompting forward or reverse direction movement. The pusher propellers are also made up of either plastic or carbon fiber.

1.2.3 Motors

Motor provides the torque for the operation of the engines of the drones and spins the propellers to lift the drones for movement.

1.2.4 Landing Gear

This gear helps in controlling the landing of the drones safely on any place or surface.

1.2.5 Flying Controller

The flying controller is the motherboard of the drone and its main function is to direct each motor's RPM in response to the inputs given. Flight controllers include sensors, compass, gyroscope, GPS modules and barometer. The order given for the multi-rotor engines to work the robot push ahead is taken care of by the regulator which controls the general functions of the robot.

1.2.6 ESC (Electronic Speed Controller)

ESC is named as an electric circuit and its most important function is to control the speed of the drones. It also helps in the setup of course and converts DC current to AC current to make the motor work perfectly. It might give switching off the engine and a dynamic breaking framework.

1.2.7 Drone GPS Module

This GPS module is responsible for the provision of latitudes, longitudes and various elevation points. GPS modules are considered to be the most important component of the drone and they help in the navigation of longer ranges along with capturing details of specific sites or locations.

1.2.8 Battery

It goes about as a wellspring of energy to the ESC and different modules that provisions to different pieces of board.

1.2.9 Radio Receiver/Transmitter

It sets up the correspondence between the flight regulator and ground station to convey controlling orders from a transmitter.

1.2.10 Antenna

Radio wire is utilized to follow the current area of the robot and to get the visual animate feed from the camera installed on the drone.

1.2.11 Camera and Accessories

Drone cameras are either inbuilt or detachable that are used to take photos or videos of particular locations.

1.2.12 Sensors

Sensors may be upward, downward, forward and backward to sense the objects nearby and do all necessary functions.

1.2.13 Power Modules

The main function of the power module is to perform motor functions, electric variable speed controls as well as amplification. They may integrate intelligence and capabilities components.

1.2.14 Sensors Used in Drones

Accelerometer: This sensor is responsible for the stability of the drones.

Gyroscope: This sensor provides angular motion to the drone.

Magnetometer: This type of sensor is present in the drones with GPS modules and helps in detecting a magnetic field of the earth and is responsible for direction for the fly to the drones.

Barometer: It is also known as a pressure sensor. The pressure variation is seen with increasing height from sea level. A barometer sensor is used to measure accurate height above mean sea level.

GPS sensor: This sensor provides the location at any place and measures the distance to be covered.

Distance sensor: A distance sensor can sense the obstacles during traveling. These distance sensors are based on ultrasonic, laser-based or LIDAR-based mechanisms.

1.2.15 Types of Drones Based on Size

Nano Size: Weight < 250–300 g.
Micro size: 250 g < Weight < 3 kg.
Small size: 3 kg < Weight < 30 kg.
Medium size: 30 kg < Weight < 150 kg.
Large size: 150 kg < Weight

1.2.16 Observation of Vegetation Reflectance by Multispectral Camera Used in Drone

With the upgraded sensors, cameras can collect images in four separate bands at the same time while maintaining the camera's frame rate. The redesigned sensor captures all of the spectrum information at the same time. RGB and near-infrared light (NIR) multispectral cameras have features of four spectral discriminating bands and red, green and blue as three sensitive bands, respectively. As demonstrated in Figure 1.2 (a) and (b), the fourth band is sensitive to NIR. The RGB and NIR bands of the multispectral camera beat competitors' dye-based color filter arrays significantly. Cross-talk between bands is significantly reduced, particularly between the NIR and color bands. The USB3 cable provides power, making setup easier. These cameras are small and light, making them ideal for a range of applications that require simultaneous color and NIR imaging. They are highly advanced and can take images from different spectral regions and operate efficiently.

The features of vegetation reflectance are utilized to create vegetation indices (VIs). The VIs are used to examine different ecologies. To study specific features of vegetation, such as total leaf area and water content, VIs are built using reflectance observations in two or more wavelengths.

1.2.17 Types of Sensors Used in Drone for Agricultural Application

Sensors are small and very simple devices that are used to measure or detect different properties or parameters very precisely with real-time-based observations. Sensors also detect the circumstances such as gesticulation, warmness or grace and transform it into digital form for better understanding and analysis of observed

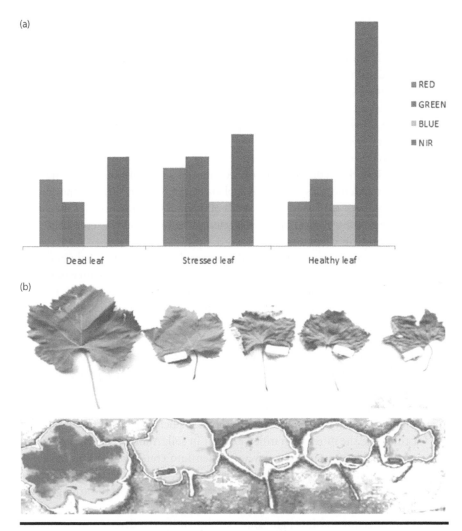

Figure 1.2 (a) Vegetation reflectance observed by different conditioned leaves (dead, stressed and healthy) of crop. (b) Vegetation reflectance.

data. Various types of sensors used for different purposes in the agricultural monitoring process are as follows:

a. **Electromagnetic Sensors**
Electromagnetic sensors use electric circuits to quantify the conduction or accumulation of electric charges by the soil particles. The whole soil system becomes a part of that circuit and any slight changes in electrical conductivity are measured in the logger.

Electromagnetic sensors are of two types:

i. Contact Electromagnetic Sensors

This sensor uses an electrode pair in which one electrode is inserted into the soil that supplies electric current and another electrode measures the voltage drop. The voltage drop data collected from the logger along with location are needed to analyze the conductivity with the help of this sensor. This sensor is very much popular in precision farming because of its large area coverage and less interference.

ii. Non-Contact Electromagnetic Sensors

This works on the principles of electromagnetic stimulation without any contact with the soil system. This appliance has a receiver coil and a transmitter; those are installed at the two ends of the non-conducting bar of the instrument. The working range of this sensor is between 300 Hz and 24 kHz.

b. **Optoelectronic Sensors**

Optoelectronic sensors integrate the electronic processes with light and optical processes. It is tranquil of a light source that emits light source of diverse frequency and a sensor that can sense these different wavelengths. It can cover the distance of several hundreds of kilometers. It can measure soil dampness and cation trade limit.

c. **Electrochemical Sensors**

These sensors measure the electrochemical phenomena of the soil system such as nutrient status and pH. Apart from that, it can detect nitrate and potassium ions.

d. **Ion-Selective Electrode Sensors**

This sensor estimates the capability of an explicit particle in an answer and can decide the nitrogen gratified existent in soil. Another reference electrode of the stable constant property was taken into consideration and the result potential was measured against this perspective. The possible contrast between two electrodes relies on the action of an explicit particle in the arrangement.

e. **Optical Sensors**

Optical sensors utilize light sources to quantify the diverse soil properties. The light energy interferes with different properties and those changes are analyzed properly.

f. **Location Sensors**

Location sensors are the sensors used to determine latitude and longitude along altitude which are needed most.

g. **Mechanical Sensors**

Mechanical sensors measure the mechanical antagonism of the soil. These devices go through the soil and measure the strength of the soil system with the help of a strain gauge. They are of two types:

i. Airflow Sensors

These sensors measure the air permeability of a particular area. The pressure created in the air system can also be analyzed by this sensor.

    ii. Acoustic Sensors

       Soil surface can be researched by estimating the progressions in the commotion level made while the instruments cooperate with soil elements.

h. **Nitrate Sensors**

   These sensors measure the nitrate content in both soil and water systems. Nitrate ions are easily leached down into the soil system and stored mostly in groundwater causing blue baby syndrome disease in humans when the nitrate concentration is > 10 ppm. These nitrate sensors are of great use to track the nitrate ion path and also to track the transformations.

i. **Soil pH Sensors**

   They measure the acidity or alkalinity of the soil system. This sensor reading is also helpful in knowing the causes of poor plant growth, fertility problems of soil, etc.

j. **Ammonium Sensors**

   They precisely determine the ammonium and nitrogen content in the soil and water system.

k. **Potassium Sensors**

   This sensor is specially designed to detect the potassium ion concentration in soil and water content.

l. **Soil-Water Sensors**

   These sensors give the details about the status of the soil-water system; thus they are helpful in irrigation management, nutrient mobility, chemical and water balance status, etc.

m. **Nanobiosensors**

   Nanobiosensors are very much advanced and important sensors used in agriculture that take the help of bio-organisms in sensing operations. Nanobiosensors are compact and analytic devices that use biologically sensitized element in their sensors for further analysis (Kumar et al., 2021).

n. **Pneumatic (Magnetic Proximity Sensor)**

   This is the most common type of sensor used for detecting the magnetic fields of the system.

1.3 Drones and Sensors in Advanced Farming

With the fitting sensors ready, the drone can be utilized for a wide assortment of utilizations, for example, valuation of plant inexperience or photosynthetic active biomass, crop stress, weed stress, etc.

1.3.1 Soil Analysis and Mapping for Field Planning

Drones are used to capture 3D images of the field so that proper analysis of soil can be performed for the planning of crops to be grown on that soil. Different

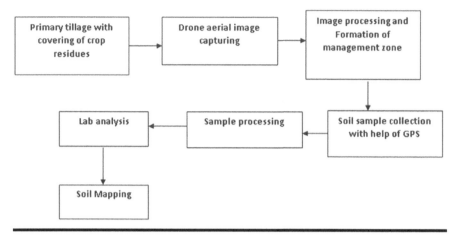

Figure 1.3 Soil sample collection and analysis with the help of GPS and drone mechanism.

high-resolution images are also analyzed to estimate the moisture percentage of soil, nitrogen content and other nutrient content in the soil. Planting-related aspects along with irrigation requirements can also be observed by using drones in agricultural fields. Sensors are also programmed to determine the various soil physical and chemical properties such as soil pH, cation exchange capacity, bulk density, moisture content and other nutrients present and the sensors used to determine such properties.

Soil sampling is performed to map the soil for its further use. The aerial images that are captured represent soil color which can be taken each year after primary tillage operation. In case of zero tillage or no-tillage system, the soil remains always covered with vegetation; thus, aerial image capturing to determine the soil color is not even possible. The process of soil sampling with the aid of aerial photography by drones is shown in Figure 1.3.

1.3.2 Seed Planting

Proper planting of seeds with maintaining distance and depth can be achieved by using drones. Drones are programmed to throw the seeds in a pod to the previously prepared soil with applied doses of fertilizer in that soil. The drones also save time and labor costs for planting to be done.

1.3.3 Soil Quality and Plant Disease Assessment

Nanobiosensors are capable to detect the various diseases caused by viruses, bacteria, fungi and other microorganisms by measuring the oxygen depletion status caused by microorganisms. The sensors are capable of detecting this oxygen depletion status, thus giving the amount of infestation of these microorganisms in the plants causing diseases which can be estimated in time so that control measures can be taken.

The soil quality assessment is also possible by using the sensors as it is based on a semi-quantitative approach. The sensors are immersed in the buffer solutions to get the exact amount of oxygen consumption by microorganisms as these help in soil quality maintenance.

1.3.4 Crop Monitoring

Crop monitoring is considered the toughest task in the field of agriculture. Large areas with standing crops are difficult to manage for the farmers on their own. The use of high-resolution drones and the field can monitor the crops on a large scale and multispectral, geospatial images captured by the drones help in analyzing crop development as well as give an idea about microclimate which is very much important for crop growth.

1.3.5 Spraying of Pesticides, Chemicals and Fertilizers on Crops

The drones integrated with sensor-based technologies can formulate and calculate the required doses of pesticides, fertilizers and other plant protection chemicals for increasing crop growth along with efficiency enhancement of applied materials. The drone-based spraying can save time and reduce the cost of operation by checking the losses and overdose of chemical application in plants. Required doses of fertilizers are important to check the toxicity of other nutrients in soil and plant systems as fertilizers are considered as plant growth substances. Nutrient losses from fertilizer materials can be checked, thus minimizing the risk of soil and environmental pollutions caused by the excess amount of nutrients.

1.3.5.1 Mechanism of Spraying Chemicals Using Drones

In the spraying mechanism, a microcontroller system is attached to the machine. An additional tank of pesticide containers is fitted with the water pump. A splitter is connected at the end with which two nozzles are attached through which spray is done. It also consists of a motor driving force circuit to regulate the speed of pesticide spray and a pesticide indicator circuit connected to a buzzer to indicate when the pesticide tank is empty.

1.3.5.2 Irrigation Scheduling

The sensors installed on irrigation machinery and in the fields can give signals when there is a need for irrigation to the crops. Crop growth stages of various crops

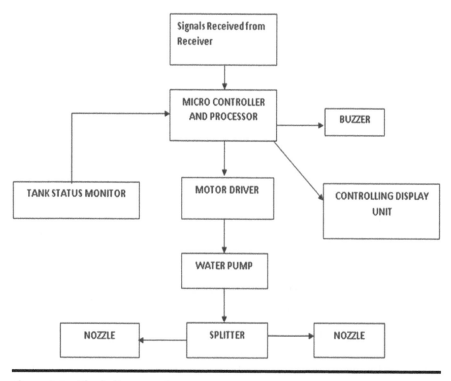

Figure 1.4   Block diagram of a sprayer.

along with irrigation requirements at each stage data are synchronized with sensor observations to fulfill the irrigation gap needed for crops, so scheduling of whole irrigation operation can be observed and maintained properly. Figure 1.4 depicts a block diagram of a sprayer. We can see that several steps are appeared.

1.3.6 Crop Health Assessment and Yield Forecasting

Various sensors used in drones are capable of capturing high-frequency and high-resolution images to assess plant health. The Normalized Difference Vegetation Index (NDVI) used in drones provides proper identification about healthy crops and unhealthy crops by giving them different colored images such as green color images for healthy plants while red color images for unhealthy crops (Figure 1.5).

The yields-related data can be collected by using drones and sensors attached to the farm tools or implements. The moisture percent and grain yield can be calculated from sensors, thus giving an idea about planning for next season cropping, storage of grains, etc.

$$NDVI = \frac{(NIR - RED)}{(NIR + RED)} \tag{1.1}$$

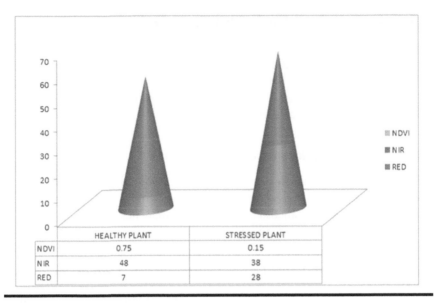

	HEALTHY PLANT	STRESSED PLANT
NDVI	0.75	0.15
NIR	48	38
RED	7	28

Figure 1.5   NDVI for healthy and stressed plants.

where NIR denotes near-infrared spectrum, and RED denotes red light wavelength spectrum.

1.3.7 Crop/Tree Biomass Estimation

The LIDAR sensors attached to drones can give details about crop/tree density and distance from the ground surface. This technique helps estimate proper forestry crop growth, its height and other important property. In sugarcane crops, harvesting time can be measured from biomass calculation.

1.3.8 Livestock and Wildlife Monitoring

Drones act as a deterrent to poachers about various animals. The drones with their thermal cameras and sensors can work efficiently in the nighttime and protect animals by monitoring wildlife animals. The livestock animals can be traced by sensors and surveyed using various drones.

1.3.9 Pest and Weeds Control

When plants are infested by insects and weeds, they emit different energy signatures and the sensors attached to the drones can detect the problems by capturing multispectral high-resolution images, thus giving the warning to protect the crops from insects and weeds. The drones are also capable of spraying pesticides and weedicides efficiently when they are programmed.

1.4 Effective Tool for Protein and DNA Detection

Carbon nanotubes and single-stranded DNA sensors can detect DNA oligonucle-otides. DNA methylation and avoidance of PCR can be performed by nanowire field biosensors. The protein biosensors can detect special protein molecules secreted by different microorganisms, thus helping in the control of microbial infestation in plants and also a nutrient deficiency in plants.

1.4.1 Nanobiosensors as Urea Detectors

Urease enzyme and glutamate dehydrogenase are responsible for the breakdown of urea molecules into NH_4 ions and cause various losses and can be detected by using nanobiosensors. Sensors can also calculate the accurate dose of urea to be applied to the crops to check the loss and toxicity.

1.4.2 Heavy Metal and Other Contaminants Detection

Biosensor method is very much accurate and rapid and integrated with techniques such as voltametry, polarography and spectroscopy which can detect heavy metals and other contaminants. Organophosphorus pesticide residues can be detected by using liposome-based biosensors even at a lower concentration. Urease-based conductometric biosensors help detect heavy metals and other contaminants in wastewater samples.

1.4.3 Food Product Quality Checking

Biosensors with advanced integrated technologies are used in food quality check-ing as well as maintenance of good quality standards of food materials. Vitamins analysis, food contamination detection, antibiotics presence on honey products, etc., can be performed by amperometric biosensors.

1.4.4 Weather Parameter Assessment

Drones are used to monitor and predict weather-based observations. Microclimates are more important from a plant growth point of view. Weather-based information is necessary to plants for cropping, protection of standing crops and to do necessary operations.

1.4.5 Resource Mapping of Farms

Various resources present in the farm are mapped precisely using GIS and GPS and also by drones. Resource mapping is important in farm management and planning for the growth of different crops and adopting integrated farming systems to ensure good income for the future.

1.4.6 Disaster Management

After disasters, the drones with their high-definition cameras and sensors give the rescue team a broad view of the field so that affected people can be rescued from unreachable areas.

1.4.6.1 Pollination of Crop Plants

Now, the drones with a proper data feed, simulation and programming can pollinate the desired crop plants for breeding as well as research projects. New and improved crop plants can be produced by pollination and drones are helpful in this situation.

1.4.6.2 Sustainability in Agriculture

The application of nano-based fertilizer materials can check nutrient loss and volatilization. Encapsulated fertilizer materials along with other encapsulated materials provide a longer supply of nutrients to the crop plants for their steady growth. Zeolites application in agriculture is known to enhance fertilizer use efficiency, nutrient loss check, optimum plant growth, improving soil quality and health status, pesticide and herbicide residue detection, etc., thus leading toward sustainability in agriculture.

The following noted points are a few outcomes of this research work for the utilization of smart technology in an agricultural application to support farmers for better crop quality production.

  i. Drone in an agricultural application is an advanced technology that refers to handling agricultural farms with required sensors to analyze the quality of crops and its product while reducing the amount of human labor required to visit the field and monitor the crops.
  ii. Collection of real data on soil properties by using drones and sensors for better analysis and executing proper soil mapping.
  iii. Plant diseases assessment through nanobiosensors gives good results for monitoring and helps analysts for right decision-making.
  iv. Crop health condition monitoring can be performed through drones by using NDVI image processing.
  v. Provided the block diagram for effective spraying of pesticides, chemicals and fertilizers on crops.

1.5 Data Analyses and Future Thrusts

The drones use various sensors (LIDAR, multispectral, thermal and hyperspectral) to capture high-resolution images that can be analyzed by using different software. Some of the image processing software are given below:

a. Drone deploy Enterprise 3D map
b. Open drone map photogrammetry
c. Precision Hawk 3D map software
d. Autodesk Recap Photogrammetry
e. Agrisoft Metashape 3D software
f. Arc GIS software (Drone 2 Map)

1.5.1 NDVI Sensor Image Analysis and Interpretations

The drones use various sensors for the capturing of high-resolution images and with the help of software the images are analyzed and the final output is given for use in agriculture which is of great significance. The NDVI sensor used in UAV or drone provides values that are processed after image analysis and gives some important interpretations as well as the health status of any crops that are presented in Tables 1.1 and 1.2.

Table 1.1   NDVI Values and Vegetation Interpretation

NDVI-Related Vegetations	
NDVI	Interpretation
0–0.12	Bare soil
0.12–0.22	No coverage completely
0.22–0.31	Very low or minimum canopy over
0.31–0.42	Low canopy cover, low vigor
0.42–0.52	Mid low canopy cover, low vigor
0.52–0.62	Average canopy cover, low vigor or mid low canopy cover
0.63–0.74	Mid high canopy cover, low vigor or average canopy cover
0.74–0.82	High canopy cover, high vigor
0.82–0.92	High canopy cover, very high vigor
0.92–0.98	Very canopy cover, very high vigor
0.98–1.0	Extremely high canopy cover, extremely high vigor

Table 1.2 Relation of NDVI Values with Crop Health Status

NDVI Value	Crop Health Status
−1–0.03	Dead plants
0.03–0.33	Unhealthy plants
0.33–0.69	Moderately healthy plants
0.69–0.85	Healthy plants
0.85–1.0	Optimum healthy plants

1.5.2 Result and Discussion

Harvest yields can differ significantly starting with one region in the field, then onto the next in light of the fact that harvests don't develop similarly over the field. These improvement disparities might be due to nutritional deficits in the soil or other styles of stress. Distant detecting licenses a rancher to select issue spots in a discipline altogether that the best kind and measure of manure, insect poison or herbicide might be applied. The farmer no longer only will increase the productiveness of his land, but additionally lowers his farm input charges and lessens environmental impact by way of the usage of this method. The effects of soil color, soil moisture and excessive density vegetation saturation on empirically expected NDVI range were studied. An attempt has been taken to improve NDVI for the agricultural field for the better health condition of the plant after proper monitoring through the drone.

The fluctuation in plant fitness status has been evaluated by the use of the NDVI maps and values of the study area during a previous couple of years of research. The density and condition of leaves within the agricultural location have measured the usage of NDVI (Figure 1.6). The quantity of ground cowl, concentration and immaturity of leaves all affect NDVI. The NDVI score of vegetation that is denser and greener can be more. As plant life get pressured, sick or die, their NDVI drops.

Standardized change red edge is seen as an additional touchy way to adapt to quantify chlorophyll awareness. Not really settled utilizing a similar condition as NDVI, besides rather than the red-light band, it uses the red edge band reflectance. The red edge is a zone that lies between the red range's assimilation limit and significant-close infrared reflectance. Therefore, it is particularly helpless against changes in vegetation well-being and nitrogen prominence.

Higher NDVI esteems in the field research region containing plants bring about a better plant than plants with lower NDVI esteems, as indicated by the analysis. On account of their high reflectance of infrared light and low reflectance of red light, solid plants have a high NDVI score. The principle boundaries that impact NDVI are phenology and force.

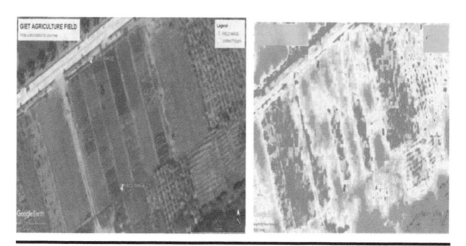

Figure 1.6 NDVI images analyzed using QGIS and Google Earth Pro (GIET University Agriculture field).

High-goal photography and multispectral imaging capacities are used for recognizing harm and checking crop's well-being. A short turnaround time from data capture to crop information delivery is one of the most important criteria in making imagery relevant to farmers.

For analysis, images were taken at certain times during the growing season and on a regular basis. An appropriate step is advisable for a farmer to take necessary actions for abnormality plant health conditions if found (Figure 1.7).

Figure 1.7 Abnormality plant health condition (GIET University, agriculture firm).

1.5.3 Rules and Regulation of Drone Use in India

In 2018, the Government of India approved the use of drones in infrastructural works. The GOI and DGCA then further formulated the plans and regulations for use of drones in agricultural works except spraying of agricultural chemicals till they got cleared. Now, the drones are fully operational in all types of agricultural works. The DGCA RPAS guidance provides all necessary operations and permits related to drones. The general laws are as follows:

a. Densely populated areas and crowd-based areas should be avoided.
b. Privacy of others should not be interfered.
c. One person should fly one UAV at a time.
d. A 5-km radius area from airports should be avoided.
e. One should fly a drone in the daytime and good weather condition.
f. The use of drones and with cameras is prohibited for flying near government facilities and military sectors.
g. There should be proper training for flying drones and the age must be more than 18 years.
h. A license plate containing all basic and important information should be on the drone during its operation.
i. The area near about 50 km from the radius of the Country's border should be avoided.
j. Visual view ought to be kept up with running drones.
k. 500 km from coastal lines into the sea area should be avoided while running drones.
l. The flying of drones above national parks and sanctuaries is also restricted.
m. A valid third party insurance policy should be covered by drone operators in case of any accidents.
n. If the drone weight is more than 250 grams, then standard laws should be followed.
o. It is not allowed to fly drones near a 5-km radius of Vijay Chowk in New Delhi.

1.6 Conclusion

Today's agriculture depends on the use of new advanced techniques and machinery, so that maximum output can be achieved to mitigate the overpopulation food crisis problems. Advanced farming follows all the principles to provide better future opportunities as well as concerned about climate changes, pollution reduction, sustainability in agriculture and minimizing soil health deterioration. Technologies like GIS, GPS, mobile applications and sensors are used in precision farming or advanced farming. Many countries are still not developed to implement this farming technique but the world food crisis is emerging as a global issue. Lack of connectivity issues and proper information is a great hurdle in rural and remote areas of India where more than 60% population are engaged in the agricultural sectors.

This chapter mentioned how a drone is equipped with sensors and detects precarious regions that need to be improved by the farmer. This information also aids in the creation of multispectral images for crop health monitoring. This chapter's main purpose is to demonstrate how quick monitoring and discovery of any unhealthy zone inform farmers to save crops.

Advanced farming is more focused on development in terms of both agricultural production and economic development. Efficient use of pesticides, fertilizers, inputs and irrigation water can be performed in this advanced farming. In the 21st century, drone technology is very common in agriculture which has provided enormous opportunities to boost up agricultural production as well as improve the socioeconomic status of the farmer and also help the growth of a nation. Advanced imaging with sensors helps the farmer to control diseases, pests and also reduce pollution by applying an adequate amount of pesticides and fertilizers in agricultural fields. Advanced farming is the talk of the hour and we all should focus on implementing these technologies in the agricultural sector for ensuring a great and sustainable future in Indian agriculture.

1.6.1 Future Thrust

India and other developing countries put a lot of effort to get maximum output from a limited piece of land to mitigate the overpopulation food crisis problem. Drone farming is emerging as a solution to the ongoing crisis and with the use of these advanced technologies, overall growth is possible in the agricultural sector. Advanced farming promises better connectivity, efficient resource utilization, and eliminates every hurdle in terms of soil quality analysis, farm management, efficient irrigation systems, improved mechanisms for pest and disease control, and weather analysis.

Agriculture is undergoing substantial changes as it strives to provide enough food while being sustainable. Within the new agricultural period, farmers can use a range of advanced sensing devices with GPS, inconsistent applications, navigation and remote sensing, followed by farm management software. Farming undergoes revolutionary changes as a result of the development and application of new and accurate farm technologies. To put it another way, contemporary farm technology has revolutionized the way farmers work.

In a nutshell, agricultural drones allow growers, service providers and researchers to scan their crops, diagnose stress, devise treatment plans and follow plant growth much more quickly and efficiently.

References

Ahirwar, S., Swarnkar, R., Bhukya, S. & Namwade, G. (2019). Application of Drone in Agriculture. Intl. J. Curr. Microbiol. App. Sci. 8(1), 2500–2505. doi: https://doi.org/10.20546/ijcmas.2019.801.264.

Chung, S. H., Sah, B. & Lee, J. (2020). Optimization for Drone and Drone-truck Combined Operations: A Review of the State of the Art and Future Directions. Comput. Oper. Res., S0305-0548(20)30121-0. doi: https://doi.org/ 10.1016/j. cor.2020.105004

Fanigliulo, R., Antonucci, F., Figorilli, S., Pochi, D., Pallottino, F., Fornaciari, L. & Costa, C. (2020). Light Drone-based Application to Assess Soil Tillage Quality Parameters. Sensors, 20(3), 728.

Farooq, W., Butt, N., Shukat, S., Baig, N. A. & Ahmed, S. M. (2016). Wirelessly Controlled Mines Detection Robot. In International Conference on Intelligent Systems Engineering (ICISE). DOI:10.1109/INTELSE.2016.7475162.

Garcia, F. M., Alvarez, L. Y., Heras, F. L., Gonzalez,V. B., Rodriguez, V. Y., Pino, A. & Arboleya, A. A. (2018). GPR System Onboard a UAV for Non-invasive Detection of Buried Objects. In 2018 IEEE Antennas and Propagation Society International Symposium and USNC/URSI National Radio Science Meeting, APSURSI 2018 – Proceedings, pp. 1967–1968. https://doi.org/ 10.1109/APUSNCURSINRSM. 2018.8608907.

García-Berná, J. A., Ouhbi, S., Benmouna B., García-Mateos G., Fernández-Alemán J. L. & Molina-Martínez J. M. (2020). Systematic Mapping Study on Remote Sensing in Agriculture, Appl. Sci., 10, 3456; doi:10.3390/app10103456.

Habibi, L., Watanabe, T., Matsui, T. & Tanaka, T. (2021). Machine Learning Techniques to Predict Soybean Plant Density Using UAV and Satellite-Based Remote Sensing. Remote Sens., 13(13), 2548. https://doi.org/10.3390/rs13132548.

Ježová, J. & Lambot, S. (2019). A Dielectric Horn Antenna and Lightweight Radar System for Material Inspection. J. Appl. Geophys. 103822. https://doi.org/10.1016/ j.jappgeo.2019.

Kabra, T. S., Kardile, A. V., Deeksha, M. G., Mane, D. B., Bhosale, P. R., & Belekar, A. M. (2017). Design, Development and Optimization of a Quad-Copter for Agricultural Applications. Intl. Res. J. Eng. Technol. 4(7), e-ISSN: 2395–0056.

Kale, S. D., Khandagale, S. V., Gaikwad, S. S., Narve, S. S. & Gangal, P. V. (2015). Agriculture Drone for Spraying Fertilizer and Pesticides. Intl. J. Adv. Res. Comput. Sci. Softw. Eng., 5(12), 804–807.

Kattenborn, T., Lopatin, J., Förster, M., Braun, A. C. & Fassnacht, F. E. (2019). UAV Data as Alternative to Field Sampling to Map Woody Invasive Species Based on Combined Sentinel-1 And Sentinel-2 Data. Remote Sens. Environ. 227, 61–73. https://doi.org/10.1016/j.rse.2019.03.025.

Keswani, B., Mohapatra, A. G., Mohanty, A., Khanna, A., Rodrigues, J. J., Gupta, D. & De Albuquerque, V. H. C. (2019). Adapting Weather Conditions Based IoT Enabled Smart Irrigation Technique in Precision Agriculture Mechanisms. Neur. Comput. Appl., 31(1), 277–292.

Klotzsche, A., Jonard, F., Looms, M. C., van der Kruk, J. & Huisman, J. A. (2018). Measuring Soil Water Content with Ground Penetrating Radar: A Decade of Progress. Vadose Zone J. 17. https://doi.org/10.2136/vzj2018.03.0052.

Kumar, S. A. & Ilango, P. (2018). The Impact of Wireless Sensor Network in the Field of Precision Agriculture: A Review. Wirel. Pers. Commun. 98, 685–698.

Lele, U. & Goswami, S. (2017). The Fourth Industrial Revolution, Agricultural and Rural Innovation, and Implications for Public Policy and Investments: A Case of India. Agric. Econ., 48(S1), 87–100.

Mattupalli, C., Moffet, C. A., Shah, K. N. & Young, C. A. (2018). Supervised Classification Of RGB Aerial Imagery to Evaluate the Impact of a Root Rot Disease. Remote Sens. 2018, 10, 917. https://doi.org/10.3390/rs10060917.

Mone, P. P., Shivaji, C. P., Tanaji, J. K. & Satish, N. A. (2017).Agriculture Drone for Spraying Fertilizer and Pesticides. Intl. J. Res. Trends Innov., 2(16): ISSN: 2456-3315.

Morey, N. S., Mehere, P. N. & Hedaoo, K. (2017). Agriculture Drone for Fertilizers and Pesticides Spraying. Intl. J. Eng. Appl. Technol. 5(3): ISSN: 2321-8134.

Nair, A. H., Krishnanand, P. P., Varghese, M., Thomas, S. B. & George, T. S. (2014). Hovercraft Based Farming System. Intl. J. Res. Dev. Technol., 1(2), 17–21.

Pederi, Y. A. & Cheporniuk, H. S. (2015). Unmanned Aerial Vehicles and New Technological Methods of Monitoring and Crop Protection in Precision Agriculture. In IEEE International Conference on Actual Problems of Unmanned Aerial Vehicles Developments (APUAVD), pp. 298–301.

Reinecke, M. & Prinsloo, T. (2017). The Influence of Drone Monitoring on Crop Health and Harvest Size. IEEE 1st International Conference on Next Generation Computing Applications (NextComp), pp. 5–10. DOI:10.1109/NEXTCOMP.2017.8016168.

Shilin, W., Jianli, S., Xiongkui, H., Le, S., Xiaonan, W., Changling, W. & Yun, L. (2017). Performances Evaluation of Four Typical Unmanned Aerial Vehicles Used for Pesticide Application in China. Intl. J. Agric. Biol. Eng., 10(4):22–31.

Shivaji, C. P., Tanaji, J. K., Satish, N. A. & Mone, P. P. (2017). Agriculture Drone for Spraying Fertilizer and Pesticides, Intl. J. Res. Trends Innov., 2(6): 34–36.

Späti, K., Huber, R. & Finger, R. (2021). Benefits of Increasing Information Accuracy in Variable Rate Technologies. Ecol. Econ., 185, 107047. https://doi.org/10.1016/j.ecolecon.2021.107047.

Spoorthi, S., Shadaksharappa, B., Suraj, S. & Manasa, V. K. (2017) Freyr Drone: Pesticide/Fertilizers Spraying Drone - An Agricultural Approach. IEEE 2nd International Conference on Computing and Communications Technologies (ICCCT - 2017), pp. 252–255.

Vaishali, S., Suraj, S., Vignesh, G., Dhivya, S. & Udhayakumar, S. (2017, April). Mobile Integrated Smart Irrigation Management and Monitoring System Using IOT. In 2017 IEEE International Conference on Communication and Signal Processing (ICCSP), pp. 2164–2167.

Vardhan, P. D. P. R. H., Dheepak, S., Aditya, P. T. & Arul, S. (2014). Development of Automated Aerial Pesticide Sprayer. Intl. J. Res. Eng. Technol. eISSN: 2319-1163, pISSN: 2321-7308.

Wang, H. H., Wang, Y. & Delgado, M. S. (2014). The Transition to Modern Agriculture: Contract Farming in Developing Economies. Am. J. Agric. Econ., 96(5), 1257–1271.

Wani, A. & Shish, L. (2015). A Review: Autonomous Agribot for Smart Farming. Proceedings of 46th IRF International Conference, 27th December 2015, Pune, India, ISBN: 978-93-85832- 97-0.

Watanabe, K., Guo, W., Arai, K., Takanashi, H., Kajiya-Kanegae, H., Kobayashi, M., Yano, K., Tokunaga, T., Fujiwara, T., Tsutsumi, N. & Iwata, H. (2017). High-Throughput Phenotyping of Sorghum Plant Height Using an Unmanned Aerial Vehicle and Its Application to Genomic Prediction Modeling. Front Plant Sci. 8:421.

Wu, K., Rodriguez, G. A., Zaj, C. M., Jacquemin, E., Clément, M., Coster, A. D. & Lambot, S. (2019). A New Drone-Borne GPR for Soil Moisture Mapping, Remote Sens. Environ., 235 (2019) 111456, https://doi.org/10.1016/j.rse.2019.111456.

Yallappa, D., Veerangouda, M., Maski, D., Palled, V., & Bheemanna, M. (2017). Development and Evaluation of Drone Mounted Sprayer for Pesticide Applications to Crops. IEEE Global Humanitarian Technology Conference (GHTC), pp. 1–7.

Yanliang, Z., Qi, L. & Wei, Z. (2017).Design and Test of a Six-Rotor Unmanned Aerial Vehicle (UAV) Electrostatic Spraying System for Crop Protection. Intl. J. Agric. Biol. Eng., 10(6):68–76.

Zhang, D., Zhou, X., Zhang, J., Lan, Y., Xu, C. & Liang, D. (2018). Detection of Rice Sheath Blight Using an Unmanned Aerial System with High-Resolution Color and Multispectral Imaging, PLoS ONE 13(5): e0187470. https://doi.org/10.1371/journal.pone.0187470.

Chapter 2

Development and Research of a Greenhouse Monitoring System

Murat Kunelbayev and Amantur Umarov
Al-Farabi Kazakh National University, Almaty, Kazakhstan

Contents

2.1 Introduction: Background and Driving Forces

In the article by Van Straten et al. (2010), a greenhouse management system is developed that produces equipment and software, and also conducts training courses on setting up the greenhouse industry. In the article by Lafont et al. (2002), Li et al. (2015), Hahn (2011), and Bennis et al. (2008), computer systems and control controllers have been developed that can be used to control the greenhouse climate in order to improve the development of culture and minimize production costs, as well as use renewable energy sources. In the articles by Heidari et al. (2011), Gupta et al. (2012), Cossu et al. (2014), Mohammadi et al. (2010), mathematical models were developed to study the impact of various energy-saving measures to determine a set of design features of an energy-efficient greenhouse. New technologies for controlling ambient temperature using cooling devices were applied in Leyva et al. (2015), Banik et al. (2014), and Castilla et al. (2006). Heat pumps are used to improve the production of vegetables in greenhouses, which are the main units for cooling systems in greenhouses. In West et al. (2014), a model for predictive control of heating, ventilation, and air conditioning for two greenhouses was developed. The article presents a new methodology for predicting the maximum daily temperature based on the regression approach of reference vectors (Paniagua-Tineo et al. 2011; Van Beveren et al. 2015). A new control system was proposed consisting of a module for minimizing energy costs and a module for implementing a specific input using existing equipment (Van Beveren et al.2015). In He et al. (2010), an algorithm and program for a neural network in a greenhouse were developed. In Yu et al. (2016), an artificial neural network was developed for modeling a greenhouse in a thermal environment. The article by Guillen et al. (2021) examines advanced computing as a solution to bridge the gap between artificial intelligence (AI) and the Internet of Things in rural areas. The paper by Saiz-Rubio et al. (2020) examines the current state of advanced farm management systems by reviewing every important step, from collecting data on crop fields to applying variable rates, so that the producer can make optimal decisions to save money while protecting the environment and transforming food production methods to sustainably match the upcoming population growth. The article by Bersani et al. (2020) provides an overview of approaches to precision and sustainable agriculture with an emphasis on a modern advanced technological solution for monitoring, tracking, and managing greenhouse systems to increase productivity more sustainably. In the article by Castañeda-Miranda et al. (2020), a new technology and architecture of the agro-industrial Internet of Things (AIIoT) for intelligent forecasting of frosts in greenhouses using hybrid AI was developed and investigated. In Pinedo-Alvarez et al. (2020), the effectiveness of the greenhouse microclimate management strategy was developed, which takes into account plant transpiration, including heating, control of various ventilation configurations, and fog generation system based on a frequency-controlled drive, which was tested using Villarreal-Guerrero computer modeling.

The main contribution in this study is that the researchers have developed a new design of a home greenhouse and a monitoring system shows the user the state of the control process, increasing the productivity of the vegetable grower user. Experimental work was also developed with the IoT and WSN functions, which have access to the application from anywhere in the world to display video instructions to the user, and the system also has manual control of three processes: cooling, watering, and lighting.

2.2 Operating Principle

2.2.1 System Architecture and Technological Equipment

The system architecture has three levels (Figure 2.1): the first level is an application level. Object management and display report operations are performed by using interface tools at this level (control buttons, charts, and histograms). The second level is a level of processing and data transfer. Data exchange operations between devices are implemented at this level. The first module ESP32 (1) acts as a transmitter – receives a signal from the sensors of the control object and transmits a signal to the second module ESP32 (2), which plays the receiver role. The ESP32 (1) and ESP32 (2) modules perform two-way data exchange, providing measurement and control operations, interacting with the third level. The third level is the object level. The greenhouse has greenhouse environmental sensors.

Spring unheated greenhouse is considered. Figure 2.2 shows the technological scheme of the mini-greenhouse. The system implements three technological processes: cooling, watering, and lighting.

The system parameters are set, respectively, air temperature $x1$, air humidity $x2$, soil moisture $x3$, and lighting intensity $x4$.

The control unit (CU) uses the feedback control principle (with deviation) (Figure 2.3). The accumulator register, which is part of the CU, compares the corresponding master action $x(i)$ (where $i = 1 \div 4$) with the corresponding output signal $y(i)$ (where $i = 1 \div 4$), and generates the control action $u(k)$ (where $k = 1 \div 3$), which is fed to the input of the corresponding actuators: fan, irrigation valve, and searchlight.

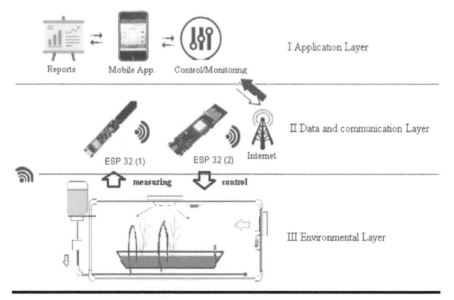

Reports   Mobile App.   Control/Monitoring   I Application Layer

ESP 32 (1)   ESP 32 (2)   Internet   II Data and communication Layer

measuring   control

III Environmental Layer

Figure 2.1   System architecture.

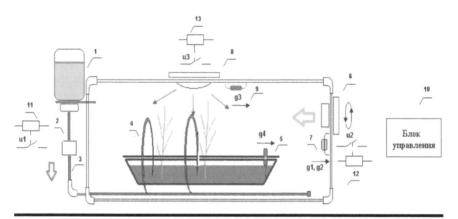

Figure 2.2 Technological circuit of greenhouse work.

The drip irrigation system works as follows. The tank is filled with water (1). The CU (10) controls the water supply (control action *u2*), that it opens/closes the water valve (2) by turning on/off the controller relay. When the valve opens, water flows down (blue arrow), passing through the main pipeline (3) and the dropper (4), and waters the plant in the pot (brown vessel). Information on soil moisture *g3* is measured by a moisture sensor (5) and transmitted to the controller; the CU is received.

The cooling system is described as follows. The CU controls the air supply to the greenhouse, forming the control action *u1*, by turning on/off the fan (6) through the relay. The air supply is indicated by a gray arrow.

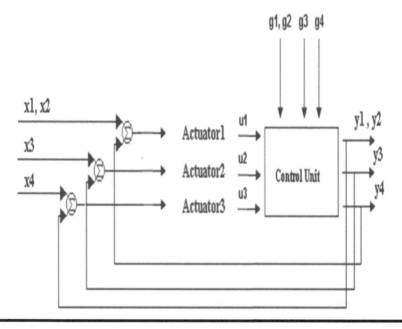

Figure 2.3 Control unit.

ESP 32 (1)   ESP 32 (2)

g_in1   u1
g_in2   u2
g_in3   u3
g_in4

Передатчик   Приемник

Figure 2.4   Transceiver and receiver.

The lighting system controls the light mode of the greenhouse. The CU generates a control action *u3*, which turns on/off the searchlight (8) via the controller relay. Lighting intensity data *g3* is measured by a light sensor (9) and is transmitted to the CU.

Figure 2.4 shows transceiver and receiver where this microcontroller consists of a microcontroller-transmitter and a microcontroller-receiver. The ESP32 (1) transmitter receives signals *g1*, *g2*, *g3*, *g4* and transmits to the ESP32 (2) receiver via a Wi-Fi or Bluetooth network. The receiver performs data processing based on control commands received from a mobile application or web interface and transmits control signals *u1*, *u2*, *u3* to the corresponding actuators.

Figure 2.5 shows the electrical connection of the signal sensors as part of the ESP32 transmitter (1). The circuit consists of an ESP32 microcontroller, a CP2104 module Wi-Fi and Bluetooth, a soil sensor, a DHT11 temperature and humidity sensor, and an LM393-based photosensor.

Figure 2.6 shows the electrical connection diagram of actuators to the ESP32 receiver (2). The diagram consists of an ESP32 microcontroller, a CP2104 Wi-Fi and Bluetooth module, a board of four relays, actuators: Dospel fan, solenoid valve from the washing machine and LED Flood Light Outdoor searchlight.

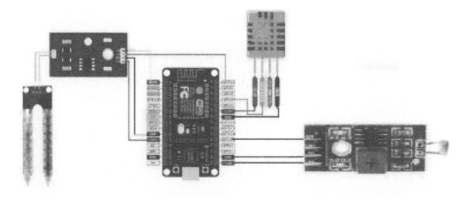

Figure 2.5   Electrical connection circuit of measure sensors in the transceiver.

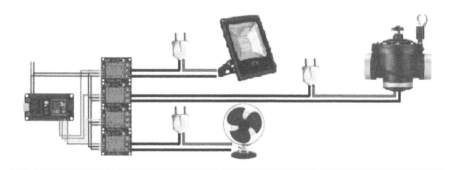

Figure 2.6   Electrical connection circuit of actuators in the receiver.

Figure 2.7 shows the system configuration parameters in the program code. The program uses libraries for communication with a Wi-Fi network, Wi-Fi Client, with a Blynk mobile phone, Widget RTC, with a DHT sensor, and a Time Lib library. The network name is STAR.

```
/* Comment this out to disable prints and save space */
#define BLYNK_PRINT Serial


#include <WiFi.h>
#include <WiFiClient.h>
#include <BlynkSimpleEsp32.h>
#include <TimeLib.h>
#include <WidgetRTC.h>
#include <DHT.h>

// You should get Auth Token in the Blynk App.
// Go to the Project Settings (nut icon).
char auth[] = "rlGQnTwlyF5M3sQ5CStocZopjzZGhPZB";

// Your WiFi credentials.
// Set password to "" for open networks.
char ssid[] = "STAR";
char pass[] = "KZ141095";


#define DHTPIN 26
#define SOILPIN 25
#define DHTTYPE DHT11


DHT dht(DHTPIN, DHTTYPE);

BlynkTimer timer;

// This function sends Arduino's up time every second to Virtual Pin (5).
// In the app, Widget's reading frequency should be set to PUSH. This means
// that you define how often to send data to Blynk App.
void sendSensor()
```

Figure 2.7   Parameters of the system configuration in program code.

2.2.2 System and Equipment Specifications

Table 2.1 provides a list and characteristics of equipment, components, and programs used in the greenhouse implementation.

The system uses low-cost, low-power microcontrollers, series ESP32 with low energy usage. They are a system on a chip with integrated Wi-Fi and Bluetooth controllers and antennas based on the Tensilica Xtensa LX6 microcontroller. These boards operate in environmental conditions from −40 to +125°C, at a frequency of 3.4 GHz, with a data transfer rate of 150 MB, with a maximum transmit power of 19.5 dB.

Table 2.1   Technological Equipment, Materials, and Programs

Equipment and Materials	Model	Specifications
Greenhouse and components		
Frame	Material – PolyVinylChloride pipes (16 m)	Dimensions: 2.0 m × 1.5 m × 1.0 m Pipe diameter 32 PN.
Pot	Material – plastics (1 pcs)	Dimensions: 120 cm × 90 cm × 50 cm. Volume – 25 kg, shelf life – 5 years.
Ground (biohumus)	Ground universal (1 pcs)	
Communication device		
Mobile phone	Samsung (1 pcs)	Model SM – T239. Operating system – Android 4.4.4
Control and communication device with a mobile phone		
Programming support environment of MK	Arduino IDE (1 pcs)	version 1.8.10
Mobile Application Development Environment	Blynk (1 pcs)	version 2.27.6
Actuators		
Air-cooling	Fan Dospel (1 pcs)	220 V, 15 W, diameter 100 mm, flow rate 100 cubic meters/hour.

(Continued)

Table 2.1 *(Continued)* **Technological Equipment, Materials, and Programs**

Equipment and Materials	Model	Specifications
Lighting Magnetic valve	Searchlight street (1 pcs) LED Flood Light Outdoor 220 V, 80 W, lighting angle	120°, 2,700 lm, white color. Service life of 50,000 hours.
	From the washing machine	220 V, 8 W, NZ contact
Drip watering system		
Hydraulic system	Tank 1 l (1 pc), PVC pipe diameter 16 PN, length 3 m (1 pc), droppers' diameter 4 mm, length 80 cm, holes 0.8–1 mm every 15 cm. (8 pcs), components (fittings, tees, plugs).	
Components	Electrical wires, clamps, contacts, trellis, lasso for the garter, etc.	

It should be noted that the main drawback of the ESP8266 board is that for each connected sensor, an additional ESP8266 microcontroller is required (it causes inconvenience of installation and increases the price), although a huge number of IoT home automation projects have been implemented based on ESP8266 to date.

2.3 Results and Discussion

The device that monitors the greenhouse's – temperature and air humidity, soil moisture, and lighting (Figure 2.8). The project is implemented on the basis of an affordable and inexpensive, multi-functional ESP32 board. The specifications of this board make it possible to provide high-quality control and management in wide climate conditions (temperature –40 to + 125°C). Monitoring and manual control of the microclimate state is carried out using a mobile device and through the user's web application (Figure 2.9). Figures 2.10 and 2.11 show the results of monitoring processes in the greenhouse during the growing season (60 days). The first graph shows the processes graphs (time series) taken from the readings of sensors g1, g2, g3, g4. The second figure shows processes graphs after the operation of smoothing data by the Moving Average method. The purpose of this operation is to identify and statistically assess the main trends in the development of the studied

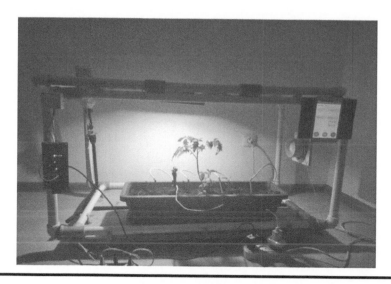

Figure 2.8   Greenhouse in working process.

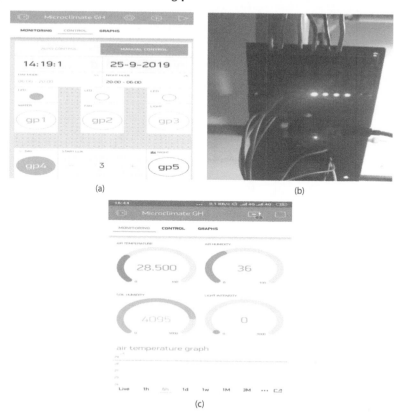

Figure 2.9   (a) Monitoring mode: show values and histograms; (b) control unit; (c) monitoring mode: plots.

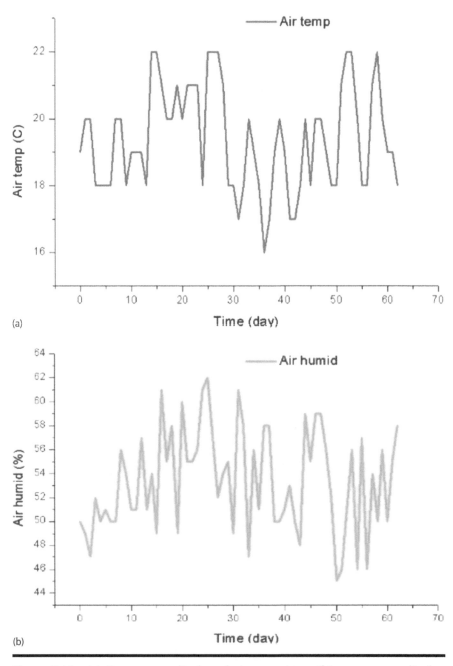

(a)

(b)

Figure 2.10 (a) Process monitoring air temperature; (b) process monitoring air humidity; (c) process monitoring soil humidity; (d) process monitoring light. *(Continued)*

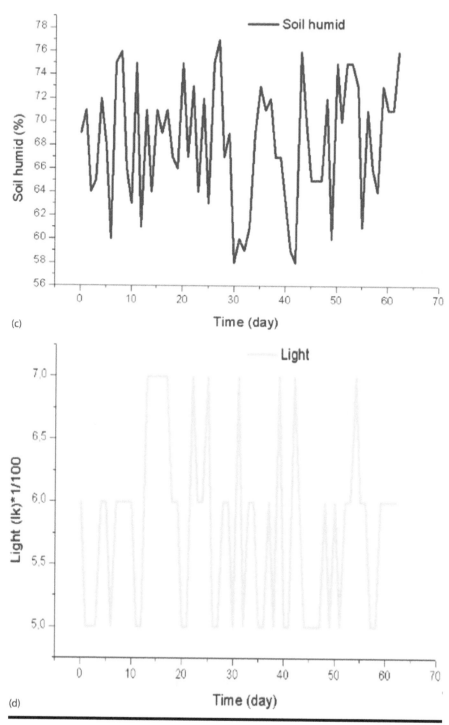

(c)

(d)

Figure 2.10 *(Continued)*

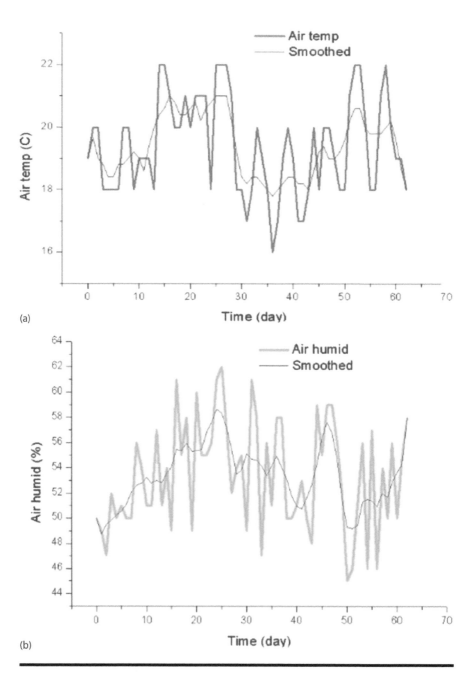

(a)

(b)

Figure 2.11 Process monitoring with smoothing operation: (a) air temperature; (b) air humidity; c) soil humidity; d) light. *(Continued)*

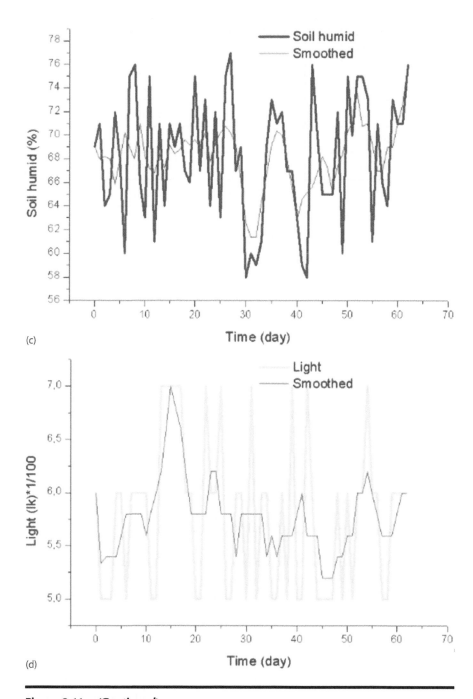

(c)

(d)

Figure 2.11 *(Continued)*

Table 2.2 Standards for Growing Tomato in a Greenhouse and Sensor Measurement Results

Parameters	Norm (task)	The Average Value of the Adjustable Value
Air temperature, C	$x1 \in [18; 22]$	$\bar{y}1 = 19.39$
Air humidity, %	$x2 \in [50; 60]$	$\bar{y}2 = 53.36$
Soil moisture, %	$x3 \in [60; 80]$	$\bar{y}3 = 68.20$
Lightning, lk	$x4 \in [500; 600]$	$\bar{y}4 = 577$

process and deviations from it. Table 2.2 shows the parameters of growing tomatoes in a greenhouse and the average values of adjustable values y (i) for this case. It is not difficult for the user to assess the state of the microclimate based on these average readings of the microclimate. According to the last table, it is necessary to make recommendations for growing vegetables in the greenhouse. The results show that the regulated values that determine the microclimate lie in the optimum region and correspond to the cultivation rate.

2.4 Conclusion

The Greenhouse Monitoring System was developed as part of the study and allows the following:

a. based on the analysis of historical data, it is possible to assess the state of the control process and help the user to take the necessary measures on time;
b. to increase the productivity of the user-vegetable grower.

The system implements the IoT and WSN functions:

the access to the application from anywhere in the world and location;
user video instruction output;
the output of reports on the results in the form of graphs, histograms, audio signals;
sending a message to the user as the monitoring process state;
manual control of three processes: cooling, watering and lighting.

It is planned to add adaptive control functions to the system. It will be implemented through neural network technologies and, depending on changes in the microclimate conditions, the system will automatically adjust and generate optimal control.

References

Banik, P., Ganguly, A. (2014). Thermal modeling and economical analysis of a solar desiccant assisted distributed fan-pad ventilated greenhouse. *Lect. Notes Eng. Comput. Sci.*, 2, 1274–1279.

Bennis, N., Duplaix, J., Enéa, G., Haloua, M., Youlal, H. (2008). Greenhouse climate modelling and robust control, *Comput. Electron. Agric.*, 61, 96–107. https://doi.org/10.1016/j.compag.2007.09.014

Bersani, C., Ouammi, A., Sacile, R., Zero, E. (2020). Model predictive control of smart greenhouses as the path towards near zero energy consumption, *Energies*, 13, 3647. https://doi.org/10.3390/en13143647

Castilla, N., Hernandez, J. (2006). Greenhouse technological packages for high-quality crop production, *Int. Soc. Hortic. Sci.*, 761, 285–297. https://doi.org/10.17660/ActaHortic.2007.761.38

Castañeda-Miranda, A., Castaño, V. (2020). Smart frost measurement for anti-disaster intelligent control in greenhouses via embedding IoT and hybrid AI methods, *Measurement*, 164, 108043. https://doi.org/https://doi.org/10.1016/j.measurement.2020.108043

Cossu, M., Murgia, L., Ledda, L., Deligios, P.A., Sirigu, A., Chessa, F. (2014). Solar radiation distribution inside a greenhouse with south-oriented photovoltaic roofs and effects on crop productivity, *Appl. Energy*, 133, 89–100. https://doi.org/10.1016/j.apenergy.2014.07.070

Guillen, M.A., Llanes, A., Imbernon, B., Martinez-Espana, R., Bueno-Crespo, A., Cano, J.-C., Cecilia, J. M. (2021). Performance evaluation of edge-computing platforms for the prediction of low temperatures in agriculture using deep learning, *J. Supercomput.*, 77, 818–840. https://doi.org/10.1007/s11227-020-03288-w

Gupta, M.J., Chandra, P. (2002). Effect of greenhouse design parameters on conservation of energy for greenhouse environmental control, *Energy*, 27, 777–794. https://doi.org/10.1016/S0360-5442(02)00030-0

Hahn, F. (2011). Fuzzy controller decreases tomato cracking in greenhouses, *Comput. Electron. Agric.*, 77, 21–27. https://doi.org/10.1016/j.compag.2011.03.003

Heidari, M.D., Omid, M. (2011). Energy use patterns and econometric models of major greenhouse vegetable productions in Iran. *Energy*, 36, 220–225. https://doi.org/10.1016/j.energy.2010.10.048

He, F., Ma, C. (2010). Modeling greenhouse air humidity by means of artificial neural network and principal component analysis, *Comput. Electron. Agric.*, 71, 19–23. https://doi.org/10.1016/j.compag.2009.07.011

Lafont, F., Balmat, J.F. (2002). Optimized fuzzy control of a greenhouse, *Fuzzy Sets Syst.*, 128, 47–59. https://doi.org/10.1016/S0165-0114(01)00182-8

Li, X., Strezov, V. (2015). Energy and greenhouse gas emission assessment of conventional and solar assisted air conditioning systems, *Sustainability*, 14710–14728. https://doi.org/10.3390/su71114710

Leyva, R., Constán-Aguilar, C., Sánchez-Rodríguez, E., Romero-Gámez, M., Soriano, T. (2015). Cooling systems in screenhouses: effect on microclimate, productivity and plant response in a tomato crop, *Biosyst. Eng.*, 129, 100–111. https://doi.org/10.1016/j.biosystemseng.2014.09.018

Mohammadi, A., Omid, M. (2010). Economical analysis and relation between energy inputs and yield of greenhouse cucumber production in Iran, *Appl. Energy*, 87, 191–196. https://doi.org/10.1016/j.apenergy.2009.07.021

Paniagua-Tineo, A., Salcedo-Sanz, S., Casanova-Mateo, C., Ortiz-García, E.G., Cony, M.A., Hernández-Martín, E. (2011). Prediction of daily maximum temperature using a support vector regression algorithm, *Renew. Energy*, 36, 3054–3060. https://doi. org/10.1016/j.renene.2011.03.030

Pinedo-Alvarez, A., Flores-Velázquez, J. (2020). Control of greenhouse-air energy and vapor pressure deficit with heating, variable fogging rates and variable vent configurations: simulated effectiveness under varied outside climates, *Comput. Electron. Agric.*, 174, 105515. https://doi.org/10.1016/j.compag.2020.105515

Saiz-Rubio, V., Rovira-Más, F. (2020). From smart farming towards Agriculture 5.0: a review on crop data management, *Agronomy*, 10, 207. https://doi.org/10.3390/ agronomy10020207

Van Straten, G., Van Willigenburg, G., Van Henten, E., Van Ooteghem, E. (2010). *Optimal Control of Greenhouse Cultivation*, CRC Press: London, UK, 326.

Van Beveren, P.J.M., Bontsema, J., Van Straten, G., Van Henten, E.J. (2015). Minimal heating and cooling in a modern rose greenhouse, *Appl. Energy*, 137, 97–109. https://doi. org/10.1016/j.apenergy.2014.09.083

West, S.R., Ward, J.K., Wall, J. (2014). Trial results from a model predictive control and optimisation system for commercial building HVAC, *Energy Build.*, 72, 271–279. https://doi.org/10.1016/j.enbuild.2013.12.037

Yu, H., Chen, Y., Hassan, S.G., Li, D. (2016). Prediction of the temperature in a Chinese solar greenhouse based on LSSVM optimized by improved PSO, *Elsevier Comput. Electron. Agric.*, 122, 94–102. https://doi.org/10.1016/j.compag.2016.01.019

Chapter 3

A Cloud-Computing Model for Implementing Smart Agriculture

M. Zhou and C. Matsika

Midlands State University, Gweru, Zimbabwe

Contents

DOI: 10.1201/9781003311782-3

3.1 Introduction

Most farmers use imprecise and crude farming methods that are unsustainable and unproductive. There is a pressing need to implement modern technologies in agriculture. The implementation of cloud-computing models and deployment strategies (CMDS) alludes to services delivery such as storage, and infrastructure over the Internet based on user demand for information management (Choudhary et al., 2016; Dašić et al., 2016; Kalghatgi & Sambrekar, 2015; Mekala & Viswanathan, 2017). Incorporating smart agricultural technologies like CMDS, Internet of Things (IoT) devices, Global Positioning Systems (GPS) tools, Artificial Intelligence and Machine Learning (AIML) tools, and robots gives a complete smart agriculture package that encourages the adoption of smart agriculture. A research study on Artificial Intelligence (AI) in agriculture only managed to reach the prototype stage and lacked detailed studies; hence, an integrated smart agriculture model is imperatively needed (O'Grady et al., 2019). There is substantial disparity in the capacity to implement Information Communication Technologies (ICTs) for agriculture; hence, cloud computing proffers a solution (Makini et al., 2020; Uriel et al., 2020). Similarly, other research studies have studied issues encountered by resource-constrained farmers in agriculture based on cloud computing, deep learning, and NB-IoT only to monitor crops through information transmission equipment (Akhtar et al., 2021; Lee et al., 2020). There is a need to harness disruptive technologies so that farmers in resource-constrained countries can obtain maximum benefits from a comprehensive smart agriculture model.

Bandi et al. (2017), Gondchawar and Kawitkar (2016a), Ji et al. (2015), Nagpure et al. (2019), Ramachandran et al. (2018), Sahu et al. (2019), and Tech-Student (2016) also reviewed methodologies that use the IoT and automation-based agricultural convergence technology with a bias toward crops in the fields and the warehouse. This research applies IoT in the context of resource-constrained environments. Mobile computing and big data analytics inform the model by integrating smart agriculture processes while promoting value from data and agricultural processes in resource-constrained countries. The development of many countries is derailed with challenges in the agricultural sector. Smart agriculture modern techniques minimize the challenges of traditional methods of agriculture (Gondchawar & Kawitkar, 2016).

According to Kumar (2021), the consistently increasing population in Asian nations such as India commands the expeditious improvement in food production technology. Kumar studied a fully automated irrigation system and a weather monitoring system that notified the farmers about climatic changes. Smart agriculture is the only solution to the issues faced by the current traditional methods of agriculture to enhance productivity (Bandi et al., 2017; Dhanasekar et al., 2018; I. M. Marcu et al., 2019; Mathur et al., 2019; Veena, 2018). In a research paper entitled *"IoT based monitoring system in agriculture,"* Dhanasekar et al. (2018) postulated IoT technologies and smart warehouse management as an integrated smart agriculture model that boosts agricultural yields and improves economies. A smart agricultural model is needed in developing countries to modernize conventional agriculture for better production (Ardiansyah & Pakuan, 2017; Bryceson, 2019; Choudhary et al., 2016; Gayathri et al., 2021; Patil et al., 2017; Sahu et al., 2019; Sushanth & Sujatha, 2018).

The book chapter contributes a model which does not only integrate disruptive technologies in agriculture. It includes facets like stakeholders and smart agriculture processes. The objectives of the book chapter are as follows:

To identify existing cloud-computing models and how they inform smart agriculture.
To discuss the disruptive technologies and apply them in agriculture.
To identify smart agriculture processes and their implementation using cloud computing and disruptive technologies.
To explore facilitation conditions to adopt and use smart agriculture in resource-constrained environments.

Divakarla and Kumari (2010) suggested investigations in risks, policy, and service models to facilitate the business aspect of cloud technology. The main contributions of the chapter are as follows:

A model that integrates disruptive technologies and CMDS.
Mapping four concepts, namely, data collection, diagnostics, decision making, and commits/actions in the model.

3.2 Background

Smart agriculture refers to information-driven farming that alludes to the management of agricultural activities using ICTs to enhance the quality and quantity of produce and concurrently optimize the human labor required by production (Bandi et al., 2017; Dehghani et al., 2020; Dhanasekar et al., 2018; Gayathri et al., 2021; Gondchawar & Kawitkar, 2016; Klerkx et al., 2019; Lee et al., 2020; I. M. Marcu et al., 2019; Meghana & Nataraj, 2016; Mekala & Viswanathan, 2017; Nagpure et al., 2019; O'Grady et al., 2019; Ramachandran et al., 2018; Ramakrishna et al., 2019; Sahu et al., 2019; Suma et al., 2017; Sushanth & Sujatha, 2018; Veena, 2018). Smart agriculture components such as robotics, sensing technologies, hardware and software applications, data analytics solutions, telecommunications systems, and GPS have been proposed and applied in different smart-farming environments.

Sustainable Development Goals 2 and 9 (SDG 2 and SDG 9) focus on sustainability and inclusiveness in better farming methodologies (smart agriculture). SDG 2 focuses on ending hunger, achieving food security and improved nutrition, and promoting sustainable agriculture. SDG 9 focuses on building resilient infrastructure, promoting inclusive and sustainable industrialization, and fostering innovation (United Nations, 2015). This book aims to develop a model for smart agriculture in resource-constrained environments.

While there exist various literatures on agricultural digitalization using disruptive technologies such as Machine Learning (ML), Block-Chain Technology (BCT), and Data Science and Analytics (DSA), the body of knowledge is scattered and disintegrated. There is no smart agriculture model for resource-constrained farmers.

3.3 Cloud-Computing Models to Support Smart Agriculture

The "cloud" alludes to a blend of networks, storage, hardware, and interfaces to deliver a service (Namani & Gonen, 2020). Cloud-computing models include Infrastructure as a Service (IaaS), Platform as a Service (PaaS), Software as a Service (SaaS), Database as a Service (DBaaS), Mobile backend as a Service (BaaS), and Big data as a Service (BDaaS) which support smart agriculture.

Figure 3.1 depicts three main cloud-computing models where SaaS refers to cloud-based software that allows farmers to access their agricultural data from any mobile device that is connected to the Internet to enhance operational efficiency, on the go. SaaS creates a versatile, conducive, and adaptable environment by leveraging cutting-edge technologies to both the modern farmer and the consumer through strategic outsourcing, convenient data storage, reduction in human labor, conservation of resources and energy, as well as by managing an IT infrastructure setup. As such, SaaS provides a more economical and scalable way to adopt and/or upgrade to smart agriculture for the marginalized farmers as they do not have to

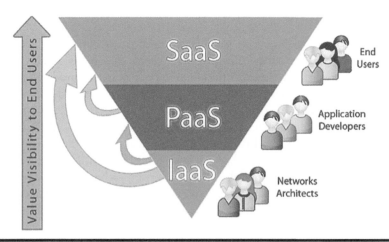

Figure 3.1   Three main cloud-computing models.

Source: SMEChannels (2016).

buy and install software on particular computers. Enterprises like CropIn utilize satellite monitoring and ML to perform a predictive analysis and produce customized reports that give actionable insights directly to farmers' screens. SaaS bridges the digital divide potentially experienced by the marginalized farmer as it enables the marginalized farmers to assess and manage their all-inclusive farm operations with one software. SaaS is a low-risk investment with either a monthly or yearly subscription. Companies providing SaaS solutions like CropIn provide one-stop inclusive solutions for the farmer. SaaS solutions drive the management of the farm, sales, risk, as well as traceability. A mobile application that will guide the farmers in their daily activities can be developed. As such, SaaS strengthens, increases efficiency, and scales up agricultural productivity through cost efficiency, marketing, compliance, scalability, improved mobile functionality, and security (Kalghatgi & Sambrekar, 2015; I. Marcu et al., 2019; Namani & Gonen, 2020; Oteyo et al., 2021; Ray, 2017; Symeonaki et al., 2017).

IaaS refers to the infrastructural services like virtual machines, networking components, and traffic redirecting, among other services, that can be rendered to aid marginalized farmers in dealing with infrastructural costs by cloud service providers. The IaaS model provides tailor-made scalable infrastructural resources to farmers in marginalized communities to promote data usage and sharing (Choudhary et al., 2016; Namani & Gonen, 2020; Pawar, 2018; Ray, 2017; Thalluri et al., 2020).

In the PaaS model, a computing platform that includes the operating system, the execution environment, the database, the web server, and the programming languages is provided to farmers; as such, they do not have to individually purchase these services but could only require an in-house software developer for the deployment of software and support. The farmer can therefore organize and run the software and applications (Kalghatgi & Sambrekar, 2015; Ray, 2017).

Cloud-computing models alleviate or reduce the costs required for hardware and software resources by farmers. Akhtar et al. (2021) suggested the need to undoubtedly incorporate the IoT in agriculture for low-income countries that heavily depend on agriculture for their gross domestic product. Farmers in developing nations do not have the appropriate infrastructure for precision agriculture. In addition, they do not have access to smart agriculture platforms that provide seamless connections across heterogeneous platforms. Therefore, it is obligatory to develop a methodological paradigm that can accommodate cloud services like IaaS which this book chapter aims to incorporate in the model to bridge the divide. The cloud allows farmers to capture information about crops, soil information, cultivators, expert information, and check information seamlessly on electronic commerce (e-commerce), and effectively share information. Cloud computing deployment models include cloud, hybrid, and on-premises strategies. The cloud-based approach fully runs in the cloud. The entire system or application runs in the cloud; hence, it is adopted in this chapter since they're no ICT and human resources required to support on-premises virtualization and resource management. Hybrid is a combination of the two concepts (Amazon, 2021).

3.4 Disruptive Technologies in Smart Agriculture

The advent of new technologies, inventions, and processes in the marketplace is coined as disruptive technologies (Girasa, 2020; Makridakis et al., 2018; Zovko & Gudlin, 2020). In a survey entitled *"Smart agriculture IoT with cloud computing,"* Mekala and Viswanathan (2017) and Ramakrishna et al. (2019) proposed that the efficient use of agricultural chemicals and other products can be done through the use of IoT technology. They concluded that there is a need to develop an optimal Agri-IoT architecture. The architecture supports very low cost, low power consumption, improved decision-making processes, quality of service (QoS), and optimal performance (I. M. Marcu et al., 2019). The interconnection of various devices like location systems, controllers, robots, sensors, motors, and relays through the Internet describes the IoT (Suma et al., 2017).

ML is part of AI which applies statistical models to train data to identify patterns for predictive purposes. In smart agriculture, an ML algorithm is applied using a given dataset. Iteratively, the algorithm is trained to perform as intended. For example, it can identify things like weeds or particular crops like wheat or corn. The algorithm will learn to identify each item precisely and improve with time.

Farmers can produce valuable information on crops status and other agricultural information. The information helps in the planning, implementation, or evaluation of processes that enhance the overall agricultural yields. ML applications in agriculture possess many benefits.

ML artifacts should be easily understood by non-technical users like farmers. The book chapter becomes a panacea to narrowing the gap as it is targeting the resource-constrained farmer. Previous research on smart agriculture has marginalized the farmers without resources and it is high time inclusive smart agricultural models are developed. The disruptive technologies include ML which supports super-intelligent decision making from existing or system-derived algorithms from the knowledge base of the data collected (big data). Other disruptive technologies include sensors and robots which are location systems enabled for monitoring and analysis of agricultural processes in the farms. The hardware elements are supported with software that is compatible with mobile devices, embedded devices, and unique devices such as sensors that are used for the collection of data to the cloud.

3.5 Smart Agriculture Processes

Smart agriculture supports several processes like data collection, diagnostics, decision making, and commits. Data collection elements include soil, air, and humidity data at a farming place using sensors that transmit the data to the server. Diagnostics and analytics are applied to the data. The data is analyzed to provide conclusions of samples collected highlighting any potential problems. Decisions are made based on the results from the data analyzed. Decision making focuses on analyzing the problems identified and deciding on actions required to resolve these. Ultimately, actions or commits are the execution of actual steps identified, and the loop continues. Diagnostics in agriculture processes result in resource optimization such as agricultural chemicals, compounds, water, and energy.

3.6 Policymakers and Other Stakeholders Involvement in Smart Agriculture

The involvement of stakeholders such as farmers, farm managers, agricultural research and specialist service providers, international and national food production organizations, software houses, and developers is critical in pulling resources together and improving processes. Akhtar et al. (2021) examined smart agriculture from an economic panorama. They suggested that supporting farmers in resource-constrained nations allows them to participate in the agricultural ecosystem seamlessly and creates synergies. Farmers can export their products from anywhere and anytime in a highly networked ecosystem and they can venture into product value-addition. The integration of the agricultural ecosystem from the seed development, farming, and production, selling and distribution, research and development is considered as an element and is facilitated through a partnership among stakeholders through the implementation of policies and regulations. The mismanagement of the agricultural ecosystem leads to food security risks and poverty globally due to imbalances in the distribution channels. These challenges affect all the aforementioned stakeholders.

3.7 Software and Applications Supporting Smart Agriculture

According to Sustainable ICTs for Agriculture & Global Trends (El Bilali et al. 2018), the digital technologies in agriculture include the use of telephony, computers and websites, satellites, mobile phones, Internet and broadband, sensor networks, and data storage and analytics processes supported by Blockchain, big data, and AI. Software and applications developed must support different devices and users in the smart agriculture ecosystem. Farmers are always on the go; hence, mobile applications and operating software must be customized to support their demands. Through ML and AI, it is now possible to have AI-enabled satellites which analyze data and then predict corn yields. An ML algorithm enables the identification of the plant conditions of plants. It is through such agriculture software and applications that farming is enhanced.

3.8 ICT Infrastructure Sharing to Support Smart Agriculture

According to Africa Infrastructure Investment Report (2013), inadequate ICTs in Africa are a drawback of sustainable development. IaaS will come in handy to help resource-constrained and marginalized farmers. Malungu and Moturi (2015) proposed an adoption framework for ICT infrastructure sharing after they established the drivers, levels, and challenges of infrastructure sharing. Infrastructure sharing results in reducing costs during the adoption and use of smart agriculture. To bridge the digital divide, services like satellites provide Wi-Fi services to farmers without an Internet connection or in marginalized regions. Drone technologies may also be used to distribute ICT gadgets or to spray fertilizers and pesticides that prevent direct human contact with harmful chemicals.

3.9 Sustainable Development Goals for Agriculture at Both Local and International Levels for Sustainable Food Security and Nutrition and Agriculture in Supporting Smart Agriculture

The European Environmental Policy (Turbé et al. 2019) coined models and assessment tools that integrate a wider range of existing and emerging measures in the agriculture sector. Instead of just concentrating on climatic issues, they also considered bridging the digital divide in smart agriculture. The key building blocks of smart agriculture identified in the *Sustainable ICTs for Agriculture & Global Trends* (2018) include computer services and applications, infrastructure, standards and interoperability, content, knowledge management, and sharing, legislation, policy and compliance, workforce and capacity development, governance and leadership, and investments and strategies. The challenges identified are categorized and related to the following:

- The coping strategies of farmers and their resilience in the face of droughts
- Lack of capacity and knowledge by farmers to adopt newer farming practices
- Population growth and diverse food habits
- Shrinking access to arable land
- Youth in agriculture, the average age of farmers
- Lack of access to quality agricultural inputs
- Lack of farm/agriculture mechanization adaptation
- Lack of access to water resources
- Inadequate supplies of improved crop varieties and certified seeds
- Insufficient access to credit by the farmers

- Inadequate extension support to farmers
- Poor on-farm management of water, crops, and pests
- Lack of post-harvest storage and logistics infrastructure access by farmers resulting in
- Post-harvest losses
- Disaster management and early warning
- Marketing, channels, access to markets and linkages
- Production and post-production processing
- Social and gender issues
- Food quality standards and monitoring

In a nutshell, digital components that need to be addressed include infrastructure issues; digital divide; interoperability issues; data analytics; data issues; capacity building; data sharing; and privacy issues; support to innovations and policies regulations are the key building blocks that need to be addressed for smart agriculture to be a success.

3.10 The Cloud-Computing Model for Smart Agriculture Processes in Resource-Constrained Environment (CSMARCE)

The CSMARCE consists of the four major elements, namely, smart agriculture adoption and use facilitators, smart agriculture processes, disruptive technologies and stakeholders as shown in Figure 3.2.

Facilitation conditions are critical for the deployment of smart agriculture in resource-constrained environments. The partnership of stakeholders such as farmers, farm managers, agricultural research and specialist services providers, international and national food production organizations, governments, and other stakeholders supports resource mobilization and utilization in smart agriculture practices. Policymakers support the cheap and easy acquisition of ICT resources. In addition, policymakers can draft infrastructure sharing models which support incentivizing owners in monetary value or compensation during replacement or maintenance. In addition, this can include innovation incentives and subsidies. The parties in this domain include the Department of Agricultural, Technical and Extension Services (AGRITEX) officers, Zimbabwe Farmers' Union (ZFU) officers, Non-Governmental Organizations supporting agriculture, and the government. The governance model is enacted to protect the owners of ICT tools and enforce responsibility in third-party users. The Ministry of Information and Communication Technologies (ICTs), Government Internet Service Provider (GISP), and Software Development Houses aid in the development and customization of applications to suit unique needs in agricultural processes. Applications

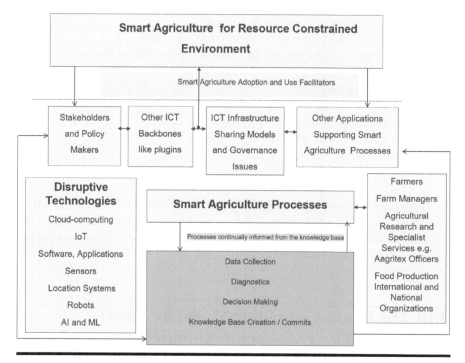

Figure 3.2 The Cloud-Computing Model for Smart Agriculture Processes in Resource-constrained Environment (CSMARCE).

include plugins that facilitate the integration of disruptive technologies tools and applications supporting agricultural processes.

Cloud computing supports the storage and sharing of data through the creation of knowledge bases to support continued knowledge creation and effective decision making in the lifecycle of the smart agriculture processes, namely, data collection, diagnostics, decision making, and decision commits. Mobile Network Operators (MNOs) and Internet Service Providers (ISPs) engagement is crucial for the provision of reliable subsidized Internet. Wireless Internet is key for IoT, sensors devices, and other ICT devices to be connected to the cloud.

The use of semi-autonomous and autonomous robots in monitoring and analysis of crops and livestock while sending data autonomously to the cloud is essential for agricultural productivity. It includes controlling pests and diseases through sensor technology, pruning, harvesting, spraying, and weed control. Equipment and tool like sprayers, harvesters are self-guided by GPS. Farmers use mobile devices to control them from anywhere and any position using customized applications. The robots eliminate the geographic barriers and inaccessibility irrespective of the time and availability of human labor. Figure 3.3 shows samples of robots used in smart agriculture.

Figure 3.3   Robots used in smart agriculture.

Sources: Association for Advanced Automation (2019); Debusmann (2021); Online Sciences (2019).

3.11 Limitations and Future Scope

The research can be further informed using primary data. Due to COVID-19 pandemic restrictions, face-to-face interviews with the farmers were not conducted to get first-hand information on the domain matter. It is also off-season for most agricultural activities in Zimbabwe as it is not yet raining; as such, most farmers were not easily reachable.

Future studies may study how Augmented and Virtual Reality (AVR) technology can enhance smart agriculture in marginalized communities. AVR technology alludes to the ability to portray the real world through overlaying digital content (augmented reality) in a two-dimensional environment (virtual reality) (Miller & Dousay, 2015). AVR technology is a tool that can be utilized by a farmer to appreciate the practical skills that enhance their farming activities. It gives the farmer, a look and feel of how the emerging technologies are being applied in smart agriculture cost-effectively. AVR technology is therefore capable of enhancing smart agriculture as it has limitless capabilities and its impact on smart agriculture should be studied further. Technology adoption models must be applied to inform further the factors affecting the adoption and use of smart agriculture.

3.12 Conclusion

Smart agriculture supports a healthy agricultural environment coupled with agricultural productivity for both high- and low-income countries. The socio-economically disadvantaged benefit from an infrastructure shared model both on physical devices and on cloud services in the use of smart agriculture equipment, and devices through rentals, waivers, and subsidies facilitated by the government and responsible authorities. The implementation of the models and their evaluation is essential for various farming environments like village farms, commercial farms, and so on. Security in the use of smart agriculture needs to be explored. The research informs the attainment of 2030 Sustainable Development Goals for Agriculture at both local and international levels for sustainable food security and nutrition and agriculture.

References

Akhtar, M. N., Shaikh, A. J., Khan, A., Awais, H., Bakar, E. A. & Othman, A. R. (2021). Smart sensing with edge computing in precision agriculture for soil assessment and heavy metal monitoring: a review. *Agriculture (Switzerland)*, *11*(6), 1–37. https://doi.org/10.3390/agriculture11060475

Amazon. (2021). Types of Cloud Computing. https://aws.amazon.com/types-of-cloud-computing/

Ardiansyah, D. & Pakuan, U. (2017). *IOT Framework for Smart Agriculture to Improve Agricultural Urgency Legal Aspects of Growth Information Technology In Indonesia* (Issue March).

Association for Advanced Automation. (2019). Agricultural Robots: Understanding Professional Service Robots in Agriculture. https://www.automate.org/a3-content/getting-started-with-automation

Bandi, R., Swamy, S. & Raghav S. (2017). A framework to improve crop yield in smart agriculture using IoT. *International Journal of Research in Science & Engineering*, *3*(1), 176–180.

Bryceson, K. (2019). *Disruptive Technologies supporting Agricultural Education. January.* https://doi.org/10.4995/head19.2019.8957

Choudhary, S., Jadoun, R. & Mandoriya, H. (2016). Role of cloud computing technology in agriculture fields. *Computing*, *7*(3), 1–7.

Dašić, P., Dašić, J. & Crvenković, B. (2016). Service models for cloud computing: search as a service (SaaS). *International Journal of Engineering and Technology*, *8*(5), 2366–2373. https://doi.org/10.21817/ijet/2016/v8i5/160805034

Debusmann, B. (2021, March 1). *Farms are going to need different kinds of robots.* https://www.bbc.com/news/business-56195288

Dehghani, M., Lee, S. H. (Mark) & Mashatan, A. (2020). Touching holograms with windows mixed reality: renovating the consumer retailing services. *Technology in Society, 63*(September), 101394. https://doi.org/10.1016/j.techsoc.2020.101394

Dhanasekar, N., Soundarya, S., Kumar, R. C., Basam, M. S. M., Kumar, S. S. & Selvan, S. S. (2018). IOT based monitoring system in smart agriculture. *International Journal of Research and Analytical Reviews, 5*(2), 1790–1795.

Divakarla, U. & Kumari, G. (2010). An overview of cloud computing in distributed systems. *AIP Conference Proceedings, 1324*(2007), 184–186. https://doi.org/10.1063/1.3526188

El Bilali, H. & Allahyari, M. S. (2018). Transition towards sustainability in agriculture and food systems: Role of information and communication technologies. *Information Processing in Agriculture, 5*(4), 456–464.

Gayathri, M., Arun Shunmugam, D. & Ishwariya, A. (2021). Smart irrigation system using IoT. *International Journal of Innovative Research in Engineering & Multidisciplinary Physical Sciences, 9*(3). https://doi.org/10.37082/ijirmps.2021.v09i03.027

Girasa, R. (2020). Artificial Intelligence as a Disruptive Technology: Economic Transformation and Government Regulation. In *Artificial Intelligence as a Disruptive Technology*. Palgrave Macmillan. https://doi.org/10.1007/978-3-030-35975-1_1

Gondchawar, N. & Kawitkar, R. S. (2016). IoT based smart agriculture. *International Journal of Advanced Research in Computer and Communication Engineering, 5*(6), 838–842.

Ji, C., Lu, H., Ji, C. & Yan, J. (2015). An IoT and Mobile Cloud Based Architecture for Smart Planting. Proceedings of the 2015 3rd International Conference on Machinery, Materials and Information Technology Applications, 35, pp. 1001–1005. https://doi.org/10.2991/icmmita-15.2015.184

Kalghatgi, S. & Sambrekar, K. P. (2015). Review: Using cloud computing technology in agricultural development. *International Journal of Innovative Science, Engineering & Technology 2*(3), 740–745.

Klerkx, L., Jakku, E. & Labarthe, P. (2019). A review of social science on digital agriculture, smart farming and agriculture 4.0: new contributions and a future research agenda. *NJAS – Wageningen Journal of Life Sciences, 90–91*(October), 100315. https://doi.org/10.1016/j.njas.2019.100315

Lee, K., Silva, B. N. & Han, K. (2020). Deep learning entrusted to fog nodes (DLEFN) based smart agriculture. *Applied Sciences (Switzerland), 10*(4). https://doi.org/10.3390/app10041544

Makini, F. M., Mose, L. O., Kamau, G., Mulinge, W., Salasya, B., Akuku, B. & Makelo, M. (2020). The status of ICT infrastructure, innovative environment and ICT4AG services in agriculture. *Food and Nutrition in Kenya, 5*(11), 1–75.

Malungu, C. B. & Moturi, C. A. (2015). ICT infrastructure sharing framework for developing countries: case of mobile operators in Kenya. *International Journal of Applied Information Systems, 9*(4), 17–24. https://doi.org/10.5120/ijais15-451392

Marcu, I. M., Suciu, G., Balaceanu, C. M. & Banaru, A. (2019). IoT Based System for Smart Agriculture. *Proceedings of the 11th International Conference on Electronics, Computers and Artificial Intelligence, ECAI 2019, June.* https://doi.org/10.1109/ECAI46879.2019.9041952

Marcu, I., Suciu, G., Bălăceanu, C., Drăgulinescu, A. M. & Dobrea, M. A. (2019). IoT Solution for Plant Monitoring in Smart Agriculture. *SIITME 2019 – 2019 IEEE 25th International Symposium for Design and Technology in Electronic Packaging, Proceedings, October,* pp. 194–197. https://doi.org/10.1109/SIITME47687.2019.8990798

Mathur, R., Pathak, V. & Bandil, D. (2019). Emerging Trends in Expert Applications and Security. In *Emerging Trends in Expert Applications and Security*, vol. 841, Issue January. Springer: Singapore. https://doi.org/10.1007/978-981-13-2285-3

Meghana, K.C. & Nataraj, K. R. (2016). IOT Based Intelligent Bin for Smart Cities. *International Journal on Recent and Innovation Trends in Computing and Communication*, *4*(5), 225–229.

Mekala, M. S. & Viswanathan, P. (2017). A Survey: Smart Agriculture IoT with Cloud Computing. *2017 International Conference on Microelectronic Devices, Circuits and Systems*, ICMDCS 2017 (August 2017), pp. 1–7. https://doi.org/10.1109/ICMDCS.2017.8211551

Miller, D. & Dousay, T. (2015). Implementing augmented reality in the classroom. *Issues and Trends in Educational Technology*, *3*(2), 1–11. https://doi.org/10.2458/azu_itet_v3i2_miller

Murali, D., Tummala, R. K., Sanjeev Kumar, A. N., Bhuvaneswari, E., & Venkatesan, R. (2021). SUSTAINABLE FARMING FOR AGRICULTURE IMPROVEMENT USING IOT. *International Journal of Modern Agriculture*, *10*(1), 106–115.

Nagpure, S., Ingale, S., Pahurkar, S., Bobade, A. M., Ghosal, M. & Dhope, T. (2019). Smart agriculture using IOT. *Helix*, *9*(3), 5081–5083. https://doi.org/10.29042/2019-5081-5083

Namani, S. & Gonen, B. (2020). Smart agriculture based on IoT and cloud computing. *Proceedings of the 3rd International Conference on Information and Computer Technologies*, ICICT 2020, pp. 553–556. https://doi.org/10.1109/ICICT50521.2020.00094

O'Grady, M. J., Langton, D. & O'Hare, G. M. P. (2019). Edge computing: a tractable model for smart agriculture? *Artificial Intelligence in Agriculture*, *3*, 42–51. https://doi.org/10.1016/j.aiia.2019.12.001

Online Sciences. (2019). Online Sciences. https://www.online-sciences.com/robotics/robotic-applications-in-agricultural-industry-autonomous-agricultural-robot-types-uses-and-importance/

Oteyo, I. N., Marra, M., Kimani, S., De Meuter, W. & Boix, E. G. (2021). A survey on mobile applications for smart agriculture. *SN Computer Science*, *2*(4), 1–16. https://doi.org/10.1007/s42979-021-00700-x

Patil, Gokul L., Gawande, Prashant S. & Bag, R. V. (2017). Smart agriculture system based on IoT and its social impact. *International Journal of Computer Applications*, *176*(1), 1–4. https://doi.org/10.5120/ijca2017915500

Pawar, D. (2018). Enhanced smart agriculture model. *International Research Journal of Engineering and Technology*, 3673–3675.

Powell, S. (2013). *Africa Infrastructure Investment Report*. https://www.un.org/ohrlls/sites/www.un.ohrlls/files/lldcs_publications/the-africa-infrastructure-investment-report-2013.pdf

Ramachandran, V., Ramalakshmi, R. & Srinivasan, S. (2018). An Automated Irrigation System for Smart Agriculture Using the Internet of Things. *2018 15th International Conference on Control, Automation, Robotics and Vision, ICARCV 2018, November*, pp. 210–215. https://doi.org/10.1109/ICARCV.2018.8581221

Ramakrishna, C., Venkateshwarlu, B., Srinivas, J. & Srinivas, S. (2019). Iot based smart farming using cloud computing and machine learning. *International Journal of Innovative Technology and Exploring Engineering*, *9*(1), 3455–3458. https://doi.org/10.35940/ijitee.A4853.119119

Ray, P. P. (2017). Internet of things for smart agriculture: technologies, practices and future direction. *Journal of Ambient Intelligence and Smart Environments*, *9*(4), 395–420. https://doi.org/10.3233/AIS-170440

Sahu, H., Modala, P., Jiwankar, A. & Wagle, S. (2019). Multidisciplinary model for smart agriculture using IoT. *International Journal of Research in Engineering, Science and Management*, *3*, 245–247.

SMEChannels. (2016). PaaS, SaaS, IaaS: The forefront of Digital India. https://www.smechannels.com/paas-saas-iaas-the-forefront-of-digital-india/

Suma, N., Samson, S. R., Saranya, S., Shanmugapriya, G. & Subhashri, R. (2017). IOT based smart agriculture monitoring system. *International Journal on Recent and Innovation Trends in Computing and Communication* 5(2), 177–181.

Sushanth, G. & Sujatha, S. (2018). IOT Based Smart Agriculture System. *2018 International Conference on Wireless Communications, Signal Processing and Networking, WiSPNET 2018*, 1(8), pp. 103–107. https://doi.org/10.1109/WiSPNET.2018.8538702

Symeonaki, E., Arvanitis, K. & Piromalis, D. (2017). Review on the trends and challenges of cloud computing technology in climate – smart agriculture. *CEUR Workshop Proceedings, 2030*, 66–78.

Tech-Student, M. (2016). A literature study on agricultural production system using IoT as inclusive technology. *International Journal of Innovative Technology and Research*, *4*(1), 2727–2731.

Thalluri, L. N., Prasad Ayodhya, J., Anjaneya Prasad, T. B., Yuva Raju, C. H., Vadlamudi, S. & Babu, P. B. (2020). A Novel and Smart IoT System for Real Time Agriculture Applications with IaaS Cloud Computing. *2020 International Conference on Computer Communication and Informatics, ICCCI 2020*, pp. 1–6. https://doi.org/10.1109/ICCCI48352.2020.9104160

Turbé, A., Barba, J., Pelacho, M., Mugdal, S., Robinson, L. D., Serrano-Sanz, F., et al. (2019). Understanding the citizen science landscape for European environmental policy: an assessment and recommendations. *Citizen Science: Theory and Practice*, *4*(1).

United Nations. (2015). Transforming our World: the 2030 Agenda for Sustainable Development. In *Transactions of the International Astronomical Union* (Vol. 10, Issue October). https://doi.org/10.1017/s0251107x00020617

Uriel, C., Sergio, S., Carolina, G., Mariano, G., Paola, D. & Martín, A. (2020). Improving the understanding of basic sciences concepts by using virtual and augmented reality. *Procedia Computer Science*, *172*, 389–392. https://doi.org/10.1016/j.procs.2020.05.165

Veena, S., Mahesh, K., Rajesh, M., & Salmon, S. (2018). The survey on smart agriculture using IOT. *Int J Innov Res Eng Manag (IJRIREM)*, *5*(2), 63-66.

Zovko, V. & Gudlin, M. (2020). Artificial Intelligence as a Disruptive Technology. *International Conference – The Future of Education*. https://doi.org/10.1007/978-3-030-35975-1

Chapter 4

Application of Conversational Artificial Intelligence for Farmer's Advisory and Communication

Anurag Sinha[1] and Den Whilrex Garcia[2]

[1]*Department of Information Technology, Amity University Jharkhand, Ranchi, India*
[2]*Department of Engineering, Lyceum of the Philippines University – Cavite Campus, Cavite, Philippines*

Contents

DOI: 10.1201/9781003311782-4

4.1   Introduction

4.1.1   State of Agriculture Sector in India

For many years, the main source of livelihood in India is from the agriculture sector. As a substantial fact, it is considered as one of the important sectors in the country as it offers abundant job and employment opportunities for the locals. Currently, India ranks second in the world in terms of the production of agricultural goods. Thus, this sector subsidizes a major share in the gross domestic product (GDP) of the country (State of Rajasthan Agriculture State of Rajasthan Agriculture, 2012; Dolci, 2017).

4.1.2   Problems and Challenges Faced by the Agriculture Segment of India

In India, the agribusiness area is as of now confronting certain troubles and difficulties. A portion of this happened quite a while past, while some are increasing a direct result of the present horticultural standards and practices. These difficulties include, but aren't limited to, the following ones (Devlin et al., 2019):

Lessening Arable Domain: Arable land turns out to be less and less due to nonstop strain from the quickly developing populace and advancing urbanization and industrialization. Truth is told, the number of inhabitants in India, floods speedier than its ability to yield wheat and rice. That squeezes the agribusiness area (Podder et al., 2021a,b).

Sluggishness Insignificant Harvest Creation: It is inconvenient that some significant yields, for example, wheat, are getting stale underway. This made a huge hole between the interest and supply of the rising populace and creation (Qiu et al., 2018).

Soil Exhaustion: Besides the positive effects, there are some adverse consequences of the Green Revolution; one of them is soil depletion. It is because of the utilization of compound composts. Likewise, the redundancy of the same yield debases the supplements in the dirt.

Decline in Fresh Ground Water: Another adverse consequence of the Green Revolution is the declining measure of groundwater. In dry areas, cultivating is refined with the assistance of water system offices done by the groundwater utilization. The constant act of such rural exercises has prompted a disturbing state in the setting of groundwater circumstances (Gao et al., 2018; N. Jain et al., 2019).

Increase Cost in Farm Inputs: Despite an increase in the expenses of homestead information sources including pesticides, manure, ranch labor, and cultivating equipment, low and medium land-holding ranchers are in a precarious position (Handrianto et al., 2019).

Effect of Global Climate Change: Increase in temperature influences agrarian practices in India too (Bhar et al., 2019).

Farmer Suicides: Farmers are ending it all; it's anything but a significant portion of submitted suicides in India. It is a significant issue looking by farming area of India. The higher self-destruction rate is accounted for in regions where there is higher commercialization and privatization of horticulture and higher worker obligation (Yan, 2018).

Refrain from Cultivating: Farmer's kids stopping from their calling is additionally a significant issue. Regardless of the arduous and monotonous work, procuring is less in contrast to its expensive homestead inputs that are making ranchers head toward different alternatives (State of Rajasthan Agriculture State of Rajasthan Agriculture, 2012).

The first section of the paper contains the problem definition and importance of NLP in farming. Similarly, the second part of the paper contains a background study and literature survey. In the rest of the paper, we have used a methodical survey of techniques for conversational Artificial Intelligence (AI) applications in farming and analysis. This paper contributes the idea which is proposed as a chapter and can be identified as an advantage in the field of agriculture. We have proposed a conceptual model and noted some significant technology for the benefit of the agriculture sector in which a Natural Language model-based system will advise and guide farmers.

4.2 The Role of Artificial Intelligence in the Agriculture Sector

4.2.1 Usability of Artificial Intelligence and Machine Learning in Agriculture

Man-made reasoning uncovers the effect of human insight on machines intended to think like people and shape their conduct, for example, learning and critical thinking. Designing is essential for computerized reasoning as

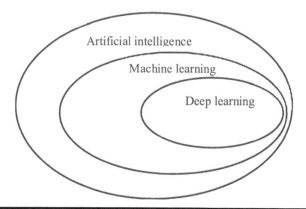

Figure 4.1   Sub-part of Artificial Intelligence (Sharma, 2021).

displayed in Figure 4.1. AI is a device used to recognize, comprehend, and dissect designs in information (Io & Lee, 2018). Quite possibly, the main space of examination on the planet is present-day natural innovation. This innovation is getting increasingly more troublesome because of the headway of innovation and its viability for issues, and the majority of them can't be successfully addressed by conventional numerical conditions just as by people (Sharma, 2021). A comparative region is especially significant for horticulture where around 30.7% of the total populace is chiefly occupied with the development of 2,781 million hectares. So ranchers need to confront numerous difficulties from seed to reap. The significant weight of cultivating is the insurance of the collect, which isn't sufficient utilization of synthetic substances, bugs and irresistible sicknesses, insufficient water system and water system, timberland of the board, and the sky is the limit from there. Agribusiness is an incredible land and conditions can't end with the installment of the normal exp. Computerized reasoning techniques have enabled us to catch explicit subtleties, everything being equal, and send the most ideal reaction to that specific issue. Fitting joining issues have been opened up through the advancement of numerous AI procedures. In Figure 4.1, it is shown that how ML and other parts of AI are a subset of AI itself (Sharma, 2021; Ruane et al., 2019; T & Ariyamala, 2020).

Several uses of AI in agriculture are as follows:

a. ***General Administration***

By and large, the worldwide seed control framework gives worldwide control of harvests that cover all parts of farming. The primary innovation for seed control was first presented by McKinion and Lemmon in 1985, in the book "Horticultural Fitness Program". An extra e-master framework was created by Boulanger for the insurance of corn seeds in his age. The framework called POMME was proposed by Roach in 1987, which was created for the control of apple plants. COTFLEX is another master program created by Stone and Taman for cropping the executives. Another master framework created by Lemmon likewise produced for cottonseed control is called COAX. 3-D laser imaging, high goal imaging, and significant distance strategies are fundamental to making bigger harvest sizes than farmland. It can achieve new changes by the way we deal with the land by ranchers with both time and exertion (S. Young, 2017).

Robinson and Mort support a diverse framework dependent on a body network intended to shield orange seeds from any sort of harm. The island of Sicily in Italy Imports and creation are set apart by a parallel model of preparing and organization testing. Comparable creation strategies are utilized by the creators to accomplish the right sort. The best kind that has quite recently shown up is 94% precise with six sections and two passages (Van Brummelen, 2019).

b. ***Disease Management***

Significant dangers to the worldwide economy, the climate, buyers, and ranchers can be brought about by plant illnesses. In India alone, 35% of yields are obliterated because of vermin and infections that cause enormous misfortunes to ranchers. The unselected culture of pesticides represents a danger to human well-being as some are biomagnified and impacts can be kept up with while taking care of the yield, assessing it, and giving legitimate consideration. Experience and key skills need to distinguish a poisonous plant and afterward do whatever it takes to recuperate computer frameworks that are utilized internationally to analyze the infection and afterward prescribe approaches to oversee it (Kumar et al., 2010). Test, test, and analysis. We shoot to guarantee that pictures of the leaves are isolated into outside regions like the debilitated region, the foundation, and the infected space of the leaves. The ailing piece of the leaf is then gathered and shipped off to the research facility for additional examination. This aids in distinguishing bugs and afterward feeling food deficiencies (Sharma, 2021; Fu et al., 2020).

c. ***Irrigation and Soil Management***

The difficult work of farming is the water system. Despite issues around water system, soils are fundamental for agribusiness (T. Young et al., 2018). Due to inappropriate soil in the board, water system prompts the expulsion of sullied yields and scenes. Simulated intelligence manufacturers who know about authentic environment designs, the kind of harvests being delivered, and soil quality can smooth out the water system interaction and increment usefulness (Kocaballi et al., 2020). Almost 70% of the world's new springs are dispensed for the water system, so this activity program can save water as

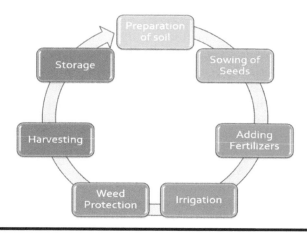

Figure 4.2   Application of AI in agriculture (Sharma, 2021).

well as assist ranchers with adapting to water issues. Companies are developing AI-based technologies and sensors to monitor home health, such as cropping using AI to reduce costs per acre, and Intello Labs using in-depth visual analytics. AI is being used in almost every part of modern agriculture; fewer of them are described above and some are given in Figure 4.2, which consist of several uses of AI in agriculture.

4.2.2 Era of Modern Agriculture Using AI

AI is silent but rapidly entering Indian farms and therefore just our society as a whole. Although machine learning (part AI) has been used for classification and predictive purposes, to say the least, food forecasting and seed production forecasts, more recently, this new group of in-depth learning algorithms has introduced a possible world for advanced research and AI applications and it is accurate (Kocaballi et al., 2020). Also, other AI techniques are coming from all directions, including farms. While there are high expectations for how AI can help the average person and change his mind, thinking and realizing the benefits it can bring, there are serious concerns about the negative impact of modern technology and also in the end, if AI methods can improve farmers in terms of health and economics, we must open up to inroads ground in the new technology coming with their own AI (Bhar et al., 2019; Bharti et al., 2020).

Natural Language Processing (NLP), Robotics, Engineering (ML), Automated Computing, Knowledge Management, Expert Process, Expert Technology, Computer Science, Voice, Automated Knowledge, Virtual Reality, Virtual Reality, Cloud Computing Internet of Things, Mathematical Computing, Advanced Research, etc., are the first in AI with the potential to solve agricultural problems. Ayog recently published a discussion paper on AI solutions in key sectors, including agriculture. In the field of agriculture, AI devices have great potential to provide information on soil quality, planting time, pesticides that can be sprayed, and pest habitat. Therefore, if AI programs can advise farmers on best practices, India can curb the agricultural rebellion. However, this type of future is a very serious challenge. A challenge that encompasses all value chains must be raised, including issues such as energy expansion and mental decline (Bhar et al., 2019).

Agribusiness will unquestionably profit immensely from AI applications. Man-made intelligence can be utilized to make keen frameworks incorporated into machines that can work with more noteworthy exactness and speed than people and simultaneously react very much like people. Man-made intelligence along with the Internet of Things (IoT) and sensor innovation can be extraordinary suppliers of exact horticulture. Man-made intelligence can likewise assume a basic part alongside distant detecting innovation in the far and wide execution of Smart Climate Agriculture. A portion of the AI methods, like versatile-based suggested frameworks and master frameworks, can significantly build the pace of appropriation of rural advancements, for example, exceptional returns or infection safe variations – others carried out by current ranches that assist with expanding livelihoods rancher. These AI procedures can likewise uphold moving the worldview of area-based directing administrations to be customized, setting explicit guidance for our country's a great many ranchers. Robotization, sensors, drones, IoT, and AI-helped sun-based energy offer new freedoms for organizations and business visionaries to offer imaginative arrangements as reasonable administrations to ranchers. Exactness cultivates in each space where we can profit with AI and can likewise help ranchers capitalize on the space they have, to be more precise about crop types, climate designs, and when and where we ought to go for planting crops. The best thing AI can do in agriculture is to avoid dizziness and distraction from many agricultural operations so that we can put our time and effort into better ways to find a range of innovative AI that is innovative to exceed human capabilities. At the national level, automatic AI-based classification and sorting are already being done for vegetables and fruits in order to create an agro-commodity standard that facilitates reliable trade across the country's borders. In-depth analysis and advanced image processing techniques are used to view photos and images, thus digitizing food quality. But increasing the utility to extend too many products and also to geographical locations requires millions of such images. It can be an exaggeration if these images have not been collected, digitized, and annotated. It is a fact that the largest agricultural data depends on the government and therefore it is entirely up to them to collect and make it available. Therefore, both quality and quantity have a direct impact on the effectiveness of in-depth studies. In addition, for other situations, such as solar or electricity planning, in-depth analysis requires several years of data to predict electricity generation. AI-based adaptive e-learning systems and decision support systems can also help students learn new concepts and identify areas where students are lacking, paying more attention to that content. These systems can cause new problems in the source material. These online systems can produce better materials and more comprehensive tests than the standard classroom curriculum (Bhar et al., 2019).

4.2.3 Curtailing Challenges of AI in Agriculture

Master frameworks are instruments for rural administration since they can give site-explicit, incorporated, and deciphered advice. Be that as it may, the improvement of master frameworks for horticulture is genuinely later, and the utilization of these frameworks in business agribusiness is uncommon to date. Despite the fact that AI has made some striking improvement in the farming area, it's anything but beneath the normal effect on the rural exercises when contrasted with its possibilities and effects in different areas. All the more actually should be done to further develop horticultural exercises utilizing AI as there are numerous limits to its execution (Ezziane, 2006).

a. *Limitation: Response Time and Accuracy*
   A significant characteristic of a keen or master framework is its capacity to execute undertakings precisely in a brief time frame. A large portion of the frameworks misses the mark according to either time or exactness, or even both. A framework postponed influences a client's choice of assignment methodology. Technique choice is speculated to be founded on an expense work joining two components: (1) the exertion needed to synchronize input framework accessibility, and (2) the precision level managed. Individuals trying to limit exertion and expand precision pick among three systems: programmed execution, pacing, and checking.

b. *Limitation: Big Data Required*
   The strength of a shrewd specialist is likewise estimated on the volume of information. A continuous AI framework needs to screen an enormous volume of information. The framework should sift through a large part of the approaching information. Nonetheless, it should stay receptive to significant or surprising occasions. An inside and out information on the assignment of the framework is needed from a field master and truth be told, pertinent information ought to be utilized working on the framework's speed and exactness. The advancement of a farming master framework requires the joined endeavors of experts from numerous fields of agribusiness and should be created with the participation of the cultivators who will utilize them.

c. *Limitation: Method of Implementation*
   The excellence of any master framework lies in its execution approach. Since it utilizes enormous information, the technique for turning upward and preparing ought to be appropriately characterized for speed and exactness.

d. *Limitation: High Data Cost*
   AI frameworks are web-based which thusly lessens or limits their utilization, especially in distant or provincial regions.

4.3 Literature Review: Conversational Artificial Intelligence

Conversational AI is a subset of AI that diagrams with talk-based or text-based AI experts that can reflect and mechanize conversations and verbal joint undertakings. Conversational AI agents like talk bots and voice associates have duplicated thinking about two central new developments. On the one hand, the methodologies expected to foster especially accurate AI models, such as AI and Deep Learning, have seen a tremendous amount of progress due to the increasing pay for research in these fields and the progress made in achieving higher selecting power with the aid of complex hardware models such as GPUs and TPUs. Furthermore, considering the Natural Language interface and the shot at their game-plan, conversational experts have been seen as a brand name fit in a wide show of employments like the clinical idea, customer care, and online business and tutoring. This move in the viable execution and their benefit has thusly made Conversational AI a pre-arranged region for development and novel evaluation. More present-day and extra-amazing models for the singular spot bits of Conversational AI planning are being presented at no other time seen rate. This assessment is planned to uncover understanding such that the most recent evaluation in Conversational AI plan moves furthermore to incorporate the overhauls that these original headways have accomplished over their standard associates. This paper is like a way which gives a wide record of a section of the evaluation openings in the Conversational AI district and along these lines sets up the stage for future examination and improvement in this field (Kulkarni et al., 2019).

In Figure 4.3, it is shown that Conversational AI agents have become standard today with the enormous progression in techniques needed to construct exact models, for example, AI and profound learning, and, also, because of the way that they are viewed as a characteristic fit in a wide scope of spaces, similar to medical services, online business, client care, the travel industry, and schooling, that intensely rely upon normal language discussions in everyday activities. In any case, the temporary rising in the investigation premium in this field has brought into the spotlight some empowering, yet fluctuating, research openings. From now on, a productive record of the middle thoughts of Conversational AI, standard procedures and back and forth movement executions there and the persistent investigation, which will go probably as a phase for future investigation and advancements, is of great importance. The Conversational AI configuration contains three essential portions, all of which are furthermore secluded into principal parts that handle more groundwork tasks. The underlying portion deals with the perception of normal language commitments from customers. This development is fundamentally a blend of two Natural Language Understanding (NLU) tasks viz. Reason Classification and Entity Extraction. Plan arrangement assists the specialist with understanding the Why of the info (Qiu et al., 2018). Instances of plans in a food requesting chatbot can be – demand, illuminate, place orders, and correspondingly for a medical services space – revealing a side effect, detailing a determination, and requesting

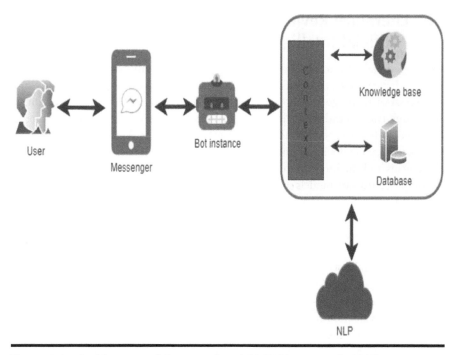

Figure 4.3   Architecture of Conversational AI (T. Young et al., 2018).

medication solution (Dong et al., 2019). Element Extraction manages the What of the information (Razzaq et al., 2017). It assists the specialist with distinguishing the discrete snippets of data got from the client, which when joined with the plan permits the specialist to completely understand the clients' input. Improved NLU techniques, such as Word Embeddings like Word2Vec, have made NLU more accurate than some of its preceding reciprocals (Devlin et al., 2019). Subsequent to understanding the clients' input, the specialist needs to settle on its arrangement of activities which ought to adequately proceed with the discussion while forestalling states where the Conversational Agent is stuck without essential data or in an inadequate circumstance. In a perfect world, the specialist should choose a bunch of activities that assist in settling the clients' demands. In any case, it might happen that the specialist doesn't have the whole data that it needs to definitively choose a particular course of activities. For instance, if the client is mentioning film timings for a theater, however, the client has not referenced which film, then, at that point, the specialist ought to perceive the missing snippet of data and react as needs are. In view of this, the specialist crosses between various explicit states, and relying on the express that the specialist winds up in, the specialist chooses its next activity. The structure module that handles this activity is known as the Dialog Management System (S. Young, 2017). Some essential ideas of discourse in the board incorporate establishing, opening filling, and setting exchanging which have been itemized in the accompanying segments of the paper. The last piece of Conversational AI collaboration is passing on the present status and results to the next included communicating substance. The answer ought to be shipped off the client in a client-justifiable organization. Regular Language Generation is utilized for this reason. Normal Language Generation is the way toward changing over organized information into client-justifiable regular language (T. Young et al., 2018).

4.3.1 Natural Language Processing

NLU is a piece of man-made mindfulness (AI) that uses PCs to understand the information made as an unstructured substance or talk. The field of NLU is a tremendous and testing subset of normal language making due to NLP. NLU is subject to chatting with lacking individuals and understanding their point, assembling that NLU goes past getting words and unravels meaning. NLU is even changed with the ability to understand the significance of paying little mind to typical human misuses like goofs or passed-on letters or words. The NLU gives a concise human-PC association. The NLU grants human vernaculars to be seen statically by the PC without the use of if/else. Regular Language Understanding (NLU) covers one of AI's phenomenal troubles. NLU for the most part contains two tasks – Named Entity Recognition (NER) and Intent Classification (IC) – which gives a depiction of NLU in AI-arranged specialists (Kulkarni et al., 2019; Ashfaq et al., 2020).

4.3.2 Applications

Conversational AI applications have extended beyond a couple perpetually with development in creative work around here. Conversational Agents would now have the choice to be found in a wide level of occupations playing out a huge load of beguiling endeavors. It used DNN (Deep Neural Network) and Restricted Boltzmann Machine (RBM) to make a chatbot in the advancement business region. Kyungyong Chun et al. upheld an AI-stimulated conversational expert that gave a web-based clinical idea illustrative assistance by using a cloud-based database. Facial development by Yuan Huang et al. fostered a chatbot that was introduced in a clinical idea application for weight of the board and gave a brand name language control system for a distant clinical benefits structure (Ali et al., 2021; Pacheco-Lorenzo et al., 2021).

4.4 Impact of Conversational Agents on Agriculture

4.4.1 Smart Chatbot for Agriculture

Chatbots are conversational remote helpers which robotize associations with end clients. Computerized reasoning fueled visit bots, utilizing AI methods, comprehending regular language, and interfacing with clients in a customized way.

In the early days' visit, bots were utilized for the most part in retail, travel, media, or protection players. Horticulture could likewise use this arising innovation by helping ranchers with answers to their inquiries, giving guidance and proposals on cultivating-related issues. This conversational partner utilizes NLP procedures to comprehend the client inquiries in their regular language. This will cause the framework to see even the syntactically not obvious sentences as info questions. The client questions go through the pre-preparing stage where the inquiry is first tokenized into words; then, at that point, the stop words like a, is, the, and so on are eliminated so it would not add to the likelihood of ordering the inquiries dependent on their classes and afterward the stemming interaction is completed where the words are changed over to their root words (Vijayalakshmi & Pandimeena, 2019; Ali et al., 2021).

The words are changed over to a pack of words and afterward changed over to a vector structure, so they can be handled effectively by the order calculation (Figure 4.4). The bot is then prepared with the preparation dataset. The UI gets the client inquiries and afterward advances them to the TalkBot application. In the TalkBot application, the text-based question goes through a pre-handling stage. Pre-handling steps incorporate Tokenization where the question sentence is tokenized into words; then, at that point, the stop words are eliminated, and afterward, the words are stemmed to their root words. In the event that the question

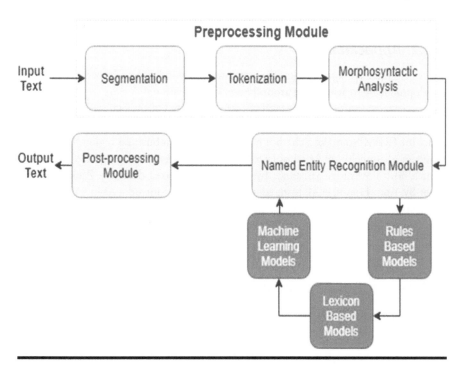

Figure 4.4 Architecture of system (Vijayalakshmi & Pandimeena, 2019).

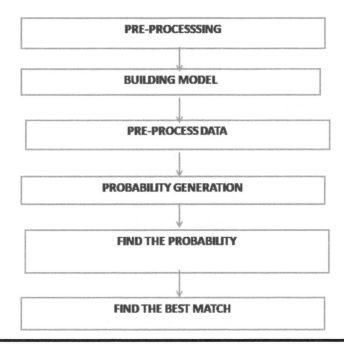

Figure 4.5   Response generation (Vijayalakshmi & Pandimeena, 2019).

is grouping-based, it would go through characterization utilizing the Naive Bayes classifier, which utilizes the information base to recover the pertinent reactions (Vijayalakshmi & Pandimeena, 2019; Razzaq et al., 2017; Ezziane, 2006).

From Figure 4.5, Response Retrieval utilizing Machine Learning. The neural organization arrangement is utilized to build a model utilizing the preparation dataset. Utilizing the model-developed probabilities is produced for the test dataset. The least probabilities are sifted through utilizing the edge esteem and arranged in plummeting requests. The most elevated likelihood is circled through to acquire the comparing reaction *(RUNNING HEAD: POWER AND DECISION MAKING Power and Decision Making: New Directions for Research in the Age of Artificial Intelligence Nathanael J. Fa*st, 2019).

4.4.2 AGRI-BOT Agriculture QA System

They collected our data from https://data.gov.in. The collection of each file requires entry of the user's name and email ID. Since we are collecting data for all states of India for the past five years, we automated the whole process through a JavaScript program that downloads and stores files as Comma Separated Values (CSV). For each state, we retrieve district-wise CSV. Each file contains the query ID, the query, query-type, query creation time, state name, district name, season, and the answer to a given query (N. Jain et al., 2019; S. Young, 2017).

The Sen2Vec model can be depicted as a technique for changing over a sentence into a vector, where the allocated weight to each element of the vector addresses that it's anything but a specific setting. The basic role of this model is to bunch the comparable sentences without contemplating the requesting of the words. Thinking about the inappropriate organization of the inquiries, we endeavor to coordinate with input questions to questions that are available in our offered dataset instead of handling the responses – the thought being that given the size of the dataset and excess, the inquiry is almost certain to be now present. We isolated the gathered information into two sections – train and test. Utilizing the preparation information, we train our model dependent on Sen2Vec and afterward for each inquiry in test information we track down the most comparative inquiry filed in the preparation information (shown in Figure 4.6) (Podder et al., 2020; Handrianto et al., 2019).

They pre-prepared the information inquiry from the test dataset likewise and converted it into a vector utilizing the implanting of the prepared model. The model yields the most comparative inquiry from the preparation information by looking at the installing vectors utilizing cosine similitude. By likeness strategies, we get a rundown of answers which fulfill the info question. They applied an answer positioning technique to yield the most appropriate answer. The appropriate response positioning takes input question figures the

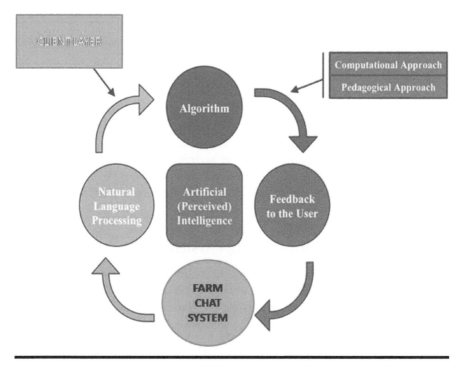

Figure 4.6   An overview of the system (N. Jain et al., 2019).

leeks score with each answer from the rundown and yield the one with the most elevated score (N. Jain et al., 2019).

4.4.3 Man-Made Intelligence and Ml-Based Advising System for Farmers Crop Production

Computerized reasoning in Agriculture: An Emerging Era of Research: in general, individuals are relied upon to appear at in excess of nine billion by 2050 which will require an improvement in green age by 70% to satisfy the premium. Basically, 10% of this general creation may begin from the accessibility of unused grounds and the rest of 90% ought to be satisfied by speed augmentation of the current age (Devlin et al., 2019). In this astonishing condition, the utilization of the most recent mechanical reactions to make growing logically convincing remains possibly the best need. Present systems to raise the cultivating age require high giganticness information sources and markets requests top-notch food. The need and growing work costs, raising expense of advance and secure bafflements related to odd yield by the greatness of diseases, blocked suspicion in precipitation, climatic strategies and loss of soil supportiveness, fluctuating business region cost in agribusiness things, and so forth, have had a gigantic restricting outcome on the financial status on this spine individual. Shockingly, the raise in individuals has made more interest in food grains working out exactly as expected with progress being created. By utilizing modernized reasoning, we can make sharp making chips away at keeping the loss of ranchers and outfit them with amazing yield. Utilizing man-made insight stages, one can collect the colossal level of information from affiliation and open districts or unending checking of different information is additionally conceivable by utilizing IoT and starting thereon can be bankrupt down with accuracy to draw in the ranchers for watching out for the total of the tricky issues looked by ranchers in the agribusiness region. By 2050, the UN expands that 86% of the inflexible individuals will live in the metropolitan areas, reducing the average workforce (T & Ariyamala, 2020; Bharati et al., 2020b; N. Jain et al., 2019).

4.4.4 Artificial Intelligence Found Farmer Supporter Chatbot

It is gathered by utilizing Naive Bayes assessment that isolates clients' solicitations and likes clients' messages. This system is a web application that offers a reaction to the solicitation of the rancher. The rancher simply needs to demand through the bot which is utilized for visiting and voice. Rancher can talk by utilizing any relationship such that there is no particular plan the client needs to follow. The system utilizes the work in Naive Bayes to answer the solicitation. The appropriate responses are sensitive to what the client questions. The user can examine any rancher-related exercises through the design. The client doesn't need a little while going to the workplace for requests. The system isolates the solicitation and sometimes later reactions to the client. The construction replies to the solicitation like it are replied by the individual.

With the assistance of Naive Bayes, the construction tends to the request presented by the rancher. The framework answers utilizing a persuading Graphical UI which induces that a genuine individual is talking with the client. The client can demand the rancher-related exercises online with the assistance of this web application. Ranchers can interface with the bot in a keyway. The complement is on empowering the bot more smartly, so that it can even comprehend not in reality well linguistically depicted sentences. The bot uses the NLP procedure to parse the customer questions. This bot is both recuperation- and generative-based. It can recuperate responses assuming the request is currently described in the informational collection or it will get responses from the inquiry bot. To make the responses more legitimate, the responses go through some savvy collaboration, so logical responses could be made. Bot furthermore can appreciate customer talk and can create talk-based yields for customer requests (Kaviya et al., 2021; Podder et al., 2020).

The proposed framework (Figure 4.7) is completely mechanized as the inquiry will be responded to premise the inquiry and information base naturally.

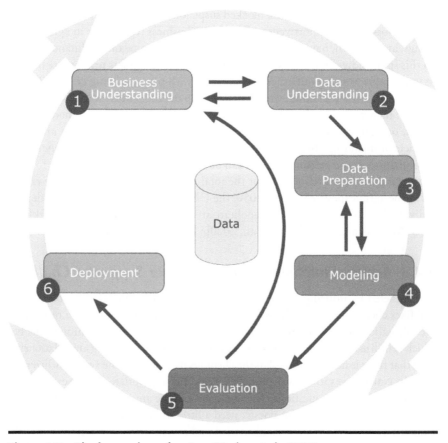

Figure 4.7   Block overview of system (Kaviya et al., 2021).

Henceforth, there is no compelling reason to have an individual to answer the inquiries and simplicity for the clients to interface with questions. Rancher can cooperate with the discussion bot in an exceptionally basic way. The emphasis is on fostering the bot more intelligently that it can even comprehend not well linguistically characterized sentences. Bot utilizes the NLP method to parse the client inquiries (Kaviya et al., 2021; Bharati et al., 2020a).

4.5 Related Studies

4.5.1 Tiger Ware Assistant: A Novel Serverless Execution of Conversational Negotiator for Customizable Surveys on Smart Devices

Tiger ware is being developed to become a complete portable overview stage that upholds both versatile applications and conversational specialists and gives some electronic review information representation and examination instruments. The proposed TigerAware Assistant and online information examination motor are new increases to the current TigerAware stage. Figure 4.8 shows the Tiger ware framework design. Its focal dataset is a NoSQL dataset containing three significant parts: a review plan store, a study reaction information store, and a client account data store (Handrianto et al., 2019).

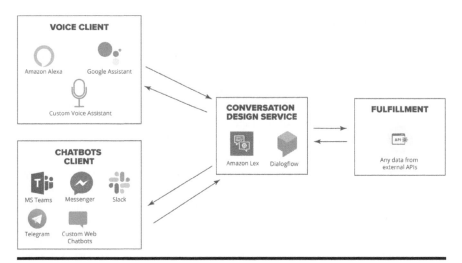

Figure 4.8   Design of tiger ware (Handrianto et al., 2019).

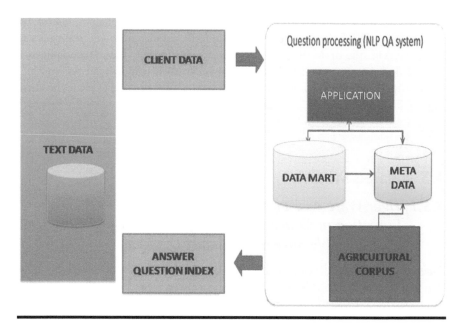

Figure 4.9   Design of bot workflow (Handrianto et al., 2019).

Figure 4.9 addresses the TigerAware Assistant work measure. It contains five critical parts:

1. A sagacious gadget or awesome speaker, like Google Home. The contraption empowers clients to pass on in standard languages to associate with TigerAware studies through Google Assistant.
2. Google Assistant, an AI-controlled humble associate made by Google that is accessible on a tremendous number of and keen home contraptions. Google Assistant unexpected spikes pursued Google Home and empowered it to converse with a client in ordinary language.
3. Dialog stream, a start to finish, construct once pass on any spot improvement suite for making conversational specialists from Google (https://cloud.google. com/dialogflow/). It is invigorated by Google AI to see a client's inspiration, which arranges an end-user's suspicion for one discussion turn. To make an informed authority, Dialog stream needs to will layout information through cloud limits. Every master has various purposes to oversee various bits of a discussion. Right when an examination part says something, Dialog stream coordinates with the clarification to the best point and executes its relating development. The activities are finished utilizing Google Cloud Functions.
4. Google Cloud Functions, Google's passed on handling association. Google Cloud Functions support workers less taking care of by permitting clients to

make, run, and direct application functionalities without the complex idea of building and remaining mindful of their figuring foundation. Cloud limits are utilized to give assessments recovered from Firebase to Dialog stream and to give changed activities of focuses.

5. A web dashboard for scientists to make and pass on traces, oversee people, and imagine and separate review reactions.

4.5.2 *Methodical Survey of Chatbots*

Chatbots are getting famous and they are at present creeping into our cells. People contribute a huge load of energy to the applications presented on the phones every day. According to another report by Flurry Analytics (2016), the overall application use in 2016 made by 11% stood separated from 2015, and the time that customers spent in applications made by 69%. The time spent in edifying and social applications loosened up by 394% in 2016 when stood separated from 2015. In China, senior customers of PDAs may not understand how to use every application; notwithstanding, by a long shot, most of them use the get-together application, like WeChat, by and large. Notwithstanding the way that they may not understand how to type messages on the cells, they can use voice messages and pictures to pass on their examinations. Late chatbots are introduced in talking applications or site pages, which enable tasks to be made through conversations, on a single cell rather than having a gigantic PC and different edges contraptions, similar to mouse and support. These are among the basic justifications for why chatbots have gotten standard. Chatbots are besides utilized in different kinds of uses (A. Sinha et al., 2020). They consolidate applications for customer care in online business destinations, authentic focus associates, language learning, or talking for entertainment reasons. Besides, there are in a like manner some prestigious chatbots from tech beasts, like IBM Watson, Facebook Messenger, Microsoft XiaoIce, and Apple Siri. Chatbots have moreover gotten essentially smarter. They can fathom human customers well in fact and they can give human-like responses. This is a direct result of the quick progression of mechanized thinking and other related advances. Various monetary supporters appreciated the ability of AI and they have made basic hypotheses to saddle the development. As monetary sponsors start placing assets into AI, chatbots are presumably going to experience further turn of events and headway later on. Presently, it is important to investigate the past assessment around here and give a report on the stream research status (Io & Lee, 2018; Razzaq et al., 2017). The information update could give a broad understanding and pieces of information into the possible destiny of chatbot research. Henceforth, the inspiration driving this assessment is to research prior investigation in chatbots using the bibliometric approach to manage recognized models and examples in this insightful assessment area. The revelations from this assessment could help with coordinating future investigations around here (Io & Lee, 2018; Verma and Sinha, 2020).

Figure 4.10 Clusters of chatbots word used and searched.

In the outline, every hub (circle) addresses a watchword (Figure 4.10). When there is a line between two hubs, it implies that these two watchwords are utilized in an equivalent paper. The bigger the hub, the more continuous it shows up. From the watchword co-events outline, we can discover significant catchphrases, for example, "correspondence", "conduct", "model", "feeling", and "plan", which are identified with the plan and advancement of a chatbot or CA. We likewise can discover a portion of the utilization of chatbots, for example, "academic specialists" and "language feelings". Nonetheless, we can't track down some mainstream catchphrases in these new years, for example, "versatile", "business insight", "profound learning", and so forth. It infers that there is a huge space of exploration freedom to investigate in the chatbot or CA region (Io & Lee, 2018).

4.6 Future Scope

Conversational intelligence is a very popular subject of AI in today's scenario. So, it has numerous applications in different diverse fields like healthcare, manufacturing, as well as in agriculture. In this chapter, we have thoroughly highlighted the main application areas of NLP in farming. So, in the future, we may implement and make AI chat system for farming, and also it gives numerous research paradigms to the future researcher so that they can implement NLP for such chat systems.

4.7 Conclusion

AI has both non-organic and human angles installed in it. Dissemination of man-made intelligence in all application fields will likewise bring a change in perspective in the manner we do investigate and advancement in horticulture now. Man-made intelligence frameworks require consistently taking care of new data furthermore, expanding the measure of data in the backend datasets utilized for performing undertakings with near precision, including planning the historical backdrop of and directing the forecasts from such frameworks. Thusly, the AI frameworks will get advanced after some time much the same as human flawlessness in expansion to versatility (M. Jain et al., 2018). The discussed framework assists ranchers with questioning about the farming, gets the reaction in the text just as discourse, and helps in anticipating the future information of cost, with the goal that they can design their exercises. The future upgrade should be possible by giving the reaction in their local language. Our chatbot can emphatically influence under-served networks by resolving questions related to cultivation, horticulture, and animal cultivating using typical language development. The farmer will need to get agricultural information similarly as confined information; for instance, the current market expenses of various yields in his/her district and environment gauge through an advising application. A farmer can directly message our AI-enabled structure in his/her language, and discover an answer. Our system would enable the farmer to present many requests, at whatever point, which will accordingly help in spreading the high-level developing advancement speedier and to a higher number of farmers (Dolci, 2017). Moreover, we found that an enormous part of the requests related to confined information, for instance, environment and market costs, were abundant. Our question-answer structure can answer most noteworthy inquiries in isolation with no human mediation with high precision (Devlin et al., 2019). This will incite better use of human resources and avoid inconsequential costs in setting up new call places. Our system is ready to do dealing with the generally large number of abundance questions and get invigorated with new requests in a rush. The structure also gives a decision that engages the farmer to present requests directly to the KCC agents if and when fundamental. Above all, we acknowledge that the structure helps in analyzing the farmers' demeanor and the plan of the Agricultural Region in India. While the structure gives a safe correspondence channel to the farmer, it moreover helps the methodology makers to grasp the necessities and stresses of the farmers. The data examination moreover gives an appreciation of which region or season farmers require thought. As such, our decision of being a sincerely strong organization uses all of the open resources wisely to deal with the issue of nonappearance of care and information in the plant region in India (M. Jain et al., 2018).

References

Ali, R., Hoque, E., Duberstein, P., Schubert, L., Razavi, S. Z., Kane, B., Silva, C., Daks, J. S., Huang, M., & Van Orden, K. (2021). Aging and engaging: a pilot randomized controlled trial of an online conversational skills coach for older adults. *American Journal of Geriatric Psychiatry*, *29*(8), 804–815. https://doi.org/10.1016/j.jagp.2020.11.004

Ashfaq, M., Yun, J., Yu, S., & Loureiro, S. M. C. (2020). I, Chatbot: Modeling the determinants of users' satisfaction and continuance intention of AI-powered service agents. *Telematics and Informatics, 54*(July). https://doi.org/10.1016/j.tele.2020.101473

Bhar, L. M., Ramasubramanian, V., Arora, A., Marwaha, S., & Parsad, R. (2019). Era of artificial intelligence: prospects for Indian agriculture. *Indian Farming, 3*(69), 10–13.

Bharati, S., Podder, P., & Mondal, M. R. H. (2020a). Artificial neural network based breast cancer screening: a comprehensive review. *International Journal of Computer Information Systems and Industrial Management Applications, 12*, 125–137.

Bharati, S., Podder, P., & Mondal, M. R. H. (2020b). Hybrid deep learning for detecting lung diseases from X-ray images. *Informatics in Medicine Unlocked, 20*, 100391. https://doi.org/10.1016/j.imu.2020.100391

Bharti, U., Bajaj, D., Batra, H., Lalit, S., Lalit, S., & Gangwani, A. (2020). Medbot: Conversational artificial intelligence powered chatbot for delivering tele-health after COVID-19. July, 870–875. https://doi.org/10.1109/icces48766.2020.9137944

Devlin, J., Chang, M. W., Lee, K., & Toutanova, K. (2019). BERT: Pre-training of deep bidirectional transformers for language understanding. *NAACL HLT 2019 – 2019 Conference of the North American Chapter of the Association for Computational Linguistics: Human Language Technologies – Proceedings of the Conference, 1*(Mlm), pp. 4171–4186.

Dolci, R. (2017). IoT solutions for precision farming and food manufacturing: artificial intelligence applications in digital food. *Proceedings – International Computer Software and Applications Conference, 2*, pp. 384–385. https://doi.org/10.1109/COMPSAC.2017.157

Dong, X., Chowdhury, S., Qian, L., Li, X., Guan, Y., Yang, J., & Yu, Q. (2019). Deep learning for named entity recognition on Chinese electronic medical records: combining deep transfer learning with multitask bi-directional LSTM RNN. *PLoS ONE, 14*(5), 1–15. https://doi.org/10.1371/journal.pone.0216046

Ezziane, Z. (2006). Applications of artificial intelligence in bioinformatics: a review. *Expert Systems with Applications, 30*(1), 2–10. https://doi.org/10.1016/j.eswa.2005.09.042

Fu, Z., Xian, Y., Zhang, Y., & Zhang, Y. (2020). Tutorial on conversational recommendation systems. *RecSys 2020 – 14th ACM Conference on Recommender Systems*, pp. 751–753. https://doi.org/10.1145/3383313.3411548

Gao, J., Galley, M., & Li, L. (2018). Neural approaches to conversational AI. *ACL 2018 – 56th Annual Meeting of the Association for Computational Linguistics, Proceedings of the Conference Tutorial Abstracts*, pp. 2–7. https://doi.org/10.18653/v1/p18-5002

Handrianto, Y., Huang, R., & Shang, Y. (2019). Short paper: Tigeraware assistant: a new serverless implementation of conversational agents for customizable surveys on smart devices. *Proceedings – 2019 1st International Conference on Transdisciplinary AI, TransAI 2019*, pp. 88–91. https://doi.org/10.1109/TransAI46475.2019.00023

Io, H. N., & Lee, C. B. (2018). Chatbots and conversational agents: a bibliometric analysis. *IEEE International Conference on Industrial Engineering and Engineering Management*, December 2017, pp. 215–219. https://doi.org/10.1109/IEEM.2017.8289883

Jain, M., Kumar, P., Bhansali, I., Liao, Q. V., Truong, K., & Patel, S. (2018). FarmChat. *Proceedings of the ACM on Interactive, Mobile, Wearable and Ubiquitous Technologies, 2*(4), 1–22. https://doi.org/10.1145/3287048

Jain, N., Jain, P., Kayal, P., Sahit, J., Pachpande, S., Choudhari, J., & Singh, M. (2019). *AgriBot: Agriculture-Specific Question Answer System*. https://doi.org/10.35543/osf.io/3qp98

Kaviya, P., Bhavyashree, M., Krishnan, M. D., & Sugacini, M. (2021). Artificial intelligence based farmer assistant chatbot. *International Journal of Research in Engineering, Science and Management 4*(4), 26–29.

Kocaballi, A. B., Quiroz, J. C., Laranjo, L., Rezazadegan, D., Kocielnik, R., Clark, L., Liao, Q. V., Park, S. Y., Moore, R. J., & Miner, A. (2020). Conversational agents for health and wellbeing. *Conference on Human Factors in Computing Systems – Proceedings, March*. https://doi.org/10.1145/3334480.3375154

Kumar, R., Ai, H., Beuth, J. L., & Rosé, C. P. (2010). Socially capable conversational tutors can be effective in collaborative learning situations. *Lecture Notes in Computer Science (Including Subseries Lecture Notes in Artificial Intelligence and Lecture Notes in Bioinformatics), 6094 LNCS*(PART 1), 156–164. https://doi.org/10.1007/978-3-642-13388-6_20

Pacheco-Lorenzo, M. R., Valladares-Rodríguez, S. M., Anido-Rifón, L. E., & Fernández-Iglesias, M. J. (2021). Smart conversational agents for the detection of neuropsychiatric disorders: a systematic review. *Journal of Biomedical Informatics, 113*(March 2021), 103632. https://doi.org/10.1016/j.jbi.2020.103632

Podder, P., Bharati, S., Mondal, M. R. H., & Kose, U. (2021a). Application of Machine Learning for the Diagnosis of COVID-19. In *Data Science for COVID-19* (pp. 175–194). Academic Press.

Podder, P., Bharati, S., Mondal, M., Paul, P. K., & Kose, U (2021b). *Artificial Neural Network for Cybersecurity : A Comprehensive Review. arXiv preprint arXiv:2107.01185.*

Podder, P., Mondal, M. R. H., Bharati, S., & Paul, P. K. (2020). Review on the security threats of internet of things. *International Journal of Computer Applications, 176*(41), 37–45. https://doi.org/10.5120/ijca2020920548

Qiu, L., Chen, Y., Jia, H., & Zhang, Z. (2018). Query intent recognition based on multi-class features. *IEEE Access, 6,* 52195–52204. https://doi.org/10.1109/ACCESS.2018.2869585

Razzaq, M. A., Khan, W. A., & Lee, S. (2017). Intent-context fusioning in healthcare dialogue-based systems using JDL model. *Lecture Notes in Computer Science (Including Subseries Lecture Notes in Artificial Intelligence and Lecture Notes in Bioinformatics), 10461 LNCS,* 61–72. https://doi.org/10.1007/978-3-319-66188-9_6

Ruane, E., Birhane, A., & Ventresque, A. (2019). Conversational AI: social and ethical considerations. *CEUR Workshop Proceedings, 2563,* 104–115.

RUNNING HEAD: POWER AND DECISION MAKING Power and Decision Making: New Directions for Research in the Age of Artificial Intelligence Nathanael J. Fast. (2019).

Saimohan Reddy T., & Ariyamala, V. (2020). Ai & Ml based advising system for farmers crop production. *International Journal of Recent Technology and Engineering, 8*(5), 3940–3943. https://doi.org/10.35940/ijrte.e6667.018520

Sharma, R. (2021). Artificial intelligence in agriculture: a review. *Proceedings – 5th International Conference on Intelligent Computing and Control Systems,* ICICCS 2021, pp. 937–942. https://doi.org/10.1109/ICICCS51141.2021.9432187

Van Brummelen, J. (2019). *Tools to create and democratize conversational artificial intelligence. 2017,* 1–195. https://hdl.handle.net/1721.1/122704

Verma, V., Sinha, A. (2020).Manipulation of email data using machine learning and data visualization. *International Journal of Advanced Science and Technology, 29*(4), 9743–9761.

Vijayalakshmi, J., & Pandimeena, K. (2019). Agriculture talkbot using AI. *International Journal of Recent Technology and Engineering, 8*(2 Special Issue 5), 186–190. https://doi.org/10.35940/ijrte.B1037.0782S519

Yan, R. (2018). "Chitty-chitty-chat bot": deep learning for conversational AI. *IJCAI International Joint Conference on Artificial Intelligence*, July, pp. 5520–5526. https://doi.org/10.24963/ijcai.2018/778

Young, S. (2017). *Statistical Spoken Dialogue Systems and the Challenges for Machine Learning*, 577–577. https://doi.org/10.1145/3018661.3022746

Young, T., Hazarika, D., Poria, S., & Cambria, E. (2018). Recent trends in deep learning based natural language processing [Review Article]. *IEEE Computational Intelligence Magazine*, *13*(3), 55–75. https://doi.org/10.1109/MCI.2018.2840738

Chapter 5

The Use of an Intelligent Fuzzy Logic Controller to Predict the Global Warming Effect on Agriculture: Case of Chickpea (*Cicer arietinum* L.)

H. Chekenbah[1], Imane El Hassani[2], S. El Fatehi[2],
Y. Hmimsa[2], M. L. Kerkeb[3], and R. Lasri[1]

[1]*Laboratory of Sciences and Advanced Technologies FPL,
Abdelmalek Essaadi University, Larache, Morocco*

[2]*Laboratory of Applied Botany, Department of Life Sciences,
FPL, Abdelmalek Essaadi University, Larache, Morocco*

[3]*Research Group, Information Systems Engineering,
Abdelmalek Essaâdi University, Tétouan, Morocco*

Contents

DOI: 10.1201/9781003311782-5

5.1 Introduction

In the last decades, the problem of global warming has become a real issue for humanity in general, and for the developing world in particular (Cline, 2007; Shackelford & Weekes-Shackelford, 2021). Most of these countries are globally centralized in Africa. The concerned countries are more affected by the problem of climate variability and change. This is due to the increase in the global temperature reached in these countries on the one hand, and the emergence of extreme phenomena in recent years such as drought, flooding, and irregular rainfall on the other hand. The developed nations already have the capability to use some adaptive techniques in order to face the problem of global warming, while the developing countries are not yet able to confront such a problem, especially since traditional agriculture is considered as a major factor of their development plans. Due to global warming, researchers have predicted multiple risks especially in the agriculture domain, where the world is being driven to achieve multiple and higher levels of dryness and hotness. This risk has already been observed over the past 10 years in most sub-Saharan countries which are already suffering from drought and desertification (Agele, 2021; Glantz, 1992), where such a small increase in temperature worsens the situation. However, the increase in temperature causes a decrease in agricultural income, since it influences the capacity of absorption and exploitation of humidity by plants in particular, and on evapotranspiration in general (Biazen, 2014). This yield diminution can reach an average of 16% of world agricultural production by 2080 according to International Monetary Fund (2008). These losses can reach catastrophic levels for some countries with more than 50% in Sudan, for example (International Monetary Fund, 2008). This makes it necessary to look up forward solutions to face the continuous increase in global warming issues.

As an African country, Morocco is considered as one of the vulnerable countries to this phenomenon, because of its critical geographical location. The effects of global warming are already being felt, for example, the severe drought of 2015, the sea-level rise, and disturbances in rainfall seasonal distribution. The latest statistics

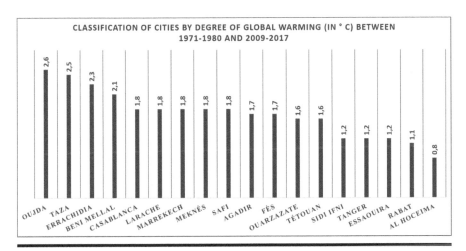

CLASSIFICATION OF CITIES BY DEGREE OF GLOBAL WARMING (IN ° C) BETWEEN 1971-1980 AND 2009-2017

Figure 5.1 Evolution of average temperatures between the periods 1971–1980 and 2009–2017 in the various weather stations in Morocco (in °C).

of the evolution of the average temperature between 1971–1980 and 2009–2013 at the different regions of Morocco has balanced between +0.8°C at Al Hoceima and +2.6°C at Oujda according to National Meteorological Directorate, Morocco. This evolution is depicted in Figure 5.1.

The most serious indicator of this anomaly is the sharp rise of the global temperature increase factor. The latest report from the Intergovernmental Panel on Climate Change (IPCC) predicts an increase in annual temperatures' average, compared to the period 1967–2005, of 1–1.5°C by 2100, in the whole Morocco (*IPCC — Intergovernmental Panel on Climate Change*, s.d.). Many adopted plans have been adopted by Morocco, in order to prevent this serious phenomenon, such as the green plan, the NOOR1 and NOOR2 concentration solar power plant, and the National Climate Plan by 2030. Despite the stimulated efforts at the national level, the situation caused by global warming keeps worsening. The factors necessitating the compensation of the provided efforts in this context, particularly the adoption of intelligent techniques in the agriculture domain, for the efficient management of the various resources used in this field with the aim of providing a friendly, safe, and sound agricultural environment. At this point, smart control with the Internet of Things (IoT) plays a key role in smart agriculture (Mekala & Viswanathan, 2017; Patil & Kale, 2016; Sushanth & Sujatha, 2018). In this work, a study of the increasing temperature effect on the growth and the income of the plants has been elaborated. In this aim, two smart greenhouses have been used on which two smart controllers are designed and implemented in the environment of the Arduino Mega boards. The study under consideration has been carried out within the Smart Farm of the Polydisciplinary Faculty of Larache, at Tangier-Tetouan-Al Hoceima region, in Morocco. The sampled plants under consideration present a "Garbanzo" variety of chickpea (*Cicer arietinum* L.). A group of this variety has been installed outdoors in natural conditions, while two other groups of the same variety are installed in the two greenhouses, on which forced stress is applied in the form of an increase of +1.5°C and +3°C in normal temperatures, respectively. The carried-out study takes into consideration three important aspects for the three different environments:

The first aspect is based on the sampling of an important factor in the evaluation of the influence of the application of temperature stress on plants, which is the chlorophyll of the leaves.

The second aspect concerns a quantitative study of the number of flowers and pods per peduncle.

In the third aspect, a chronological study based on which precise dates and durations have been taken into consideration such as the date of the first flower and the flowering date.

In the aims of achieving significant and efficient results, some required specifications have been fixed. To comply with these specifications, a real-time and self-adaptive Fuzzy Logic Controller (FLC) has been developed and embedded in each greenhouse.

5.2 Methodology

An empirical study is established aiming to follow the influence of the application of temperature stress conditions on the growth and productivity of the cultivar "Garbanzo" of chickpea (*Cicer arietinum* L.). This stress is applied in specific growth stages which are the flowering stage and the pod development stage (Figure 5.2).

5.2.1 Material and Methods

In this experience, 50 seeds were used to accomplish the experimental required protocol. Each seed was sown in a pot with a depth of 3 cm. The pots were watered twice a week with an average of 25% per pot. During the early stages of development, and under the same conditions, the pots were placed and randomized. The sampled plants have been separated into three different groups:

Ten plants have been left in the outside environment, considered as witnesses (Figure 5.3 (a)).

At the flowering stage, 10 plants have been moved to the inside of the first greenhouse, where we applied a +1.5°C temperature stress (Figure 5.3 (b)),

Figure 5.2 Plant stages ((a) stage of seed germination, (b) flowering stage, and (c) pod development stage).

while 10 other plants have been moved to the inside of the second green-house (Figure 5.3 (c)), where we applied a +3°C temperature stress.

At the pod development stage, 10 plants have been moved to the inside of the first greenhouse, where we applied a +1.5°C temperature stress, while 10 other plants have been moved to the inside of the second greenhouse, where we applied a +3°C temperature stress.

Figure 5.3 **Environments of the experience ((a) witnesses, (b) 1ˢᵗ greenhouse (+1.5°C), and (c) 2ⁿᵈ greenhouse (+3°C)).**

5.2.1.1 Parameters Studied

In order to preside over the growth of the sampled plants, a daily supervising of the phenological, vegetative development, and physiological parameters of plants in the three environments was carried out as shown in Figure 5.4.

a. **The phenological parameters**

  The phenological parameters considered are, respectively:

  The date of the first flower (DFF, in days after sowing (DAS)) corresponds to the date of blooming of the first flowers in the plant.

  The flowering date (FD, in DAS): the blooming date of 50% of the flowers.

b. **Vegetative development parameters**

  The vegetative development parameters considered are, respectively: the number of leaflets per leaf (NLL), the leaf area (LA), and the number of branches per plant (NBP).

  To carry out this task, 10 sheets of each stress are chosen and analyzed.

c. **Physiological parameters**

  Regarding collecting the physiological parameters, the measurement of chlorophyll was effectuated. It has been measured using an *SPAD 502 Plus*

Figure 5.4 Supervising of the phenological and physiological parameters' plants.

chlorophyll meter device. These measurements were carried out on sheets two times: 40 days after stress application (40 DAS) and 80 days after stress application (80 DAS).

5.2.2 Implementation of the Smart Controller

To guarantee the stress temperature conditions set by the research team, it has been necessary to design and implement an intelligent controller that will be installed in each greenhouse.

5.2.2.1 Required Specifications

In order to achieve the study process, the researcher's group has fixed several particular specifications, concerning the conditions under which the study was conducted, such as:

Before the separation of the variety considered on the three environments, the sampled plants have undergone the same living conditions since the stage of germination of the seeds.

The instantaneous temperature values inside each greenhouse must be equal to the ambient temperature added to a critical stress value, which is +1.5°C in the first greenhouse, and +3°C in the second one.

The tolerated temperature error value is set at ±0.1°C.

The automated control of the temperature inside the greenhouses is effectuated based on an air conditioner, from the brand *KROHLER*; this air conditioner effectuates three principal actions which are Heating, Cooling, and Dehumidification.

The tolerated humidity error value is set at ±10%.

The examination of the meteorological parameters should be a real-time remote consultation.

5.2.2.2 The Adopted Concept

To meet the strict specifications set by the research group, a real-time self-adaptive FLC has been designed and implemented on an Arduino Mega board. The choice of a Fuzzy Controller is not arbitrary but based on different criteria such as stability, error minimization, and low energy consumption since they act directly on the actuators and do not require additional blocks. The temperature inside the greenhouses reaches high values due to the global warming effect, which causes an overload on the operation of the air conditioner (AC). To overcome this problem, a humidification system is used at the same time along with the AC; everything is controlled in real time with the Fuzzy Controller. The humidification system is provided by water sprays installed at the edges of each greenhouse; the effectuated control is carried out by a solenoid valve (SV).

To simplify the monitoring of greenhouses from a weather condition point of view, we are using sensors connected with the IoT technology for instant and remote consultation of both, temperature, and humidity inside the greenhouses. In case of an unexpected failure of the control system, an alert is broadcasted to the various members of the search group, once the interior temperature has reached a critical value defined at +3°C from the ambient temperature.

5.2.2.2.1 Concept of the Fuzzy Logic Controller

Fuzzy Controller is characterized by its flexibility compared to the classic controller since it offers a multitude of choices in input and output by bringing into play the

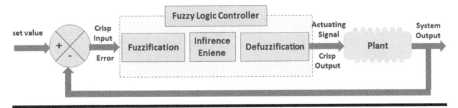

Figure 5.5   Fuzzy control loop.

notion of membership function degree and activation degree instead of binary values (all or nothing) (Passino & Yurkovich, 1998). It is well known that Fuzzy Logic techniques have proved their efficiency in the control domain especially in controlling complex and nonlinear systems, where the Jacobian Matrix is not always available (Lasri et al., 2012). The basic architecture of the FLC is illustrated in Figure 5.5.

The first step which is fuzzification consists of converting numerical input variables (crisp values) into linguistic input variables, using the notion of membership function and membership degree. The membership degree refers to the average of an element belonging to a specific fuzzy set; typically, this degree takes the form of a crisp value between zero and one (Passino & Yurkovich, 1998). The fuzzy inference system (FIS) consists of accomplishing the second step which is evaluating the membership degree of the input variables and returning the responsible membership functions of such state of the plant. A well-defined rule base is extracted through the knowledge of a domain expert, from where the FIS evaluates the activation degree of each rule. These rules are expressed linguistically, taking the form of Equation (5.1) (Chekenbah et al., 2021; Lasri et al., 2014).

$$IF\ x_1\ is\ X_1^{i1}\ AND\ x_2\ is\ X_2^{i2}\ AND\ ...\ x_N\ is\ X_N^{iN}\ THEN\ u = R_{i1i2....iN} \quad (5.1)$$

where $X_m^{im} \in \left\{ X_m^1, X_m^2, ..., X_m^{im} \right\}$ are the MFs of the input X_m, nm is the number total of membership functions, and $R_{i1i2....iN}$ are the consequences of the rule.

An evaluation of the activated rules called aggregation makes it possible to have a single set of fuzzy outputs; this step converts the fuzzy inputs into fuzzy outputs. While the defuzzification which is the last step of the process aims to transform the fuzzy output to crisp output, the principle of a Fuzzy Controller is explained in the diagram in Figure 5.6.

There are two main types of FIS: the Mamdani- and the Sugeno-type FIS. They both have almost the same structures, the only difference being in the level of the generated crisp output (the defuzzification) (Sari et al., 2016). In the case of Sugeno's model, the consequences of the inference rules depend on the values taken by the antecedent inputs; they take values which are represented as spikes-singleton

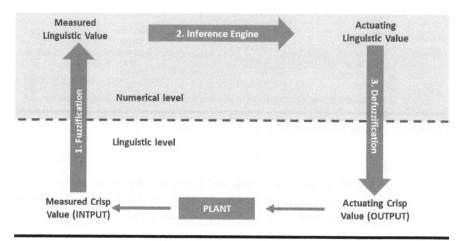

Figure 5.6   Fuzzy Logic Controller block diagram.

with an amplitude as a function of one or more input variables; this function is a mathematic linear function or constant (Zero-Order Takagi-Sugeno-Kang) (Qin et al., 2021; Yulianto et al., 2017).

In contrast, Mamdani's type relies on the fact that the consequence is represented in the same way as the antecedent part. In this work, we have adopted the Zero-Order Takagi-Sugeno-Kang FLC because of its simplicity of implementation, and the discontinuous character of the desired control signal to control the ACs installed in both greenhouses. To accomplish this process, we had chosen the MIN-MAX method to effectuate the evaluation rules action. The rule base consists of 15 rules; each one takes the form of Equation (5.2).

$$\text{If } (E_H \text{ is } X_1^H) \text{ and } (E_T \text{ is } X_1^T) \text{ Then } (U_C = K_1^{SV}) \text{ and } (X_{AC} = C_1^{AC}) \quad (5.2)$$

The adopted Fuzzy Controller has two inputs and two outputs (MIMO); the input variables are, respectively, the humidity error E_H and the temperature error E_T, which are expressed by (5.3), (5.4), and (5.5).

$$E_H = H_{in} - H_{out} \quad (5.3)$$

$$E_T = T_{in} - T_r \quad (5.4)$$

$$T_r = Tout + Stress \quad (5.5)$$

To measure the temperature inside and outside greenhouses, we chose the *DS18B20* sensor, thanks to its high degree of precision since the admissible error set at the start is of the order of 10^{-1}. For humidity measurement, the *DH11* sensor was chosen.

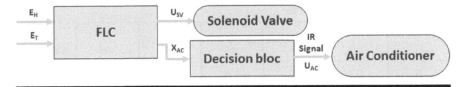

Figure 5.7   Input and outputs (I/O) of the Fuzzy Logic Controller.

The output variables are, respectively:

The control of the solenoid valve (SV) is responsible for the triggering of air
 humidifiers installed at the boundaries of the greenhouses.
The command signal for the AC.

A set of triangular and trapezoidal membership functions has been assigned
to the inputs (three for the first input and five for the second one). A set of
crisp sets is used to describe both output variables MFs in the form of singleton
spikes (two for the first input and eight for the second one). The consequents
and their pre-defuzzified crisp values for the first output are On ON(K1=0)
and Off OFF(K2=1), and for the second one are Fast Cooling FC(C1=−3),
Medium Cooling MC(C2=−2), Low Cooling LC(C3=−1), Off OFF(C4=0),
Low Heating LH(C5=1), Medium Heating MH(C6=2), and Fast Heating
FH(C7=3). The internal structure of the FLC under consideration is depicted in
Figures 5.7 and 5.8.

The set of fuzzy rules used is summarized in Table 5.1.

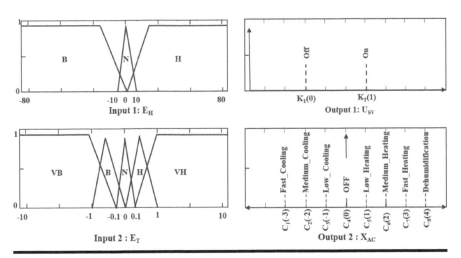

Figure 5.8   Internal structure of the FLC.

Table 5.1   Rule Table for FIS

E_T E_H	VB	B	N	H	VH	Outputs
B	C7	C5	C4	C3	C1	X_{AC}
	K2	K2	K2	K2	K2	U_{SV}
N	C7	C6	C4	C2	C1	X_{AC}
	K1	K1	K1	K1	K2	U_{SV}
H	C7	C6	C8	C2	C1	X_{AC}
	K1	K1	K1	K1	K2	U_{SV}

The illustration shows beside the FLC a block of decisions aiming to convert the crisp output of the FLC X_{AC} to an infrared (IR) signal U_{AC} to command our plant which is the AC. The conversion process is well elaborated in Table 5.2.

The different parts of the control carried out are summarized in Figure 5.9.

5.2.2.2.2 Online Self-Organization of the Internal Structure of the Membership Functions

The internal structure of such an FLC plays an important role in its performance, which makes its design a decisive step. However, determining this structure requires a deep knowledge of the behavior of the plant to control, which is not the case in most complex systems where several parameters influence the process of the system.

Among the important parameters in the design of a Fuzzy Controller are membership functions, in terms of shape and parameters. Determining optimal parameters is not always possible, which seeks an optimization step after the design task.

In this work, to ensure online self-optimization of the internal structure of the Fuzzy Controller, a step of self-organization of membership functions is applied. The regard of this step is to balance the membership functions to

Table 5.2   Associated Actions with the Decision Block

Crisp output (FLC)	C1	C2	C3	C4	C5	C6	C7	C8
Decision (IR Signal)	Cooling-16	Cooling-18	Cooling-20	Off	Heating-32	Heating-30	Heating-28	Dehumidi-fication

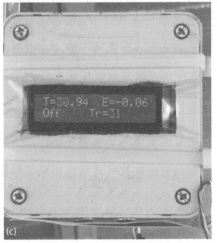

Figure 5.9 Controller parts: (a) air conditioner, (b) solenoid valve, and (c) realized controller.

obtain an adapted structure over the entire input space for each input variable. This step is based on the online Square-Error Integral assessment which can be determined by (5.6).

$$ISE_k^l = \frac{1}{\delta_y^2}\left(\int e^2(t)dt\,\big/_{u_k(t)\in[S_k^{l-1},S_k^l]} - \int e^2(t)dt\,\big/_{u_k(t)\in[S_k^l,S_k^l+1]}\right) \qquad (5.6)$$

The equation compares the recorded error to the right and left of each membership function center and for each entry. This comparison makes it possible to decide to resize and/or move the membership function, according to Equations (5.7) and (5.8).

In the case where the error recorded on the left is greater than that on the right, a displacement of the center of the membership function to the left is performed according to Equation (5.7). The most activated functions (which will be a great contribution to ISE) will be resized according to (5.8) to have at all times a balanced distribution of membership functions around the universe of discourse.

$$\Delta a_k^l = \frac{a^{l-1} - a^l}{2} \cdot \frac{ISE_k^l}{ISE_k^l + \dfrac{1}{\rho^l}} \tag{5.7}$$

$$\Delta b_k^l = \frac{\Delta c_k^l}{\varnothing^l}, \Delta b_k^{l\pm1} = -\frac{\Delta c_k^l}{\varnothing^l} \tag{5.8}$$

where a_k^l is the center of the l membership function of the input u_k, ρ^l and $\varnothing^l$ are the normalizations factors, and b_k^l is the basis of the l membership function of the input u_k.

The reverse operation is performed otherwise, that is, a displacement (5.9) and a resizing (5.10).

$$\Delta a_k^l = \frac{a^{l+1} - a^l}{2} \cdot \frac{\left|ISE_k^l\right|}{\left|ISE_k^l\right| + \dfrac{1}{\rho^l}} \tag{5.9}$$

$$\Delta b_k^l = -\frac{\Delta c_k^l}{\varnothing^l}, \Delta b_k^{l\pm1} = +\frac{\Delta c_k^l}{\varnothing^l} \tag{5.10}$$

This step of self-organization of the membership functions makes it possible to obtain at any time a self-optimized structure and to guarantee that at least two membership functions are activated for each input value.

5.2.2.2.3 Integration of Internet of Things Technology

The integration of the IoT into the various fields of remote monitoring and control has become a necessity in recent years (Eriyadi et al., 2021). This is, thanks to the remote solutions, what it offers for organized energy management, which has a positive impact on the rationalization of resources and energy efficiency in general (Shahzad et al., 2016). The integration of IoT in the field of agriculture has been of major importance, thanks to the advantages mentioned above, and thanks to the fact that this field requires significant human and energy resources. The main elements used in IoT are connected sensors (objects), as they replace humans in measuring, observing, monitoring, and sending measured data in real-time. These data are usually stored in databases for then decision-making.

In this work, the IoT is mainly used to check the weather conditions in each greenhouse, since the control of the air conditioning is done automatically. The data to be consulted are the temperature and humidity inside the greenhouses.

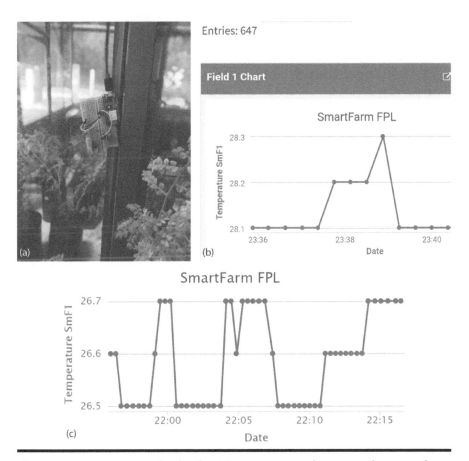

Figure 5.10 Remote monitoring by IoT: (a) connected sensors, (b) smartphone consultation, and (c) computer consultation.

These data are transmitted to an onboard computer in the smart farm and stored in a database for further manipulation. These data are sent via a wireless protocol; for this, a *NodeMCU ESP8266-WiFi* model integrated into a Wi-Fi network is used with *DS18B20* and *DH11* sensors measuring both values: the temperature and the air humidity (Figure 5.10).

5.3 Results and Discussion

5.3.1 Smart Control and IoT

Figure 5.11 shows a comparison between the temperature values in the three environments. It can be seen that the implementation of a self-adapting Fuzzy Controller makes it possible to comply with the required specifications to experiment with

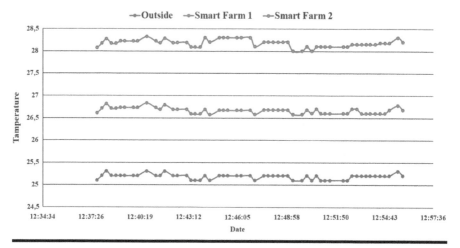

Figure 5.11   Temperature of the three environments.

precision. In fact, the error between the setpoint temperature and the desired temperature is of the order of 10^{-2}. This controller also helps to reduce the operating time of the AC, thereby minimizing the overload on the AC and thus reducing energy consumption.

The use of connected objects (sensors) makes it possible to simplify the observation and sampling of meteorological conditions, which makes it possible to avoid the influence on interior climates due to the opening of the greenhouse doors at all times.

5.3.2 Phenological Information

Table 5.3 summarizes the global phenological information of sampled plants.

From experience, it was found that flowering of the "Garbanzo" variety of chickpea started after 32 days of sowing. Subsequently and after 8 days, the different plants reach 50% of flowering. From the point of view of the anatomy of the plant, the number of branches, which is an indication of branching of chickpea plants, thus contributing to the development of above-ground biomass, was found to be 2.84 ± 0.79 twigs per plant. This number showed a variation of two to four branches per plant. But this remains relatively variable taking into account the coefficient of variation (27.88%) which confirms the heterogeneity of the number of branches between the different plants. Conversely, the number of leaflets per plant, which is 12.74±0.63, did not record many variations between different chickpea plants.

Table 5.3   Phenological Information

	AVERAGE	AND	MIN	MAX	Coefficient of Variation (%)
Number of branches per plant	2.84	0.79	2	4	27.88
Number of leaflets per leaf	12.74	0.63	11	13	4.96
1st flowering days	32 days				
50% flowering days	8 days				

From a point of a physiological view, exposing plants to high temperatures during the vegetative stages can damage components of the photosynthetic system of the leaves (Figure 5.12), thereby reducing carbon dioxide uptake rates compared to environments with optimal temperatures. In this context, the preliminary results of the experiment carried out showed that depending on the increase in temperature, a reduction in the chlorophyll content begins to appear. However, taking into account the duration of exposure to heat stress applied, this decrease becomes more significant especially during the flowering stage and during the pod development stage (Figure 5.13).

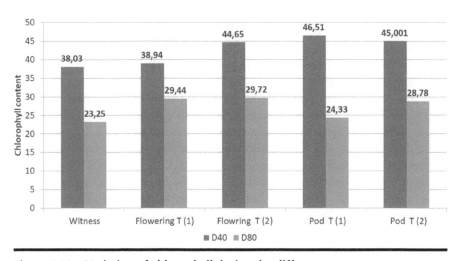

Figure 5.12   Variation of chlorophyll during the different stages.

Figure 5.13   Influence of the application of temperature stress on plants.

5.4 Conclusion

This work presents the results of a predictive study of the effect of heat stress caused by temperature increase on agricultural growth and production. The study adopts a multidisciplinary approach, based on an experience carried out at the level of the smart farm of the Polydisciplinary Faculty of Larache, Morocco. In this context, a study on the response of the "Garbanzo" variety of chickpea (*Cicer arietinum* L.) to heat stress was carried out.

For a more precise application of the applied temperature stresses, two self-organizing Fuzzy Controllers were designed and implemented in the two green-houses used in this experiment. Connected sensors were used with IoT technology to facilitate the observation of weather conditions. The use of self-organized Fuzzy Controllers allows the experiment to be carried out under optimal conditions in terms of precision (of the order of 10–1) and even in terms of energy efficiency. Several comparative studies have been carried out to assess the influence of the application of stress. These studies focus on the phenological and vegetative development and physiological parameters of the plants. The results obtained clearly show the influence of the temperature increase on the yield of *chickpea* plants. This influence becomes more important especially at the flowering stage and the pod development stage.

5.5 Limitations and Scope for Future Work

5.5.1 Limitations of the Study

The limits of the study carried out can be summarized by the following two points: the use of a limited number of seeds used in the experiment (50 seeds), and the limitation on a single type of plant which is the "garbanzo," a variety of chickpeas (*Cicer arietinum* L.).

5.5.2 Scope for Future Work

The study made can be developed using several types of plants with the use of a large number of seeds. It can also be generalized to the different seasons of the year, taking into account the effect of water scarcity on agricultural production.

From a technological point of view, the study can be improved by integrating more developed climate sensors (gas sensors, soil property sensors, etc.) and instant monitoring tools such as cameras connected to cloud computing and smart farming tools.

References

Agele, S. (2021). Global warming and drought, agriculture, water resources, and food security: Impacts and responses from the tropics. *Handbook of Climate Change Management*, pp. 1–20. https://doi.org/10.1007/978-3-030-22759-3_183-1

Biazen, M. (2014). The effect of climate change and variability on the livelihoods of local communities: In the case of Central Rift Valley Region of Ethiopia, *Open Access Library Journal*, 1(453), 1–10.

Chekenbah, H., El Abderrahmani, A., Aghanim, A., Maataoui, Y., & Lasri, R. (2021). Solving problem of partial shading condition in a photovoltaic system through a self-adaptive fuzzy logic controller. *International Journal on Technical and Physical Problems of Engineering*, 13(2), 130–137.

Cline, W. R. (2007). *Global warming and agriculture: End-of-century estimates by country*. Peterson Institute. Washington, D.C.

Eriyadi, M., Abdullah, A. G., Hasbullah, H., & Mulia, S. B. (2021). Internet of things and fuzzy logic for smart street lighting prototypes. *IAES International Journal of Artificial Intelligence (IJ-AI)*, 10(3), 528. https://doi.org/10.11591/ijai.v10.i3.pp528-535

Glantz, M. H. (1992). Global warming and environmental change in sub-Saharan Africa. *Global Environmental Change*, 2(3), 183–204. https://doi.org/10.1016/0959-3780(92)90002-O

International Monetary Fund. (2008). *Finance and Development, March 2008*. International Monetary Fund. http://www.elibrary.imf.org/view/IMF022/09127-9781451922349/09127-9781451922349/09127-9781451922349.xml

IPCC — Intergovernmental Panel on Climate Change. (s.d.). Consulté 26 juin 2021, à l'adresse https://www.ipcc.ch/

Lasri, R., Rojas, I., Pomares, H., & Valenzuela, O. (2014). A new adaptive and self organizing fuzzy policy to enhance the real time control performance. *International Journal of Computational Intelligence Systems*, 7(3), 582–594. https://doi.org/10.1080/1875689 1.2013.865403

Lasri, R., Rojas, I., Pomares, H., & Valenzuela, O. (2012). A new adaptive fuzzy control policy against conventional methods. Statistical analysis of real time control performance. *2012 IEEE International Conference on Complex Systems (ICCS)*, pp. 1–6. https://doi.org/10.1109/ICoCS.2012.6458535

Mekala, M. S., & Viswanathan, P. (2017). A survey: Smart agriculture IoT with cloud computing. *2017 International Conference on Microelectronic Devices, Circuits and Systems (ICMDCS)*, pp. 1–7. https://doi.org/10.1109/ICMDCS.2017.8211551

Passino, K. M., & Yurkovich, S. (1998). *Fuzzy control.* United States: Addison-Wesley.

Patil, K. A., & Kale, N. R. (2016). A model for smart agriculture using IoT. *2016 International Conference on Global Trends in Signal Processing, Information Computing and Communication (ICGTSPICC)*, pp. 543–545. https://doi.org/10.1109/ICGTSPICC.2016.7955360

Qin, B., Chung, F.-L., & Wang, S. (2021). KAT: A knowledge adversarial training method for zero-order Takagi-Sugeno-Kang fuzzy classifiers. *IEEE Transactions on Cybernetics*, 1–15. https://doi.org/10.1109/TCYB.2020.3034792

Sari, W. E., Wahyunggoro, O., & Fauziati, S. (2016). A comparative study on fuzzy Mamdani-Sugeno-Tsukamoto for the childhood tuberculosis diagnosis. 070003. https://doi.org/10.1063/1.4958498

Shackelford, T. K., & Weekes-Shackelford, V. A. (Éds.). (2021). Global Warming. In *Encyclopedia of Evolutionary Psychological Science* (p. 3453). Springer International Publishing. https://doi.org/10.1007/978-3-319-19650-3_302065

Shahzad, G., Yang, H., Ahmad, A. W., & Lee, C. (2016). Energy-efficient intelligent street lighting system using traffic-adaptive control. *IEEE Sensors Journal, 16*(13), 5397–5405. https://doi.org/10.1109/JSEN.2016.2557345

Sushanth, G., & Sujatha, S. (2018). IOT based smart agriculture system. *2018 International Conference on Wireless Communications, Signal Processing and Networking (WiSPNET)*, pp. 1–4. https://doi.org/10.1109/WiSPNET.2018.8538702

Yulianto, T., Komariyah, S., & Ulfaniyah, N. (2017). Application of fuzzy inference system by Sugeno method on estimating of salt production. 020039. https://doi.org/10.1063/1.4994442

Chapter 6

Using Machine Learning Algorithms to Mapping of the Soil Macronutrient Elements Variability with Digital Environmental Data in an Alluvial Plain

Fuat Kaya and Levent Başayiğit

Department of Soil Science and Plant Nutrition, Isparta University of Applied Sciences, Isparta, Türkiye

Contents

DOI: 10.1201/9781003311782-6

6.1 Introduction

Soils are the focus of the agro-ecosystem. Soils can provide nutrients to plants, store these nutrients, provide usable water, and contribute significantly to the sustainability of agricultural production to feed humanity (Ließ et al., 2021). Sustainable and economical production in agriculture can only be possible with the optimal nutrition of plants. All plants need carbon and oxygen in the atmosphere and soil air, hydrogen in soil water, 14–16 other essential elements, and several useful elements from nutrient resources in the soil. The basic elements come from the mineral components of the soil. Plant growth is not possible without them. In this regard, according to the number of elements needed by the plant, it is generally possible to make distinctions as macro- or micronutrients (Blume et al., 2016). The nutrient content of the soil is determined by traditional analysis methods and fertilization recommendations can be made for the needs of the plant. In areas where intensive agricultural activities are carried out, the spatial distribution of nutrients that occupy an important place in plant nutrition is highly influenced by land use (Shahbazi et al., 2019). Fertilization caused by land use is excessive and environmentally harmful as a result of the loss of nutrients such as nitrogen and phosphorus from the soil which can lead to eutrophication in surface waters (Blume et al., 2016). For this reason, it is also critically important that sensitive areas can be determined spatially with high accuracy. The distribution of nutrients in the soil is inherently heterogeneous. To determine the distribution of this heterogeneous situation, geostatistical methods have been used for half a century, with a systematic sampling methodology, in areas where there are no sudden spatial changes (Ließ et al., 2012; Mponela et al., 2020). However, this methodology cannot be performed effectively, especially in areas where land cover or land-use changes are high in short distances such as our study area. In the agricultural areas, different nutrient inputs occur mainly through mineral fertilization bound to land use (Kacar & Katkat, 2015). Soil map, which has a unit-based small-scale (rough resolution) depiction size, has limited use for detailed spatial planning on a regional scale (Hengl et al., 2015). Therefore, it cannot support the activities of precision agriculture and the management of small-scale farms. In this context, with pedometrics, a field that continues to develop under the science of soil survey and mapping, continuous, site-specific soil information can be produced with pedometric modeling approaches (Wadoux et al., 2021). Pedometrics can be defined as an interdisciplinary science that integrates with the application of mathematical and statistical methods to study the distribution and formation of soils (Heuvelink, 2013). One of the main reasons for advances in the science of pedometrics is the 21st century of accessible digital data (Wadoux et al., 2021). Digital soil mapping (DSM) is a method for the generation of spatial soil information through numerical models which are extracted as spatial variations of soil properties from observation and environmental covariates that digitally represent soil formation factors (McBratney et al., 2003). DSM is carried out by creating pixel-based soil maps using mathematical or statistical models in which environmental variables are related to soil information. DSM offers major novelties in removing some of the unconformities in traditional soil mapping (Caubet et al., 2019; Ma et al., 2019). DSM, the formation of soils where knowledge has accumulated for centuries, and several centuries of soil survey and mapping follow the progress of science. To understand spatial soil distribution at the area scale, pedometric modeling relies on the conceptional model of pedogenesis (Jenny, 1941), in which soils and their site-specific properties are the product of the interaction of soil-forming factors over long periods. The DSM framework was defined by McBratney et al. (2003) to perform the soil and related environmental factors in a spatial context and to express these relationships quantitatively. The modeling in this framework is based on how well the soil function of interest captures its causes or any functional relationship between them (Ließ et al., 2021). To approximate soil-forming factors in this direction, spatially digital geographic data on a global scale can be obtained free of charge from multiple sources. The production and usefulness of functional maps are important in DSM science. Accordingly, Jones et al. (2005) report the major impact of land cover on organic carbon dynamics in soils. As a matter of fact, differentnesses in land use and land cover in short distances significantly affect the distribution of soil macronutrients (de Brogniez et al., 2015). Land cover classes maps (European Union, Copernicus Land Monitoring Service, 2018) produced as a result of the CORINE project, which has been carried out for a quarter of a century, can be used as a predictive environmental variable in the production of spatially functional digital soil properties and maps (Gardi & Yigini, 2012; FAO, 2017; FAO, 2018).

To determine the macroelement contents of soil sample points in a test area is important to find the spatial distribution in non-sampled areas (Campbell et al., 2019; Shahbazi et al., 2019). Nutrient levels, which are important in plant cultivation, are one of the most important edaphological factors (Goss & Ulery, 2013).

Studies on the spatial distribution of edaphological factors with DSM methodology are relatively new. In this regard, the production of spatial maps of macronutrients with the most useful models may provide an advantage for fertilization studies.

In our study, we discuss (i) the results of using the CORINE land cover classes map as an environmental variable in an area where intensive agricultural activities are carried out, in addition to topographic and remote sensing product indices used in the literature in DSM science. (ii) We compared machine learning algorithms that are effectively used in information extraction in areas where there are extremely complex relationships in determining the relationships between environmental covariates and soil macronutrients and in producing spatial maps. To determine the spatial distribution of soil macronutrients, researchers have focused on the production of prediction model-based maps in DSM (Hengl & MacMillan, 2019). We used the random forest algorithm, one of the effective machine learning algorithms. In addition, (iii) we evaluated the modeling performance of the support vector machine (SVM), one of the most useful estimation tools (Taghizadeh-Mehrjardi et al., 2021) in recent years. (iv) We also compared the results with the multiple linear regression method.

6.2 Material and Methods

6.2.1 Study Area

The study area was located in the western Mediterranean region of Türkiye. It was within the borders of Isparta province. This covers an area of approximately 100 km² located between the coordinates of UTM 36 Zone 4192000 to 4204000 North, and 298000 to 304000 East (Figure 6.1). According to the Java Newhall Simulation Model, the study area has a Mesic soil temperature regime and a Xeric soil moisture regime (Van Wambeke, 2000).

Isparta Atabey plain is an agricultural plain where irrigated agriculture activities have been carried out for a quarter of a century (GDSHW, 2020). The distribution of CORINE land cover classes of the study area is given in Figure 6.2. Agricultural production is carried out in approximately 84% of the study area (Figure 6.2).

6.2.2 Method

The study was carried out in three stages: field, laboratory, and office studies. Soil samples were taken in the field studies and were analyzed in the laboratory studies. In the office studies, environmental variables were produced from the digital elevation model (DEM) (NASA, 2021), Sentinel 2A MSI Satellite

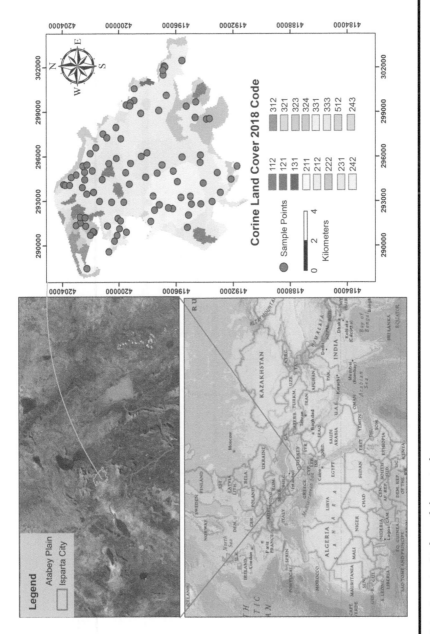

Figure 6.1 Isparta Atabey plain – study area.

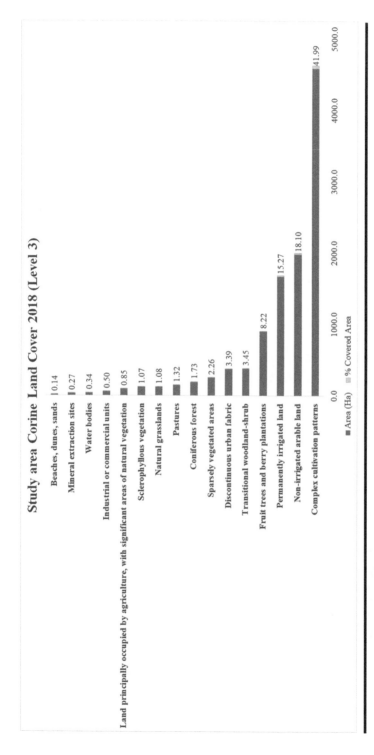

Figure 6.2 Land cover classes of the study area.

images (ESA, 2015), CORINE land cover class (European Union, Copernicus Land Monitoring Service, 2018), and knowledge discovery studies were carried out with modeling. A flowchart of the procedures followed in this work is presented in Figure 6.3.

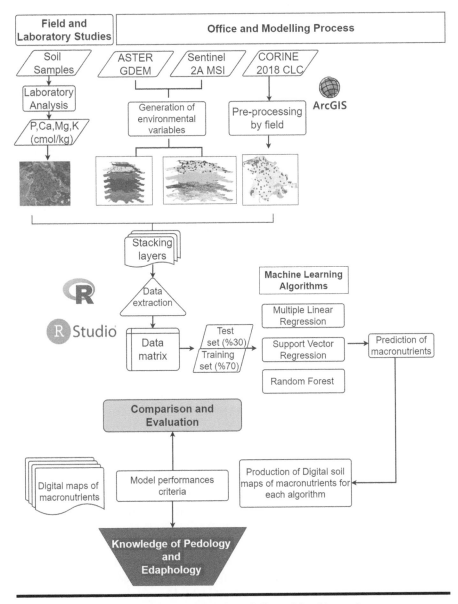

Figure 6.3   Flowchart of the methodology followed in this study.

6.2.2.1 Soil Sampling and Laboratory Analyses

The soil surface sampling scheme was performed by applying a stratified method (Soil Science Division Staff, 2017). A total of 91 soil samples were collected from 0 to 30-cm surfaces using stratified random sampling in 2019 in Figure 6.1. In this study, we only considered soil available Mg (Magnesium), K (Potassium), P (Phosphorus), and Ca (Calcium) (associated with fertility). Soil available P uses the Olsen method with a spectrophotometer (Olsen et al., 1954), with Ca, Mg, and K contents being extracted with 1 N ammonium acetate (NH_4OAc) (pH 7) and determined by an atomic absorption spectrophotometer (Varian- AA240FS) (Soil Survey Staff, 2014). The NH_4OAc-extracted cations, Ca^{2+}, Mg^{2+}, and K^+, are reported in meq 100 g^{-1} soil or cmol(+) kg^{-1} and P is ppm or mg kg^{-1} (Soil Survey Staff, 2014).

6.2.2.2 Environmental Covariates

Soil formation factors were generated from multiple digital sources while predicting functional soil macronutrients in DSM. To assess the soil organism factor, we used indices (Table 6.1) derived from the satellite image (downloaded from Copernicus Open Access Hub "https://scihub.copernicus.eue" within the framework of T36STH dated 11/16/2019. Registration number S2A_MSIL2A_20191116T085231_N0213_R107_T36STH) and obtained near the date of soil samples which were taken from the Sentinel 2A MSI Satellite. The spatial and spectral resolution information of the satellite image used is given in Sentinel-2 User Handbook (ESA, 2015). The temporal resolution of each Sentinel 2 satellite is 10 days, and the temporal resolution for the integrated 2 satellites is 5 days. Series A and B of the Sentinel 2 satellite can take images of the same area on earth at a temporal resolution of 5 days. Radiometric resolution is 12-bit (ESA, 2015). CORINE land cover classes 2018 V 2.0 data, standardized to a positional accuracy of 100 m and a 25-ha minimum mapping unit, was downloaded from "https://land.copernicus.eu/pan-european/corine-land-cover" (European Union, Copernicus Land Monitoring Service, 2018). In CORINE land cover class, all categorical predictors were recoded into dummy variables (Gardi & Yigini, 2012; FAO, 2018; Ließ et al., 2021). DEM was downloaded from the "https://search.earthdata.nasa.gov" Aster GDEM (NASA, 2021) database to derive the topographic attributes. The terrain attributes were derived from the DEM. The topographic variables derived following Hengl and Reuter (2008), and Gruber and Peckham (2009) that were used as environmental (independent) covariates in the modeling are given in Table 6.1. All covariates must have the same projection system and pixel size and the projected reference system used in this study was WGS1984 UTM Zone 36 (EPSG: 32636) (Malone et al., 2017). Therefore, all covariates resampling was done at a resolution of 30×30 m^2 using the

Table 6.1   Environmental Covariates

Soil-Forming Factors	Environmental Covariates	Definition
TOPOGRAPHY (R)	Elevation (m)	The elevation is commonly used in DEM, as it is often indicative of climatic processes.
	Slope (%)	The slope is the angle formed between any part of the earth and the horizontal.
	Aspect (0° to 360°)	This was defined as the slope direction.
	Profile curvature	Profile curvature affects the acceleration and deceleration of the flow, and thus erosion and accumulation.
	Planform curvature	Planform curvature affects the convergence and decomposition of the flow.
	Topographic wetness index	$$TWI = \ln\left(\frac{As}{tan\beta}\right) \qquad (7.1)$$ *As*, specific catchment area (contributing area per unit contour length) *tanβ*, specific catchment area slope, in radians. *As* is a parameter of water intake tendency; *tanβ* defines the local slope and contour length, and the tendency to transfer water (Agren et al., 2014).
PARENT MATERIAL(P)	Topsoil grain size index (Xiao et al., 2006)	$$\frac{(Red - Green)}{(Blue + Green + Red)} \qquad (7.2)$$ It is associated with the fine sand content on the soil surface.
	Brightness index (Hounkpatin et al., 2018)	$$\sqrt{(Blue^2 + Green^2 + Red^2)}\Big/ 3 \qquad (7.3)$$

(Continued)

Table 6.1 *(Continued)* Environmental Covariates

Soil-Forming Factors	Environmental Covariates	Definition
	Normalized clay index (Brown et al., 2017)	$$\frac{(\textbf{SWIR1} - \textbf{SWIR2})}{(\textbf{SWIR1} + \textbf{SWIR2})} \quad (7.4)$$ SWIR, Shortwave infrared Clay index (CI) was calculated to represent the parent material throughout the study area.
ORGANISM(O) AND ANTHROPOGENIC EFFECT	Normalized difference vegetation index – NDVI (Tucker, 1979)	$$\frac{(\textit{Near Infrared} - \textit{Red})}{(\textit{Near Infrared} + \textit{Red})} \quad (7.5)$$ Normalized Difference Vegetation Index (NDVI) combines the vegetation-specific reflection properties of the 0.6–0.7 μm (Red) and 0.7–1.3 μm (NIR) wavelength ranges, thus providing an insight into the vitality of the plant. It is in the range of –1 to 1.
	CORINE land cover Class	Soil samples were collected from 7 of them in the area with 16 land cover classes at level 3.

ArcGIS-Arctoolbox-Raster processing-toolset-Resample tool (ESRI, 2010). All environmental variables are given in Figure 6.4.

6.2.2.3 Creating the Data Matrix

All topographic, land cover class, and satellite-based environmental covariates were stacked as a single layer for the extract process (Figure 6.4). The environmental variable values of the 91 coordinated soil sampling locations were extracted. These procedures were carried out using the R "raster" package (Hijmans, 2020).

6.2.2.4 Correlation Analysis and Descriptive Statistics

Descriptive statistics parameters were determined by using the "describe" function in the "psych" package (Revelle, 2019). The Pearson correlation coefficient was calculated to determine the degree of relationship between the soil macronutrients'

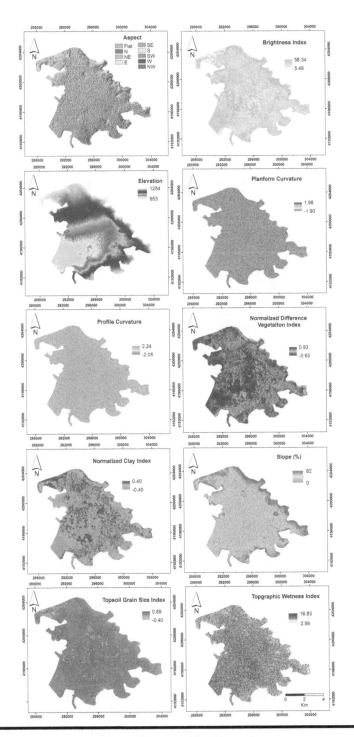

Figure 6.4 Environmental covariates used in this study.

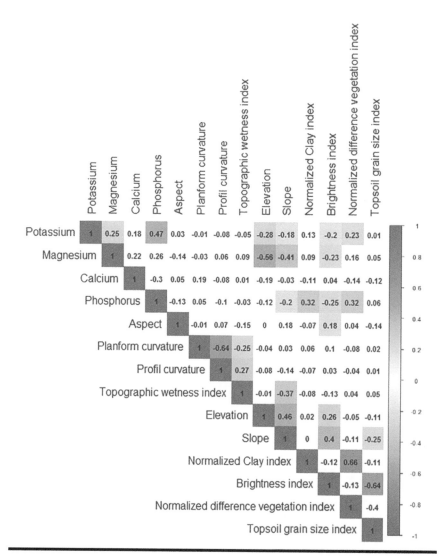

Figure 6.5 The correlation graph of soil nutrients and environmental variables.

values and the environmental covariates. Correlations were performed in the "stats" package, and graphs were created using the "corrplot" (Wei & Sinyo, 2017) package to determine the significant ones at p <0.05 (Figure 6.5).

6.2.2.5 Modeling

The data matrix is divided into two subsets (training set (70%; N:63) and a test set (30%; N:28)) (FAO, 2018). The applicability of random forest, support vector regression, and multiple linear regression models in the study area is compared for each target variable (macronutrients). The three models are described in more detail below.

6.2.2.5.1 Multiple Linear Regression

Linear regression models purpose to explain a dependent variable by a linear combination of estimators (independent variables-environmental covariates (Forkuor et al., 2017)). In this study, while spectral, topographic, and land cover variables were independent variables, various soil macroelement contents were considered as dependent variables (Hengl & Macmillan, 2019).

$$y = \alpha + \sum_{i=1}^{n} bi * xi \pm \varepsilon \qquad (7.6)$$

where y is the dependent variable (soil macronutrients), x_i denotes the independent variables (spectral, topographic, and land cover classes), n is the number of variables, b_i are the partial regression coefficients, α is the intercept, and ε is the standard error of the estimate. It can also be used in the equation by converting categorical environmental variables (land cover class) to dummy variables (binary, 0–1; FAO, 2018; Hengl & Macmillan, 2019; Hounkpatin et al., 2021). In our study area, seven categories of CORINE land cover class overlapped with soil samples at the same point and were added to the data set.

For multiple linear regression, we used the "lm" function in the R Core Environment program (R Core Team, 2020). A matrix was produced by stacking soil sampling points on spectral, topographic, and land cover spatial raster layers and extracting the corresponding values. Stepwise regression identifies a subset of predictors based on the statistical significance of the predictors (using stepwise, forward selection, or backward elimination) (Venables & Ripley, 2013). In this study, the "step" function as performed in the "MASS" package (Venables & Ripley, 2013) of the R statistical package was used for the stepwise regression. The importance of the environmental variables used in the model was determined based on the absolute value of the t statistical value for each model parameter with the "VarImp" function available in the "caret" (Kuhn et al., 2015) package in the R Core Environment (R Core Team, 2020).

In many practical situations, seeking and formulating linear relationships can be very restrictive. Therefore, statistical learning or machine learning techniques have been used to establish the relationship between dependent and independent variables (Hengl & Macmillan, 2019).

6.2.2.5.2 Random Forest Algorithm

The random forest algorithm developed by Breiman (2001) has been used many times as a regression method for predicting soil macronutrients content in DSM studies (Shahbazi et al., 2019). The approach of combining many random decision trees and their estimates with means is preferred in DSM because it is multiple enough to be applied to large-scale studies and provides information on the importance of the variables (Ließ et al., 2012; Hengl et al., 2015; Hengl et al., 2021).

The "randomForest" package (Liaw & Wiener, 2002) was used in this study. The amount of data in the calibration set used for the detection of out-of-bag (OOB) errors was 36.8%, which also permitted the determination of the importance of the variable. The random forest algorithm requires three parameters: (i) The default value for "ntree" defined in the package is 500. (ii) The "nodesize" value of 5 was used for each terminal node, which is a standard value in regression studies. While creating each tree in the regression estimates, the more value, which defines the number of variables to be changeably selected, was selected to have a default value of one-third of the total number of independent variables (Liaw & Wiener 2002; Biau & Scornet, 2016).

The importance of the environmental covariates used in the model was calculated for each model with the "importance" function in the "randomforest" package (Liaw & Wiener, 2002). In software packages, a regression approach computes two important measures of %IncMSE (increase in mean standard error) and IncNodePurity. For each tree in the regression model, the prediction error for the OOB part is listed as the mean square error (MSE). The significance of each variable is estimated by changing each variable in the unutilized OOB samples. The change in the OOB error is a mark of the importance of these independent covariates. Variables with a relatively large increase in the OOB error are more important.

The percentage increase in mean square error (% Inmse) is the most commonly used (Sahragard & Pahlavan-Rad, 2020). Upper orders in the variable importance graph indicate important common variables. To interpret the relative importance, the % Inmse is shown between 0 and 100 (Stum et al., 2010; Pahlavan-Rad et al., 2020; Sahragard & Pahlavan-Rad, 2020).

6.2.2.5.3 Support Vector Regression

SVMs were developed by Cortes and Vapnik (1995). Although they are used extensively in classification problems, which is one of the first purposes of use, they can also be used in regression problems. Drucker et al. (1997) detail the use of support vector regression. It is a popular machine learning algorithm with relatively high accuracy and low computational cost (Taghizadeh-Mehrjardi et al., 2021). It has been used in modeling studies of various soil properties with the use of kernel functions (Pasolli et al., 2011).

When we received, consider a "y" variable (soil macronutrient) with observation points belonging to a feature set x = (x1, x2,....xn) with different types of independent variables (indices produced from satellite imagery, topographic indices, and categorical land cover data) from an analytical point of view, we can express this prediction problem with the following equation:

$$y = f(x) + e \tag{7.7}$$

where "f" denotes the desired and unknown input-output mapping, and "e" denotes a Gaussian variable with zero mean and unit variance that affects the estimation process being considered. Here, the estimation of "y" in the case of determining a function f is as close as possible to the closest match to reality for the target under consideration. Given a set of N reference samples, the goal of the ε-insensitive SVR technique is to find a smooth function f approaching f while maintaining at most one ε deviation from the "y" targets. Data is projected into higher-dimensional space through kernel techniques to allow separation in the case of nonlinear. The radial basis function (RBF) (i.e. Gaussian function) kernel is commonly applied for this purpose (Ballabio, 2009; Kovačević et al., 2010; Taghizadeh-Mehrjardi, 2021; Ma et al., 2021). The first term ε is calculated according to an insensitive loss function, where ε measures tolerance to errors, thus allowing an insensitive tube to be defined surrounding the f function. Therefore, the robustness of this technique will be increased against minor errors and noise in the training set. The parameter C measures the distance (in the corresponding feature space) of the training samples outside the ε insensitive tube from the tube itself. Here, C can be expressed with non-negative ξ ve ξˣ slack variables (variables included in linear programming problems so that inequalities representing constraints can be replaced with equations). C is a regulation parameter that allows adjusting the balance between the complexity (flatness) of the function and tolerance to empirical errors. The constrained optimization problem can be reformulated by the Lagrange function, which leads to the convex quadratic problem in the dual formulation and thus a unique solution. The modeling process of support vector regression was performed using the "svm" function in the "e1071" package, which allows the LIBSVM library (Chang & Lin, 2011) to be implemented in the R Core Environment interface (Meyer et al., 2020). The variables that are important in the model were calculated and interpreted as stated in FAO (2018).

6.2.2.6 Model Evaluation

The coefficient of determination (R^2) and root mean square error (RMSE) was used to evaluate the model performance (Malone et al., 2017; Zeraatpisheh et al., 2019):

$$Coefficient\ of\ Determination\ \left(R^2\right) = \left[\frac{\sum_{i=1}^{n}(Gi - Gort)(Ti - Tort)}{\sqrt{\sum_{i=1}^{n}(Gi - Gort)^2 (Ti - Tort)^2}}\right]^2 \quad (7.8)$$

$$Root\ Mean\ Square\ Error\ (RMSE) = \sqrt{\frac{\sum_{i=1}^{n}(Gi - Ti)2}{n}} \quad (7.9)$$

Gi and *Ti* are the observed and predicted values, respectively. G_{ort} and T_{ort} values are the average of observed and predicted values, respectively, while *n* is the number of samples in the data set. The lowest RMSE values were interpreted with the assumption that it might be the most useful model.

6.2.2.7 Generating Digital Maps of Macronutrients

Produced models were applied to the environmental variable data set in the raster environment in R Studio V 1.3, which is the Integrated Development Environment (IDE) of the R Core Environment program (RStudio Team, 2019). In this application, all layers must have the same projection system and pixel size.

6.3 Results and Discussion

6.3.1 Results of the Correlation Analysis and Descriptive Statistics

The descriptive statistics results for macronutrient values are given in Table 6.2. By determining the degree of variability of soil properties by considering the coefficient of variation, it was reported that coefficient values (CV) of 0–15% represent a low variation, 16–35% represent a medium variation, and more than 36% represent a high variation (Bishop & McBratney, 2018). Descriptive statistics of environmental variables that take continuous values (numeric) for 91 samples in the data set are also given in Table 6.2. Mg and P have higher variability in the study area than other macroelements (Table 6.2). It can be seen that in the rock structure, the soils present in the study area are formed and the variability of soil formation factors affects the decomposition processes. Therefore, this is to be expected in areas where agricultural activities are maintained and land use varies short distances. Shahbazi et al. (2019) reported that the available P contents of soils have a very high coefficient of variation in the area they studied. Similarly, Maleki et al. (2021) reported that long-term agricultural activities are effective on the variations of soil properties on different landforms.

The correlation between the macronutrient values and the environmental variables (continuous-numerical) is given in Figure 6.5. In the study area, negative relationships were determined between K and elevation and slope values. A similar situation exists in Mg. Especially in sloping areas, it is more likely that large particles can be formed from primary minerals, whereas 2:1-type clay minerals are more likely to form in old stream beds in the deposition and weathering process. No significant relationship was found between other topographic

Table 6.2 Descriptive Statistical Results for the Soil Properties and Environmental Variables (SD: Standard Deviation; CV: Coefficient of Variation (%); Skew: Skewness; Kurt.: Kurtosis, NDVI: Normalized Difference Vegetation Index)

Variable	SD	CV	Min.	Mean	Max.	Skew.	Kurt.
K (cmol kg⁻¹)	0.62	44.00	0.46	1.40	3.92	1.15	2.43
Mg (cmol kg⁻¹)	3.10	57.32	1.14	5.40	13.65	0.62	−0.34
Ca (cmol kg⁻¹)	10.54	30.67	7.45	34.38	51.38	−0.81	0.04
P (mg kg⁻¹)	32.98	114.54	3.86	28.80	214.08	3.53	15.29
Aspect	100.30	55.53	−1.00	180.60	348.70	−0.35	−0.68
Planform curvature	0.46	−769.59	−1.28	−0.06	1.28	0.00	0.82
Profile curvature	0.50	1269.21	−1.15	0.04	0.96	−0.13	−0.91
Topographic wetness index	1.78	25.95	4.23	6.84	12.75	1.06	0.69
Elevation	40.80	4.02	955.00	1015.20	1122.00	0.38	−0.75
Slope	4.15	63.35	0.00	6.55	18.94	0.76	0.15
Normalized clay index	0.03	17.31	0.11	0.17	0.24	0.59	−0.10
Brightness index	2.40	14.55	10.91	16.51	22.46	0.12	−0.69
NDVI	0.08	39.66	0.10	0.21	0.58	2.01	5.25
Topsoil grain size index	0.05	30.31	−0.06	0.15	0.26	−0.84	4.47

variables and soil macronutrients in the dominant flat plain, as in similar flat areas (John et al., 2020).

A significant positive correlation was determined between the P and the NDVI. It is an accepted approach to correlate the surface soil properties of soils with reflectance values obtained from remotely sensed images to provide a means of measuring spatial heterogeneity. As a matter of fact, considering that the satellite image studied is in the period after the natural plant development period is over, it shows that remote sensing indices can be used effectively in terms of reflecting applications in agricultural areas rather than natural vegetation. There are moderate positive relationships between K and Mg among macronutrients. Similarly, the relationship between K and P values is moderately positive.

6.3.2 Spatial Prediction, Model Interpretation, and Evaluation

Results for three different models and four macroelements are given comparatively in Table 6.3. In the estimation of all soil macronutrients, the highest R^2 values and the lowest RMSE values in the training set were obtained with the random forest algorithm (Table 6.3). This situation is reported in different study areas regardless of scale. Hengl et al. (2015) reported that the random forest algorithm gave the highest performance results to map soil characteristics at a resolution of 250 m on the African scale. Support vector regression, which can capture nonlinear relationships, thanks to the kernel function used, showed the best model performance after the random forest algorithm. All algorithms could not show the performance that is achieved in the training set in the test sets (Table 6.3). In addition, the most decrease has been in the multiple linear regression model, which can capture linear relationships and has limited use. The soil properties may not increase and decrease in certain linearity with the environmental variable values in the feature space in

Table 6.3   Comparison of the Approaches Used to Predict Soil Properties (MLR: Multiple Linear Regression, SVM: Support Vector Machine, RF: Random Forest)

		Training		Test	
Macronutrient	*Model*	R^2	*RMSE*	R^2	*RMSE*
P (mg kg⁻¹)	**MLR**	0.17	23.58	0.05	42.88
	SVM	0.34	29.06	0.09	23.27
	RF	0.79	16.39	0.29	20.56
Ca (cmol kg⁻¹)	**MLR**	0.47	7.39	−0.41	13.13
	SVM	0.66	5.91	0.002	11.02
	RF	0.83	4.12	0.12	10.33
Mg (cmol kg⁻¹)	**MLR**	0.59	1.74	0.29	3.09
	SVM	0.76	1.32	0.36	2.95
	RF	0.85	1.03	0.22	3.25
K (cmol kg⁻¹)	**MLR**	0.36	0.51	−2.03	0.87
	SVM	0.52	0.44	−0.63	0.63
	RF	0.82	0.26	−0.78	0.66

data sets where soils obtained from alluvial plains are available. As a matter of fact, in these areas where the elevation value is very similar, the land cover changes in a short distance; in this case, it affects the distribution of soil macronutrients. This situation causes linear relationships not to be formed and makes the multiple linear regression model that can model linear relationships fail. However, decreases in the test set in nonlinear models may be an indication that the models may tend to overfitting.

The reason for this is that although nonlinear machine learning algorithms are used, it is difficult to cope with the overlaps that occur in the feature space in an alluvial plain (Hengl et al., 2007). The support vector regression algorithm executed using the radial basis kernel function also appears to be sensitive to overlaps in the feature space (Table 6.3). The value of C can be important in parameter optimization. This parameter, which is important in determining the complexity (or flatness) of the function (Pasolli et al., 2011), should be used carefully against the problem of overfitting.

In addition to the accuracy of the models, the interpretation of the graphics showing the importance levels of the variables in the model plays an important role in increasing the knowledge discovery in DSM science (Wadoux et al., 2020; Wadoux & McBratney, 2021). The graphics for the important environmental variables in the model for each soil macronutrient are given in Figure 6.6.

It can be seen that the most important environmental variables in the models used in the spatial estimation of macroelements are the land cover classes, excluding K (Figure 6.6). Accordingly, knowledge of land cover classes can provide us with predictions in modeling. Wiesmeier et al. (2011) reported that the most important variables controlling soil chemical properties are land use. In this regard, maps of land cover classes that have been updated at certain ranges for a quarter of a century can also depict the orientation of agricultural product patterns of farmers living in the studied area. This may also require collecting additional information and observations from the study area.

Macroelements maps produced according to three different model algorithms will be given separately under each model title.

6.3.2.1 Multiple Linear Regression

In multiple regression, residuals (predicted minus observed values) are assumed to be normally distributed (i.e. follow the normal distribution). It can generate histograms of residuals as well as normal probability plots to examine the distribution of residual values (FAO, 2018). In this direction, as a result of the modeling created for the macroelements, the histogram and the Qqnorm and Qqline graphs, showing the distribution of the residuals of each macroelement for the training set, were produced in the R Core Environment (R Core Team, 2020) by using

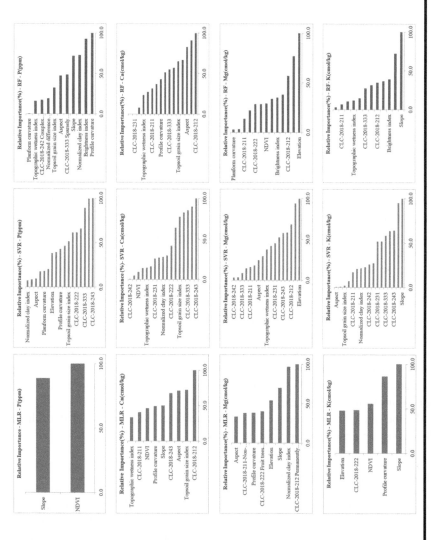

Figure 6.6 Important environmental variables in predicting soil macronutrients.

the "hist", "qqnorm", and "qqline" functions (Figure 6.7). In the histograms of P and Mg (Figure 6.7, A, C), curves were tended to be right, and the residuals move away from the normal distribution (Webster, 2001; FAO, 2018). P and Mg showed the highest coefficient of variation among macroelements (Table 6.2). The high-variation coefficient, which is also an indicator of spatial variability in an alluvial

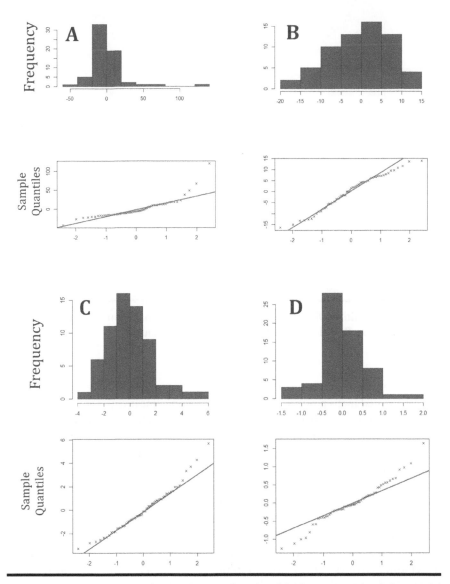

Figure 6.7 Histogram and QQ plot graphs of residuals as a result of the model using multiple linear regression (A: Phosphorus, B: Calcium, C: Magnesium, D: Potassium).

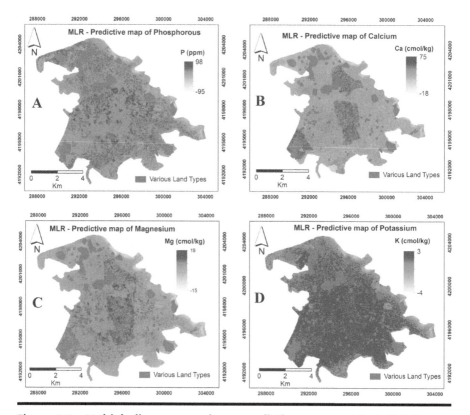

Figure 6.8 Multiple linear regression – predictive macronutrient digital maps (A: Phosphorus, B: Calcium, C: Magnesium, D: Potassium).

agricultural plain, causes the failure of linear modeling algorithms. As a matter of fact, the spatial maps produced by using the multiple linear regression model to the raster environmental variable data set (Figure 6.8), it can be seen that the model predicts negative macronutrient content. This is a factually inaccurate result. However, negative values may also represent areas with extreme values in the environmental variable set in the study area. The importance of the masking process can be demonstrated. The most important environmental variables for P in the multiple linear regression model were NDVI and slope (Figure 6.6). P was correlated negatively with slope and positively with NDVI (Figure 6.5). The most important variable in the spatial modeling of Ca and Mg with the multiple linear regression model was the "CLC-2018-212 Permanently irrigated land" categorical land cover class. Irrigated agriculture activities were carried out in this class for many years, the minerals were present in the irrigation water in this process, and the capillary structure of the soil as a result of irrigation may tend to increase Ca and Mg on the surface with the upward movement of water (Figure 6.8) (Maleki et al., 2021). As a matter of fact,

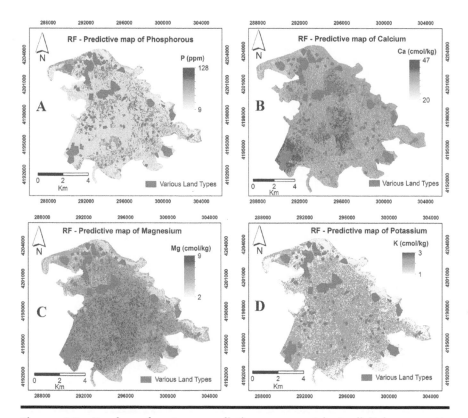

Figure 6.9 Random forest – predictive macronutrient digital maps (A: Phosphorus, B: Calcium, C: Magnesium, D: Potassium).

there is a similar situation for Ca and Mg in maps created as a result of modeling with other algorithms (Figures 6.9 and 6.10).

6.3.2.2 Random Forest

Considering the training set model results for all macroelements evaluated within the scope of the study, the lowest RMSE values were obtained with the random forest algorithm.

Considering the minimum and maximum values of the predicted dependent variables (macroelements) (Table 6.2), the random forest algorithm produced the closest predictions to these values compared to other model algorithms (Figure 6.9). The most useful maps spatially are the maps of this model. The most important environmental variable in the model for Ca was the CLC-2018-212 Permanently irrigated land categorical land cover class (Figure 6.6). For the prediction of K, the most important variables in the random forest algorithm were topographic

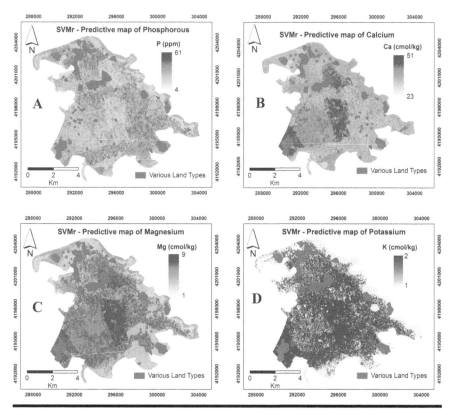

Figure 6.10   Support vector regression – predictive macronutrient digital maps (A: Phosphorus, B: Calcium, C: Magnesium, D: Potassium).

variables, as in other algorithms (Figure 6.6). This may indicate that the K element is not much affected by land uses and may be related to the primary and secondary minerals in the soil structure. The relationships between the amount of clay and the slope and elevation values in an alluvial plain have been revealed (Kaya & Başayiğit, 2021). In mineral soils, most of the K is bound as lattice constituents in silicate minerals, particularly alkaline feldspars, micas, and illites. This situation is closely related to the pedogenesis of the soils and the exchangeable K amounts may differ (Blume et al., 2016).

6.3.2.3 Support Vector Regression

The support vector regression algorithm, which we used to capture nonlinear relationships, showed similar model performances to the random forest algorithm by force of the radial basis kernel function (Table 6.2). It can also be seen from the result maps of the model that the categorical land class "CLC-2018-212 Permanently irrigated land" affects the estimation for Ca and Mg (Figures 6.6 and 6.10). In the prediction of P with support vector regression, very close RMSE values were obtained from the training and test sets. Indeed, the RMSE value was not increased in the test set (Table 6.3). Notably, the categorical land cover classes "CLC-2018-231 Pastures" and "CLC-2018-243 land-primarily occupied by agriculture, with significant areas of natural vegetation" are important variables in the model in the phosphorous estimation (Figure 6.6). Indeed, the performance of support vector regression in data sets with sparse samples has been reported (Drucker et al., 1997; Taghizadeh-Mehrjardi et al., 2021).

6.4 Conclusions

In this study, different machine learning algorithms were compared for making digital spatial maps of macronutrients in an alluvial agricultural plain. Based on the increase in the importance of edaphological approaches in DSM, field-specific inferences were made from the most useful models produced and evaluations were presented. As a result of the study, it was determined that CORINE land cover classes with a history of several decades were an important predictor of the distribution of soil macronutrients, which are dynamic soil properties. In an alluvial agricultural plain with complex phenomena, the multiple linear regression model has had low success in predicting the minimum values for capturing linear relationships. Random forest and support vector regression algorithms, which have the potential to reveal nonlinear relationships, produced similar results and it was determined that the most useful algorithm was the random forest. Evaluation of the obtained model results under the control of the soil scientist is an opportunity to increase the useful information to be obtained from the model. There may be criticism of the absolute accuracy of maps. But it may be important to consider in the context of field conditions, for example, in the creation of site-specific fertilizer recommendations. However, it can be an alternative to obtain information about soil properties in areas where soil sampling has not been done, especially in the context of small-scale agriculture. As in our study area, geostatistical approaches are limited in areas with socio-ecologically heterogeneous farms, i.e. different land uses. However, hybrid modeling techniques (for example, Regression Kriging) that take into account the spatial location of the sample points should be investigated in future studies of macronutrients with dynamic soil properties. In general, good-resolution soil maps are useful for many soil scientists and land managers in Türkiye. We suggest that the comparative approach can be used to mapping using soil databases and environmental variable sets available in other regions of Türkiye because agro-ecological regions differ significantly across. Considering the analytical accuracy of the model results, the digital macroelement maps produced not only serve for expert knowledge but may also be suitable data for integration into precision agriculture systems based on agriculture 5.0.

References

Agren, A. M., Lidberg, W., Strömgren, M., Ogilvie, J., & Arp, P. A. (2014). Evaluating digital terrain indices for soil wetness mapping – a Swedish case study. *Hydrology and Earth System Sciences*, Discussion, *18*(9), 3623–3634. https://doi.org/10.5194/hess-18-3623-2014

Ballabio, C. (2009). Spatial prediction of soil properties in temperate mountain regions using support vector regression. *Geoderma, 151*, 338–350. https://doi.org/10.1016/j.geoderma.2009.04.022

Biau, G., & Scornet, E. (2016). A random forest-guided tour. *Test, 25*(2), 197–227. https://doi.org/10.1007/s11749-016-0481-7.

Bishop, T. F. A., & McBratney, A. B. (2018). Soil Statistical Description and Measurement Scales. In McBratney, A. B., Minasny, B., & Stockmann, U. (Eds.), *Pedometrics* (pp. 43–57). Springer.. https://doi.org/10.1007/978-3-319-63439-5_2.

Blume, H. P., Brümmer, G. W., Fleige, H., Horn, R., Kandeler, E., Kögel-Knabner, I., & Wilke, B. M. (2016). Soil-Plant Relations. In Blume, H. P., Brümmer, G. W., Fleige, H., Horn, R., Kandeler, E., Kögel-Knabner, I., & Wilke, B. M. (Eds.), *Scheffer/SchachtschabelSoil Science* (pp. 409–484). Springer, Berlin, Heidelberg. https://doi.org/10.1007/978-3-642-30942-7_9.

Brown, K. S., Libohova, Z., & Boettinger, J. (2017). Digital Soil Mapping. In Ditzler, C., Scheffe, K., & Monger, H.C. (Eds.), *Soil Survey Manual, USDA Handbook 18* (pp. 295–354.), Government Printing Office, Washington, DC.

Breiman, L. (2001). Random forests. *Machine Learning, 45*(1), 5–32.

Campbell, P. M. M., Francelino, M. R., Filho, E. I. F., Rocha, P. A., & Azevedo, B. C. (2019). Digital mapping of soil attributes using machine learning. *Revista Ciência Agronômica, 50*(4), 519–528. https://doi.org/10.5935/1806-6690.20190061

Caubet, M., Dobarco, M. R., Arrouays, D., Minasny, B., & Saby, N. P. A. (2019). Merging country, continental and global predictions of soil texture: lessons from ensemble modelling in France. *Geoderma. 337*, 99–110. https://doi.org/10.1016/j.geoderma.2018.09.007

Chang, C. C., & Lin, C. J. (2011). Libsvm. *ACM Transactions on Intelligent Systems and Technology, 2*, 1–39. https://doi.org/10.1145/1961189.1961199

Cortes, C., & Vapnik, V. (1995). Support-vector networks. *Machine Learning, 20*, 273–297. https://doi.org/10.1007/BF00994018

de Brogniez, D., Ballabio, C., Stevens, A., Jones, R. J. A., Montanarella, L., & van Wesemael, B. (2015). A map of the topsoil organic carbon content of Europe generated by a generalized additive model. *European Journal of Soil Science, 66*(1), 121–134. https://doi.org/10.1111/ejss.12193

Drucker, H., Burges, C. J. C., Kaufman L., Smola, A. J., & Vapnik, V. (1997). Support vector regression machines. *Advances in Neural Information Processing Systems, 9*, 155–161.

ESA (2015). *Sentinel-2 User Handbook*. European Space Agency, European Union.

ESRI (2010). ArcGIS user's guide, http://www.esri.com.

European Union, Copernicus Land Monitoring Service (2018). *Corine land cover class 2018 V 2.0 data*. https://land.copernicus.eu/pan-european/corine-land-cover. Accessed date: 04 May 2021.

FAO. (2017). *Soil Organic Carbon Mapping Cookbook* (First edition). FAO, Rome, Italy.

FAO. (2018). *Soil Organic Carbon Mapping Cookbook* (Second edition). FAO, Rome, Italy.

Forkuor, G., Hounkpatin, O. K., Welp, G., & Thiel, M. (2017). High resolution mapping of soil properties using remote sensing variables in south-western Burkina Faso: a comparison of machine learning and multiple linear regression models. *PloS One*, *12*(1), e0170478. https://doi.org/10.1371/journal.pone.0170478

Gardi, C., & Yigini, Y. (2012). Continuous mapping of soil pH using digital soil mapping approach in Europe. *Eurasian Journal of Soil Science*, *2*, 64–68.

GDSHW. (2020). *General Directorate of State Hydraulic Works. Isparta Atabey Plain Irrigation Rehabilitation Project Resettlement Action Plan*. November 2020. 150 pp.

Goss, R. M., & Ulery, A. L. (2013). Edaphology. *Reference Module in Earth Systems and Environmental Sciences*, Elsevier. https://doi.org/10.1016/B978-0-12-409548-9.05143-5.

Gruber, S., & Peckham, S. (2009). Land-surface parameters and objects in hydrology. *Developments in Soil Science*, *33*, 171–194. https://doi:10.1016/S0166-2481(08)00007-X

Hengl, T., Heuvelink, G. B., Kempen, B., Leenaars, J. G., Walsh, M. G., Shepherd, K. D., & Tondoh, J. E. (2015). Mapping soil properties of Africa at 250 m resolution: random forests significantly improve current predictions. *PloS One*, *10*(6), e0125814. https://doi.org/10.1371/journal.pone.0125814

Hengl, T., Miller, M. A. E., Križan, J., Shepherd, K. D., Sila, A., Kilibarda M., et al. (2021). African soil properties and nutrients mapped at 30 m spatial resolution using two-scale ensemble machine learning. *Scientific Reports*, *11*, 6130. https://doi.org/10.1038/s41598-021-85639-y.

Hengl, T., & Reuter, H.I. (2008). Geomorphometry: concepts, software, applications. *Developments in Soil Science*, *33*, 772 pp.

Hengl, T., Toomanian, N., Reuter, H. I., & Malakouti, M. J. (2007). Methods to interpolate soil categorical variables from profile observations: lessons from Iran. *Geoderma*, *140*(4), 417–427. https://doi.org/10.1016/j.geoderma.2007.04.022.

Hengl, T., & Macmillan, R. A. (2019). *Predictive Soil Mapping with R*. OpenGeoHub Foundation, Wageningen, Netherlands.

Heuvelink, G. (2013). The definition of pedometrics. *Pedometron*, *14*, 2–3.

Hijmans R. J. (2020). raster: Geographic Data Analysis and Modeling. R package version 3.4-5.

Hounkpatin, K. O., Schmidt, K., Stumpf, F., Forkuor, G., Behrens, T., Scholten, T., & Welp, G. (2018). Predicting reference soil groups using legacy data: a data pruning and Random Forest approach for tropical environment (Dano catchment, Burkina Faso). *Scientific Reports*, *8(1)*, 1–16. https://doi.org/10.1038/s41598-018-28244-w

Hounkpatin, K. O., Stendahl, J., Lundblad, M., & Karltun, E. (2021). Predicting the spatial distribution of soil organic carbon stock in Swedish forests using a group of covariates and site-specific data. *SOIL*, *7*(2), 377–398. https://doi.org/10.5194/soil-7-377-2021.

John, K., Isong, I. A, Kebonye, N. M., Ayito, E. O., Agyeman, P. C., & Afu, S. M. (2020). Using machine learning algorithms to estimate soil organic carbon variability with environmental variables and soil nutrient indicators in an alluvial soil. *Land*, *9*(12), 487. https://doi.org/10.3390/land9120487

Jenny, H. (1941). *Factors of Soil Formation: A System of Quantitative Pedology*, 1st edn. McGraw-Hill Inc., New York.

Jones, R. J. A., Hiederer, R., Rusco, E., & Montanarella, L. (2005). Estimating organic carbon in the soils of Europe for policy support. *European Journal of Soil Science*, *56*, 655–671.

Kacar, B., & Katkat, A. V. (2015). Plant nutrition. Nobel Publications (Six Edition), Ankara. (In Turkish)

Kaya, F., & Başayiğit, L. (2021). *Digital Mapping of Soil Particle Size Distribution in an Alluvial Plain Using the Random Forest Algorithm.* In EGU General Assembly Conference Abstracts EGU21-7828. https://doi.org/10.5194/egusphere-egu21-7828

Kovačević, M., Bajat, B., & Gajić, B. (2010). Soil type classification and estimation of soil properties using support vector machines. *Geoderma, 154*(3–4), 340–347. https://doi.org/10.1016/j.geoderma.2009.11.005

Kuhn, M., Wing, J., Weston, S., Williams, A., Keefer, C., Engelhardt, A., Cooper, T., Mayer, Z., Kenkel, B., R Core Team, Benesty, M., Lescarbeau, R., Ziem, A., & Scrucca, L. (2015). *caret: Classification and regression training.*

Liaw, A., & Wiener, M. (2002). Classification and regression by randomForest. *R News, 2*(3), 18–22.

Ließ, M., Gebauer, A., & Don, A. (2021). Machine learning with GA optimization to model the agricultural soil-landscape of Germany: an approach involving soil functional types with their multivariate parameter distributions along the depth profile. *Frontiers in Environmental Science, 9*, 692959. https://doi.org/10.3389/fenvs.2021.692959

Ließ, M., Glaser, B., & Huwe, B. (2012). Uncertainty in the spatial prediction of soil texture: comparison of regression tree and Random Forest models. *Geoderma. 170*, 70–79. https://doi.org/10.1016/j.geoderma.2011.10.010.

Ma, Y., Zhang, Z., Kang, Y., & Özdoğan, M. (2021). Corn yield prediction and uncertainty analysis based on remotely sensed variables using a Bayesian neural network approach. *Remote Sensing of Environment, 259*, 112408. https://doi.org/10.1016/j.rse.2021.112408

Ma, Y. X., Minasny, B., Malone, B. P., & McBratney, A. B. (2019). Pedology and digital soil mapping (DSM). *European Journal of Soil Science, 70*, 216–235. https://doi.org/10.1111/ejss.12790

Maleki, S., Karimi, A., Zeraatpisheh, M., Poozeshi, R., & Feizi, H. (2021). Long-term cultivation effects on soil properties variations in different landforms in an arid region of eastern Iran. *Catena, 206*, 105465. https://doi.org/10.1016/j.catena.2021.105465

Malone, B. P., Minasny, B., & McBratney, A. B. (2017). Continuous Soil Attribute Modeling and Mapping. In Malone, B. P., Minasny, B., & McBratney, A. B. (Eds.), *Using R for Digital Soil Mapping* (pp. 151–167). Springer.https://doi.org/10.1007/978-3-319-44327-0_6

McBratney, A. B., Santos, M. M., & Minasny, B. (2003) On digital soil mapping. *Geoderma. 117*, 3–52. https://doi.org/10.1016/S0016-7061(03)00223-4.

Meyer, D., Dimitriadou, E., Hornik, K., Weingessel, A., & Leisch, F. (2020). e1071: Misc Functions of the Department of Statistics, Probability Theory Group (Formerly: E1071), TU Wien. R package version 1.7-4.

Mponela, P., Snapp, S., Villamor, G. B., Tamene, L., Le, Q. B., & Borgemeister, C. (2020). Digital soil mapping of nitrogen, phosphorus, potassium, organic carbon and their crop response thresholds in smallholder managed escarpments of Malawi. *Applied Geography*, 124, 102299. https://doi.org/10.1016/j.apgeog.2020.102299.

NASA, (2021). National Aeronautics and Space Administration - Aster Global Digital Elevation Model (Aster GDEM) NASA Official) Retrieved 02.06.2020, http://www.gdem.aster.ersdac.or.jp

Olsen, S. R., Cole, C. V., Watanabe, F. S., & Dean, L. A. (1954). *Estimation of available phosphorus in soils by extraction with sodium bicarbonate.* U.S. Govt. Print. Office, Washington, DC.

Pahlavan-Rad, M. R., Dahmardeh, K., Hadizadeh, M., Keykha, G., Mohammadnia, N., & Gangali, M., et.al. (2020). Prediction of soil water infiltration using multiple linear regression and random forest in a dry flood plain, eastern Iran. *Catena. 194*, 104715. https://doi.org/10.1016/j.catena.2020.104715.

Pasolli, L., Notarnicola, C., & Bruzzone, L. (2011). Estimating soil moisture with the support vector regression technique. *IEEE Geoscience and Remote Sensing Letters, 8*, 1080–1084. https://doi.org/10.1109/LGRS.2011.2156759.

R Core Team (2020). *R: A Language and Environment for Statistical Computing*. R Foundation for Statistical Computing, Vienna, Austria.

Revelle, W. (2019). *psych: Procedures for Personality and Psychological Research*, Northwestern University, Evanston, Illinois, USA.

RStudio Team. (2019). *RStudio: Integrated Development for R*. RStudio, Inc., Boston, MA URL http://www.rstudio.com/. Accessed 11 February 2021.

Sahragard, H. P., & Pahlavan-Rad, M. R. (2020). Prediction of soil properties using random forest with sparse data in a semi-active volcanic mountain. *Eurasian Soil Science, 53*(9), 1222–1233. https://doi.org/10.1134/S1064229320090136

Shahbazi, F., Hughes, P., McBratney, A. B., Minasny, B., & Malone, B. P. (2019). Evaluating the spatial and vertical distribution of agriculturally important nutrients—nitrogen, phosphorous and boron—in North West Iran. *Catena, 173*, 71–82. https://doi.org/10.1016/j.catena.2018.10.005

Soil Science Division Staff. (2017). *Soil Survey Manual*. Ditzler, C., Scheffe, K., & Monger, H. C. (Eds.). USDA Handbook 18. Government Printing Office, Washington, DC.

Soil Survey Staff. (2014). *Kellogg soil survey laboratory methods manual. Soil Survey Investigations Report No. 42, Version 5.0*. R. Burt and Soil Survey Staff (Eds.). U.S. Department of Agriculture, Natural Resources Conservation Service.

Stum, A. K., Boettinger, J. L., White, M. A., & Ramsey, R. D. (2010). Random Forests Applied as a Soil Spatial Predictive Model in Arid Utah. In Boettinger J. L., Howell D. W., Moore, A. C., Hartemink A. E., & Kienast-Brown, S.,(Eds.), *Digital Soil Mapping. Progress in Soil Science* (pp. 179–190). 2, Springer, Dordrecht. https://doi.org/10.1007/978-90-481-8863-5_15.

Taghizadeh-Mehrjardi, R., Schmidt, K., Toomanian, N., Heung, B., Behrens, T., Mosavi, A., & Scholten, T. (2021). Improving the spatial prediction of soil salinity in arid regions using wavelet transformation and support vector regression models. *Geoderma, 383*, 114793. https://doi.org/10.1016/j.geoderma.2020.114793

Tucker, C. J. (1979). Red and photographic infrared linear combinations for monitoring vegetation. *Remote Sensing of Environment, 8*(2), 127–150. https://doi.org/10.1016/0034-4257(79)90013-0

Van Wambeke, A. R. (2000). *The Newhall Simulation Model for Estimating Soil Moisture and Temperature Regimes*. Department of Crop and Soil Sciences, Cornell University, New York.

Venables, W. N., & Ripley, B. D. (2013). *Modern Applied Statistics with S-PLUS*. Springer Science & Business Media.

Wadoux, A. M. C., Román-Dobarco, M., & McBratney, A. B. (2021). Perspectives on data-driven soil research. *European Journal of Soil Science, 72*, 1675–1689. https://doi.org/10.1111/ejss.13071

Wadoux, A. M. C., & McBratney, A. B. (2021). Hypotheses, machine learning and soil mapping. *Geoderma, 383*, e114725. doi.org/10.1016/j.geoderma.2020.114725. https://doi.org/10.1016/j.geoderma.2020.114725

Wadoux, A. M. C., Minasny, B., & McBratney A. B. (2020). Machine learning for digital soil mapping: applications, challenges and suggested solutions. *Earth-Science Reviews*, *210*, e103359. https://doi.org/10.1016/j.earscirev.2020.103359

Webster, R. (2001). Statistics to support soil research and their presentation. *European Journal of Soil Science, 52*(2), 331–340. https://doi.org/10.1046/j.1365-2389.2001.00383.x

Wei, T., Simko, V. (2017). *R package "corrplot": Visualization of a Correlation Matrix* (Version 0.84).

Wiesmeier, M., Barthold, F., Blank, B. et al. (2011). Digital mapping of soil organic matter stocks using Random Forest modeling in a semi-arid steppe ecosystem. *Plant Soil, 340*, 7–24. https://doi.org/10.1007/s11104-010-0425-z

Xiao, J., Shen, Y., Tateishi, R., & Bayaer, W. (2006). Development of topsoil grain size index for monitoring desertification in arid land using remote sensing. *International Journal of Remote Sensing, 27*(12), 2411–2422. https://doi.org/10.1080/01431160600554363

Zeraatpisheh, M., Ayoubi, S., Jafari, A., Tajik, S., & Finke, P. (2019). Digital mapping of soil properties using multiple machine learning in a semi-arid region, central Iran. *Geoderma, 338*, 445–452. https://doi.org/10.1016/j.geoderma.2018.09.006

Chapter 7

A Smart IoT Framework for Soil Fertility Enhancement Assisted via Deep Neural Networks

Sannidhan Manjaya Shetty, Jason Elroy Martis, and Sudeepa Keregadde Balakrishna

NMAM Institute of Technology, Karnataka, India

Contents

DOI: 10.1201/9781003311782-7

7.1 Introduction

A huge part of South Asian geography comprises agricultural land, and hence agriculture is treated as a prime occupation. Farming in these regions of the globe is also very challenging as there is an unexpectedly large variation in the climatic conditions leading to the greater deterioration in crop productivity. The unexpected variations in the climatic conditions made the farmer's life very difficult. Also, they demotivated many younger generations to continue with an agricultural profession as there is a greater element of risk involved in terms of investment to profit ratio. A well-adopted resolution against the abrupt climatic variations is to follow seasonal cropping that involves cultivating a suitable crop based on the weather conditions and quality of the farmland. Hence, farmers are accustomed to prescheduling seasonal cropping based on a particular month/season. But as the modern world is constantly exposed to an increasing amount of pollution, a frequent variation is observed both in climatic aspects and in the quality of the farmland. Farmers are still facing many issues in adapting to seasonal cropping (Aryal et al. 2020; Knox et al. 2012).

Many nations around the subcontinent have considered frequent weather fluctuations as a serious threat to the agricultural occupation and the welfare of the farmers. Several measures have been taken by the national authorities and concerned centers to deal with abrupt climatic conditions and to promote efficient seasonal farming. Many countries have even established a dataset acting as a guide for suggesting relevant crops based on climatic factors and soil nourishment attributes. Still, there are many challenges faced in seasonal cropping. It stresses real-time retrieval of changing conditions of the climate and the quality of the soil to take substantial action (Mahabub et al., 2020). The possible solution to the problem can be achieved by designing intellectual technical systems to access climatic conditions and soil parameters and suggest a suitable crop along with relevant fertilizers for the upgradation of soil nourishment.

Researches have been accomplished with the application of Internet of Things (IoT) systems to deal with the issues related to seasonal cropping. The accomplished research subjugated the problem by evolving an appropriate resolution to gather parameters related to soil quality and climatic conditions. Out of many, very limited research predicted suitable crop cultivation based on atmospheric and geographical traits (Sannidhan et al. 2018; Zhao et al. 2020; Salam and Shah 2019). However, the systems failed in implementing time-invariant prediction for seasonal cultivation practices based on the atmospheric conditions, attributes of soil nourishment. Implemented systems could not also suggest using relevant fertilizers to upgrade the quality of soil under deteriorating conditions.

Considering the missing ailments of previous research works, in this work, we propose the engagement of an economical and state-of-the-art deep learning IoT framework to broadcast instantaneous information corresponding to the attributes of the soil. The gathered data is analyzed to predict suitable crops for the cultivation and required soil nourishment to increase its fertility factor. The prediction system consists of the utilization of transformer networks trained from the readings obtained from different sensors deployed at different geographical locations.

Following are the contributions incorporated into the proposed system to fulfill the necessary objectives:

1. Assimilation of sensors into IoT board to collect soil parameters concerning the farmland.
2. An efficient cloud storage system to accumulate the gathered sensor data.
3. Expansion of a deep learning classification model for foreseeing macronutrient earth constraints.
4. To project a time-invariant prototypical network using transformers for seasonal yield estimation.
5. Implementation of a customized regression model to aid the real-time fertilizer prediction to enhance soil nourishment.

The remainder of the chapter is further split into four different sections. Section 7.2 presents an exhaustive literature work, Section 7.3 labels the idea of the proposed arrangement in detail, Section 7.4 contains results and discussions, and finally, Section 5 offers the conclusion and future scope of the claimed research work.

7.2 Literature Survey

An exhaustive literature review was conducted to suffice the objectives of the proposed system. The review covered the referral of journal papers, web resources related to IoT, and deep learning systems.

Lee et al. (2013) developed an IoT-based innovative framework to accumulate atmospheric parameters in real-time to recommend competent harvesting procedures for boosting production rate. Experimental analysis on a yearly basis proved that the technique improved the yield of tomato fruit.

Truong et al. (2017) proposed an IoT system with sensor devices to collect data corresponding to climatic conditions. The data is then accumulated onto the cloud to predict fungal disease using an SVM regression model. Outcomes of the research article evidenced the assistance of the system in providing timely maintenance against fungal infection.

Kose et al. et al. (2022) designed an IoT-based technology for agriculture by incorporating big data analytics. IoT system accumulates collected data onto a cloud, and big data analytics is implemented via a map-reduce technique to predict fertilizer utilization. Outcomes of research evidence that the technique achieved a higher production rate assisting the farmers. The observed fact is that the work failed in predicting soil fertility based on varying climatic attributes.

Pereñiguez-García et al. (2017) implemented a system to track frost conditions in the climate around the regions of Murcia as the unanticipated discrepancies in the frost instigated significant temperature variations. The authors efficiently dealt with the problem through the incorporation of IoT to acquire real-time data. The proposed system estimates the occurrence of the frost with the aid of standard forecast data available, and the presented outcomes achieved accurate frost prediction. Part of the future work endorses the utilization of soil sensors to improve the quality of soil through the required enrichment.

Vijayabaskar et al. (2018) implemented an IoT framework with NPK sensors to collect nutrients from the soil. The system was developed to predict soil nourishment and acclaim pertinent crops to enhance production. Based on the collected data, the system also suggests the utilization of appropriate fertilizer. For the purpose of predictive analysis, researchers have taken the benefit of the Hadoop technique's agro algorithm.

Rezk et al. (2021) developed a system based on the IoT framework to efficiently predict crop productivity and drought conditions. The core concept of the prediction model is reinforced via WPART, an amalgamation of wrapper extractor and PART classifier. Outcomes and analysis presented in the research article attained a maximum accuracy rate of 98%. Future work mentioned in the article recommended incorporating classification based on time series.

Pravallika et al. (2020) developed an economic IoT framework for classifying crop suitability through the assessment of soil fertility. The artifact concentrated on promoting seasonal cropping depending on frequent climatic variations by collecting required data from the incorporated sensors. However, there is a gap in the research that exposes the need to utilize machine learning algorithms for better prediction.

Priya and Yuvaraj (2019) implemented IoT with ANN systems to predict the crop to boost productivity. Model is incorporated with sensors to acquire atmospheric attributes and then classified using a pretrained ANN for crop prediction. Model is also frequently enhanced by frequently retraining it with the recently acquired data. The system successfully gained 97% accuracy. However, as an extended scope, authors stressed incorporating a module to predict the utilization of relevant fertilizers to enhance the soil's richness.

Venkatesan and Tamilvanan (2018) developed an IoT-based automatic irrigation system controlled via relevant sensors. The model was developed with the intention of preventing the wastage of water resources. Even though the application introduced novelty by offering a first-of-its-kind service, there was a large scope for further extension based on data acquired from the sensors. Thus, the chapter paves the way for further extending the work by including a crop prediction module based on climatic conditions.

Gupta et al. (2020) developed a node MCU IoT system with sensors connected to obtain soil attributes. Gathered data is classified using statistical data mining models for the classification of the crops. Outcomes portrayed higher efficiency of KNN with an accuracy rate of 88%. In the future section, the authors suggested the usage of ANN to boost the rate of accuracy.

Gao et al. (2019) analyzed the use of BERT for contextual awareness. Though BERT uses a transfer learning sequence to sequence approach, its usage is not well discovered and used. Modifying their BERT model (TD-BERT) worked very well with sequence-based embeddings and showed stable context-aware improvement. Hence, the nature of the work highlights the future scope of BERT and its variants in the sequential prediction of time-invariant data.

Le et al. (2021) used transformers' BERT architecture in order to predict DNA sequences. Since the field is challenging and has never been applied before, outcomes from this research have proven that BERT successfully increased the prediction sequence features by 5–10% in sensitivity, specificity, and accuracy. The authors also further explored the use of BERT in CNN and concluded that it has a lot of potential in sequence prediction.

Zhao et al. (2020) explored the potential of BERT in sequence prediction in agricultural diseases. They have chosen a variant of BERT known as BERT-CRF and applied the model to predict Chinese agricultural diseases. Outcomes from this research have shown that there is a significant improvement in disease detection and classification. Hence, it is once again proved from this chapter that incorporating a transformer-based deep learning model will surely boost up the prediction performance for time-invariant data classification.

7.3 Proposed System

Considering the various drawbacks of the literature survey, we have tweaked our system to undermine the fallacies. Figure 7.1 shows an architecture diagram of our proposed system.

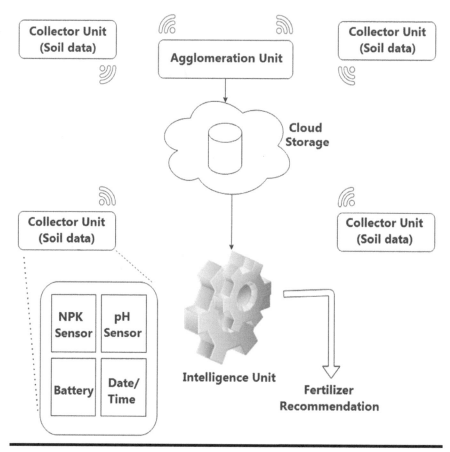

Figure 7.1   Overall architecture of our proposed system.

As portrayed in Figure 7.1, our proposed arrangement is sketchily separated into four units, namely the (1) collector unit, (2) intermediate and agglomerative unit, (3) cloud storage unit, and (4) intelligence unit. All of them toil in sync with one another to accomplish flawless work of solutions. These units are elucidated in aspect under their subsequent sections.

7.3.1 Collector Unit

These units are numerous and form the tail end of the pipeline. They collect data from the surroundings and relay the collected information back to the intermediate unit. The drawing of the data assortment arrangement for the end nodes is revealed in Figure 7.2. Further subsections describe the subunits of the collector unit in detail.

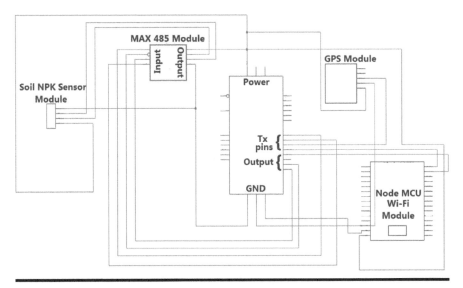

Figure 7.2   Schematic of our collector component equipped through sensors.

7.3.1.1 Nutrient Sensor

The nutrient sensor does the job of recognizing nutrients in the soil. The crucial nutrients required for plant growth are NPK, designated as Nitrogen-Phosphorous-Potassium. The sensor cannot detect these nutrients directly but estimates these by sensing the ions present in their salts. The sensor measures these salts in mg/kg. The readings obtained from the sensor are very erroneous since they fluctuate due to weather conditions. A turnaround method is used to calibrate these problems by taking a median and average among a fixed time frame. Equations (7.1) and (7.2) show the calibrated solution (Harshani et al. 2018).

$$Frame_{average} = \left\{ \frac{\sum_i^n Reading_i}{tot} \right\} \ for \ t_i \in (i.n) \tag{7.1}$$

$$Frame_{median} = \left\{ med\left(Reading_i\right) \right\} \ for \ t_i \in (i.n) \tag{7.2}$$

Here, $Frame_{average}$ and $Frame_{median}$ symbolize the normal and intermediate analyses, respectively, from the instrument in a fixed time interval.

7.3.1.2 Acidity Sensor (pH Meter)

This instrument helps the collector to grab the tartness of the earth. The reading obtained denotes the number of hydrogen ions in the soil symbolized as H^+.

The higher the concentration of H⁺ ions, the additional acidic the soil. The reading has a series in between fourteen to one, where one denotes acidity and fourteen indicates nonacidic earth soil. Diverse florae require superlative circumstances of acidity to raise judiciously. These readings are relatively stable and do not change drastically unless supplemented by external factors (Ananthi et al. 2018).

7.3.1.3 GPS Sensor

This device's duty is used to discover out the exact position of the sensor on the field. This sensor consumes a lot of power, ranging from a range of 14 mW to 250 mW. Hence, too many readings can drain the battery, causing malfunction. Fortunately, we don't move the sensor once it is placed, so this avoids numerous unwanted readings, thereby saving battery life. This sensor is referred to once every fifteen days to see any movement if any accidental movement occurred (Basu et al. 2019).

7.3.2 Intermediate and Agglomerative Unit

This unit's chief purpose is to create a federal middle that amasses statistics from numerous instruments and assemble them in a unique solitary position. The collector interconnects by means of Wi-Fi and LoRa. The intermediate unit also creates a repeater router for long-range infrastructures. When statistics is composed in the agglomerative unit, it develops a hard-to-assess problem like supposing out the position where the data was invented. We accomplish this issue by creating a sensory table ID in which the sending collector unit adds its ID along with the sensory data. If any new entry is added, the intermediate unit tries to authenticate it. MQTT is the protocol used for subscribing and publishing data to and fro from the sensors. We have also created a framework that is tailored to custom fit this type of infrastructure (Yassein et al. 2018; Atmoko et al. 2017; Pradeep et al. 2020). After this, the storage unit takes over.

7.3.3 Storage Unit

The storage unit's primary job is to store data received from the agglomerative unit. It forms nothing but a simple log of all information collected by it. This unit is deployed on the cloud for the ease of safekeeping. Any cloud platform could be utilized for this purpose. We have chosen Google Cloud to store data. Note that the data is stored in a tabular format. The reason for selecting cloud is connectivity and reliability from loss of sensory reading (Islam et al. 2019).

7.3.4 Intelligence Unit

The intelligence component arranges the intelligence of the system. It turns numerous machine-level procedures and confident deep learning procedures to evaluate the superlative conceivable calculation of harvests and their condition to improve soil fertility too. Data from the storage unit serves as supervision for the running algorithms, which then predicts back data to match the constraints.

We have employed transformers' classification for time series classification. Also, we have classified soil fertility based on the reading received by the collectors. Our intelligence unit also assesses soil fertility and grants-guided methods to enhance it.

7.3.4.1 Transformer Model for Crop Prediction

We perform crop prediction with the help of classification. We have limited our classification to predict only six to seven types of crops. Since the prediction must depend on previous data in a selected time frame, it is imperative to use algorithms that even consider older time frames (Sannidhan et al. 2019; Pallavi et al. 2021; Martis and Balasubramani 2020). Here is where recursive neural networks come into the picture. They help by considering trending lines and forgetting the least cycles to predict newer entries. The only drawback of these is that they are slow. This fallacy is enhanced using a recent neural network called the transformer. The architecture of the transformer is shown in Figure 7.3.

As we can see from Figure 7.3, the transformer uses the idea of attention by evaluating the input data ports. It possesses an encoder-decoder architecture that is used by assessing sequences and has various applications in natural language processing. Rather than sequences used in RNN, transformers employ attention to add the context of data, thereby granting higher parallelization than RNN. Our transformer performs coding using a pretrained model called BERT, abbreviated as Bidirectional Encoder Representations from the transformer, which can be used by fine-tuning to our tasks. The chief function of the encoder coating is to encode the data used by the attention layer to generate contexts as an output to the decoder. Likewise, there are several encoder attention decoder layers in the transformer. All these layers are arranged in a feed-forward fashion which is common in other networks. The attention units employ a mathematical formulation called scaled dot product, as shown in Equation (7.3).

$$q_i = x_i * W_Q \tag{7.3}$$

Here, q_i is the query vector acting as output. x_i forms the sequence embedding, and W_Q forms the weights of that transformer neuron. i represents a specific layer in the transformer. Applying Equation (7.3) for all layers, we get the output as shown in Equation (7.4).

$$Output = \bigcup_{i=0}^{n} \left(x_i * W_Q \right) \tag{7.4}$$

$$Input = \bigvee x_i \tag{7.5}$$

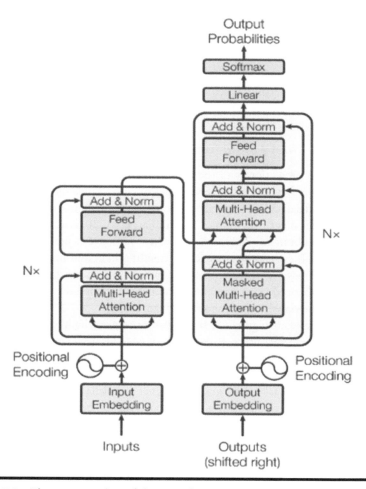

Figure 7.3   The construction of the transformer.

Here, *Input* forms to be the vectorized embeddings of x_i generated by the encoder.

7.3.4.2 Neural Network Model for Fertility Classification

We have designed our network for classifying the fertility factor of the soil. The fertility factor is assessed based on the rating of NPK, pH values, and crop type sensed by the collector. The fertility factor is fixed into five categories, namely Depleted (0), Deficient (1), Adequate (2), Sufficient (3), and Surplus (4). The categories set for pH are (0) Extremely Acidic, (1) Lightly Acidic, (2) Neutral, (3) Lightly Basic, and (4) Highly Basic. The crop types prefixed are lawn, fruit-bearing, flowering, shrubs, vegetables, and trees. Figure 7.4 shows the architecture of our network.

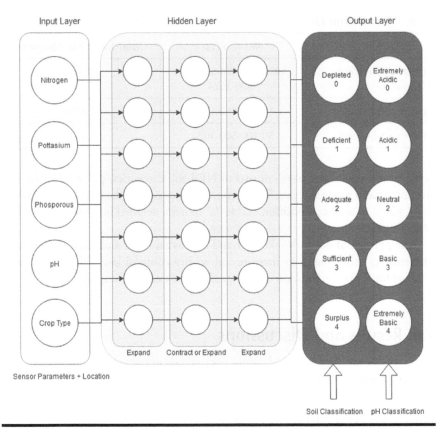

Figure 7.4 **Detailed architecture of the fertility classifier.**

As we can observe from Figure 7.4, our network is divided into three basic layers: the input layer, the hidden layer, and the output layer (Sannidhan et al. 2021; Martis et al. 2020). The input layer takes the input of NPK, pH, and crop type. The output layer assesses the fertility factor category, as discussed earlier. The hidden layer consists of neurons in different levels to form hyperparameters in the network. For the sake of comparison, we have divided our hidden layer into three categories, namely (1) Expand-Contract-Expand, (2) Expand-Contract, and (3) Contract-Expand. The expand term indicates a higher number of neurons, and the contract term indicates a lower number of neurons. Table 7.1 shows the expanded architecture of our proposed neural networks in terms of the number of neurons and its trainable parameters.

7.3.4.3 Neural Network Model for Fertilizer Recommendation

Our neural network for soil fertility enhancement is a regression-type network designed for the type of fertilizers that must be added to enhance soil nutrient

Table 7.1 Neuron Distribution in Different Categories

Architecture	Neuron List	Total Trainable Parameters
Expand-Contract-Expand	1024-500-100-50-100-500-1024	10,53,253
Expand-Contract	1024-500-100-50	8,42,987
Contract-Expand	50-100-500-1024	5,45,825

composition. The input layer consists of NPK soil categories, pH values, and cultivation area in square meters. The output layer consists of the amount of fertilizer to be added to each composition. Table 7.2 shows a detailed fertilizer composition of the NPK.

The pH neural network takes pH and area as an input and recommends a list of fertilizers to be added to increase soil acidity composition. Table 7.3 shows a detailed fertilizer composition to change the pH category if required.

7.4 Results and Discussions

Here, we discuss the results and graphs obtained by implementing our system. Our segment is separated into subsequent subdivisions.

7.4.1 Hardware Components

The following hardware components were used for the successful running of our system.

1. The collector unit has a GPS modem as well as a nutrient sensor. The GPS modem installed was GPS NPO072MV and JBXS-5002-RT. The nutrient sensor used was JXCIOT. We also installed a soil pH sensor module from Robu robotics.

Table 7.2 Fertilizer Recommendations of NPK

Nutrient	Fertilizers Used	
Nitrogen	Dehydrated Plasma (11%)	Sodium Nitrates (16%)
Phosphorous	Crushed Bones finely powdered (19%)	Tri-Superphosphate (46%)
Potassium	Muriate of Potash (60%)	-

Table 7.3   Fertilizer Recommendations for pH Balancing

pH Category	Fertilizers Used
Highly Acidic	Dolomitic
Acidic	Calcic Limestone
Neutral	–
Basic	Iron Sulfate
Highly Basic	Aluminum Sulfate

2. The agglomerate unit is a central station and includes a Raspberry Pi running a custom-made framework on Raspbian OS. The 3B+ model of Raspberry Pi suits our structure perfectly.
3. Our intelligence unit requires more complicated hardware, and it consists of Double Intel Tesla PS-3709V84C 1.9 THz 5M 7.4TFLOPS/s with 256 GB RAM possessing Twin Nvidia Tesla p100TPU with 3,854 Cores. They have an operational speed of 19.1 Tera Flops.

7.4.2 Cloud Systems

The main receiver station, i.e. the intermediate units, collects data and stores them on the cloud. For known reliability, we have used the services of Google Drive and created a Google Sheet for data addition. Every entry added is event-based and accomplished by a free app called IFTTT, which is well known for IoT data addition models. Since Google allows free data of about 20 GB, it would take about ten years to exhaust the free space provided.

7.4.3 Data Collection

The outcomes attained from the NPK sensor are vulnerable, and standards are directed only when investigation surrounds are directed to the instrument via the MAX844 module. The frame arrangement corresponding to investigation and reply formats associated with diverse instrument nodes are presented consecutively from Table 7.4 to Table 7.9. In each frame, ADC represents Address Code, RSA abbreviates to register start address, FuC stands for Function Code, and RL denotes Register length. The CRC standards are used to confirm the statistical integrity of the analysis. The comeback frame value is hexadecimal in nature and must be converted to digital.

On reception, from the investigational findings, attained values from the nitrogen instrument are 45 mg/kg, potassium sensor is 25 mg/kg, and phosphorus sensor is 26 mg/kg.

Table 7.4   Investigation Frame Format for N

AdC	RL	FuC	RSA	CRC_H	RC_L
0 × 02	0 × 30 0 × 04	0 × 05	0 × 01 0 × 1e	0 × E4	0 × 0c

Table 7.5   Reply Frame Format for N

AC	Number of Bytes	FuC	CRC_H (FuC)	N Value	CRC_L
0 × 01	0 × 04 0 × 01	0 × 03	0 × 9d	0 × 00 0 × 21	0 × b9

Table 7.6   Investigation Frame Format for P

AdC	FuC	AdC	P Value	CRC_H	CRC_L
0 × 03	0 × 04	0 × 1f 0 × 01	0 × 00 0 × 01	0 × e5	0 × dc

Table 7.7   Reply Frame Format for P

AC	FC	Number of Bytes	P Value	CRC_L	CRC_H
0 × 01	0 × 03	0 × 02	0 × 00 0 × 025	0 × b5	0 × cd

Table 7.8   Investigation Frame Format for K

AdC	FuC	RSA	K Value	CRC_H	CRC_L
0 × 01	0 × 03	0 × 00 0 × 20	0 × 00 0 × 01	0 × r5	0 × dc

Table 7.9   Reply Frame Format for K

AdC	FuC	Number of Bytes	K Value	CRC_H	CRC_L
0 × 05	0 × 03	0 × 02	0 × 00 0 × 031	0 × c4	0 × dc

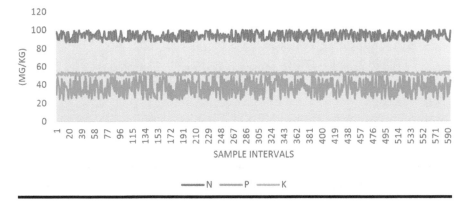

Figure 7.5   Graph showing the typical NPK values of a single sensor.

We have taken reading from the collector unit for every fifteen-minute interval. The values attained, as shown in Figure 7.5, are taken from 11th March 2020 to 17th May 2021 in Udupi District of Karnataka. We have placed a total of ten nodes at 300 meters, carefully selecting a garden containing lawn, fruit-bearing, flowering, shrubs, vegetables, and trees. In Figure 7.5, the plot corresponds to a sample reading of a sensor placed at Kundapura at 13.2245° N, 75.1134° E.

From Figure 7.5, we can observe that the values of N range between 85.30 and 99.45 milligrams per kilogram. P ranges between 22.354 and 55.611, and K ranges between 50.912 and 55.12. Table 7.10 shows the statistical details of values concerning the NPK parameters.

Likewise, Figure 7.6 portrays the soil acidity readings in connection to pH values obtained via a sensor placed at the Kundapura town of Udupi district in the Karnataka state of India.

From Figure 7.6, we infer that pH values ranged between 5.98 and 6.32, signifying that pH does not typically vary a lot. Table 7.11 shows the statistical summary of the pH values with respect to the readings obtained from the graphical chart depicted in Figure 7.6.

Table 7.10   Summary of NPK Values Obtained from Sensor

Parameter	Nitrogen (N)	Phosphorous (P)	Potassium (K)
MIN	85.304	22.354	50.912
MAX	99.45	55.611	55.12
STD DEV	4.064269	8.010896	1.153863
AVERAGE	93.20474	36.66649	51.94183
Variance	16.51828	64.17446	1.331401

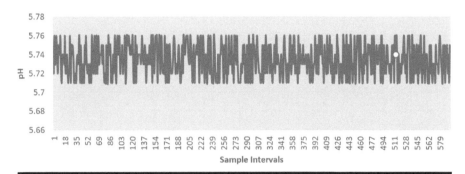

Figure 7.6   Graph depicting the pH readings of a sensor placed at Kundapura.

7.4.4 Intermediate and Agglomerative Unit

Readings gained from various collector units are composed at the chief station. The reading frame format and sample data received from each collector are shown in Figure 7.7.

7.4.5 Intelligence Unit

The reading attained from the central station acts as a supervisor for this unit. Note that the NPK values are attained from various collectors and their latitude and longitude use transformers to assess crop precision.

7.4.5.1 Transformer Accuracy

Our transformer model used BERT as a precursory trainer and passed on to a dense classification of 1000-500-300-200-150-50 nodes. We also ran our model several times to assess the training and validation accuracy of our network. Our dataset formed an 80%–20% split. Table 7.12 shows the training accuracy of our model.

Table 7.11   Statistical Summary of pH and Electrical Conductivity Values Obtained from the Sensor

Parameter	pH
MAX	5.76
MIN	5.71
STD DEV	0.017036
Variance	0.00029
AVERAGE	5.74345

Node Id	Location	Time Stamp	N	P	K	EC	pH	Location

(a)

{ "Node": { "Status": { "-health": "Active", "-Battery": "73%", }, "ID": "8fcb1245", "loc": { "-lat": "13.2391° N", "-long": "75.1068° E" }, "time": { "-date": "13/2/2021", "-time": "12:45 AM" }, "data": {"Macro": {"-N": "90.345", "-P": "25.243", "-K": "51.674" }, "Others": { "-pH": "5.81", "-EC": ".04" }}}}

(b)

Figure 7.7 (a) Frame format for receiver collector unit. (b) Sample frame data to the intermediate unit.

Noting the values depicted, it is observed that the evaluation accuracy in real-time slides down by 2.72% due to varying climatic conditions.

For comparison purposes, we have used other models and also compared their accuracies. Table 7.13 shows the comparison with other models.

It is evident from Table 7.13 that our BERT model attained higher accuracy when compared to other LSTM and transformer models. Figure 7.8 depicts the comparison graphically.

7.4.5.2 Fertility Classifier Statistics

We have implemented all three models for the sake of comparison of accuracies. Table 7.14 shows the summary chart of all models.

It is evident from Table 7.14 that the expanded contract architecture of our neural network model performs remarkably in all factors for classifying soil fertility. Figure 7.9 displays the graphical characteristics of Table 7.14.

We have also used the confusion matrix as a metric for all classification categories. Table 7.15 depicts the precision and recall characteristics of the expanded contract model employed by us.

Table 7.15 stresses that there is high precision and recall when it comes to adequate classes. This is true because it is proven from satellite data and ground chemical studies of a particular region.

Table 7.12 Accuracy Values of Transformer-Induced Model

Network Type	Training Accuracy	Validation Accuracy	Evaluation Accuracy
Transformer (pretrained BERT)	93.33%	90.46%	87.74%

Table 7.13   Accuracy Values of Dissimilar Models

Network Type	Training Accuracy	Evaluation Accuracy	Validation Accuracy
Transformer (pretrained BERT)	93.33%	87.74%	90.46%
Transformer (pretrained GPT)	92.13%	83.45%	89.56%
LSTM	89.32%	83.32%	85.46%

Table 7.14   Fertilizer Model Classifiers Accuracy Percentages

Architecture	Neuron List	Training Accuracy	Validation Accuracy	Evaluation Accuracy
Expand-Contract-Expand	1024-500-100-50-100-500-1024	65.32%	54.33%	34.55%
Expand-Contract	1024-500-100-50	95.33%	92.46%	90.74%
Contract-Expand	50-100-500-1024	61.32%	45.33%	25.34%

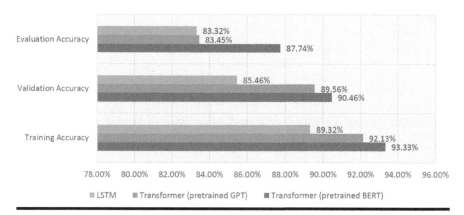

Figure 7.8   Accuracy comparison with other models.

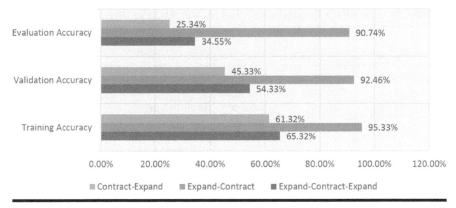

Figure 7.9 Graphical comparison of other model accuracies in Table 7.11.

7.4.5.3 Fertilizer Recommendation Statistics

Our fertilizer recommendation model is a custom-built recommendation regression-type network that assesses soil characteristics, area, duration, location, and crop type to recommend the exact quantity of fertilizer required for optimal nourishment. As our previous statistics have suggested, an Expand-Contract architecture worked better in classifying fertility classes. We have chosen a similar architecture for our regression network. Table 7.16 displays the characteristics of our network.

It is evident from Table 7.16 that some of our input to the fertilizer model is classification-based; it becomes difficult to assess the accuracy. To develop a turnaround to this problem, we developed an ingenious solution to assign qualitative numbers to categories based on rank correlation. Note that our fertilizer model has an output of six nodes, but they are decided for alternate solutions for the farmer.

Table 7.15 Confusion Matrix of Expand Contract Model

	Depleted	Deficient	Adequate	Sufficient	Surplus	Precision
Depleted	63	1	2	5	5	82.89%
Deficient	5	65	2	4	3	82.278%
Adequate	5	1	80	1	2	89.88%
Sufficient	1	1	2	80	2	93.023%
Surplus	2	7	7	7	63	73.256%
Recall	82.3%	86.67%	86.022%	82.474%	84%	Overall 83.32%

Table 7.16   Fertilizer Recommendation Model Architecture

Network Type	Architecture	Input Nodes	Output Nodes	Hyperparameters Nodes
Regression (Classifier characteristics)	Expand-Contract	N, P, K, Area, Application Duration, location, crop type	Dehydrated Blood (11%) Sodium Nitrate (16%) Powdered and Crushed meal (19%) Tri-Superphosphate (46%) Muriate of Potash (60%)	1000-750-500-250-100-50

Solution 1 consists of the quantity in kilogram per hectare of dried blood, bone meal, and muriate of potash. Solution 2 consists of nitrate of soda, triple superphosphate, and muriate of potash in kilogram per hectare. The farmer can select any one of the two solutions.

Our pH balancer model is also developed on a similar architecture as shown in Table 7.16 and recommends fertilizers as shown in Table 7.3. The accuracy of both models is portrayed in Table 7.17.

As we can observe from Table 7.17, our two models have surpassed our expectations by providing an overall accuracy of about 93%, which is considered acceptable. Figure 7.10 depicts Table 7.17 graphically.

We have applied this model in one of the villages of Kundapur taluk of Udupi district and marked readings over twelve months. The values are tabulated in Table 7.18, and Figure 7.11 shows the appreciation graphically.

In Figure 7.11, the bar graph shows a dramatic change in soil macronutrient fertility by about 22%, causing an increase in crop productivity of that farmer to about 29%.

Table 7.17   Accuracy Statistics of Fertilizer and pH Model

Model Type	Epochs	Architecture	Training Accuracy	Validation Accuracy	Evaluation Accuracy
Fertilizer recommender	4000	Expand-Contract	90.32%	93.21%	92.34%
pH balancer	4000		94.23%	94.56%	93.21%

Table 7.18   Nutrient Value Readings Obtained from a Village in Kundapur Taluk

Reading Value	Macronutrient reading			Crop Value (Crop Units Overall)
	Nitrogen (mg/kg)	Phosphorous (mg/kg)	Potassium (mg/kg)	
Beginning	87.323 (Adequate)	23.56 (Depleted)	30.23 (Depleted)	200,000
+2 months	94.323 (Excess)	27.453 (Scarce)	33.56 (Lacking)	225,000
+2 months	96.323 (Excess)	32.453 (Satisfactory)	40.85 (Satisfactory)	257,000
Summary	**Upsurge**	**Upsurge**	**Upsurge**	**Upsurge**
Percentage	**10.3%**	**36.9%**	**26.6%**	**28.5%**

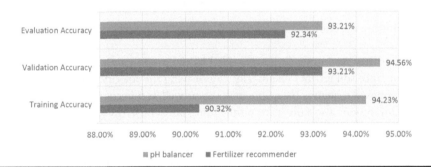

Figure 7.10   Graphical comparison of other model accuracies for pH balance and fertilizer recommendation.

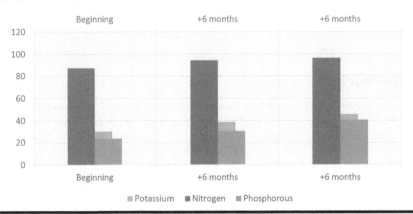

Figure 7.11   Graphical chart showing the increase in soil fertility.

7.5 Conclusion

Agriculture prevails as one of the primary income standards for Southeast Asia and its territories due to its advantage over geographic areas. Recently, due to climatic changes, weather patterns are disturbed, causing havoc among crops and soil, thereby raising concerns over farming and its practices. Many farmers have shifted toward chemical farming, further causing other issues to the soil as well as other ecology. Our proposed system tries to omit the loophole caused by introducing micromanagement of soil nutrients as well as cropping patterns. It also provides timely suggestions of adding fertilizers in desired amounts to preserve and maintain soil quality. We accomplish this feat by utilizing the ability of a myriad of deep learning techniques coupled with machine learning methodologies. Implementation of our system in some parts of India has shown remarkable progress in the soil macronutrient constituency as well as boosted the income of farmers by 22%.

7.6 Limitations and Future Scopes

Following are the limitations identified out of the proposed system:

1. Fertilizer recommendation provided by the proposed system only focuses to enhance soil fertility chemically, thus leaving the soil dry and flaky.
2. Proposed system is incapable to detect as well as prevent diseases and pests.
3. Our system also fails in recommending efficient irrigation practices in tandem with fertilizer endorsement.

Considering the limitations of the system we have presented, our future work can focus on implementing organic farming practices to boost soil quality and enhance water retention. To prevent diseases and pests, the system could be extended to function as a micromanagement solution. Further, our system can act as a knowledge assistant and as a boon to farmers' productivity and their well-being.

References

Ananthi, N., Divya, J., Divya, M., & Janani, V. (2018). IoT Based Smart Soil Monitoring System for Agricultural Production. *Proceedings of 2017 IEEE Technological Innovations in ICT for Agriculture and Rural Development, TIAR 2017, 2018-January,* pp. 209–214. https://doi.org/10.1109/TIAR.2017.8273717

Aryal, J. P., Sapkota, T. B., Khurana, R., Khatri-Chhetri, A., Rahut, D. B., & Jat, M. L. (2020). Climate change and agriculture in South Asia: adaptation options in smallholder production systems. *Environment, Development and Sustainability,* 22(6), 5045–5075. https://doi.org/10.1007/s10668-019-00414-4

Atmoko, R. A., Riantini, R., & Hasin, M. K. (2017). IoT real time data acquisition using MQTT protocol. *Journal of Physics: Conference Series*, *853*(1), 12003. https://doi.org/10.1088/1742-6596/853/1/012003

Basu, D., Gui, X., Zhang, Y., & Nag, A. (2019, November 1). Non-Centralised and Non-GPS Navigation Mechanism Using IoT Sensors: Challenges and trade-offs. *2019 29th International Telecommunication Networks and Applications Conference, ITNAC 2019.* https://doi.org/10.1109/ITNAC46935.2019.9078003

Gao, Z., Feng, A., Song, X., & Wu, X. (2019). Target-dependent sentiment classification with BERT. *IEEE Access*, *7*, 154290–154299. https://doi.org/10.1109/ACCESS.2019.2946594

Gupta, G., Setia, R., Meena, A., & Jaint, B. (2020). Environment Monitoring System for Agricultural Application Using IoT and Predicting Crop Yield Using Various Data Mining Techniques, pp. 1019–1025. https://doi.org/10.1109/icces48766.2020.9138032

Harshani, P. R., Umamaheswari, T., Tharani, R., Rajalakshmi, S., & Dharani, J. (2018, December 11). Effective Crop Productivity and Nutrient Level Monitoring in Agriculture Soil Using IOT. *ICSNS 2018 – Proceedings of IEEE International Conference on Soft-Computing and Network Security.* https://doi.org/10.1109/ICSNS.2018.8573674

Islam, M. M., Khan, Z., & Alsaawy, Y. (2019). A framework for harmonizing internet of things (IoT) in Cloud: analyses and implementation. *Wireless Networks*, 1–12. https://doi.org/10.1007/s11276-019-01943-6

Knox, J., Hess, T., Daccache, A., & Wheeler, T. (2012). Climate change impacts on crop productivity in Africa and South Asia. *Environmental Research Letters*, *7*(3), 34032. https://doi.org/10.1088/1748-9326/7/3/034032

Kose, U., Prasath, V. S., Mondal, M. R. H., Podder, P., & Bharati, S. (Eds.). (2022). *Artificial Intelligence and Smart Agriculture Technology.* CRC Press

Le, N. Q. K., Ho, Q.-T., Nguyen, T.-T.-D., & Ou, Y.-Y. (2021). A transformer architecture based on BERT and 2D convolutional neural network to identify DNA enhancers from sequence information. *Briefings in Bioinformatics.* https://doi.org/10.1093/bib/bbab005

Lee, M., Hwang, J., & Yoe, H. (2013). Agricultural Production System Based on IoT. *Proceedings – 16th IEEE International Conference on Computational Science and Engineering, CSE 2013*, pp. 833–837. https://doi.org/10.1109/CSE.2013.126

Mahabub, A., Habib, A. Z. S. B., Mondal, M., Bharati, S., & Podder, P. (2020, December). Effectiveness of ensemble machine learning algorithms in weather forecasting of Bangladesh. In *International Conference on Innovations in Bio-Inspired Computing and Applications* (pp. 267–277). Springer, Cham

Martis, J. E., & Balasubramani, R. (2020). Reckoning of emotions through recognition of posture features. *Journal of Applied Security Research*, *15*(2), 230–254. https://doi.org/10.1080/19361610.2019.1645530

Martis, J. E., Sudeepa, K. B., Sannidhan, M. S., & Bhandary, A. (2020). A Rapid Automated Process for Organizing Bacterial Cluster Segments Using Deep Neural Networks. *Proceedings of the 3rd International Conference on Smart Systems and Inventive Technology, ICSSIT 2020*, pp. 963–968. https://doi.org/10.1109/ICSSIT48917.2020.9214173

Pallavi, S., Sannidhan, M. S., & Bhandary, A. (2021). Retrieval of facial sketches using linguistic descriptors: an approach based on hierarchical classification of facial attributes. *Advances in Intelligent Systems and Computing, 1133*, 1131–1149. https://doi.org/10.1007/978-981-15-3514-7_84

Pereñíguez-García, F., Ángel Guillén-Navarro, M., & Martínez-España, R. (2017). IoT-based system to forecast crop frost. *Proceedings of the 2017 13th International Conference on Intelligent Environments, IE 2017, 2017-January*, pp. 28–35. https://doi.org/10.1109/IE.2017.38

Pradeep, B., Balasubramani, R., Martis, J. E., & Sannidhan, M. S. (2020). Generic IoT Platform for Analytics in Agriculture. In *Studies in Big Data* (vol. 2, pp. 225–248). Springer, Singapore. https://doi.org/10.1007/978-981-15-0663-5_11

Pravallika, G. S., Kundana, L., Thanvi, K. S., Sirisha, G., & Rupa, C. (2020). Proficient Smart Soil based IoT System for Crop Prediction. *Proceedings of the 2nd International Conference on Inventive Research in Computing Applications, ICIRCA 2020*, pp. 752–757. https://doi.org/10.1109/ICIRCA48905.2020.9183054

Priya, P. K., & Yuvaraj, N. (2019). An IoT based gradient descent approach for precision crop suggestion using MLP. *Journal of Physics: Conference Series*, 1362(1), 12038. https://doi.org/10.1088/1742-6596/1362/1/012038

Rezk, N. G., Hemdan, E. E. D., Attia, A. F., El-Sayed, A., & El-Rashidy, M. A. (2021). An efficient IoT based smart farming system using machine learning algorithms. *Multimedia Tools and Applications, 80*(1), 773–797. https://doi.org/10.1007/s11042-020-09740-6

Salam, A., & Shah, S. (2019). Internet of things in smart agriculture: Enabling technologies. *IEEE 5th World Forum on Internet of Things, WF-IoT 2019 – Conference Proceedings*, pp. 692–695. https://doi.org/10.1109/WF-IoT.2019.8767306

Sannidhan, M. S., Ananth Prabhu, G., Robbins, D. E., & Shasky, C. (2019). Evaluating the performance of face sketch generation using generative adversarial networks. *Pattern Recognition Letters, 128*, 452–458. https://doi.org/10.1016/j.patrec.2019.10.010

Sannidhan, M. S., Prabhu, G. A., Chaitra, K. M., & Mohanty, J. R. (2021). Performance enhancement of generative adversarial network for photograph–sketch identification. *Soft Computing*, 1–18. https://doi.org/10.1007/s00500-021-05700-w

Sannidhan, M. S., Sunil Kumar Aithal, S., Martis, J. E., & Bhandary, A. (2018). A Cost Effective Approach for Detecting Electricity Theft using Raspberry Pi Board. *International Conference on Current Trends in Computer, Electrical, Electronics and Communication, CTCEEC 2017*, pp. 132–138. https://doi.org/10.1109/CTCEEC.2017.8455088

Truong, T., Dinh, A., & Wahid, K. (2017, June 12). An IoT environmental data collection system for fungal detection in crop fields. *Canadian Conference on Electrical and Computer Engineering*. https://doi.org/10.1109/CCECE.2017.7946787

Venkatesan, R., & Tamilvanan, A. (2018). A sustainable agricultural system using IoT. *Proceedings of the 2017 IEEE International Conference on Communication and Signal Processing, ICCSP 2017, 2018-January*, pp. 763–767. https://doi.org/10.1109/ICCSP.2017.8286464

Vijayabaskar, P. S., Sreemathi, R., & Keertanaa, E. (2018). Crop prediction using predictive analytics. *6th International Conference on Computation of Power, Energy, Information and Communication, ICCPEIC 2017, 2018-January*, pp. 370–373. https://doi.org/10.1109/ICCPEIC.2017.8290395

Yassein, M. B., Shatnawi, M. Q., Aljwarneh, S., & Al-Hatmi, R. (2018). Internet of Things: Survey and open issues of MQTT protocol. *Proceedings of the 2017 International Conference on Engineering and MIS, ICEMIS 2017, 2018-January*, pp. 1–6. https://doi.org/10.1109/ICEMIS.2017.8273112

Zhao, Y., Liu, L., Xie, C., Wang, R., Wang, F., Bu, Y., & Zhang, S. (2020). An effective automatic system deployed in agricultural Internet of Things using multi-context fusion network towards crop disease recognition in the wild. *Applied Soft Computing Journal, 89*, 106128. https://doi.org/10.1016/j.asoc.2020.106128

Chapter 8

Plant Disease Detection with the Help of Advanced Imaging Sensors

Shivam Singh[1], Raina Bajpai[2], Md. Mahtab Rashid[3], Basavaraj Teli[2], and Gagan Kumar[4]

[1]Department of Plant Pathology, School of Agriculture Lovely Professional University, Punjab, India
[2]Department of Mycology and Plant Pathology, Institute of Agricultural Sciences, Banaras Hindu University, Varanasi, India
[3]Department of Plant Pathology, Bihar Agricultural University, Sabour, Bhagalpur, Bihar, India
[4]Krishi Vigyan Kendra Narkatiaganj, Dr. Rajendra Prasad Central Agricultural University, Pusa, Samastipur, Bihar, India

Contents

DOI: 10.1201/9781003311782-8

8.1 Introduction

Agricultural production entails overseeing numerous processes in order to maximize yield throughout all seasons. It includes a thorough examination of the land, the seeds used, each crop's key nutritional requirements, and several other factors. Agricultural production and other kinds of income are utilized to fulfill the everyday requirements of not just farmers, but others as well. However, as with any other field, agricultural production has significant challenges as a result of plant disease. Aside from natural disasters such as droughts and landslides, diseases are also responsible for significant crop production losses (Liu *et al.*, 2020; Mishra *et al.*, 2020). The incidence of different plant diseases is regularly increased as a result of new farming techniques (Gewin, 2003; Oerke and Dehne, 2004). There are numerous explanations for it though. Plant diseases spread quickly as a result of globalization and human activities (Anderson *et al.*, 2004; Brasier, 2008; Fisher *et al.*, 2012). Climate change-related favorable conditions are another determinant for emergent trends (Coakley, 1988; Rosenzweig, 2001; Bebber *et al.*, 2014). Such activities seem difficult to manage; even a strict monitoring system using quarantine or protective methods cannot stop insect pests and diseases from spreading across the world (Brasier, 2008). Other factors that increase plant vulnerability to fungal infections depend on current production techniques. High-yielding major crops have been used and bred in modern times. Such genotypes are frequently unadapted to local conditions and become less resistant to different pathogens than their wild species. Moreover, pathogen genetic alterations have led to a loss of formerly reliable approaches of host plants resistance, and different strains have evolved that can defeat previously effective disease management techniques by developing chemical resistance (Boyd *et al.*, 2013; Parnell *et al.*, 2017). Imbalance fertilizers, wide farming of same plants, less rotation in crops, and farming using less tillage may indeed lead to increased insect pest and disease prevalence (Veresoglou *et al.*, 2000; Oerke and Dehne, 2004; Walters and Bingham, 2007). Crop disease prevalence and spread within agroecosystems continue to have and will continue to have huge ramifications for crop yields (Fisher *et al.*, 2012; Parnell *et al.*, 2017). Production is decreased in terms of quality or quantity because of numerous forms of diseases (Bos and Parlevliet, 1995; Fletcher *et al.*, 2006). Crop diseases can be defined as any type of alteration that interferes with the plant's regular functions.

The management of the big proportion of agricultural production includes a variety of regular operations, like keeping a close eye out for diseases that reduce crop production to unacceptable items (Kogan, 1998; Walters *et al.*, 2012).

Since a long time, plant disease identification has been done by specialists using their own eyes, knowledge, and their experiences. Finding a specialist and contacting them isn't just a time-taking and labor-intensive effort, but it is also a lengthy and costly process (Miller *et al.*, 2009). As a result, the entire procedure might take a long time, making it difficult to exterminate any disease and also extremely laborious in a larger proportion (Liu *et al.*, 2020; Mishra *et al.*, 2020). Technological advances for the detection of crop illness, such as preparation, similar assessment, and approaches based on deep learning for categorization, are more time-efficient than traditional methods (Kulkarni and Patil, 2012; Nagasubramanian *et al.*, 2019; Jasim and Tuwaijari, 2020; Nagaraju and Chawla, 2020; Sun *et al.*, 2020). These assist farmers in improving crop value while also reducing the prevalence of disease through early prediction and prompt curing (Sinha and Shekhawat, 2020). Additionally, artistic evaluation of crop disease prevalence and incidence likely leads to inaccuracies because contact points of plant and pathogen, and initial infections may not always be observable, and the rater's evaluation is subjective. To combat such situations, crop protection requires new and inventive ways to handle upcoming difficulties as well as advances in crop yields, which will necessitate high accuracy than ever before owing to consumer supervision. For better plant disease identification above visual evaluation methods, improved and automatic techniques with great specificity, sensitivity, as well as dependability are required (Nutter and Schultz, 1995; Nutter *et al.*, 2006; Bock *et al.*, 2010). A variety of imaging techniques are used to detect diseases in plants. Photoacoustic (PA) imaging, which helps make use of absorption of the light in tissues, is among the imaging technology generally used. It takes advantage of the characteristic of light immersion by tissues and converts it into energy, leading to the formation of PA signals. The total pressure emitted by tissue has been traced and employed for imaging purposes in this case. Magnetic resonance imaging (MRI) is a very important technique that provides accurate pictures that are often needed to study various diseases. Powerful magnets are being used in this technique to establish a powerful magnetosphere, which results in accurate proton alignments. The motion among those protons is caused afterward by the applied electric field. Lastly, switching off the rf field sensors aids throughout the identification of energy emitted during motion.

One of the most modern techniques of spectroscopy is fluorescence spectroscopy, which employs this measurement, which is discharged following the interaction of light via a field of concern. Laser-stimulated fluorescence is commonly employed on a broad scale for plant disease detection and mostly required to recognize various physiological conditions of various plants. Chlorophyll or blue-green luminescence are the most common tests performed on the leaf. It facilitates timely detection of any form of changes due to serious nutrient deficiency (Sankaran *et al.*, 2010). Hyperspectral imaging (HSI) is the effective imaging technique among all recent techniques used. Electromagnetic spectrum within a pixel of any image is employed in this method to detect the presence of any disease in plants and to analyze pixel of every picture, the light spectrum is generally used. Different plant diseases can be detected in a very appropriate way with this technique. When combined with microscopy, HSI can generate high-quality pictures (Rumpf *et al.*, 2010). Summary of works done by many authors by using different imaging techniques is given below:

- Early identification of groundnut diseases was studied by EwisOmran (2016). In this study, early and late leaf spot diseases were identified with the help of spectroscopy under *in-situ* conditions. Further, thermal and spectral studies were also involved to study the difference between healthy and infected leaves of groundnut.
- Martinelli *et al.* (2015) studied the recent technique of disease identification which was based on protein and nucleic acid analysis and described various mobility spectrometers and lateral flow devices which help in the early detection of infection in plants. They have also concluded that remote sensing technologies combined with spectroscopy-based approaches produce great spatialization, which aids in the early detection of plant diseases.
- Different noninvasive sensors were studied for plant disease detection by Mahlein *et al.* (2012) which includes thermography, chlorophyll fluorescence, and hyperspectral sensors. They have compared all these sensors and observed that huge data was recorded in hyperspectral systems and temperature was a very critical variable in thermography. They have suggested that these technologies need to be fully explored.
- Different direct and indirect technologies/methods were studied for plant diseases categorization. In this, Immuno Fluorescence (IF), Polymerase Chain Reaction (PCR), Fluorescence in situ hybridization, Flow cytometry (FCM), and Enzyme-Linked Immunosorbent Assay (ELISA) were involved in direct methods and Fluorescence and Hyperspectral imaging were involved in indirect methods. They have observed that direct methods are very difficult to handle; it consumes time and requires experts, and indirect methods lack specification of different types of diseases (Fang and Ramasamy, 2015).
- HSI was used for the detection of disease at the early stage of infection and studied about the health of the plant by Lowe *et al.* (2017). They have observed that many indices are there which are increasing on a daily basis and all are very important for the detection of specific vegetation.
- Different Disease Indexes (DIs) were developed and studied to identify different diseases like leaf spot in sugar beet and on other crops (Mahlein *et al.*, 2013). They have used hyperspectral sensors to study healthy as well as infected leaves at different stages of plants.
- Different imaging techniques like SWIR and VNIR were studied to identify *Tomato spotted wilt virus* (Moghadam *et al.*, 2017).

8.2 Disease Detection in Plants by Different Imaging Sensors

In many years, digital picture processing has progressed. It all started when the phase of two-dimensional (2-D) picture analysis arrived. Later, expertise methodologies utilizing MRI and CT altered development, and finally, a three-dimensional (3-D) picture analysis was presented. Digital design methodologies were established in the beginning, and then modern imaging and computer techniques have been used since 1999 to provide improved and even more real visualization as needed. Sensors for digital imaging are being used to collect information to study leaves from various angles in order to identify different diseases in the plant. There are different imaging methods that can be beneficial like MRT, HSI, MSI, thermal imaging, visible imaging, and 3-D imaging. A huge set of new advancements in various fields of plant pathology have been revealed, employing various kinds of extremely sensitive sensors as well as several data processing pipelines. Details of different imaging methods along with their application are discussed.

8.2.1 NMR/MRI

It is commonly recognized for its strong magnets. The magnets are effective because it effectively polarizes and stimulates the focused proton individually incorporated in atoms of water existing within tissue, resulting in a traceable signal geographically coded with distinct representations of a host. MRI equipment releases frequency band waves (radio frequency) which only attach to O_2. This technology performs by first producing pulses and then sending this to the part of the host being studied. Then, assimilation of sent energy causes them to rotate in a new inclination. It is referred to as MRI's resonance procedure, initially defined in the 1930s and 1940s (Klioze, 2013). The first MRI scan on a human was accomplished in 1977 and it took 5 hours to take a single image. The key benefit of NMR is that it can precisely solve both dynamic and static variables, but it also provides information from the material's structure in a non-corrosive manner. The morphological characteristics of opaque materials of any dimension, type, or constitution could be photographed in this technique, while a number of chemical characteristics can be assessed at the same time. As a result, a long-term dynamic response of living plant tissue like leaves and stems may now be visualized. It is feasible to create metabolic layouts of living plant bodies and utilize this information to track different physiological procedures. For example, an MRI scan of a stem can indicate the position of the xylem vessels in a living plant and also reveal if they are hydrated, and estimate velocity as well as the direction of liquid's flow. It also identifies the compounds or metabolites dissolved in it (Van As *et al.*, 2009; Windt *et al.*, 2009).

8.2.2 Spectroscopic Imaging

Profile-based and spectroscopy-based techniques are being employed to identify different diseases in leaves. The benefit of applying such techniques would be that these techniques detect different diseases in plants with high accuracy (Table 8.1). The obstacles that such methods confront involve the selection of the best approach for the specific plant disease as well as automation of techniques for constant

Table 8.1 Analysis of Various Techniques with Their Application and Accuracy in Different Plant Diseases

Optical Techniques	Application	Accuracy (%)	References
Leaf spectral reflectance	Identification of grapevine leaf roll	75	Sankaran *et al.*, 2010
Decision tree	To identify sugar beet powdery mildew	86	Cao *et al.*, 2015
Multispectral Imaging	To identify defects in photographs of apple	90	Sankaran *et al.*, 2010
Hyperspectral imaging through SWIR and VNIR	Detection of TSWV in capsicum	90	Moghadam *et al.*, 2017
Neural Network Ensemble	Identification of diseases of tea	91	Sladojevic *et al.*, 2016
QDA	To identify yellow rust of wheat	92	Bravo *et al.*, 2003
Decision tree	To identify sugar beet rust	92	Cao *et al.*, 2015
Decision tree	To identify Cercospora leaf spot (sugar beet crop)	95	Cao *et al.*, 2015
Particle Sworm Optimization	To identify spots in infected leaves of cotton	95	Sladojevic *et al.*, 2016
Spectral Information Divergence	To check different diseases and insect damage in grape	95.2	Qin *et al.*, 2009

(Continued)

Table 8.1 *(Continued)* Analysis of Various Techniques with Their Application and Accuracy in Different Plant Diseases

Optical Techniques	Application	Accuracy (%)	References
NN-SOM	Identification of a disease caused by reniform nematode in cotton	97	Lawrence *et al.*, 2004
Support Vector Machine	To compare fresh and infected leaves of sugar beet	97	Rumpf *et al.*, 2010
Hyperspectral sensing, MLP and RBF	Identification of Laurel wilt of avocado	98	Abdulridha *et al.*, 2016
MLP and SOM	Identification of wheat rust	99	Moshou *et al.,* 2004

monitoring of diseases in plants (Sankaran *et al.*, 2010). In contrast to an RGB imaging technique, spectroscopic imaging refers to a set of methods that captures more than red, green, and blue wavelength ranges. It can be studied in various types of EMR (Electromagnetic Radiation), like high-energy X-rays and very low-energy microwaves (Li *et al.*, 2014). There are three components in an SI, like a light source, spectrograph, and detector which helps in image generation. These components are designed to fulfill the selectivity and sensitivity requirements. SI produces three types of images, i.e. one spectral dimension (z), two spatial ($X \times Y$), and 3-D. The data is extremely consecutive in the 400–2,500-nm range of the spectrum, and extracting and modeling patterns need advanced multidimensional statistical methods (Mishra *et al.*, 2017; Lowe *et al.*, 2017).

8.2.3 *Multispectral and Hyperspectral Imaging*

The multispectral technique captures any forms of pictures of different crops, whether they are visible or invisible, by using various kinds of wavelength bands like red, green, or infrared. Multispectral pictures are used along with machine learning as well as algorithms to detect different diseases in plants. Hyperspectral employs many classic imaging techniques, such as spectrometry, that combines multiple spectral data sets at the same time. Its goal is to detect the wavelength for each concerned pixel of the pictures under consideration. Through a typical computerized vision system, an ultra-spectrum scanning sensor is often used for wavelength distribution, as well as a conveyance phase is provided (Rumpf *et al.*, 2010; Li *et al.*, 2017). Human eye does have the ability to see a certain span of wavelengths in the electromagnetic spectrum ranging between 400 and 700 nm (Lowe et al., 2017). Throughout a frequency range, this imaging method often incorporates a range of confined wavelengths. It thus provides a color data collection comprising valuable information, and a semantic resolution having the large number of pixels of information on a leaf (Table 8.1) (Lowe *et al.*, 2017). First spectral sensors were multispectral. Spectral information of object is often assessed by such sensors in multiple reasonably broad wavebands. Data for RGB wavebands and a near-infrared spectrum may be provided by multispectral imaging cameras. With a spectrum range (350–2,500 nm) and a limited spectral resolution (1 nm), advanced hyperspectral sensors have enhanced the intricacy of observed data (Steiner *et al.* 2008).

The HIS model is preferred over non-imaging technologies for several applications because a spatial dimension gives additional details on the structure, gradient, and color (Behmann *et al.,* 2015). Multispectral sensors are almost similar to hyperspectral sensors in terms of data complexity and information richness. Typically, this sensor detects spectrum information of an object across a number of rather large wavebands. Multispectral imaging cameras, for example, may provide data in both RGB and NIR bands. Because all these sensors are light as well as inexpensive, they are frequently employed in aerial operations on UAVs (Unmanned Aerial Vehicles) (Mahlein, *et al.,* 2012). Recent HIS research has resulted in innovations in components, detectors, as well as software, along with new programs/applications and research sectors for HSI, such as agriculture and food production, and medical (Cheng *et al.,* 2017; Mahlein, 2016; Mulla, 2013; Sendin *et al.,* 2016; Wahabzada *et al.,* 2017).

Sensor with 1-m spatial resolution is insufficient for detecting individual symptoms or infected stems and leaves; proximal sensor modules are ideal in this case (Oerke *et al.,* 2014). Various studies have already been done but the use of HIS in the field of plant pathology (Table 8.2) is still in its early stage of development (Bock *et al.,* 2010).

8.2.4 Optoacoustic Imaging (OAI/PAI)

It is also known as PA imaging which is a type of clinical imagery with a hybrid component that is based on the PA effect. It is a modern, intra-operative, and X-ray-free imaging technique that combines many advantages, like absorbance contrasts and ultrasonic magnification in deep scanning of diffusional and also other regimes. It is possible to observe the interior structure and textural properties of a subject by strategically placing ultrasonic sensors with frequencies/wavelengths tailored to the objects. There is no exposure to X-rays or hazardous energy because it's an intra-operative technology. It does not necessitate radiation and magnetism shielding facilities or enclosed spaces. This could result in the creation of diagnostic equipment that could be utilized anytime, anywhere, and by anyone. In PAI, pulsed laser light with a wavelength adjusted to the absorber to be viewed is irradiated, causing ultrasonic waves to be detected by ultrasonic sensors. The absorber distribution inside the topic can therefore be built in three dimensions. This section describes the technical components of PA imaging, the imaging principle, and the technique's most notable feature, "color visualization." Alexander Graham Bell invented it in 1880 and also observed the absorption of EMR by a medium that produces sound waves. Later, Kruger (1994) proved its effectiveness in the extensively scattered medium. It was later used in biomedical (Hoelen *et al.*, 1998). As per the findings, this technique can be utilized for a variety of reasons, including tumor analysis, to map blood-oxygen levels, scanning of brain function, and for detection of many other diseases. The PA effect describes how electromagnetic power is consumed and transformed into waves. PA imaging benefits from the strengths of pure optical imaging while avoiding the major drawbacks of every method. PAT blends the strong contrast provided by optical emission with high resolution and penetration depth provided by ultrasonic photography (Ntziachristos *et al.*, 2005).

8.2.5 Tomography

It is one of the detection methods that produce a tomogram by photographing a plane or object. It is classified into various types, like linear, poly and computed tomography, positron emission, and zonography. Recent attempts to remunerate for insufficiency of molecular and serological biology approaches have shown difficulties in developing alternative instruments for early diagnosis. Microscopy and clinical procedures such as X-ray tomography (Tollner *et al.*, 2002), as well as PET (Positron Emission Tomography), have been used to differentiate diseased plants among healthy ones (McKay *et al.*, 1988). The majority of such methods are suitable for intra-operatively obtaining structural and morphological crop photographs, but they have limits. For example, while a microscope has a very better resolution, but it has restrictions in its deep scan range and requires extra preparation for histopathology. Poor picture resolutions of X-ray tomography make this difficult to discern micro-scale characteristics in specimens. PET employs a detector to improve functional photography/imaging, though images are difficult to present in actual time. OCT (Optical Coherence Tomography) is a noninvasive optical imaging method that employs a low-consistency interferometer to get a high-resolution and cross-sectional image of the tissue. It is an improved version of another technology known as OCDR (Optical Coherence Domain Reflectometry), which was invented in 1987 (Huang *et al.*, 1991; Bouma and Tearney, 2002). For a different variety of biological applications, this technology has proven to be a valuable imaging technique and it has essential implications in different medical domains, such as dermatology and ophthalmology, because of its actual imaging capacity and micrometer-scaled resolution (Bouma and Tearney, 2002; Hee *et al.*, 1995; Muscat *et al.*, 2002; Srinivas *et al.*, 2004). This technology has recently developed new industrial uses, such as security equipment construction, fracture identification, and electrical gadgets detection (Gambichler *et al.*, 2005; Dunkers *et al.*, 2001; Cheng and Larin, 2006). OCT has a 2-mm (approximately) scanning depth range in plant tissue. Because the scanning depth range of OCT is suited for analyzing the inner structure of plant leaves, these properties are extremely beneficial to plant researchers. Ten years ago, OCT was used for the first time to investigate internal structures of different crop plants, such as kiwifruit, orach, tomato, and spiderwort (Kutis *et al.*, 2005; Sapozhnikova *et al.*, 2003; Reeves *et al.*, 2002; Clements *et al.*, 2004). This technology was recently employed in 2009, for diagnosis of viral diseases in orchid and onion (Chow *et al.*, 2009; Meglinski *et al.*, 2010).

8.2.6 Thermography

It is a test for detecting temperature variations and blood circulation in host tissues using an infrared camera. It is mostly used technique to capture images of breast. There are mainly three types of thermography, like contact-, dynamic angio-, and tele-thermography. The thermal imaging technological advances take full advantage of the metabolic rate principle. DITI (digital infrared thermal imaging) is a form of thermal imaging used for the diagnosis of breast cancer. It detects breast cancer by detecting heat variations on the breast's surface. Thermography, hyperspectral, and chlorophyll fluorescence devices/sensors have mostly been utilized to detect different diseases of plants in which hyperspectral devices gather a huge quantity of information; that's why, specific methods for obtaining results are needed (Mahlein *et al.*, 2012).

8.2.7 Fluorescence Techniques

These methods have now been frequently employed to study photo-respirational activities in different plants. The technology is extremely important to monitor crops since it allows us to reduce strain/stress in an early stage of crops, resulting in significant losses in crops. Plant photosynthetic activity is evaluated using a number of chlorophyll fluorescence measures. A functional sensor with an LED is often used to monitor the photosynthetic transfer of electrons in this technology (Bauriegel *et al.*, 2014; Chaerle *et al.*, 2004; Murchie and Lawson, 2013). Over leaves, such a technique is being used to investigate changes in a photosynthetic activity driven by biotic and abiotic factors (Burling *et al.*, 2011; Scholes and Rolfe, 2009). The use of fluorescence imaging in collaboration with image processing techniques has been found to be effective in the detection and quantification of fungal infections (Konanz *et al.*, 2014). A drawback of present chlorophyll fluorescence imaging techniques is that plants must be prepared according to a rigorous routine, making it difficult to utilize in regular agriculture conservatories or agricultural locations (Table 8.2). As a result, research has focused on obtaining fluorescence metrics from field-induced reflectance, which might be used to diagnose diseases in plants at the canopy or fields (Rossini *et al.*, 2014).

Table 8.2 Use of Optical Sensors to Examine Different Diseases in Plants

Sensors	Crops and Their Diseases	References
Thermal	Cercospora leaf spot (sugar beet)	Chaerle et al., 2004
	Downy and powdery mildew (cucumber)	Berdugo et al., 2014; Oerke et al., 2006
	Scab diseases (apple)	Oerke et al., 2011
	Downy mildew (rosa)	Gomez, 2014
Spectral	Net blotch, brown rust and powdery mildew (barley)	Kuska et al., 2015; Wahabzada et al., 2015
	Yellow rust and head blight (wheat)	Huang et al., 2007; Moshou et al., 2004; Bauriegel et al., 2011; Bravo et al., 2003
	Leaf spot, rust and powdery mildew (sugar beet)	Bergstrasser et al., 2015; Hillnhutter et al., 2011; Mahlein et al., 2010, 2012, 2013; Rumpf et al., 2010
	Late blight (tomato)	Wang et al., 2008
	Scab disease (apple)	Delalieux et al., 2007
	Virus (tulip)	Polder et al., 2014
	Orange rust (sugarcane)	Apan et al., 2004
Fluorescence	Rust and powdery mildew (wheat)	Burling et al., 2011
	Leaf spot (sugar beet)	Chaerle et al., 2004, 2007; Konanz et al., 2014
	Bacterial blight (bean)	Rousseau et al., 2013
	Downy mildew (lettuce)	Bauriegel et al., 2014; Brabandt et al., 2014
RGB	Bacterial blight (cotton)	Camargo and Smith, 2009
	Leaf spots and rust (sugar beet)	Neumann et al., 2014
	Canker (orange)	Bock et al., 2010
	Anthracnose (tobacco)	Wijekoon et al., 2008
	Scab (apple)	
	Rust (Canadian Goldenrod)	

8.2.8 Thermal Imaging

It's a method of converting the numerous forms of radiation detected in an item into multiple sorts of pictures in order to obtain different attributes, analyze, and categorize them. It was first deployed in defense, but it has since been utilized in a wide range of agricultural industries such as engineering. Thermal imaging of plants has been created using a variety of devices and methodologies. This technology can be used for a variety of agricultural activities for every stage of crops. It's a prominent element in which the interaction between water, soil, and plants has been thoroughly investigated (Vadivambal and Digvir, 2011). Crop temperature can be measured using infrared thermography (IRT), which is linked to water status in crops, microclimate, and variations in transpiration caused by early plant disease infections. Thermal imaging and infrared camera can capture emitted infrared radiation in the thermal infrared region of 8–12 mm, which is displayed in false color images with each image pixel, including the temperature value of the observed object. IRT can be applied in plant science at a variety of temporal and spatial dimensions, from aerial to small-scale applications. It is, however, frequently affected by external elements such as temperature, daylight, rain, and airspeed (Oerke *et al.*, 2006). Plant-virus interactions in tobacco and *Cercospora beticola* in sugar beet have both been linked to local temperature fluctuations caused by pathogen infection (Chaerle *et al.*, 2004). Oerke *et al.* (2006) studied downy mildew of cucumber caused by *Pseudoperonospora cubensis* and scab of apple caused by *Venturia inaequalis* successfully by IRT. Thermography was also able to visualize the pathogen's spatial colonization of apple tissues beyond obvious symptoms in the plant-pathosystem for apple and *V. inaequalis*, where hyphae and conidia were only microscopically discernible (Oerke *et al.*, 2011). Infection of *Peronospora sparsa* and dissemination on several Rosa cultivars were studied by Gomez (2014) (Table 8.2).

8.2.9 3-D Imaging

The requirement of 3-D imaging seems to be important for the automatic detection of different plant diseases. In agricultural approaches, there are a variety of methods for acquiring 3-D images (Jarvis, 1983; Blais, 2004; Bellmann *et al.*, 2007) by using 2-D along with 3-D technology (Grift, 2008; McCarthy *et al.*, 2010). Volume and surface presentations are the two most used 3-D formats. Volume presentation describes frequency as well as volumetric components in the coordinates of the given model.

A variety of low-cost sensors are now accessible. Such sensors are now being employed to investigate different leaf diseases better since the information obtained would be used to measure earlier reported output aspects (Vázquez-Arellano *et al.*, 2016). Light velocity is used by these sensors, such as LIDARs and TOF cameras, to estimate depths (Underwood *et al.*, 2013; Lachat *et al.*, 2015).

8.2.10 RGB Imaging

Plant pathology relies heavily on digital photographic pictures to evaluate the health of plants. It's very easy to handle digital cameras which are a convenient source of red, green, and blue pictures to detect, identify, and count different plant diseases. Almost everyone, either scientists or farmers, used to carry digital camera sensors now in mobile phones or portable computers. Alternatives to assess digital photographs of various parts of plants include recording devices and scanners. In a growing season of the crop, these sensors can be employed on all scales of resolution to monitor different plants. Plants' biotic stress can be detected by using all three channels (red, green, and blue) of RGB images. HSV, LAB, or YCBCR color spaces also give a valuable information of crop diseases, same as RGB (Bock *et al.* 2010).

In addition, color, levels of gray, structure, dispersal, association, as well as structures all can be used to identify and detect different symptoms of crop diseases. Different techniques to recognize patterns and to study different appliances have been employed to identify and to detect different diseases in plants using RGB photographs (Camargo and Smith 2009; Neumann *et al.* 2014). Furthermore, the structured collection of essential information from RGB pictures enhances the accuracy of classification (Behmann *et al.*, 2014). Digital picture inspection is a well-known technique to assess plant diseases. Many software packages, like Leaf Doctor, Custom-made, Scion Image, and ASSESS 2.0, are available now (Tucker and Chakraborty 1997; Wijekoon *et al.*, 2008; Bock *et al.*, 2010; Pethybridge and Nelson 2015).

8.3 Methods of Image Classification to Detect Diseases in Plants

Segmentation is the most crucial phase in the analysis of leaf photographs. The segmentation process starts with a photograph and divides this into sub-segments. Such segments generally represent different types of plant parts for categorization purposes. Low contrast and certain optical uncertainties, as well as noise, make picture segmentation difficult under this situation.

Sensor offers a variety of chances as well as technological capabilities for automated, impartial, and replicable evaluation of diseases in plants. There are a large number of existing sensors which give superior information of different crops in the field and that can also be used to detect and identify different diseases in plants. The level of advances made to create these techniques and to apply them to detect diseases in plants for more than 40 years is remarkable (Brenchley, 1964; Jackson and Wallen, 1975; Nilsson, 1995; Seelan *et al.*, 2003; West *et al.*, 2003). Specialized plant approaches have been introduced as a result of advancements in agriculture (Steddom *et al.*, 2005; Furbank and Tester, 2011; Fiorani *et al.*, 2012; Cobb *et al.*, 2013). Most effective sensors are now being applied for intra-operative assessment of nutrition in crops. The introduction of alternative economical sensor technologies having excellent execution in the market is indeed an essential step in agricultural systems (Paulus *et al.*, 2014; Grieve *et al.*, 2015).

8.4 Conclusions, Limitations, and Future Scopes

One of the most prevalent issues around the world is the loss of a large portion of output due to plant disease. Timely detection of existing plant diseases requires the implementation of appropriate strategies to diagnose and minimize loss. As a result, researchers are concentrating on reliable methods for detecting plant diseases. In future, sensor-based smartphone is expected to be available for farmers which will help to know more about diseases in the field and to detect these very easily. As conditions in plant phenotyping are frequently under control, sensor applications are expected to take precedence over the time-consuming visual evaluation by technicians. Linking complementing study domains, like phytopathology, development of sensors, bioinformatics, as well as machine learning, is essential for future scientific research. An interdisciplinary approach along with practical agriculture can lead to effective solutions for diagnosis and detection of plant diseases with maximum accuracy as well as sensitivity which will improve the management of plant diseases. Furthermore, there are other fields of study that require further investigation:

■ Proposed algorithm should be improved more to reduce the error in classification.
■ It is required to characterize different pathogens like fungi, bacteria, and viruses.
■ It is necessary to explore the effects of combined infections on plant optical characteristics.
■ Automation in the detection of disease severity should be there and for automatic early tracing, a reliable and efficient system should be designed.
■ The interaction between foliar and soil-borne pathogens/pests must be assessed.
■ It is necessary to investigate the interaction between biotic and abiotic factors.
■ Plant optical qualities must be explored in terms of their genetic, transcriptomic, and metabolic features.
■ Work also necessitates the study of various variations in the environment.
■ The prospect of early infection before the appearance of apparent symptoms has yet to be explored.

References

Abdulridha, J., Ehsani, R. and Castro, A. (2016). Detection and differentiation between laurel wilt disease, Phytophthora disease, and salinity damage using a hyperspectral sensing technique. *Agriculture*, 6 (4):56.

Anderson, P. K., Cunningham, A. A., Patel, N. G., Morales, F. J., Epstein, P. R. and Daszak, P. (2004). Emerging infectious diseases of plants: pathogen pollution, climate change and agro-technology drivers. *Trends Ecol. Evol.*, 19:535–44.

Apan, A., Held, A., Phinn, S. and Markley, J. (2004). Detecting sugarcane 'orange rust' disease using EO-1 Hyperion hyperspectral imagery. *Int. J. Remote Sens.*, 25:489–498.

Bauriegel, E., Brabandt, H., G"arber, U. and Herppich, W. B. (2014). Chlorophyll fluorescence imaging to facilitate breeding of *Bremia lactucae*-resistant lettuce cultivars. *Comput. Electron. Agric.*, 105:74–82.

Bauriegel, E., Giebel, A., Geyer, M., Schmidt, U. and Herppich, W. B. (2011). Early detection of *Fusarium* infection in wheat using hyper-spectral imaging. *Comput. Electron. Agric.*, 75:304–312.

Bebber, D. P., Holmes, T. and Gurr, S. J. (2014). The global spread of crop pests and pathogens. *Glob. Ecol. Biogeogr.*, 23:1398–1407.

Behmann, J., Mahlein, A. K., Rumpf, T., R"omer, C. and Pl"umer, L. (2014). A review of advanced machine learning methods for the detection of biotic stress in precision crop protection. *Precis. Agric.*, 16:239–260.

Behmann, J., Mahlein, A. K., Rumpf, T., Romer, C. and Plumer, L. (2015). A review of advanced machine learning methods for the detection of biotic stress in precision crop protection. *Precis. Agric.*, 16:239–60.

Bellmann, A., Hellwich, O., Rodehorst, V. and Yilmaz, U. (2007). A benchmarking dataset for performance evaluation of automatic surface reconstruction algorithms. IEEE Conference on Computer Vision and Pattern Recognition. IEEE, Minneapolis, MN, USA, pp. 1–8.

Berdugo, C., Zito, R., Paulus, S. and Mahlein, A. K. (2014). Fusion of sensor data for the detection and differentiation of plant diseases in cucumber. *Plant Pathol.*, 63:1344–1356.

Bergstrasser, S., Fanourakis, D., Schmittgen, S., Cendrero-Mateo, M. P., Jansen, M., Scharr, H. and Rascher, U. (2015). HyperART: non-invasive quantification of leaf traits using hyperspectral absorption-reflectance-transmittance imaging. *Plant Methods*, 11(1):1–17.

Blais, F. (2004). Review of 20 years of range sensor development. *J. Electron. Imaging*, 13: 231–240.

Bock, C. H., Poole, G. H., Parker, P. E. and Gottwald, T. R. (2010). Plant disease severity estimated visually, by digital photography and image analysis, and by hyperspectral imaging. *Crit. Rev. Plant Sci.*, 29:59–107.

Bos, L. and Parlevliet, J. E. (1995). Concepts and terminology on plant/pest relationships: toward consensus in plant pathology and crop protection. *Annu. Rev. Phytopathol.*, 33:69–102.

Bouma, B. E. and Tearney, G. J. (2002). *Handbook of Optical Coherence Tomography*. Marcel Dekker, New York, USA.

Boyd, L. A., Ridout, C., O'Sullivan, D. M., Leach, J. E. and Leung, H. 2013. Plant-pathogen interactions: disease resistance in modern agriculture. *Trends Genet.*, 29:233–40.

Brabandt, H., Bauriegel, E., G"arber, U. and Herppich, W. B. (2014). ΦPSII and NPQ to evaluate *Bremia lactucae* infection in susceptible and resistant lettuce cultivars. *Sci. Hortic.*, 180:123–129.

Brasier, C. M. (2008). The biosecurity threat to the UK and global environment from international trade in plants. *Plant Pathol.*, 57:792–808.

Bravo, C., Moshou, D., West, J., McCartney, A. and Ramon, H. (2003). Early disease detection in wheat fields using spectral reflectance. *Biosyst. Eng.*, 84 (2):137–145.

Brenchley, G. H. (1964). Aerial photography for the study of potato blight epidemics. *World. Rev. Pest Cont.*, 3:68–84.

Burling, K., Hunsche, M. and Noga, G. (2011). Use of blue-green and chlorophyll fluorescence measurements for differentiation between nitrogen deficiency and pathogen infection in wheat. *J. Plant Physiol.*, 168:1641–1648.

Camargo, A. and Smith, J. S. (2009). Image pattern classification for the identification of disease causing agents in plants. *Comput. Electron. Agric.*, 66:121–125.

Cao, X., Luo, Y., Zhou, Y., Fan Xu, X., West, J. S. et al. (2015). Detection of powdery mildew in two winter wheat plant densities and prediction of grain yield using canopy hyperspectral reflectance. *PLoS One*, 10 (3): e0121462.

Chaerle, L., Hagenbeek, D., De Bruyne, E. and Van der Straeten, D. (2007). Chlorophyll fluorescence imaging for disease-resistance screening of sugar beet. *Plant Cell Tiss. Org.*, 91:97–106.

Chaerle, L., Hagenbeek, D., De Bruyne, E., Valcke, R. and Van Der Straeten, D. (2004). Thermal and chlorophyll-fluorescence imaging distinguish plant pathogen interactions at an early stage. *Plant Cell Physiol.*, 45:887–896.

Cheng Y. and Larin, K. V. (2006). Artificial fingerprint recognition by using optical coherence tomography with autocorrelation analysis. *Appl. Opt.*, 45:9238–9245.

Cheng, J. H., Nicolai, B. and Sun, D. W. (2017). Hyperspectral imaging with multivariate analysis for technological parameters prediction and classification of muscle food: a review. *Meat Sci.*, 123:182–91.

Chow, T. H., Tan, K. M., B. K. Ng, Razul, S. G., Tay, C. M., Chia, T. F. and Poh, W. T. (2009). Diagnosis of virus infection in orchid plants with high-resolution optical coherence tomography. *J. Biomed. Opt.*, 14:014006.

Clements, J. C., Zvyagin, A. V., Silva, K. K. M. B. D., Wanner, T., Sampson, D. D. and Cowling, W. A. (2004). Optical coherence tomography as a novel tool for non-destructive measurement of the hull thickness of lupin seeds. *Plant Breeding*, 123:266–270.

Coakley, S. M. (1988). Variation in climate and prediction of disease in plants. *Annu. Rev. Phytopathol.*, 26:163–81.

Cobb, J. N., DeClerck, G., Greenberg, A., Clark, R. and McCouch, S. (2013). Next generation phenotyping: requirements and strategies for enhancing our understanding of genotype-phenotype relationships and its relevance to crop improvement. *Theor. Appl. Genet.*, 126:867–887.

Delalieux, S., van Aardt, J., Keulemans, W. and Coppin, P. (2007). Detection of biotic stress (*Venturia inaequalis*) in apple trees using hyperspectral data: non-parametric statistical approaches and physiological implications. *Eur. J. Agron.*, 27:130–143.

Dunkers, J. P., Phelan, F. R., Sanders, D. P., Everett, M. J., Green, W. H., Hunston, D. L. and Parnas, R. S. (2001). The application of optical coherence tomography to problems in polymer matrix composites. *Opt. Laser Eng.*, 35:135–147.

EwisOmran, El-Sayed (2016). Early sensing of peanut leaf spot using spectroscopy and thermal imaging. *Arch. Agron. Soil Sci.* https://doi.org/10.1080/03650340.2016.1247952.

Fang, Yi and Ramasamy, R. P. (2015). Current and prospective methods for plant disease detection. *Biosensors* https://doi.org/10.3390/bios5030537.

Fiorani, F., Rascher, U., Jahnke, S. and Schurr, U. (2012). Imaging plants dynamics in heterogenic environments. *Curr. Opin. Biotechnol.*, 23:227–235.

Fisher, M. C., Henk, D. A., Briggs, C. J., Brownstein, J. S., Madoff, L. C. et al. (2012). Emerging fungal threats to animal, plant and ecosystem health. *Nature*, 484:186–94.

Fletcher, J., Bender, C., Budowle, B., Cobb, W. T., Gold, S. E. et al. (2006). Plant pathogen forensics: capabilities, needs, and recommendations. *Microbiol. Mol. Biol. Rev.*, 70:450–71.

Furbank, R. T. and Tester, M. (2011). Phenomics – technologies to relieve the phenotyping bottleneck. *Trends Plant Sci.*, 16:635–644.

Gambichler, T., Moussa, G., Sand, M., Sand, D., Altmeyer, P. and Hoffmann, K. (2005). Applications of optical coherence tomography in dermatology. *J. Dermatol. Sci.*, 40:85–94.

Gewin, V. (2003). Bioterrorism: agriculture shock. *Nature*, 421:106–108.

Gomez, S. (2014). Infection and spread of Peronospora sparsa on Rosa sp. (Berk.) – a microscopic and a thermographic approach. Dissertation, University of Bonn, Germany.

Grieve, B., Hammersley, S., Mahlein, A. K., Oerke, E. C. and Goldbach, H. (2015). Localized multispectral crop imaging sensors: engineering & validation of a cost effective plant stress and disease sensor. Sensors Applications Symposium (SAS). pp. 1–6.

Grift, T. (2008). A review of automation and robotics for the bioindustry. *J. Biomech. Eng.*, 1:37–54.

Hee, M. R., Izatt, J. A., Swanson, E. A., Huang, D., Schuman, J. S., Lin, C. P., Puliafito, C. A. and Fujimoto, J. G. (1995). Optical coherence tomography of the human retina. *Arch. Ophthalmol.*, 113:325–332.

Hillnhutter, C., Mahlein, A. K., Sikora, R. A. and Oerke, E. C. (2011). Remote sensing to detect plant stress induced by *Heterodera schachtii* and *Rhizoctonia solani* in sugar beet fields. *Field Crops Res.*, 122:70–77.

Hoelen, C. G., de Mul, F. F., Pongers, R. and Dekker, A. (1998). Three-dimensional photoacoustic imaging of blood vessels in tissue. *Opt. Lett.*, 23:648–650.

Huang, D., Swanson, E. A., Lin, C. P., Schuman, J. S., Stinson, W. G., Chang, W., Hee, M. R., Flotte, T., Gregory, K., Puliafito, C. A. and Fujimoto, J. G. (1991). Optical coherence tomography. *Science*, 254:1178–1181.

Huang, W., Lamb, D. W., Niu, Z., Zhang, Y., Liu, L. and Wang, J. (2007). Identification of yellow rust in wheat using *in-situ* spectral reflectance measurements and airborne hyperspectral imaging. *Precis. Agric.*, 8:187–197.

Jackson, H. R. and Wallen, V. R. (1975). Micro-densiometer measurements of sequential aerial photographs of field beans infected with bacterial blight. *Phytopathology*, 65:961–968.

Jarvis, R. (1983). A perspective on range finding techniques for computer vision. *IEEE Trans. Patt. Anal. Mach. Intell.*, PAMI-5:122–139.

Jasim, M. A. and Tuwaijari, J. M. A. L. (2020). Plant leaf diseases detection and classification using image processing and deep learning techniques. International Conference on Computer Science and Software Engineering (CSASE), Duhok, Iraq, pp. 259–265.

Jones, H. G., Stoll, M., Santoa, T., de Sousa, C., Chaves, M. M. and Grant, O. M. (2002). Use of infrared thermography for monitoring stomatal closure in the field: Application to grapevine. *J. Exp. Bot.*, 53:2249–2260.

Klioze, D. (2013). MRI: Basic Physics a Brief History. Retrieved from Youtube: https://www.youtube.com/watch?v=djAxjtN7VE

Kogan, M. (1998). Integrated pest management: historical perspectives and contemporary developments. *Annu. Rev. Entomol.*, 43:243–270.

Konanz, S., Kocs´anyi, L. and Buschmann, C. (2014). Advanced multi-color fluorescence imaging system for detection of biotic and abiotic stresses in leaves. *Agriculture*, 4:79–95.

Kruger, R. (1994). Photoacoustic ultrasound. *Med. Phys.*, 21:127–131.

Kulkarni, A. H. and Patil, A. R. K. (2012). Applying image processing technique to detect plant diseases. *Int. J. Mod. Eng. Res.*, 2 (5):3661–3664.

Kuska, M., Wahabzada, M., Leucker, M., Dehne, H. W., Kersting, K., Oerke, E. C., Steiner, U. and Mahlein, A. K. (2015). Hyperspectral phenotyping on microscopic scale-towards automated characterization of plant-pathogen interactions. *Plant Methods*, 11:1-15

Kutis, I. S., Sapozhnikova, V. V., Kuranov, R. V. and Kamenskii, V. A. (2005). Study of the morphological and functional state of higher plant tissues by optical coherence micros-copy and optical coherence tomography. *Russ. J. Plant Physiol.* 52:559–564.

Lachat, E., Macher, H., Mittet, M., Landes, T. and Grussenmeyer, P. (2015). First experi-ences with Kinect v2 sensor for close range 3D modeling. The International Archives of the Photogrammetry, Remote Sensing and Spatial Information Sciences. ISPRS, Avila, Spain, pp. 93–100 Vol. XL-5/W4.

Lawrence, G. W., Kelly, A. T., King, R. L., Vickery, J., Lee, H. K. and McLean, K. S. (2004). Remote sensing and precision nematicide applications for *Rotylenchulus reni-formis* management in cotton. In *Proceedings of the Fourth International Congress of Nematology, 8-13 June 2002, Tenerife, Spain* (pp. 13-21). Brill

Lenthe, J. H., Oerke, E. C. and Dehne, H. W. (2007). Digital infrared thermography for monitoring canopy health of wheat. *Precis. Agric.* 8:15–26.

Li, L., Zhang, Q. and Huang, D. F. (2014). A review of imaging techniques for plant pheno-typing. *Sensors-Basel*, 14:20078–20111.

Li, Xiaona, Li, Ruolan, Wang, Mengyu, Liu, Yaru, Zhang, Baohua and Zhou, Jun (2017). Hyperspectral imaging and their applications in the non-destructive quality assessment of fruits and vegetables. *Hyperspectral Imaging in Agriculture, Food And Environment*, 27–63

Liu, L., Dong, Y., Huang, W., Xiaoping, D., Ren, B., Huang, L., Zheng, Q. and Ma, H. (2020). A disease index for efficiently detecting wheat fusarium head blight using Sentinel-2 multispectral imagery. *IEEE Access* 8:52181–52191.

Lowe, A., Harrison, N. and French, A. P. (2017). Hyperspectral image analysis techniques for the detection and classification of the early onset of plant disease and stress. *Plant Methods*, 13. https://doi.org/10. 1186/s13007-017-0233-z.

Lowe, A., Harrison, N., French, A. P. (2017). Hyperspectral image analysis techniques for the detection and classification of the early onset of plant disease and stress. *Plant Methods*, 13(1), 1-12.

Mahlein, A. K. (2016). Plant disease detection by imaging sensors—parallels and specific demands for precision agriculture and plant phenotyping. *Plant Dis.*, 2:241–251.

Mahlein, A. K., Oerke, E. C., Steiner, U. and Dehne, H. W. (2012). Recent advances in sensing plant diseases for precision crop protection. *Eur. J. Plant Pathol.*, 133:197–209.

Mahlein, A. K., Rumpf, T., Welke, P., Dehne, H. W., Pl¨umer, L., Steiner, U. and Oerke, E. C. (2013). Development of spectral vegetation indices for detecting and identifying plant diseases. *Remote Sens. Environ.*, 128:21–30.

Mahlein, A. K., Steiner, U., Dehne, H. W. and Oerke, E. C. (2010). Spectral signatures of sugar beet leaves for the detection and differentiation of diseases. *Precis. Agric.*, 11:413–431.

Mahlein, A. K., Steiner, U., Hillnh¨utter, C., Dehne, H.-W. and Oerke, E. C. (2012). Hyperspectral imaging for small-scale analysis of symptoms caused by different sugar beet disease. *Plant Methods*, 8(1):1–13.

Martinelli, F., Scalenghe, R., Davino, S., Panno, S., Scuderi, G., Ruisi, P., Villa, P., Stroppiana, D., MircoBoschtti, L., Goulart, R., Davis, C. E. and Dandekar, A. M. (2015). Advanced methods of plant disease detection. *Agron. Sustain. Dev.*, 35 (1):1–25.

McCarthy, C. L., Hancock, N. H. and Raine, S. R. (2010). Applied machine vision of plants: a review with implications for field deployment in automated farming operations. *Intell. Serv. Robot.*, 3:209–217.

McKay, R. M. L., Palmer, G. R., Ma, X. P., Layzell, D. B. and McKee, B. T. A. (1988). The use of positron emission tomography for studies of long-distance transport in plants: uptake and transport of 18F. *Plant Cell Environ.*, 11:851–861.

Meglinski, I. V., Buranachai, C. and Terry, L. A. (2010). Plant photonics: application of optical coherence tomography to monitor defects and rots in onion. *Laser Phys. Lett.*, 7:307–310.

Miller, S. A., Beed, F. D. and Harmon, C. L. (2009). Plant disease diagnostic capabilities and networks. *Annu. Rev. Phytopathol.*, 47:15–38.

Mishra, P., Asaari, M. S. M., Herrero-Langreo, A., Lohumi, S., Diezma, B. and Scheunders, P. (2017). Close range hyperspectral imaging of plants: a review. *Biosyst. Eng.*, 164: 49–67. (Key review paper describing the general application of spectral imaging in plant analysis.)

Mishra, P., Polder, G. and Vilfan, N. (2020). Close range spectral imaging for disease detection in plants using autonomous platforms: a review on recent studies. *Curr. Robot. Rep.*, 1:43–48.

Moghadam, P., Ward, D., Goan, E., Jayawardena, S., Sikka, P. and Hernandez, E. (2017). Plant disease detection using hyperspectral imaging. International Conference on Digital Image Computing: Techniques and Applications (DICTA), Sydney, NSW, pp. 1–8.

Moshou, D., Bravo, C., West, J., Wahlem, S., McCartney, A. and Ramon, H. (2004). Automatic detection of "yellow rust" in wheat using reflectance measurement and neural networks. *Comput. Electron. Agric.*, 44 (3):173–188.

Mulla, D. J. (2013). Twenty five years of remote sensing in precision agriculture: key advances and remaining knowledge gaps. *Biosyst. Eng.*, 114:358–371.

Murchie, E. H. and Lawson, T. (2013). Chlorophyll fluorescence analysis: a guide to good practice and understanding some new applications. *J. Exp. Bot.*, 64:3983–3998.

Muscat, S., McKay, N., Parks, S., Kemp, E. and Keating, D. (2002). Repeatability and reproducibility of corneal thickness measurements by optical coherence tomography. *Investigative Ophthalmology & Visual Science*, 43(6), 1791–1795.

Nagaraju, M. and Chawla, P. (2020). Systematic review of deep learning techniques in plant disease detection. *Int. J. Syst. Assur. Eng. Manag.*, 11:547–560.

Nagasubramanian, K., Jones, S., Singh, A. K. et al. (2019). Plant disease identification using explainable 3D deep learning on hyperspectral images. *Plant Methods*, 15(1):1–10.

Neumann, M., Hallau, L., Klatt, B., Kersting, K. and Bauckhage, C. (2014). Erosion band features for cell phone image based plant disease classification. Proceedings of the 22nd International Conference on Pattern Recognition (ICPR), Stockholm, Sweden, 24–28 August 2014. pp. 3315–3320.

Nilsson, H. E. (1995). Remote sensing and imaging analysis in plant pathology. *Can. J. Plant Pathol.*, 17:154–166.

Ntziachristos, V., Ripoll, J., Wang, L. V. and Weissleder, R. (2005). Looking and listening to light: the evolution of whole-body photonic imaging. *Nature Biotech.*, 23:313–320.

Nutter, F. W. and Schultz, P. M. (1995). Improving the accuracy and precision of disease assessments: selection of methods and use of computer-aided training programs. *Can. J. Plant Pathol.*, 17:174–184.

Nutter, F. W., Esker, P. D. and Netto, R. A. C. (2006). Disease assessment concepts and the advancements made in improving the accuracy and precision of plant disease data. *Eur. J. Plant Pathol.*, 115:95–103.

Oerke, E. C. and Dehne, H. W. (2004). Safeguarding production—losses in major crops and the role of crop protection. *Crop Prot.*, 23:275–285.

Oerke, E. C., Fr"ohling, P. and Steiner, U. (2011). Thermographic assessment of scab disease on apple leaves. *Precis. Agric.*, 12:699–715.

Oerke, E. C., Mahlein, A. K. and Steiner, U. (2014). Proximal sensing of plant diseases. *Detection and Diagnostic of Plant Pathogens, Plant Pathology in the 21st Century*. M. L. Gullino and P. J. M. Bonants, eds. Springer Science and Business Media, Dordrecht, The Netherlands. pp. 55–68.

Oerke, E. C., Steiner, U., Dehne, H. W. and Lindenthal, M. (2006). Thermal imaging of cucumber leaves affected by downy mildew and environmental conditions. *J. Exp. Bot.*, 57:2121–2132.

Parnell, S., van den Bosch, F., Gottwald, T. and Gilligan, C. A. (2017). Surveillance to inform control of emerging plant diseases: an epidemiological perspective. *Annu. Rev. Phytopathol.*, 55:591–610.

Paulus, S., Behmann, J., Mahlein, A. K., Pl"umer, L. and Kuhlmann, H. (2014). Low-cost 3D systems: suitable tools for plant phenotyping. *Sensors* 14:3001–3018.

Pethybridge, S. J. and Nelson, S. C. (2015). Leaf doctor: a new portable application for quantifying plant disease severity. *Plant Dis.*, 99:1310–1316.

Polder, G., van der Heijden, G. W. A. M., van Doorn, J. and Baltissen, T. A. H. M. C. (2014). Automatic detection of *Tulip breaking virus* (TBV) in tulip fields using machine vision. *Biosyst. Eng.*, 117:35–42.

Qin, J., Burks, T. F., Ritenour, M. A. and Bonn, W. G. (2009). Detection of citrus canker using hyperspectral reflectance imaging with spectral information divergence. *Journal of food engineering*, 93(2), 183–191

Reeves, A., Parsons, R. L., Hettinger, J. W. and Medford, J. I. (2002). *In-vivo* three-dimensional imaging of plants with optical coherence microscopy. *J. Microsc.*, 208:177–189.

Rosenzweig, C. (2001). Climate change and extreme weather events—implications for food production, plant diseases, and pests. *Glob. Change Hum. Health*, 2:90–104.

Rossini, M., Alonso, L., Cogliati, S., Damm, A., Guanter, L., Julietta, T., Meroni, M., Moreno, J., Panigada, C., Pinto, F., Rascher, U., Schickling, A., Sch"uttemeyer, D., Zemek, F. and Colombo, R. (2014). Measuring suninduced chlorophyll fluorescence: an evaluation and synthesis of existing field data. 5th International Workshop on Remote Sensing of Vegetation Fluorescence, 22–24 April 2014, Paris. pp. 1–5.

Rousseau, C., Belin, E., Bove, E., Rousseau, D., Fabre, F., Berruyer, R., Guillaumes, J., Manceau, C., Jaques, M. A. and Boureau, T. (2013). High throughput quantitative phenotyping of plant resistance using chlorophyll fluorescence image analysis. *Plant Methods*, 9(1):1–13.

Rumpf, T., Mahlein, A. K., Steiner, U., Oerte, E. C., Dehne, H. W. and Plumer, L. (2010). Early detection and classification of plant disease with support vector machine based on hyperspectral reflectance. *Comput. Electron. Agric.*, 74:91–99.

Sankaran, S., Mishra, A., Ehsani, R. and Davis, C. (2010). A review of advance techniques for detecting plant diseases. *Comput. Electron. Agric.*, 72 (1):1–13.

Sapozhnikova, V. V., Kamenskii, V. A. and Kuranov, R. V. (2003). Visualization of plant tissues by optical coherence tomography. *Russ. J. Plant Physiol.*, 50:282–286.

Scholes, J. D. and Rolfe, S. A. (2009). Chlorophyll fluorescence imaging as tool for understanding the impact of fungal diseases on plant performance: a phenomics perspective. *Funct. Plant Biol.*, 36:880–892.

Seelan, S. K., Laguette, S., Casady, G. M. and Seielstad, G. A. (2003). Remote sensing applications for precision agriculture: a learning community approach. *Remote Sens. Environ.*, 88:157–169.

Sendin, K., Williams, P. J. and Manley, M. (2016). Near infrared hyperspectral imaging in quality and safety evaluation of cereals. *Crit. Rev. Food Sci. Nutr.*, 58:575–590.

Sinha A. and Shekhawat, R. S. (2020). Review of image processing approaches for detecting plant diseases in. *IET Image Process.* 14 (8):1427–1439.

Sladojevic, S., Arsenovic, M., Anderla, A., Culibrk, D. and Stefanovic, D. (2016). Deep neural networks based recognition of plant diseases by leaf image classification. *Comput. Intell. Neurosci.*, 2016:1–11.

Srinivas, S. M., de Boer, J. F., Park, H., Keikhanzadeh, K., Huang, H. E., Zhang, J., Jung, W. Q., Chen, Z. and Nelson, J. S. (2004). Determination of burn depth by polarization sensitive optical coherence tomography. *J. Biomed. Opt.*, 9:207–212.

Steddom, K., Bredehoeft, M. W., Khan, M. and Rush, C. M. (2005). Comparison of visual and multispectral radiometric disease evaluations of Cercospora leaf spot of sugar beet. *Plant Dis.*, 89:153–158.

Steiner, U., Bürling, K. and Oerke, E. C. (2008). Sensorik für einen präzisierten Pflanzenschutz. *Gesunde Pflanz.* 60:131–141.

Sun, J., Yang, Y., He, X. and Wu, X. (2020). Northern maize leaf blight detection under complex field environment based on deep learning. *IEEE Access*, 8:33679–33688.

Tollner, E. W., Shahin, M. A., McClendon, R. W. and Arabnia, H. R. (2002). Apple classification based on surface bruises using image processing and neural networks. *Trans. ASABE*, 45:1619–1627.

Tucker, C. C. and Chakraborty, S. (1997). Quantitative assessment of lesion characteristic and disease severity using digital image processing. *J. Phytopathol.*, 145:273–278.

Underwood, J., Calleija, M., Nieto, J. and Sukkarieh, S. (2013). A robot amongst the herd: remote detection and tracking of cows. In: Ingram, L., Cronin, G., Sutton, L. (Eds.), *Proceedings of the 4th Australian and New Zealand Spatially Enabled Livestock Management Symposium.* The University of Sydney, Camden, Australia, p. 52.

Vadivambal, R. and Digvir, J. (2011). Applications of thermal imaging in agriculture and food industry—a review. *Food Bioprocess Technol.*, 4:186–199.

Van As, H., Scheenen, T. and Vergeldt, F. J. (2009). MRI of intact plants. *Photosynth. Res.*, 102:213–222.

Vázquez-Arellano, M., Griepentrog, H. W., Reiser, D. and Paraforos, D. S. (2016). 3-D imaging systems for agricultural applications—a review. *Sensors*, 16 (5):618.

Veresoglou, S. D., Barto, E. K., Menexes, G. and Rillig, M. C. (2000). Fertilization affects severity of disease caused by fungal plant pathogens. *Plant Pathol.* 62:961–969.

Wahabzada, M., Besser, M., Khosravani, M., Kuska, M. T., Kersting, K. et al. (2017). Monitoring wound healing in a 3D wound model by hyperspectral imaging and efficient clustering. *PLoS One* 12(12):e0186425.

Wahabzada, M., Mahlein, A. K., Bauckhage, C., Steiner, M., Oerke, E. C. and Kersting, K. (2015). Metro maps of plant disease dynamics—automated mining of differences using hyperspectral images. *PLoS One*, 10:e0116902.

Walters, D. R. and Bingham, I. J. (2007). Influence of nutrition on disease development caused by fungal pathogens: implications for plant disease control. *Ann. Appl. Biol.*, 151:307–324.

Walters, D. R., Avrova, A., Bingham, I. J., Burnett, F. J. and Fountaine, J. (2012). Control of foliar diseases in barley: towards an integrated approach. *Eur. J. Plant Pathol.*, 133:33–73.

Wang, X., Zhang, M., Zhu, J. and Geng, S. (2008). Spectral prediction of *Phytophthora infestans* infection on tomatoes using artificial neural network (ANN). *Int. J. Remote Sens.*, 29:1693–1706.

West, J. S., Bravo, C., Oberti, R., Lemaire, D., Moshou, D. and McCartney, H. A. (2003). The potential of optical canopy measurement for targeted control of field crop diseases. *Annu. Rev. Phytopathol.*, 41:593–614.

Wijekoon, C. P., Goodwin, P. H. and Hsiang, T. (2008). Quantifying fungal infection of plant leaves by digital image analysis using Scion Image software. *J. Microbiol. Methods*, 74:94–101.

Windt, C. W., Gerkema, E. and Van As, H. (2009). Most water in the tomato truss is imported through the xylem, not the phloem: a nuclear magnetic resonance flow imaging study. *Plant Physiol.*, 151:830–842.

Chapter 9

Artificial Intelligence-Aided Phenomics in High-Throughput Stress Phenotyping of Plants

Debadatta Panda[1], M. Kumar[1],
L. Mahalingam[1], and M. Raveendran[2]

[1]Department of Genetics and Plant Breeding,
CPBG, Tamil Nadu Agricultural University, Coimbatore, Tamil Nadu, India
[2]Department of Plant Biotechnology, CPMB, Tamil Nadu
Agricultural University, Coimbatore, Tamil Nadu, India

Contents

DOI: 10.1201/9781003311782-9

9.1 Introduction

For feeding the population of billions in the scenario of the shrinking area and water availability, it is essential to focus on enhancing the crop's productivity while taking sufficient care to sustain the natural resources. The crop varieties need to be armored against disease, pest incidence, and a necessary level of climate resilience to survive and perform optimally in varying climatic conditions (Kahiluoto *et al.,* 2019). For climate-resilient breeding, high-throughput phenotyping is an essential part that aims to get a large amount of data per unit time with an optimized cost. It is primarily used for large-scale automation experiments (Jin *et al.,* 2020). Connecting genotype to phenotype for enhanced understanding is still a significant obstacle, and it limits employing advanced breeding programs for getting the most out of high-throughput genomics and phenomics. For this aspect, the ability to process vast volumes of data to derive biologically meaningful conclusions is essentially required (Harfouche *et al.,* 2019).

Conventionally, breeders try different methods to filter the desirable traits from reliable sources and incorporate them in the varieties with superior agronomic background by advancing the populations for further selecting the best plant with all the superior properties to be released as varieties. For this process, getting the correct and precise phenotypic and genotypic data cost-effectively with a high level of accuracy is needed. Usually, phenotyping many traits manually is very labor-intensive and costly too. The assured accuracy of observations is impossible to judge as they are generated on a sufficiently large amount in a brief span of time. Since this data will form the basis for the upcoming work of 10 years or so and the hope for feeding the population better, anything that can aid to speed, accuracy, and reliability of data is worth investing.

Nowadays, the idea of predictive breeding is flourishing, thanks to the concepts like genomic selection and the availability of enormous genomics databases. However, polygenic control and epistatic effects of the genes cause a nonlinear relationship among genotype and phenotype. Due to an epistatic impact, the predicted product of the gene gets modified in different downstream pathways. Then, accurate phenotype becomes difficult to be detected statistically. Hence, judging plants based on phenotype and integrating them with the genotyping data are challenging to achieve. Apart from that, Yang *et al.* (2020) have also pointed out that inefficient execution field phenotyping has been the primary restricting aspect in obtaining potential gain in breeding programs.

Evaluation of the high technical demanding experiments like mutagenesis, genetically modified organisms (Blum, 2014), or genome editing also depends on the quality of phenotyping (Yang *et al.,* 2020). In general, the traditional method of phenotyping using destructive sampling cannot produce data as faster and sounds accurate as the way the omics data are produced. This shortcoming in the linking directly or indirectly affects the efficiency of plant selection and further crop improvement (Jin *et al.,* 2020). To solve the quest underlying the functionality of the genes and further use in breeding programs, access to the very detailed data from a bigger sample size is beneficial (Harfouche *et al.,* 2019). In this context, artificial intelligence (AI)-aided phenomics can undoubtedly help in getting a clearer understanding by speed and precision of the data, thus presenting a more comprehensive outlook about the relationship between genotype and phenotype.

Streich *et al.* (2020) have also suggested that AI can help in achieving the sustainable development goals of United Nations by using a multi-omics approach, AI-assisted crop ideotype designing, etc. Hence, the current chapter aims to explain the basics of AI along with the techniques and equipment based on AI in brief, and it will also throw light on how AI is helping in various aspects of stress phenotyping of plants. The content of the chapter in the upcoming section can be put in a nutshell as follows:

- Plant phenomics is the study of various attributes of the plant, basically utilizing manual observations by generating huge data with accuracy and precision of the data is often doubtful.
- Currently, AI is facilitating services in various fields of agriculture like the development of smart devices, early predictions about disease monitoring, yield assessment, and irrigation automation.
- Emerging technologies of AI have enormous potential to enhance the speed and the accuracy of data collection with high precision.
- Different AI-aided devices like imaging sensors, aerial and ground phenotyping platforms are gaining popularity in the field of plant phenomics.
- LemnaTec, WIWAM, and Phenospex are successful phenotyping platforms developed in different parts of the world.

9.2 What Is Phenomics

Phenomics is one of the omics technologies which encompasses a wide range of methodologies designed for phenotypic characterization of the plant through manual or automatic sampling by destructive or non-destructive means to derive meaningful outlooks about the organism in various aspects (Egea-Cortines & Doonan, 2018). High-throughput phenotyping aims to obtain more amounts of phenotyping data per unit cost and per unit time involved. The central prospective area of work for phenomics is for studying the morphological development of shoot, root, and leaf in terms of its behavior to specific circumstances like availability of specific growth factors, presence of various stresses, study of the photosynthetic indices, and yield prediction (Demidchik *et al.*, 2020). Most phenotyping platforms are currently working in a single domain; however, it is imperative to integrate data from multiple domains at different levels (Zhao *et al.*, 2019). The fusion of these phenomics technologies along with genomics will hasten the development of crops resilient to different climate conditions; nevertheless, these omics technologies are producing massive, mixed, and complex data at a rate far quicker than the capacity of evaluation at the moment (Harfouche *et al.*, 2019).

9.3 Why It Is Necessary to Get an Understanding of the Phenotypes

Selecting the plants with better yield, quality, or taste and further raising them have been practiced since time immemorial. According to Fiorani and Schurr (2013), phenotyping is the process by which the different characteristics of the organism are assessed from cellular level to whole-plant level, starting from how it looks its size, the shape of different parts to every other aspect, which ultimately defines that organism. The observed phenotype usually is the interplay of the genotype and the environment where it is present (Pieruschka and Poorter, 2012). It helps in a comprehensive understanding of the object investigated. A genotype is a collection of hereditary features, whereas a phenotype is a collection of quantifiable or observable characteristics (Gjuvsland *et al.*, 2013). Flexibility in the growth condition of the plants enables a single genotype that can express different phenotypes. As a result, a crop's performance can be understood as a manifestation of genetic background, necessitating a study of the phenotypic-genetic link (Houle *et al.*, 2010). In this perspective, the emerging sector of AI has enormous scope to join this link by speeding up the process. The science and technology of AI are explained in a more detailed way in the subsequent parts of the chapter.

9.4 Artificial Intelligence

AI is the modeling of human intellectual knowledge such as visual processing, voice recognition, decision-making, and language processing in digital platforms and trained to imagine, interpret the situation, and behave like humans in learning and problem-solving. AI is swiftly becoming prevalent due to its excellent usefulness in situations that cannot be addressed well by the people or traditional computing architectures and its rapid technological improvement and wide range of applications

(Rich and Knight, 1991). Several approaches have been proposed to aid and overcome the current difficulties in phenotyping plants in agriculture, ranging from managing databases (Martiniello, 1988) to decision support systems (Thorpe *et al.*, 1992) from time to time. Systems employing AI have shown to be outstanding performers in terms of effectiveness and reliability among these solutions. Capturing the intricacies of each problem using the AI approach can offer a more acceptable answer for it and has become much convenient (Bannerjee *et al.*, 2018).

9.4.1 History of AI in Agriculture

McKinion and Lemmon first discussed employing AI techniques in crop production and supervision in the article "Expert Systems for Agriculture" (McKinion and Lemmon, 1985) in 1985. For managing apple plantations, Roach and his team designed the POMME expert system in 1987 (Roach *et al.*, 1987). The COTFLEX system (Stone and Toman, 1989) by Stone and Toman and the COMAX system by Lemmon were designed for cotton crop management (Lemmon, 1990). During that concurrent time, an artificial neural network with several layers was devised to safeguard the lemon crop against cold damage (Robinson and Mort, 1997). Since then, AI has been spreading in different areas of agriculture and will enter newer areas in days to come.

9.4.2 Artificial Intelligence in Different Areas of Agriculture

Considering its quick scientific growth and a broad spectrum of potential utilities, AI has turned out to be one of the exciting and eye-catching areas of research in software engineering. AI's core concept in agriculture lies in better adaptability, high speed, precision, and cost-effectiveness (Eli-Chukwu, 2019). AI also assists farmers in using their farming knowledge, and helps in changing the approach to directed farming to achieve larger yields and better quality with minimal resource use (Khandelwal and Chavhan, 2019). AI-based systems assist farmers in enhancing efficiency in all sectors and management challenges faced during crop harvesting, irrigation, and other agricultural services, sensitivity to composition of the soil, surveillance of the crops, and pest management (Sujawat, 2021). Its sensors can even detect and identify weeds in agriculture as well as recognize crop ailments, various infestations, or nutritional status. With the assistance of machine learning (ML) along with deep learning (DL),

AI may indeed deliver an efficient plus realistic solution for future progress (Murugesan *et al.*, 2019).

9.4.3 Classes of AI

Despite the fact that first-generation AI has been employed to explore as well as categorize omics outputs, and is being applied to survey as well as categorize omics outputs, it is equipped to handle activities in single omics data sets rather than multiple omics data available. Next-generation AI has the potential to alter the nature of experiment planning, leading to greater data acquisition, assessment, and getting better insight out of the data (Harfouche *et al.*, 2019). By limiting environmental deterioration, AI can solve various problems while protecting our valuable resources (Sujawat, 2021).

9.4.4 Fields of AI in the Agricultural Sector

As per the review by Sujawat (2021), AI has a vast potential for use in agriculture. The various paradigms of use of AI for different purposes in agriculture are summarized below.

9.4.4.1 Use of Internet of Things (IoT) in Agriculture

In agriculture, IoT provides farmers with decision-making tools and smart devices that smoothly connect the crop production, information, and service systems intended for increased productivity, reliability, and higher return.

9.4.4.2 Graphical Information Acquisition and Interpretation

Aerial photography is taken using drones that aid crop surveillance and overall detailing of the field. When this platform gets combined with imaging technology and the IoT, it ensures quick and effective completion of the operations.

9.4.4.3 Disease Detection

The crop images are divided into surface areas such as the background of the crop and diseased leaf areas using image sensing and analysis. Then, the contaminated or sick region is worked out and sent to a laboratory for further analysis.

9.4.4.4 Expert System

The necessity of expert systems in the transmission of technical data across agricultural systems may be appreciated by assessing the challenges in the current knowledge dissemination system and proving that expert systems may assist in overcoming those challenges and are likely to improve.

9.4.4.5 Field Management

Using extremely detailed photographs from drone and copter systems, the concurrent assessment may be done throughout the cultivation cycle, mapping details of the entire crop and detecting spots where which particular input supplementation is required.

9.4.4.6 Robotics in Agriculture

Agribot or Agbot, a type of agricultural robot, assists the farmer in increasing crop efficiency while minimizing the need for manual labor. Agricultural robots are expected to handle the tilling, sowing, and harvesting processes automatically in the future.

9.4.4.7 Advancement in Irrigation System

Devices equipped with AI trained with prior meteorological trends, growing area, in addition to detailed information regarding crop varieties grown could help in the automation of irrigation and enhancement of total production, allowing farmers to better manage their water issues.

9.4.4.8 Crop Health Monitoring

Crop metrics can be constructed for vast tracts of cultivable land using imaging in hyperspectral range apart from systems like 3D laser scanning.

Some successful application models of AI have been further summarized in Table 9.1. As the table denotes, various AI-based systems have been developed and employed for different processes in agriculture. In cotton, for aiding in crop management, a system like COTFLEX and COMAX was developed. Dr. Wheat and TEAPEST are tools used in wheat and tea, respectively, for disease diagnosis and management of pest attacks. Similarly, a soil moisture analysis system has been developed in paddy which symbolizes another successful use of AI in agriculture.

9.5 Stress Phenotyping and Artificial Intelligence: In Duo

Stress phenotyping deals with the study of all the aspects of the plant characteristics observable under stress conditions for facilitating a better understanding of the basis of the stress on the plant and its ultimate impact on the economic parameters. Given that the crop plants are affected by many types of biotic or abiotic stresses, in turn, affecting their growth and performance, faster and detailed stress phenotyping is the need of the hour. Commonly, it is observed by calculating various indices for different stresses, data collection by imaging, further processing to get a broader idea about the impact of particular stress on the plant. This information forms the basis for the selection of elite plants with a better ability to combat stress. Phenotyping at greater dynamic resolutions of tissue and cellular scales is more tedious than whole-plant phenotyping methods (Hall *et al.*, 2016). The processing of samples to unveil the crop micro-phenotypes is time-consuming and complicated, with several steps (Zhao *et al.*, 2019). Again, dealing with a larger population in segregating generations of crops needs much more accuracy since all the plants

Table 9.1   AI in Diverse Domains of Agriculture

Purpose	AI-Based System	Crop	Reference
Crop management	COTFLEX	Cotton	Stone and Toman, 1989
Crop management	COMAX	Cotton	Lemmon, 1986
Crop management	POMME	Apple	Roach et al., 1987
Frost damage	–	Citrus	Robinson and Mort,1997
Crop management, pest related issues	–	Soybean	Prakash et al., 2013
Pest management	SMARTSOY		Batchelor et al., 1989 Batchelor et al., 1992
Pest management	IPEST	–	Van Der Werf and Zimmer, 1998
Pest management	TEAPEST	Tea	Ghosh and Samanta, 2003
Pest management	Redesigned TEAPEST	Tea	Samanta and Ghosh, 2012
Diagnosis of wheat diseases	Dr. Wheat	Wheat	Khan et al., 2008
Soil water content determination	–	Paddy	Arif et al., 2013

in that population are a unique representation of themselves; any mistake in their phenotyping will cause a potential loss in the future.

AI intervention in agriculture assists farmers in regaining their farming efficiency and reducing harmful environmental influences (Saxena *et al.*, 2020). Disease and the resulting loss not only degrade the quantity but also reduce the quality of the produce. Farmers must be equipped with the latest technology and procedures to get the highest yield from their crops. AI has an extended range of applications in a variety of fields (Salam, 2020). Due to its ability to recognize and reason the problems and establish practical solutions, AI can be a massive help to farming (Sujawat, 2021).

9.6 Phenotyping Interventions in Various Stages of Crop Improvement

At different dimensions ranging from cell to canopy, crop phenotyping strives to correctly and precisely obtain attributes connected to plant growth condition, level of production, and vulnerability to biotic and abiotic stress (Fiorani and Schurr, 2013).

The main goal of high-throughput phenotyping is simultaneous evaluation of the multiple traits on a large scale at various developmental stages. For achieving this goal, there is a need for scientists and experts from different backgrounds like crop breeding, electronic engineering, molecular biology, data science, statistics, and agronomy to come together and work together for the further sustainable development of the phenotyping process. Unmanned aerial vehicles (UAVs), robotics, and remotely operated devices are used in the available crop phenotyping platforms for monitoring crop growth stage and performance. These devices are equipped with various sensors and image processing and analysis technology (Jin *et al.*, 2020).

9.7 Components of AI Used in Phenotyping

9.7.1 Sensors

Sensors are of different types based on the level of working – leaf level, near-canopy level, and airborne sensor working in aerial level. Airborne sensors include RGB, multispectral, hyperspectral, and thermal camera, whereas near-crop sensors include stereo cameras and LIDAR. Photosynthesis and fluorescence sensors are leaf-level instruments (Jin *et al.*, 2020).

9.7.1.1 Photosynthetic Sensors

These produce image outputs and hence cannot be used with the ground or aerial imaging platforms (Kose *et al.*, 2022), e.g. Li-COR. Further development of quick, image-based sensors can help researchers comprehend the photosynthetic sensitivity to environmental changes in a more efficient way.

9.7.1.2 Fluorescence Sensors

Fluorescence signals act best under uniform light availability showing greater activity starting UV range to near-infrared (Zhou *et al.*, 2018). This forms two types of signals in the color spectrum based on a multicolor fluorescence photographic concept (Chaerle and Van Der Straeten, 2001). They are frequently employed to assess a crop's metabolic resiliency under stressful situations (Thoren and Schmidhalter, 2009). The fluorescence sensor generates an image that can investigate the variation of leaf photosynthetic status in different regions and detect early signs of crop stress caused by diseases and pests (Fang and Ramasamy, 2015). Here at a time, four different color bands can be seen from a single wavelength of light, e.g. Plant Explorer. Fluorescence sensors are currently used at the level of leaves. Sensor and background noise limit chlorophyll fluorescence on the canopy, lowering the proportion of noise in the received signal (Fahlgren *et al.*, 2015). The availability of better fluorescence sensors will certainly improve the field applications of these tools in the future.

9.7.1.3 Stereo Cameras

These are equipped with multiple lenses and distinct sensors (Li *et al.*, 2016). Structures of single plants are observed in 3D at a meager cost. Its significant drawbacks are poor spatial resolution, sensitivity to changing external lighting conditions, and difficulty determining canopy-level features in the field (Biskup *et al.*, 2007). Still, the resolution, as well as illumination of the stereo cameras, is needed to be refined further in the future.

9.7.1.4 RGB Cameras

RGB cameras are affordable devices that capture bands in red, green, and blue colors (Jin *et al.*, 2017), providing very informative and sharper aerial images (Zhang *et al.*, 2020). A computer-based image that closely resembles human sight perception portrays characters like the density of the plant, level of compactness of ear, the extent of coverage of canopy, the height of the plant, amount of leaf rolling, angle of the leaf, level of lodging, along with other phenotypic characteristics. These qualities acquired by an RGB camera enhance the understanding of the crop. One of its shortcomings is the availability of color information and gray values only in three visual spectral bands (Araus and Cairns, 2014). However, overlapping leaves cause trouble getting decent picture segmentation results (Geipel *et al.*, 2016).

9.7.1.5 Multi- and Hyperspectral Cameras

The interplay amidst sun rays with the crop is the basis for multispectral and hyperspectral cameras (Araus and Cairns, 2014). Moreover, they have several bands in the visible and infrared spectra. Hyperspectral cameras have been shown to have a better spectral resolution (Jay *et al.*, 2017), combined with more sensitivity to minor variations in leaf pigments like carotenoids and chlorophyll (Zarco-Tejada *et al.*, 2018). It can calculate parameters such as compactness of plant, the extent of coverage of canopy, stay-green trait, crop surveillance, various infections, and infestation of insect and pathogens throughout the crop season. Vegetative index-based parameters, like photosynthetic state and fluorescence, are primarily measured with multispectral cameras. With the availability of spectral information, this system allows merging data of GPS for multiple images to derive more useful information (Jin *et al.*, 2020).

9.7.1.6 Thermal Cameras

For detecting water stress experienced by the plants, these cameras are employed. It works in the thermal spectrum by computing radiation with infrared wavelength (Zarco-Tejada *et al.*, 2008). Spatial patterns derived from thermal pictures are used to carry out image segmentation that distinguishes stressed from unstressed plants.

Thermal cameras are more expensive than multispectral cameras. Light-weight forms of the camera are more likely to become thermally unsteady because of the changing exterior conditions (Jones *et al.*, 2009). These cameras are suitable to be used for imaging at both grounds and different heights after being mounted on the platforms. These are primarily utilized to record the growth of the plant, illness, stress, and temperature sensitivity faced by the plants. With the wide spectrum of this camera, the assessment of temperature at canopy level, parameters concerning water stress, deficiencies, and extent of lodging have become quite amenable (Baluja *et al.*, 2012, Calderón *et al.*, 2013, Calderón *et al.*, 2015, Kelly *et al.*, 2019). The major challenge is improving plant phenotyping traits' functionality and assessment accuracy by combining image information from different optical sensors.

9.7.1.7 Examples of the High-Throughput Sensors Available

a. **Li-COR**

Li-COR is a system through which net photosynthesis is calculated by analyzing CO_2 uptake, the conductance of water, CO_2 concentration inside the cell, temperature, and humidity parameters (Arfan *et al.*, 2007). These parameters are used for crop growth analysis and gaseous exchanges studies.

b. **Plant Explorer**

Plant Explorer system includes parameters like the level of fluorescence at initial condition, level of maximum fluorescence, the efficiency of conversion of light to energy, and amount of quantum yield generated (Steele, 2004). Crop stress assessments, photosynthetic functions, and chloroplast content projections can be made using these parameters (Buschmann *et al.*, 2000).

c. **LIDAR**

LIDAR is a geo-observation system that specifically gets the three-dimensional coordinates of particular object surface that focuses through information like positions, distances, and angles (Guo *et al.*, 2016) with an accuracy level up to a millimeter with less influence of the environmental fluctuations. LIDAR captures one object distinct from another utilizing beam of laser light (Thapa *et al.*, 2018), and time between signal emission and return is used to calculate the distance. The LIDAR system in combination with platforms both at ground level and different heights has also been developed for enhanced usability (Jimenez-Berni *et al.*, 2018). However, to characterize 3D crop structures properly, the amount of possible 3D point clouds should be enhanced in the future.

9.7.2 Aerial Phenotyping Platforms

Micro Air Vehicles (MAVs) along with UAVs and nanosatellites are effective forms of aerial phenotyping devices that give high-spatial-resolution photos of the plants at varying heights (Tattaris *et al.*, 2016, Chapman *et al.*, 2012). Swift flying with excellent efficiency even at high altitudes is indeed a major advantage of fixed-wing UAVs. Another class of multi-rotor UAVs can hover (can stay at a particular space in the air) and have low takeoff and landing requirements with slower speed, limited endurance duration (Zhang and Kovacs, 2012).

The benefit of UAVs is the significantly higher-resolution photographs that can be obtained in a short period; yet, owing to the vehicles' limited range and speed, it is challenging to cover vast areas. However, MAVs can cover more extensive areas in a shorter amount of time with a lesser image resolution.

Micro/nanosatellites offer information from the various spectra and they show high sensitivity toward field architecture, green pigmentation, and moisture content. Optical satellites (e.g. *QuickBird* and *RapidEye*) and synthetic aperture radar (SAR) satellites (e.g. *ENVISAT* and *RADARSAT*) are different classes of micro/nanosatellites used for phenotyping for large-scale phenotyping.

9.7.3 Ground Phenotyping Platforms

9.7.3.1 Phenopoles

Phenopoles are poles constructed of aluminum, plastic, or other materials; these equipment carry required sensors directly while the field data is collected. Out of two types of phenopoles, fixed peoples are similar to field weather stations; here, the RGB sensor placed at a particular height on the pole captures photos and is sent at particular time intervals to a server (Araus *et al.*, 2018), e.g. PhenoCam. The compactness of plants in the field, canopy coverage, flowering time, and other parameters are measured using fixed and mobile phenopoles.

9.7.3.2 Phenomobile

Because of their proximity to ground level (1–3 m), mobile phenopoles are manually handled and operated using wireless data or mobile phones, allowing for higher-resolution photos. However, gathering photographs for the field requires manpower. Phenomobiles are self-driving, human-driven, and tractor-driven vehicles. Different sensors, GPS systems, panel controlling navigation, and a system for data collection along reliable supply systems of power are all standard components of an automatic phenomobile (Comar *et al.*, 2012).

9.7.4 Machine Learning

Conventional informatics is ineffective in interpreting the massive amounts of graphical data generated by phenotyping process through modern high-quality sensors. The approach of ML overcomes these limitations.

Advanced image analysis approaches strive to extract meaningful data straight from raw images and train the recognition algorithms, predict outcomes when the data is being collected, and essentially explain the constituents of the image in detail (Zhang *et al.*, 2017). This aspect of phenotyping is solved by another tool of AI called ML.

To comprehend the data, ML employs statistics, probabilistic reasoning, visualization, and optimization. The learning opportunity is created by providing a platform that boosts the level of perfection of estimates gradually with the passage of time predicted upon previous outcomes. It is instrumental in situations where the data structure and patterns of linkages are not understood ahead of time.

Efficient, dependable, and versatile software tools like R-packages, MATLAB toolkits, Theano, and Caffe are now available, thanks to recent technological advancements (Bau and Cardé, 2016, Chu *et al.*, 2013). It has made features like facial recognition systems, speech processing, and language recognition readily available in a user-friendly manner in general fields but yet to be fully actualized in agriculture. They are used for annotating the genomes. Convolution neural networks have been successfully employed for locating and characterizing the features of disease damage on maize leaves (DeChant *et al.*, 2017), and forecasting the strength and development of leaf chlorosis because of iron deficit (Bai *et al.*, 2018).

9.8 General Workflow of Stress Phenotyping by AI

The use of AI starts from photographing the object to further processing it to ultimately deliver much more information than as obtained by a manual analysis in a particular time. The generalized workflow as derived from Sujawat (2021) is explained further.

9.8.1 Image Acquisition

The sample plan imaging is done with various photographic sensors placed in-ground or areal platforms, and these images are read using MATLAB software.

9.8.2 Image Pre-Processing

Here, the background noise surrounding the object is removed, and scaling different images is done to bring them to a particular pixel size for further processing.

9.8.3 Image Segmentation

Image segmentation annotates pixels or photographs into groups or classes based on similarity and dissimilarity in the areas. It is applied for labeling the image by AI rather than intensive manual work.

9.8.4 Extraction of Feature

It is a method leading to dimensionality reduction, the way to reduce the initially available massive data into smaller sizes, focusing on essential features of the image or data. It brings out the most crucial feature by selecting and combining the variables. Features like color, texture, and morphology are used for the identification of the particular stress.

9.8.5 Detection and Classification of Stress

In this stage, finally, the stresses are identified and further processed through DL technique-based models (like Convolutional Neural Network (CNN)) and correlated with the previously available data sets for comparison and the newly generated data is then added to the storage system.

9.9 Application of AI Techniques in the Agricultural Sector

9.9.1 Image Processing

Image processing is a method used to measure the affected area by disease and helps find differences in the color of the affected area. The surveys show detection of disease by using image processing (Ganatra and Patel, 2018). An introduction of a robot in agriculture that detects the leaf disease using image processing is explained (Kumar and Vani, 2018).

9.9.2 Machine Learning

ML AI application has been effectively made in the present world for disease diagnosis. ML algorithms are quick and precise in detecting many diseases. Using ML, publicly available massive data sets can be processed, providing a better way to identify diseases in plants on a massive scale (Ramesh *et al.*, 2018). Algorithms based on this system can be utilized to identify and categorize diseases of different crops (Tripathi and Maktedar, 2016).

9.9.3 Deep Learning

It helps in detecting crucial correlations among various aspects of the data. In the case of human medicine, it learns the data concerning presently available patients which apids in disease detection process of upcoming patients with similar complaints (Mishra *et al.*, 2021). In case of plants, the DL-aided disease detection model has the ability to conquer the dynamics of the environment and enhance the accuracy of identification (Guo *et al.*, 2020).

9.9.4 Convolutional Neural Networks (CNNs)

These help in the process of image recognition and can provide a prompt and definite diagnosis (Sujawat, 2021, Zarco-Tejada *et al.*, 2019).

9.9.5 Expert System

Expert systems in agriculture can help in integrated crop management, irrigation, nutritional disorders, fertilizer application, and weed control (Sujawat, 2021, Ganesan, 2004).

9.10 Application of AI Platforms in Phenotyping Different Stresses

9.10.1 Nitrogen Stress

Nitrogen deficit condition causes lower chlorophyll content, slower growth, lesser photosynthesis, and increased susceptibility to diseases and pests (DeTurk, 1941). The stress is tracked using near-infrared and visible spectral reflectance sensors and cameras mounted on UAVs or phenomobiles (Schmidhalter *et al.*, 2003, Barmeier & Schmidhalter., 2017). These technologies, when used together, can identify stress early.

9.10.2 Water Stress

Underwater stress, stomata close, crop growth, and photosynthesis are affected. Again, transpirational cooling also varies from normal. All these parameters are drastically reduced on intensifying crop heat stress (Sankaran *et al.*, 2015). The temperature of the crop at canopy level is also a valuable indication of a crop's response toward limited water availability and subsequent stress caused by it (Jackson *et al.*, 1977) and the selection of suitable cultivars for the concerned situation (Winterhalter *et al.*, 2011, Thompson *et al.*, 2018, Chapman *et al.*, 2014, Jones *et al.*, 2009).

Compared to ground-based techniques, the use of thermal cameras in combination with UAVs and mobile platforms capture faster images concerning crop temperature at different levels (Tattaris *et al.*, 2016). It may aid in the selection of water-stress-resistant genotypes. Apart from near-infrared sensors, other sensors in the visible spectrum also aid in evaluating water stress (Gutierrez *et al.*, 2010).

Thermal, multispectral, and hyperspectral cameras can provide quantitative and qualitative data sets for selecting water-stress-resistant genotypes. These technologies will encourage high-throughput, non-destructive sensors in the field to estimate crop phenotyping traits.

9.10.3 Diseases

Globally, techniques like remote sensing are widely used to have a forecast on disease epidemics (Li *et al.*, 2016) and monitor emerging outbreaks (Zarco-Tejada *et al.*, 2018). To diagnose blight infestation in potatoes, Nebiker *et al.* (2016) employed NDVI index values derived from multispectral pictures. Optical sensors working close to the ground (such as hyperspectral, RGB, and thermal cameras) are used for crop stress profiling especially for the diseases (Sankaran *et al.*, 2013, Yamamoto *et al.*, 2017); this has been experimentally validated for Huanglongbing (HLB) disease with great accuracy in the citrus crop. Experiments in different crops such as tomato and sugar beet have clearly shown that disease prevalence and crop variety's resistance to infection can be accurately predicted using UAV-based sensors near the ground. In comparison to other devices, the fluorescence sensors proved more productive to detect crop diseases. It could be combined with hyperspectral, multispectral, RGB, and thermal cameras to detect crop disease severity early.

9.10.4 Lodging

Crop lodging is defined as a crop plant's permanent displacement from its upright position (Pinthus, 1974). It affects the harvest operation and reduces the yield and quality of the produce (Fischer and Stapper, 1987). Changes in crop structure (Hosoi and Omasa, 2012), biochemical characteristics (Baret *et al.*, 2007), and morphology (Murakami *et al.*, 2012) in the lodging situation alter reflectance and light backscatter at different wavelengths. Starting from the use of linear polarization from backscatter (Fitch *et al.*, 1984) to the motor-driven camera (Ogden *et al.*, 2002), hyperspectral sensors (Liu *et al.*, 2011), RGB sensors (Liu *et al.*, 2018), and UAV-mounted thermal cameras (Chapman *et al.*, 2014). RADAR-mounted satellite images (Yang *et al.*, 2015) have been used to detect the lodging in various scales in crops like wheat and rice.

9.11 Successful Phenotyping Platforms across the World

Devices for automatic weighing, watering, illumination, and maintaining a microenvironment; sensors for tracking well-being and cycle passage; digital surveillance systems for various processes; platforms for calibrating and shifting the sample plants; navigation systems; structures for automatic measurement of weight, watering, brightness, and information storage and processing, as well as infrastructure and software for more in-depth picture analysis using machine vision and learning systems are available. Some platforms are highly specialized, such as DIRT or SmartGrain, and platforms with a broader scope (LemnaTec or PSI lines). The gathering of valuable data together, characterizing the phenotype's morphological and physiological properties and their analysis and visualization interpretation, is the foundation of phenotyping platforms' operation.

Using ground-penetrating radars (GPRs) and electromagnetic soil inductance systems, mapping of intra-soil conductivity has been conducted in a nondestructive method. This process assembled a clearer picture of root propagation and underlying soil structures (Sandhu *et al.*, 2018). LemnaTec and Heinz Walz from Germany along with other platforms like Photon Systems Instruments from the Czech Republic, Qubit Phenomics from Canada, Phenomics from France, and Phenospex from Australia are the successful phenotyping platforms, to name a few.

9.11.1 LemnaTec

This is one of the world's biggest manufacturers of platforms for various processes of phenotyping. These have enclosed labs, greenhouses, open trial venues, field settings, and aerial platforms under construction. An approach for documenting injury in sugar beet crops apart from soybean leaves for the impact of weedicide chemicals was also devised with its assistance (Weber *et al.*, 2017). A novel technique for regulating the water status in cereals was established using the Phenocenter platform (Fahlgren *et al.*, 2015). A technique for evaluating the efficacy of photosynthesis for the major classes of higher plants was developed (Cabrera-Bosquet *et al.*, 2016). Perhaps for the first time, a system like LemnaTec Scanalyzer FIELD explains the phenotypic expressions for many genes and correlates their role in phenomena like photosynthesis, respiratory process, resistance against different stresses, and architectural development of the shoot (Cendrero-Mate *et al.*, 2017).

9.11.2 Photon Systems Instruments (PSI) Platforms

These are developed in a scalable way to cater to the requirements of each scientific investigation. PSI's camera and sensor manufacturing is a standout feature. It also showcases mobile platforms such as autonomous tractors, unmanned aerophenomics complexes, and one-of-a-kind in-sea containers. Using PSI equipment, Mishra *et al.* (2014) demonstrated that the fluorescence of chlorophyll in the leaves of higher plants could be a signal of water scarcity.

9.11.3 WIWAM

WIWAM XY system, a product of WIWAM, is recently utilized by Skirycz *et al.* (2011) to illustrate the reduction in growth, which can act as a tool for enhancing biomass production in stress conditions. Clauw et al. (2015) discovered the response pattern of Arabidopsis ecotypes to drought.

9.12 National and International Agencies Working in Artificial Intelligence Research in Agriculture

USDA National Institute of Food and Agriculture, in collaboration with the National Science Foundation, has laid out a plan for establishing Artificial Intelligence Research Institute to form an infrastructure potential to carry out research ahead. Agriculture and Food Research Initiative (AFRI) Foundational and Applied Science also provide funding for the various research projects (National Institute of Food and Agriculture, 2020). International Crops Research Institute for the Semi-Arid Tropics (ICRISAT) and Microsoft in collaboration have developed an AI-enabled sowing app that provides information to farmers on the date of sowing, fertilizer recommendation based on soil testing, and seed treatment (InsightIAS, 2019). FAMWES (Fall Armyworm Monitoring and Early Warning System) is a mobile application working across Sub-Saharan Africa along with parts of Asia. This app uses an AI tool called PlantVillage, which helps recognize fall armyworm attack-related information and advice (FAO, 2018).

9.13 Status of AI Innovations for Agriculture in India

In India, in June 2020, the Indian Government unveiled India's AI, a specialized AI portal built jointly by MeitY and NASSCOM, which is expected to serve as a primary center for all AI-related projects and advances in India. Govt. of India has taken the schemes and initiatives like National Mission on Natural Language Translation, Atal Innovation Mission, Digital India, and National Skill Development Mission (NSDM) for uplifting the research in the sector of AI (IndiaAI, https://indiaai. gov.in/initiatives). Niti Ayog, Govt. of India has formed a "National Strategy for Artificial Intelligence" in 2018, focusing on leveraging the revolutionary technologies and implementing AI in health, agriculture, and education (Niti Ayog, 2018).

9.14 Advantages of Using AI in Stress Phenotyping

Root phenotyping for various stresses has become amenable with the use of AI. Set-up like Rhizotron has made the study of roots and underground environment interactions more amenable and fast for further experiment. Accurate judgment of yield parameters is possible with AI use, which has dramatically broadened the selection scope. The advent of ML approaches has enhanced the pace of predictive breeding approaches like genomic selection. It has also opened avenues for discovering and validating new traits in wild forms and wild relative crop plants to form new material for pre-breeding. The data gathered from the platforms will also aid in genomic studies to derive more meaningful conclusions.

9.15 Opportunities and Prospects for AI in Plant Breeding

While advances in high-throughput crop phenotyping technologies have continued, additional development opens a new path for more precise estimations of most crop phenotyping features. Sophisticated sensors, combined with superior ground and aerial phenotyping platforms, have led to a considerable need for advanced phenotyping and image processing with higher accuracy levels. Since field environmental circumstances frequently influence plant phenotyping sensors, more robust and refined crop phenotyping sensors are required for field crop phenotyping studies. The majority of sensors and platforms used for phenotyping are very costly and difficult to afford in regular breeding programs. Nevertheless, with the fast advancements in the production of minute sensors, various cost-effective and potent sensors are now available for use. Combining the data output from different camera sensors will give much more insights into the trait concerned. With the availability of economic, highly informative genotyping facilities, crop phenotyping approaches and subsequent methods of study and interpretation of data need to be upgraded further. More research interventions are needed to simulate models for predictive breeding for dealing with various stresses.

9.16 Conclusion

Agriculture has been the backbone of society since time immemorial, and it will continue to do so for eternity. Various revolutionary discoveries gradually made the world a civilized one, and agriculture is not an exception. In the process of trying to harvest goods and breed superior, our farmers and scientists have faced huge setbacks from the various stresses. Albeit earlier scientists succeeded in isolating plant types through phenotypic observations, complexity in understanding quantitative traits necessitates the aids from IoT/AI. Especially from a breeder's perspective, predicting the stress and its outcomes is highly challenging and the response of plants to various types of stresses is difficult to understand. There is some literature available to show that different varieties behave differently for varied stresses. The emerging technology of AI has a significant role in this regard. It has already started sprinkling its magic on omics research, whether genomics, phenomics, or applied sections like predictive breeding. Again, it can also be stated that all the developments of AI in stress breeding and phenotyping are in budding condition only; much more development is awaited in the future. Synergized efforts from engineering and biological sciences can certainly materialize this goal. With reasonable endeavor and innovation, AI will undoubtedly bring a brighter horizon for stress breeding.

References

Araus, J. L., & Cairns, J. E. (2014). Field high-throughput phenotyping: the new crop breeding frontier. *Trends in Plant Science, 19*(1), 52–61.

Araus, J. L., Kefauver, S. C., Zaman-Allah, M., Olsen, M. S., & Cairns, J. E. (2018). Translating high-throughput phenotyping into genetic gain. *Trends in Plant Science, 23*(5), 451–466.

Arif, C., Mizoguchi, M., & Setiawan, B. I. (2013). Estimation of soil moisture in paddy field using artificial neural networks. *arXiv preprint arXiv`1303.1868*.

Arfan, M., Athar, H. R., & Ashraf, M. (2007). Does exogenous application of salicylic acid through the rooting medium modulate growth and photosynthetic capacity in two differently adapted spring wheat cultivars under salt stress?. *Journal of Plant Physiology, 164*(6), 685–694.

Bai, G., Jenkins, S., Yuan, W., Graef, G. L., & Ge, Y. (2018). Field-based scoring of soybean iron deficiency chlorosis using RGB imaging and statistical learning. *Frontiers in Plant Science, 9*, 1002.

Baker, D. N., Lambert, J. R., & McKinion, J. M. (1983). GOSSYM: A simulator of cotton crop growth and yield. *South Carolina. Agricultural Experiment Station. Technical Bulletin (USA)*.

Baluja, J., Diago, M. P., Balda, P., Zorer, R., Meggio, F., Morales, F., & Tardaguila, J. (2012). Assessment of vineyard water status variability by thermal and multispectral imagery using an unmanned aerial vehicle (UAV). *Irrigation Science, 30*(6), 511–522.

Bannerjee, G., Sarkar, U., Das, S., & Ghosh, I. (2018). Artificial intelligence in agriculture: a literature survey. *International Journal of Scientific Research in Computer Science Applications and Management Studies, 7*(3), 1–6.

Baret, F., Houlès, V., & Guerif, M. (2007). Quantification of plant stress using remote sensing observations and crop models: the case of nitrogen management. *Journal of Experimental Botany, 58*(4), 869–880.

Barmeier, G., Mistele, B., & Schmidhalter, U. (2016). Referencing laser and ultrasonic height measurements of barley cultivars by using a herbometre as standard. *Crop and Pasture Science, 67*(12), 1215–1222.

Barmeier, G., & Schmidhalter, U. (2017). High-throughput field phenotyping of leaves, leaf sheaths, culms and ears of spring barley cultivars at anthesis and dough ripeness. *Frontiers in Plant Science, 8*, 1920.

Batchelor, W. D., McClendon, R. W., Adams, D. B., & Jones, J. W. (1989). Evaluation of SMARTSOY: an expert simulation system for insect pest management. *Agricultural Systems, 31*(1), 67–81.

Batchelor, W. D., McClendon, R. W., & Wetzstein, M. E. (1992). Knowledge engineering approaches in developing expert simulation systems. *Computers and Electronics in Agriculture, 7*(2), 97–107.

Bau, J., & Cardé, R. T. (2016). Simulation modeling to interpret the captures of moths in pheromone-baited traps used for surveillance of invasive species: the gypsy moth as a model case. *Journal of Chemical Ecology, 42*(9), 877–887.

Biskup, B., Scharr, H., Schurr, U., & Rascher, U. W. E. (2007). A stereo imaging system for measuring structural parameters of plant canopies. *Plant, Cell & Environment, 30*(10), 1299–1308.

Blum, A. (2014). Genomics for drought resistance–getting down to earth. *Functional Plant Biology, 41*(11), 1191–1198.

Buschmann, C., Langsdorf, G., & Lichtenthaler, H. K. (2000). Imaging of the blue, green, and red fluorescence emission of plants: an overview. *Photosynthetica, 38*(4), 483–491.

Cabrera-Bosquet, L., Fournier, C., Brichet, N., Welcker, C., Suard, B., & Tardieu, F. (2016). High-throughput estimation of incident light, light interception and radiation use efficiency of thousands of plants in a phenotyping platform. *New Phytologist, 212*(1), 269–281.

Calderón, R., Navas-Cortés, J. A., Lucena, C., & Zarco-Tejada, P. J. (2013). High-resolution airborne hyperspectral and thermal imagery for early detection of Verticillium wilt of olive using fluorescence, temperature, and narrow-band spectral indices. *Remote Sensing of Environment, 139*, 231–245.

Calderón, R., Navas-Cortés, J. A., & Zarco-Tejada, P. J. (2015). Early detection and quantification of Verticillium wilt in olive using hyperspectral and thermal imagery over large areas. *Remote Sensing, 7*(5), 5584–5610.

Caus, M., & Dascaliuc, A. (2013). Seasonal dynamics of soluble peroxidase in Buxussempervirens L. leaves. *Vytauto Didžiojouniversiteto Botanikossodoraštai*, 2013, t. 17, 80–90.

Cendrero-Mateo, M. P., Muller, O., Albrecht, H., Burkart, A., Gatzke, S., Janssen, B., …, & Rascher, U. (2017). Field phenotyping: concepts and examples to quantify dynamic plant traits across scales in the field. In *Terrestrial Ecosystem Research Infrastructures* (pp. 53–81). CRC Press, Boca Raton.

Chaerle, L., & Van Der Straeten, D. (2001). Seeing is believing: imaging techniques to monitor plant health. *Biochimicaet Biophysica Acta (BBA) – Gene Structure and Expression, 1519*(3), 153–166.

Chapman, S. C., Merz, T., Chan, A., Jackway, P., Hrabar, S., Dreccer, M. F., …, & Jimenez-Berni, J. (2014). Pheno-copter: a low-altitude, autonomous remote-sensing robotic helicopter for high-throughput field-based phenotyping. *Agronomy, 4*(2), 279–301.

Chapman, A., Mesbahi, M., Valavanis, K. P., & Vachtsevanos, G. J. (2012). UAV swarms: models and effective interfaces. *Handbook of Unmanned Aerial Vehicles*, pp. 1987–2019. Springer Publishing Company, Incorporated

Chu, K. W., Lee, W. S., Cheng, C. Y., Huang, C. F., Zhao, F., Lee, L. S., …, & Tsai, M. J. (2013). Demonstration of lateral IGBTs in 4H-SiC. *IEEE Electron Device Letters, 34*(2), 286–288.

Clauw, P., Coppens, F., De Beuf, K., Dhondt, S., Van Daele, T., Maleux, K., …, & Inzé, D. (2015). Leaf responses to mild drought stress in natural variants of Arabidopsis. *Plant Physiology, 167*(3), 800–816.

Comar, A., Burger, P., de Solan, B., Baret, F., Daumard, F., & Hanocq, J. F. (2012). A semi-automatic system for high throughput phenotyping wheat cultivars in-field conditions: description and first results. *Functional Plant Biology, 39*(11), 914–924.

DeChant, C., Wiesner-Hanks, T., Chen, S., Stewart, E. L., Yosinski, J., Gore, M. A., …, & Lipson, H. (2017). Automated identification of northern leaf blight-infected maize plants from field imagery using deep learning. *Phytopathology, 107*(11), 1426–1432.

Demidchik, V. V., Shashko, A. Y., Bandarenka, U. Y., Smolikova, G. N., Przhevalskaya, D. A., Charnysh, M. A., …, & Medvedev, S. S. (2020). Plant phenomics: fundamental bases, software and hardware platforms, and machine learning. *Russian Journal of Plant Physiology, 67*, 397–412.

DeTurk, E. E. (1941). Plant nutrient deficiency symptoms. Physiological basis. *Industrial & Engineering Chemistry, 33*(5), 648–653.

Dharmaraj, V., & Vijayanand, C. (2018). Artificial intelligence (AI) in agriculture. *International Journal of Current Microbiology and Applied Sciences, 7*(12), 2122–2128.

Egea-Cortines, M., & Doonan, J. H. (2018). Phenomics. *Frontiers in Plant Science, 9,* 678.

Eli-Chukwu, N. C. (2019). Applications of artificial intelligence in agriculture: a review. *Engineering, Technology & Applied Science Research, 9*(4), 4377–4383.

Fahlgren, N., Gehan, M. A., & Baxter, I. (2015). Lights, camera, action: high-throughput plant phenotyping is ready for a close-up. *Current Opinion in Plant Biology, 24,* 93–99.

Fang, Y., & Ramasamy, R. P. (2015). Current and prospective methods for plant disease detection. *Biosensors, 5*(3), 537–561.

Fiorani, F., & Schurr, U. (2013). Future scenarios for plant phenotyping. *Annual Review of Plant Biology, 64,* 267–291.

Fitch, B. W., Walraven, R. L., & Bradley, D. E. (1984). Polarization of light reflected from grain crops during the heading growth stage. *Remote Sensing of Environment, 15*(3), 263–268.

Fischer, R. A., & Stapper, M. (1987). Lodging effects on high-yielding crops of irrigated semidwarf wheat. *Field Crops Research, 17*(3–4), 245–258.

Food and Agriculture Organization.(2018). Pest control on the goa mobile app for monitoring and early detection of fall armyworm. http://www.fao.org/3/ca4493en/ca4493en.pdf

Ganatra, N., & Patel, A. (2018). A survey on diseases detection and classification of agriculture products using image processing and machine learning. *International Journal of Computer Applications, 180*(13), 1–13.

Ganesan, V. (2004). Agricultural expert system for the diagnosis of pests and diseases. *IFAC Proceedings Volumes, 37*(2), 107–110.

Geipel, J., Link, J., Wirwahn, J. A., & Claupein, W. (2016). A programmable aerial multispectral camera system for in-season crop biomass and nitrogen content estimation. *Agriculture, 6*(1), 4.

Ghosh, I., & Samanta, R. K. (2003). TEAPEST: an expert system for insect pest management in tea. *Applied Engineering in Agriculture, 19*(5), 619.

Gjuvsland, A. B., Vik, J. O., Beard, D. A., Hunter, P. J., & Omholt, S. W. (2013). Bridging the genotype-phenotype gap: what does it take?. *The Journal of Physiology, 591*(8), 2055–2066.

Gutierrez, M., Reynolds, M. P., Raun, W. R., Stone, M. L., & Klatt, A. R. (2010). Spectral water indices for assessing yield in elite bread wheat genotypes under well-irrigated, water-stressed, and high-temperature conditions. *Crop Science, 50*(1), 197–214.

Guo, Q., Wu, F., Pang, S., Zhao, X., Chen, L., Liu, J., ..., & Chu, C. (2016). Crop 3D: a platform based on LiDAR for 3D high-throughputcrop phenotyping. *Scientia Sinica Vitae, 46*(10), 1210–1221.

Guo, Y., Zhang, J., Yin, C., Hu, X., Zou, Y., Xue, Z., & Wang, W. (2020). Plant disease identification based on deep learning algorithm in smart farming. *Discrete Dynamics in Nature and Society, 2020.*

Hall, H. C., Fakhrzadeh, A., Luengo Hendriks, C. L., & Fischer, U. (2016). Precision automation of cell type classification and sub-cellular fluorescence quantification from laser scanning confocal images. *Frontiers in Plant Science, 7,* 119.

Harfouche, A. L., Jacobson, D. A., Kainer, D., Romero, J. C., Harfouche, A. H., Mugnozza, G. S., ..., & Altman, A. (2019). Accelerating climate-resilient plant breeding by applying next-generation artificial intelligence. *Trends in Biotechnology, 37*(11), 1217–1235.

Hassan, M. A., Yang, M., Rasheed, A., Jin, X., Xia, X., Xiao, Y., & He, Z. (2018). Time-series multispectral indices from unmanned aerial vehicle imagery reveal senescence rate in bread wheat. *Remote Sensing, 10*(6), 809.

Houle, D., Govindaraju, D. R., & Omholt, S. (2010). Phenomics: the next challenge. *Nature Reviews Genetics, 11*(12), 855–866.

Hosoi, F., & Omasa, K. (2012). Estimation of vertical plant area density profiles in a rice canopy at different growth stages by high-resolution portable scanning lidar with a light-weight mirror. *ISPRS Journal of Photogrammetry and Remote Sensing, 74*, 11–19.

India AI. Agritech case studies. Ministry of Electronics and Information Technology (MeitY). https://indiaai.gov.in/initiatives

InsightIAS. (2019). India's Approach to Leadership in Artificial intelligence (AI). https://www.insightsonindia.com/wp-content/uploads/2019/06/India%E2%80%99s-Approach-to-Leadership-in-Artificial-intelligence-AI.pdf

Jackson, R. D., Reginato, R. J., & Idso, S. (1977). Wheat canopy temperature: a practical tool for evaluating water requirements. *Water Resources Research, 13*(3), 651–656.

Jay, S., Maupas, F., Bendoula, R., & Gorretta, N. (2017). Retrieving LAI, chlorophyll and nitrogen contents in sugar beet crops from multi-angular optical remote sensing: comparison of vegetation indices and PROSAIL inversion for field phenotyping. *Field Crops Research, 210*, 33–46.

Jimenez-Berni, J. A., Deery, D. M., Rozas-Larraondo, P., Condon, A. T. G., Rebetzke, G. J., James, R. A., ..., & Sirault, X. R. (2018). High throughput determination of plant height, ground cover, and above-ground biomass in wheat with LiDAR. *Frontiers in Plant Science, 9*, 237.

Jin, X., Liu, S., Baret, F., Hemerlé, M., & Comar, A. (2017). Estimates of plant density of wheat crops at emergence from very low altitude UAV imagery. *Remote Sensing of Environment, 198*, 105–114.

Jin, X., Zarco-Tejada, P. J., Schmidhalter, U., Reynolds, M. P., Hawkesford, M. J., Varshney, R. K., ..., & Li, S. (2020). High-throughput estimation of crop traits: a review of ground and aerial phenotyping platforms. *IEEE Geoscience and Remote Sensing Magazine, 9*(1), 200–231.

Jones, H. G., Serraj, R., Loveys, B. R., Xiong, L., Wheaton, A., & Price, A. H. (2009). Thermal infrared imaging of crop canopies for the remote diagnosis and quantification of plant responses to water stress in the field. *Functional Plant Biology, 36*(11), 978–989.

Kahiluoto, H., Kaseva, J., Balek, J., Olesen, J. E., Ruiz-Ramos, M., Gobin, A., ..., & Trnka, M. (2019). Decline in climate resilience of European wheat. *Proceedings of the National Academy of Sciences, 116*(1), 123–128.

Kelly, J., Kljun, N., Olsson, P. O., Mihai, L., Liljeblad, B., Weslien, P., ..., & Eklundh, L. (2019). Challenges and best practices for deriving temperature data from an uncalibrated UAV thermal infrared camera. *Remote Sensing, 11*(5), 567.

Khan, F. S., Razzaq, S., Irfan, K., Maqbool, F., Farid, A., Illahi, I., & Amin, T. U. (2008, July). Dr. Wheat: a Web-based expert system for diagnosis of diseases and pests in Pakistani wheat. In *Proceedings of the World Congress on Engineering, 1* (2–4).

Khandelwal, P. M., & Chavhan, H. (2019). Artificial Intelligence in Agriculture: An Emerging Era of Research. *Research Gate Publication.*

Klose, R., Penlington, J., & Ruckelshausen, A. (2009). Usability study of 3D time-of-flight cameras for automatic plant phenotyping. *Bornimer Agrartechnische Berichte, 69*(93–105), 12.

Kose, U., Prasath, V. B. S., Mondal, M. R. H., Podder, P., & Bharati, S. (Eds.). (2022). *Artificial Intelligence and Smart Agriculture Technology*. CRC Press, Boca Raton, FL, Unites States.

Kumar, V., & Vani, K. (2018). Agricultural robot: leaf disease detection and monitoring the field condition using machine learning and image processing. *International Journal of Computational Intelligence Research, 14*(7), 551–561.

Lemmon, H. (1986). COMAX: an expert system for cotton crop management. *Science, 233*(4759), 29–33.

Lemmon, H. (1990). Comax: an expert system for cotton crop management. *Computer Science in Economics and Management, 3*(2), 177–185.

Li, W., Niu, Z., Chen, H., Li, D., Wu, M., & Zhao, W. (2016). Remote estimation of canopy height and aboveground biomass of maize using high-resolution stereo images from a low-cost unmanned aerial vehicle system. *Ecological Indicators, 67*, 637–648.

Liu, Z., Li, C., Wang, Y., Huang, W., Ding, X., Zhou, B., …, & Shi, J. (2011, October). Comparison of spectral indices and principal component analysis for differentiating lodged rice crop from normal ones. In *International Conference on Computer and Computing Technologies in Agriculture* (pp. 84–92). Springer, Berlin, Heidelberg.

Liu, T., Li, R., Zhong, X., Jiang, M., Jin, X., Zhou, P., …, & Guo, W. (2018). Estimates of rice lodging using indices derived from UAV visible and thermal infrared images. *Agricultural and Forest Meteorology, 252*, 144–154.

Martiniello, P. (1988). Development of a database computer management system for retrieval on varietal field evaluation and plant breeding information in agriculture. *Computers and Electronics in Agriculture, 2*(3), 183–192.

McKinion, J. M., & Lemmon, H. E. (1985). Expert systems for agriculture. *Computers and Electronics in Agriculture, 1*(1), 31–40.

Mitran, T., Meena, R. S., & Chakraborty, A. (Eds.). (2021). *Geospatial Technologies for Crops and Soils*. Springer Nature, Singapore.

Mishra, A., Heyer, A. G., & Mishra, K. B. (2014). Chlorophyll fluorescence emission can screen cold tolerance of cold acclimated Arabidopsis thaliana accessions. *Plant Methods, 10*(1), 1–10.

Murakami, T., Yui, M., & Amaha, K. (2012). Canopy height measurement by photogrammetric analysis of aerial images: application to buckwheat (*Fagopyrum esculentum* Moench) lodging evaluation. *Computers and Electronics in Agriculture, 89*, 70–75.

Murugesan, S., Malik, S., Du, F., Koh, E., & Lai, T. M. (2019). Deepcompare: visual and interactive comparison of deep learning model performance. *IEEE Computer Graphics and Applications, 39*(5), 47–59.

Mishra, S., Dash, A., & Jena, L. (2021). Use of deep learning for disease detection and diagnosis. In *Bio-inspired Neurocomputing* (pp. 181–201). Springer, Singapore.

National Institute of Food and Agriculture. (2020). Artificial Intelligence. U.S. Department of Agriculture. https://nifa.usda.gov/artificial-intelligence

Nebiker, S., Lack, N., Abächerli, M., & Läderach, S. (2016). Light-weight multispectral UAV sensors and their capabilities for predicting grain yield and detecting plant diseases. *International Archives of the Photogrammetry, Remote Sensing & Spatial Information Sciences, 41*, 963–970.

Niti Ayog. (2018). National strategy on artificial intelligence. https://www.niti.gov.in/sites/default/files/2019-01/NationalStrategy-for-AI-Discussion-Paper.pdf

Ogden, R. T., Miller, C. E., Takezawa, K., & Ninomiya, S. (2002). Functional regression in crop lodging assessment with digital images. *Journal of Agricultural, Biological, and Environmental Statistics, 7*(3), 389–402.

Perez-Sanz, F., Navarro, P. J., & Egea-Cortines, M. (2017). Plant phenomics: an overview of image acquisition technologies and image data analysis algorithms. *Gigascience, 6*(11), gix092.

Pieruschka, R., & Poorter, H. (2012). Phenotyping plants: genes, phenes and machines. *Functional Plant Biology, 39*(11), 813–820.

Pinthus, M. J. (1974). Lodging in wheat, barley, and oats: the phenomenon, its causes, and preventive measures. In *Advances in Agronomy* (vol. 25, pp. 209–263). Academic Press.

Prakash, C., Rathor, A. S., & Thakur, G. S. M. (2013). Fuzzy based Agriculture expert system for Soyabean. In *International Conference on Computing Sciences WILKES100-ICCS2013*, Jalandhar, Punjab, India (vol. 113).

Ramesh, S., Hebbar, R., Niveditha, M., Pooja, R., Shashank, N., & Vinod, P. V. (2018, April). Plant disease detection using machine learning. In *2018 International Conference on Design Innovations for 3Cs Compute Communicate Control (ICDI3C)* (pp. 41–45). IEEE.

Rich, E., & Knight, K. (1991). *Artificial Intelligence.* McGraw Hill, Inc, New York, NY, United States.

Roach, J., Virkar, R., Drake, C., & Weaver, M. (1987). An expert system for helping apple growers. *Computers and Electronics in Agriculture, 2*(2), 97–108.

Robinson, C., & Mort, N. (1997). A neural network system for the protection of citrus crops from frost damage. *Computers and Electronics in Agriculture, 16*(3), 177–187.

Salam, A. (2020). Internet of things for sustainable community development: introduction and overview. In *Internet of Things for Sustainable Community Development* (pp. 1–31). Springer, Cham.

Samanta, R. K., & Ghosh, I. (2012). Tea insect pests classification based on artificial neural networks. *International Journal of Computer Engineering Science (IJCES), 2*(6), 1–13.

Sandhu, D., Coleman, Z., Atkinson, T., Rai, K. M., & Mendu, V. (2018). Genetics and physiology of the nuclearly inherited yellow foliar mutants in soybean. *Frontiers in Plant Science, 9*, 471.

Sankaran, S., Maja, J. M., Buchanon, S., & Ehsani, R. (2013). Huanglongbing (citrus greening) detection using visible, near-infrared and thermal imaging techniques. *Sensors, 13*(2), 2117–2130.

Sankaran, S., Khot, L. R., Espinoza, C. Z., Jarolmasjed, S., Sathuvalli, V. R., Vandemark, G. J., ..., & Pavek, M. J. (2015). Low-altitude, high-resolution aerial imaging systems for row and field crop phenotyping: A review. *European Journal of Agronomy, 70*, 112–123.

Saxena, A., Khanna, A., & Gupta, D. (2020). Emotion recognition and detection methods: a comprehensive survey. *Journal of Artificial Intelligence and Systems, 2*(1), 53–79.

Schmidhalter, U., Jungert, S., Bredemeier, C., Gutser, R., Manhart, R., Mistele, B., & Gerl, G. (2003). Field-scale validation of a tractor based multispectral crop scanner to determine biomass and nitrogen uptake of winter wheat. In *Programme Book of the Joint Conference of ECPA-ECPLF* (pp. 615–619).

Skirycz, A., Vandenbroucke, K., Clauw, P., Maleux, K., De Meyer, B., Dhondt, S., ..., & Inze, D. (2011). Survival and growth of Arabidopsis plants given limited water are not equal. *Nature Biotechnology, 29*(3), 212–214.

Stone, N. D., & Toman, T. W. (1989). A dynamically linked expert-database system for decision support in Texas cotton production. *Computers and Electronics in Agriculture, 4*(2), 139–148.

Sujawat, G. S. (2021). Application of artificial intelligence in detection of diseases in plants: a survey. *Turkish Journal of Computer and Mathematics Education (TURCOMAT)*, *12*(3), 3301–3305.

Srikanth, V., Rajesh, G. K., Kothakota, A., Pandiselvam, R., Sagarika, N., Manikantan, M. R., & Sudheer, K. P. (2020). Modeling and optimization of developed cocoa beans extractor parameters using box behnken design and artificial neural network. *Computers and Electronics in Agriculture*, *177*, 105715.

Steele, R. (Ed.). (2004). *Understanding and Measuring the Shelf-life of Food*. Woodhead Publishing, Sawston, Cambridge.

Stone, N. D., & Toman, T. W. (1989). A dynamically linked expert-database system for decision support in Texas cotton production. *Computers and Electronics in Agriculture*, *4*(2), 139–148.

Streich, J., Romero, J., Gazolla, J. G. F. M., Kainer, D., Cliff, A., Prates, E. T., …, & Harfouche, A. L. (2020). Can exascale computing and explainable artificial intelligence applied to plant biology deliver on the United Nations sustainable development goals?. *Current Opinion in Biotechnology*, *61*, 217–225.

Tattaris, M., Reynolds, M. P., & Chapman, S. C. (2016). A direct comparison of remote sensing approaches for high-throughput phenotyping in plant breeding. *Frontiers in Plant Science*, *7*, 1131.

Thapa, S., Zhu, F., Walia, H., Yu, H., & Ge, Y. (2018). A novel LiDAR-based instrument for high-throughput, 3D measurement of morphological traits in maize and sorghum. *Sensors*, *18*(4), 1187.

Thompson, A. L., Thorp, K. R., Conley, M., Andrade-Sanchez, P., Heun, J. T., Dyer, J. M., & White, J. W. (2018). Deploying a proximal sensing cart to identify drought-adaptive traits in upland cotton for high-throughput phenotyping. *Frontiers in Plant Science*, *9*, 507.

Thoren, D., & Schmidhalter, U. (2009). Nitrogen status and biomass determination of oil-seed rape by laser-induced chlorophyll fluorescence. *European Journal of Agronomy*, *30*(3), 238–242.

Thorpe, K. W., Ridgway, R. L., & Webb, R. E. (1992). A computerized data management and decision support system for gypsy moth management in suburban parks. *Computers and Electronics in Agriculture*, *6*(4), 333–345.

Tripathi, M. K., & Maktedar, D. D. (2016, August). Recent machine learning-based approaches for disease detection and classification of agricultural products. In *2016 International Conference on Computing Communication Control and Automation (ICCUBEA)* (pp. 1–6). IEEE.

Tripathi, M. K., & Maktedar, D. D. (2018). A framework with OTSU'S thresholding method for fruits and vegetables image segmentation. *International Journal of Computer Applications*, *975*, 8887.

Van Der Werf, H. M., & Zimmer, C. (1998). An indicator of pesticide environmental impact based on a fuzzy expert system. *Chemosphere*, *36*(10), 2225–2249.

Venkatesh, M. S., & Raghavan, G. S. V. (2004). An overview of microwave processing and dielectric properties of agri-food materials. *Biosystems Engineering*, *88*(1), 1–18.

Vickers, N. J. (2017). Animal communication: when I'm calling you, will you answer too?. *Current Biology*, *27*(14), R713–R715.

Weber, J. F., Kunz, C., Peteinatos, G. G., Santel, H. J., & Gerhards, R. (2017). Utilization of chlorophyll fluorescence imaging technology to detect plant injury by herbicides in sugar beet and soybean. *Weed Technology*, *31*(4), 523–535.

Winterhalter, L., Mistele, B., Jampatong, S., & Schmidhalter, U. (2011). High through-put phenotyping of canopy water mass and canopy temperature in well-watered and drought stressed tropical maize hybrids in the vegetative stage. *European Journal of Agronomy, 35*(1), 22–32.

Yamamoto, K., Togami, T., & Yamaguchi, N. (2017). Super-resolution of plant disease images for the acceleration of image-based phenotyping and vigor diagnosis in agriculture. *Sensors, 17*(11), 2557.

Yang, H., Chen, E., Li, Z., Zhao, C., Yang, G., Pignatti, S., ..., & Zhao, L. (2015). Wheat lodging monitoring using polarimetric index from RADARSAT-2 data. *International Journal of Applied Earth Observation and Geoinformation, 34*, 157–166.

Yang, H., Yang, J. P., Li, F. H., & Liu, N. (2018). Replacing the nitrogen nutrition index by SPAD values and analysis of effect factors for estimating rice nitrogen status. *Agronomy Journal, 110*(2), 545–554.

Yang, W., Feng, H., Zhang, X., Zhang, J., Doonan, J. H., Batchelor, W. D., ... & Yan, J. (2020). Crop phenomics and high-throughput phenotyping: past decades, current challenges, and future perspectives. *Molecular Plant, 13*(2), 187–214

Zarco-Tejada, P. J., Berni, J. A., Suárez, L., & Fereres, E. (2008). A new era in remote sensing of crops with unmanned robots. *SPIE Newsroom, 10*(2.1200812), 1438.

Zarco-Tejada, P. J., Camino, C., Beck, P. S. A., Calderon, R., Hornero, A., Hernández-Clemente, R., ..., & Navas-Cortes, J. A. (2018). Previsual symptoms of Xylellafastidiosa infection revealed in spectral plant-trait alterations. *Nature Plants, 4*(7), 432–439.

Zarco-Tejada, P. J., Hornero, A., Beck, P. S. A., Kattenborn, T., Kempeneers, P., & Hernández-Clemente, R. (2019). Chlorophyll content estimation in an open-canopy conifer forest with Sentinel-2A and hyperspectral imagery in the context of forest decline. *Remote Sensing of Environment, 223*, 320–335.

Zhang, C., & Kovacs, J. M. (2012). The application of small unmanned aerial systems for precision agriculture: a review. *Precision Agriculture, 13*(6), 693–712.

Zhang, J., Naik, H. S., Assefa, T., Sarkar, S., Reddy, R. C., Singh, A., ..., & Singh, A. K. (2017). Computer vision and machine learning for robust phenotyping in genome-wide studies. *Scientific Reports, 7*(1), 1–11.

Zhao, C., Zhang, Y., Du, J., Guo, X., Wen, W., Gu, S., ..., & Fan, J. (2019). Crop phenomics: current status and perspectives. *Frontiers in Plant Science, 10*, 714.

Zhang, M., Zhou, J., Sudduth, K. A., & Kitchen, N. R. (2020). Estimation of maize yield and effects of variable-rate nitrogen application using UAV-based RGB imagery. *Biosystems Engineering, 189*, 24–35.

Zhou, R., Hyldgaard, B., Yu, X., Rosenqvist, E., Ugarte, R. M., Yu, S., ..., & Zhao, T. (2018). Phenotyping of faba beans (*Vicia faba* L.) under cold and heat stresses using chlorophyll fluorescence. *Euphytica, 214*(4), 1–13.

Chapter 10

Plant Disease Detection Using Hybrid Deep Learning Architecture in Smart Agriculture Applications

Murugan Subramanian[1], Nelson Iruthayanathan[2], Annadurai Chinnamuthu[2], Nirmala Devi Kathamuthu[3], Manikandan Ramachandran[4], and Ambeshwar Kumar[4]

[1]Department of Computer Science and Engineering, Sri Aravindar Engineering College, Tamil Nadu, India

[2]Department of ECE, Sri Sivasubramaniya Nadar College of Engineering, Kalavakkam, Chennai, Tamil Nadu, India

[3]Department of CSE, Kongu Engineering College, Perundurai, Erode, Tamil Nadu, India

[4]School of Computing, SASTRA Deemed University, Tamil Nadu, India

Contents

DOI: 10.1201/9781003311782-10

10.1 Introduction

Indian economy is mainly contributed by agriculture and nowadays due to the migration of people and population escalation declining constantly and still, it remains a main division of employment (Liu et al. 2017). The pace for competitiveness, productivity, expanded and maintainable agriculture are needed to be accelerated. Agricultural research, productivity and quality of food are increased for enhancement (Behmann et al. 2015). Diseases in the crop are diagnosed accurately and the following classification is widely difficult to process and it is prejudiced by various parameters like nutrition, environment and climate (Petrellis 2018). Technology and science are developed progressively depending on machine vision to achieve intelligent farming with active computation of research fields. Furthermore, when it comes to growing crops, gardeners are frequently perplexed by plants that exhibit symptoms (Prasad et al. 2016). The pathology of plants is considered by farmers and researchers as the main domain and is frequently queried about the plant diseases and their eliminating measures. At that time when the disease occurs, it is difficult to cure it, so the diseases are prevented before they start their spread to other plants (Ali et al. 2017). It is necessary to design software for identifying the plant disease as soon as possible in the beginning stage. An approach suitable for this process is a smartphone app and it is convenient for an untrained person to get knowledge about plant disease types (Howard et al. 2017). Disease Identifier or Garden Compass Plant available as an application in the app store for iPhone users and A&L Plant Disease Diagnosis available as an application in the Google Play store for Android users are some of the applications used to find plant diseases. The pictures of plant diseases are submitted to plant team experts for the symptom diagnosis (Mohanty et al. 2016). Moreover, the results are provided to the farmers after a long time and required to be paid by the farmers. The main limitation of the method mentioned above is that it identifies only the type of disease and doesn't provide any suggestion for curing the disease (Kavitha 2018). Advancement deep learning relies on the mobile application for meeting criteria such as picture analysis, ailment diagnosis, and classification of disease, which is provided at no cost after a long time of waiting (Brahimi et al. 2018).

Several concepts like image processing, deep learning (DL) methods and applications are available for detecting diseases in plants and classifying them. DL techniques are employed in image processing and extraction of patterns which considerably reduces the classification accuracy. Recently, DL techniques are widely involved in pattern recognition as they effectively identify various outlines. Hybridization of DL techniques provides automated feature extraction (Ferentinos 2018) and even reduces the error rate and computational time, thereby achieving higher classification accuracy than conventional approaches. The motivation behind this research work is plant disease detection and providing solutions for recovering plants from these diseases using AlexNet with a stacking concept (Lee et al. 2018).

Contribution of the Research

The contributions made here are three-fold:

- Initially, a novel stacking-based AlexNet method is employed to learn plant diseases representations and a comparison is made to estimate the performance level.
- Next, it is quantitatively proved that a stacking-based AlexNet method outperforms the approaches in the literature.
- At last, it is also qualitatively proved that this novel approach precisely detected infected areas by using neuron activations.

The full work is organized and presented in various sessions where Section 10.2 discusses the works related to this work. Section 10.3 describes the proposed stacking-based AlexNet architecture. Section 10.4 elaborates the implementation by presenting the experimental results. Finally, this work is concluded with future scope in Section 10.5.

10.2 Related Works

Many approaches were established for precise identification and obtained accurate outcomes. These developed models used class labels for training and thus constructed a better system for image classification. In Zhang et al. in the year 2019, plant diseases were detected with an approach using hybrid clustering which was developed by using leaf images. In Patil and Kumar (2017), **Content-Based Image Retrieval (CBIR)**, was developed where color and texture data were gathered by Patil et al. (2017) and a **Support Vector Machine** (SVM) classifier is used to categorize them. The main aim was to construct an image analyzing and classifying approach which possibly extracts the features and identifies them more accurately. In Ferentinos (2018), a novel image selection system based on short text descriptions was developed to assist the non-experts in the identification of plant diseases. Moreover, this system can be remotely used from a desktop/smart mobile/PDA

(Personal Digital Assistant). In Pertot et al. (2012), a real-time system was modeled which involved mobiles for on-field imaging of the plants having a disease. Moreover, the leaf image was segmented and the diseased patch was identified using the improvised **k-clustering** technique. In Yang et al. (2019), a microscopic method was introduced for image detection based on the features like shape, size and texture using a matrix for deciding called a **Tree – Confusion**. In addition, for disease identification, **CNN – Convolutional Neural Network** has been widely utilized. In DeChant et al. (2017), an automatic system was established which had the ability to identify plant disease in images captured from the maize field. In Ni et al. (2019), Deep CNN (DCNN) was used to establish an automated corn detector. Lu et al. (2017) developed a novel approach depending on DCNN for identifying rice diseases. In Zhang et al. (2019), a network of agricultural machinery image recognition was designed using the DL approach. In Zhang et al. (2018), the existing DCNN was enhanced to obtain improved identification accuracy of maize leaf disease. In Rangarajan et al. (2018), two architectures, namely AlexNet and VGG-16 net DL, were used to detect (Coulibaly et al. 2019), and transfer learning was established to extract the feature. Aditya Khampari et al. (2021) emphasize the process of transfer learning for breast cancer detection. 2D and 3D images of mammogram datasets are implemented in modified VGG (MVGG). A novel hybrid DL framework was proposed by Bharati et al. (2020) by a combination containing augmentation of the data, VGG, STN – Spatial Transformer Network using CNN based on Artificial Neural Network (ANN) was reviewed systematically by Bharati et al. (2020) to diagnose breast cancer through a mammogram. The drawbacks and advantages of various models of ANN which include SNN – Spiking Neural Network, DBN – Deep Belief Network, CNN – Convolutional Neural Network, etc., were reviewed in this paper. This model of DL applications is described by Bharati et al. (2021) for medical imaging and in the management of discovering drug which is useful in the treatment of COVID-19. CT and X-ray images combined with DL methods are used to classify pneumonia with COVID-19. Applications in DL of COVID-19 analysis with the images of X-ray are introduced in Bharati et al. (2021).

As more hardware resources were required and conventional models based on neural networks required a huge amount of quality datasets for training consuming more time which is not appropriate to promote and use this model. This research suggests a model based on transfer learning integrated with a pre-trained model for identification which uses the dataset of diseased leaves for training.

10.3 System Model

The framework involved for training comprises three different approaches, namely classification, transfer learning and a stacking ensemble approach. The first two construct DL classification models which use a single input image, while the last

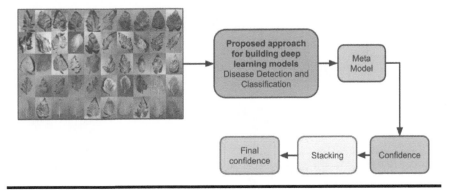

Figure 10.1   Proposed deep convolutional neural network-based classification architecture.

one combines these models. Classification is applied to separate the steps of training by classifying healthy and diseased cases. Transfer learning constructs the classification model to classify healthy cases with diseased cases based on the obtained knowledge after detecting the disease. For diagnosing the disease, transfer learning is used from a pre-trained model. At last, a stacking ensemble approach combined the DL models to produce the overall result as shown in Figure 10.1.

10.4 Dataset Description

This proposed hybridization model is applicable for detecting the bacterial spots from plants affected by the disease in plants. The leaf images from plants are extracted using the Plant Village dataset which comprises 4,457 leaf images. These images were distributed evenly into two groups, namely healthy (2,160 images) and bacterial spotted diseased images (2,297 images). The pathologic plant leaves were cut before they were captured, and furthermore, the picture goals were 3,072 × 2,304 pixels. To reduce computation time for picture processing, the sore area color leaf picture was segmented from each plant disease picture utilizing Photoshop 7.0 programming, and each segmental sub-picture estimate was standardized to 345 × 245 pixels.

10.5 Transfer Learning Process

In the transfer learning process, a particular pre-trained model dataset is provided with weights for achieving efficient dataset classification. Generally, transfer learning is conducted through two ways which are described as follows:

- Feature Extraction: In the feature extraction technique, the model is trained with a standard Plant Village dataset. Then, classification is included in the

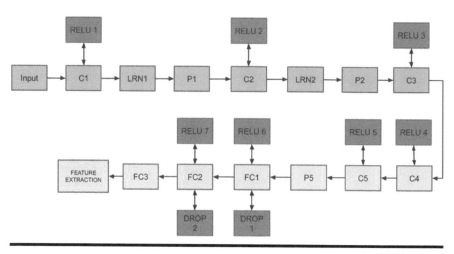

Figure 10.2   Extraction of the feature using AlexNet.

model for the elimination of redundancy. The other part of the network performs feature extraction for running the classification algorithm. AlexNet
model which learns the image features from a scene is used where the scene is
a series of transformations during training like convolution and max-pooling.
The feature extraction process is specifically illustrated in Figure 10.2.

■ Fine Tuning: In this stage, rather than supplant and classifier, the training
pre-trained model is adjusted with the progression of training each layer of
the network model. Generally, transfer learning is applied for the limited
availability of data, and it prevents weight overfitting and randomization
effects for achieving better training. To minimize the time taken for training by the CNN model, this research work employs transfer learning based
on ResNet to drift the shallow neural network for the source to target task
and improve the speed of convergence. Initially, two aspects, namely domain
and task, have to be discussed. Let D represent the domain, including two
contents *X* and *P(X)*:

$$D = X, P(X) \tag{10.1}$$

X is the feature space containing every possible feature value, while *P(X)* is the
specific instance of feature sampling in feature space.

Let *T* represent the task, including two concepts *y* and *f(x)*:

$$T = Y, f(x) \tag{10.2}$$

Y represents the label space which is a vector containing all labels. *f(x)* is a
learned prediction function based on labels and characteristics of the input.

10.6 Construction and Fine-tuning of Stacked AlexNet

The dataset is partitioned into three sets, namely training, validating and testing sets. Pre-trained models like ResNet 101, Xception, NASNet, MobileNet, VGGNet and InceptionV3 were applied in which the last network layers were fine-tuned. Four conventional convolutional and max-pooling layers were added on top of transfer learning architecture. Finally, two dense layers were used with 2 and 64 neurons. For classification, the last layer is the function of activation as softmax, batch size of 20 epochs was involved in training where the hyper-parameters like an optimizer, size of the batch, learning rate and pre-trained weights were altered. 30% dropouts were utilized for reducing the overfitting among layers and normalization of the batch for minimizing internal covariate shift. Thus, a local optimum or a saddle point stuck up is prevented in this prototype. The measure chosen for evaluating the model is multi-class log loss. A Rectified Linear Unit (ReLU) activation function was employed in all layers other than the last layer in which sigmoid was involved as it was a binary classification problem. Moreover, two data generators for training and testing were involved which were able to directly load the required data from the source, then convert them as training data and training targets.

10.7 Classification Using Stacked AlexNet

The key objective of the Stacked AlexNet model proposed is an automatic differentiation of images of the collected dataset. The analysis is based on plant disease and non-disease classification with minimization of detection time with an increase in efficacy. To eliminate trade-off problems transfer learning as well as multiple pre-trained AlexNet is applied. This AlexNet model adopts suitable methods so that training is done faster and avoids complex structure overfitting, more number of training parameters and a huge volume of training data. So the AlexNet model is directly constructed by using a ReLU which makes the model more consistent and directly trains the network from the starting point to improve the speed of training; "Near-suppression" operation performed Local Response Normalization (LRN) where the local input regions are normalized such that the performance of this model is enhanced more effectively. Figure 10.3 shows the Stacked AlexNet architecture.

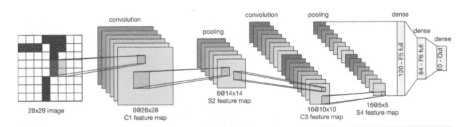

Figure 10.3   Stacked AlexNet architecture.

The layer m with input is represented by $I^{(m)}$. The pre-trained CONV layer m with input is $n_1^{(m-1)} \times n_2^{(m-1)} \times n_3^{(m-1)}$ object in three-dimensional $n_c^{(m-1)}$ so $I^{(m-1)} \epsilon \mathbb{R}^{n1(m-1) \times n_2^{(m-1)} \times n_3^{(m-1)}}$ entries represented as $I(m,)$ i,j,k in this j, k, i in three-dimensional volume are indexed. For CONV layer m, the result is given by $n_1^{(m)} \times n_2^{(m)} \times n_3^{(m)}$ as its dimensions and filter count or channels $n_c^{(m)}$. The CONV layer m's output with a filter is estimated as follows: $I_{i,j,k}^{(m,l)} = f_{tanh}\left(b^{(m,l)}\right) + \Sigma_{i,j,k,l} I_{i,j,k}^{(m-1,l)} W_{i-i,j-j,k-k,l}^{(m-l)}$, where $W^{(m,l)}$ and $b^{(m,l)}$ are the parameters defining the filter of lth in layer m. Finally, a hyperbolic tangent activation function with $f_{tanh(a)} = \tanh(a)$ was used.

The spatial structure of the inputs is preserved by the ReLU layers and creates a more complex input representation. The FC layer of the network takes the single-vector output of CONV layers as an input for by ignoring the spatial and channel structures. The 1D vector $I^{(m)}$ is the output of FC layer. In layer m, the output of neuron i is defined as follows:

$$I_i^{(m)} = f_{ReLu}\left(b^{(m,i)} + \sum_j I_j^{(m-1)} W_j^{(m,i)}\right) \tag{10.3}$$

where $W^{(m,i)}$ and $b^{(m,i)}$ represent m as the ith parameters; the j's total is the total of all dimensions given. $f_{ReLu}(.)$ activation function is selected as a ReLU with $f_{ReLu}(a) = \max(0,a)$ which is involved in numerous domains and hopefully assists particularly for classification. Moreover, the sparsity in outputs separates classes while learning. The output layer takes the final FC layer as an input. For the output layer, its structure is based on the specific task and two various output functions are considered. While classifying with K classes, the common softmax output function is:

$$f_i = \frac{\exp\left(I_i^{(o)}\right)}{\sum_j \exp\left(I_j^{(o)}\right)} \tag{10.4}$$

$$I_i^{(o)} = b^{(o,i)} + \sum_{k=1}^{k} W_k^{(o,i)} I_k^{(N)} \tag{10.5}$$

Here, N represents the index of the final FC layer, $b^{(o,i)}$ and $W^{(o,i)}$ denote the output unit I's parameters and $f_i \epsilon [0,1]$ indicates I as the output and is described as the probability of that class. The difference in the logistic output function is considered as follows:

$$f = a + (b-a)(1+\exp\left(b^{(o)} + \sum_j W_j^{(o)} I_j^{(N)}\right)^{-1} \tag{10.6}$$

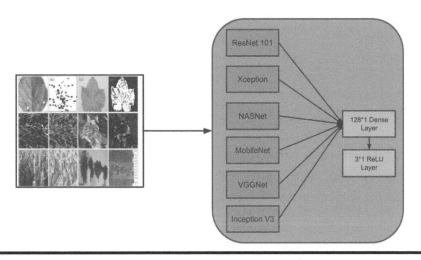

Figure 10.4   Stacking process in a network.

Providing continuous output f is limited to be within (*a*, *b*) with parameters $b^{(o)}$ and $W^{(o)}$. This is termed as the scaled logistic output function. If a ranking multi-class classification is considered, this function may perform better.

Figure 10.4 indicates the stacking process in a network. For the data collected and the structure of the network, the major objective is to select the network parameters for that data. To achieve this, an objective function is defined and optimization based on a gradient approach is used for searching the parameters that can minimize the objective function. Assume that $D = n_i, y_i i = 1$ represent the *D* training samples where n and y indicate the input and output, respectively. Input is the part of the CT scan, while output indicates the malicious class representing the beginning malicious where Θ is gathering every W weight, b biases each network layer. The format of the function of objective is

$$E(\theta) = \sum_{i=1}^{D} L\left(y_i, f\left(n_i, \Theta\right)\right) + \lambda E_{prior}\left(\Theta\right) \qquad (10.7)$$

where f (ni, Θ) denotes the output for input n with parameters Θ, Loss function L(yi, f(ni, Θ)) gives the difference between the observed and predicted results of the network y and yˆ, respectively. $E_{prior}\left(\Theta\right) = \|W\|^2$ is a function in which weight decay prior supports in preventing the overfitting and the strength is controlled by λ.

Based on the output function, two objective functions are used. The standard cross-entropy loss function $L\left(y_i, \hat{y}\right) = -\sum_{k=1}^{k} y_k \log\left(\hat{y}k\right)$ is used in the softmax output function where y and yˆ are the binary indicator vector and vector of probabilities for every K class, respectively. The limitation here is that every class error produced is considered equal, thus leading to mislabel. The malignancy at the first level is considered second level by mislabeling as 5. To overcome this issue, the squared error loss function is used as the scaled logistic function. Generally, $L(y_i, \hat{y}) = (y_i, \hat{y})^2$, y, y^ are assumed as real values. Particularly, the parameters are updated as $\Theta_{t+1} = \Theta_t + \Delta\Theta_{t+1}, \Delta\Theta_{t+1} = \rho\Delta\Theta_t - \varepsilon\nabla E_t(\Theta_t)$ at iteration t, where the momentum parameter $\rho = 0.9$, $\Delta\Theta_{t+1}$ represents the momentum vector, t indicates the learning rate and the gradient of the objective function $\nabla E_t(\Theta_t)$ is determined using the training samples chosen at t.

10.8 Algorithm for Classification

Multivariate Function ← MF()
Initialize Target Vector ← Target
Random Integer + Target Vector = Base

for each iteration do

$$\text{TempVector1} = \text{Target} + \text{Random Deviation}$$

$$\text{TempVector2} = \text{Target} - \text{Random Deviation}$$

$$\text{Weighted} = \text{Weighted Difference}\left(\text{TempVector1, Temp Vector2}\right)$$

$$\left\{\left(yj', \, xj\right)\right\} j =, \text{ where } xj = 0, 1$$

$$r =,\ldots R$$

$$\omega r, \text{ in amount to } \sum \omega r, jnj = 1 = 1$$

In case of every feature, a weak classifier is trained.
In case of error ϵi of a classifier hi is designed matching to the weight ωr, ..., $\omega r, n$:

$$\epsilon i = \sum \omega r, j \left| hi\left(yj'\right) - xj \right| nj = 1$$

Weighted + Base = Base
Aggregate (Target, Base) =Trial
if MF(Trial) < MF(Base) then
Trial=Base
else
Target = Base
end if
end for
return Base

10.9 Experimental Theory

Experimental theory is performed for different methods, and the results are shown in Table 10.1. Comparing the existing classification networks such as Convolutional Encoder Network (CEN) and ResNet-50 + Support Vector Machine (SVM) with proposed Stacked AlexNet considering accuracy, precision, score, RMSE and RAE is selected.

- **Accuracy** gives capability in the projected network model. True negative (TN) and true positive (TP) are used to calculate the classifier's capacity which is used to be lacking in identifying the leaf disease. False negative (FN) and false positive (FP) are used to find the number of wrong calculations made in the models.

$$Accuracy = \frac{TP + TN}{TP + TN + FP + FN} \tag{10.8}$$

Table 10.2 shows the difference in existing CEN and ResNet-50+SVM with proposed Stacked AlexNet method for accuracy.

Figure 10.5 compares accuracy between existing CEN, ResNet-50+SVM and proposed Stacked AlexNet, where the X-axis shows the count, while the Y-axis gives accuracy. When compared, the first formula gives 92% and 93%, while the proposed method achieves 95% which is 3% better than CEN and 2% better than ResNet-50+SVM.

- **Precision** gives the success of the model used in classification. This classification function acts as a predictor to result in true identification in the case of leaf disease. TP gives the value of true positive, which is used to calculate precision by

$$Precision\ (P) = \frac{TP}{TP + FP} \tag{10.9}$$

Table 10.1 Operational Parameters

Operational Parameters	Values
Epochs	150
Batch Size	16
Hidden Layers	7
Learning Rate Drop	1e-2
Learn Rate Drop Period	40
Initial Learn Rate	1e-2
Batch Normalization Epsilon	10^{-4}
Loss Function Error	$L=L_{class}+L_{box}+L_{mask}$

Table 10.2   Analysis of Accuracy

Number of Datasets	CEN	ResNet-50+SVM	Stacked AlexNet
200	86	88	89
400	87	90	91
600	89	91	92
800	90	92	93
1,000	92	93	94

Table 10.3 represents the comparison of existing CEN and ResNet-50+SVM with the proposed Stacked AlexNet method for precision.

Figure 10.6 compares precision between existing CEN, ResNet-50+SVM and proposed Stacked AlexNet, where the X-axis denotes the number of datasets, while the Y-axis shows the precision in percentage. When compared, the existing method achieves 90% and 91%, while the proposed method achieves 93% which is 3% better than CEN and 2% better than ResNet-50+SVM.

■ **Recall** gives the absence of disease in the system by a negative value which is named as R where TN gives the true negative value and it is given by

$$Recall\ (R) = \frac{TP}{TP + FN} \tag{10.10}$$

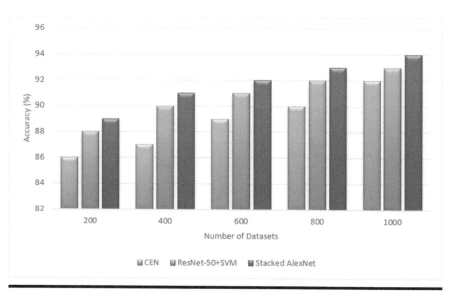

Figure 10.5   Comparison of accuracy.

Table 10.3 Analysis of Precision

Number of Datasets	CEN	ResNet-50+SVM	Stacked AlexNet
200	82	85	86
400	84	87	88
600	87	88	89
800	88	90	91
1,000	90	91	93

Table 10.4 shows the comparison of existing CEN and ResNet-50+SVM with the proposed Stacked AlexNet method for recall.

Figure 10.7 compares recall between existing CEN, ResNet-50+SVM and proposed Stacked AlexNet, where the X-axis gives the count of datasets, while the Y-axis gives the value recall. When compared, the first system achieves 86% and 88%, while the proposed method achieves 89% which is 3% better than CEN and 1% better than ResNet-50+SVM.

Table 10.5 compares the existing CEN model with ResNet-50+SVM with the proposed Stacked AlexNet method for F1-score.

Figure 10.8 compares the F1-score between existing CEN, ResNet-50+SVM and proposed Stacked AlexNet, where the X-axis gives the count of

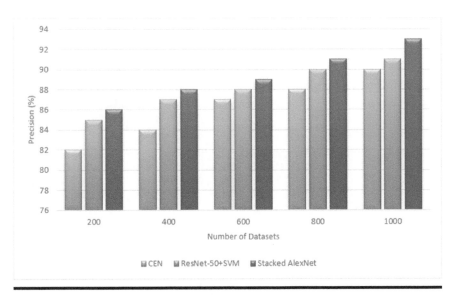

Figure 10.6 Comparison of precision.

Table 10.4 Analysis of Recall

Number of Datasets	CEN	ResNet-50+SVM	Stacked AlexNet
200	80	81	83
400	82	83	84
600	83	84	85
800	85	86	87
1,000	86	88	92

Table 10.5 Analysis of F1-Score

Number of Datasets	CEN	ResNet-50+SVM	Stacked AlexNet
200	75	76	79
400	76	78	81
600	78	79	82
800	80	81	84
1,000	81	82	85

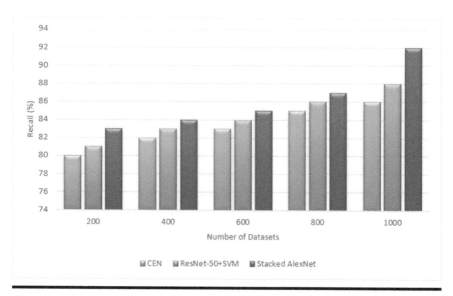

Figure 10.7 Comparison of recall.

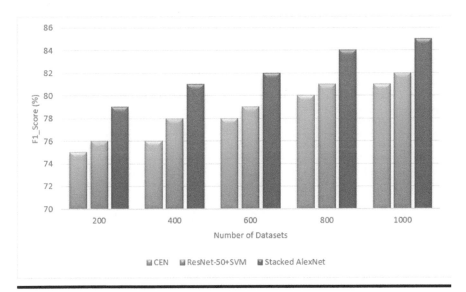

Figure 10.8   Comparison of F1-score.

datasets, while the Y-axis gives the F1-score. When compared, the first system gives 81% and 82%, while the proposed method achieves 85% which is 4% better than CEN and 3% better than ResNet-50+SVM.

■ **Root Mean Square Error (RMSE)**
RMSE gives the difference between predicted and observed values by the model.

$$RMSE = \sqrt{\sum_{t}^{T}(y'(t) - y(t))} \qquad (10.11)$$

Table 10.6 shows the comparison of existing CEN and ResNet-50+SVM with a proposed Stacked AlexNet method for RMSE.

Figure 10.9 compares RMSE between existing CEN, ResNet-50+SVM and proposed Stacked AlexNet, where the X-axis gives the count of datasets, while the Y-axis gives the value of RMSE. When compared, the existing method achieves 63% and 51%, while the proposed method achieves 40% which is 23% better than CEN and 11% better than ResNet-50+SVM.

■ **Relative Absolute Error (RAE)**
RAE compares the mean error to the errors of a trivial or naive model.

$$RAE = \frac{\sum_{i=1}^{n}(pi - Ai)^2}{\sum_{i=1}^{n} Ai} \qquad (10.12)$$

Table 10.6   Analysis of RMSE

Number of Datasets	CEN	ResNet-50+SVM	Stacked AlexNet
200	70	59	55
400	69	57	50
600	67	55	48
800	65	53	43
1,000	63	51	40

Table 10.7 shows the comparison of existing CEN and ResNet-50+SVM with the proposed Stacked AlexNet method for RAE.

Figure 10.10 compares RAE between existing CEN, ResNet-50+SVM and proposed Stacked AlexNet, where the X-axis gives the number of datasets, while the Y-axis gives RAE. When compared, the first model gives 50% and 50%, while the proposed method achieves 35% which is 10% better than CEN and 10% better than ResNet-50+SVM.

Table 10.8 shows the overall comparison of existing CEN and ResNet-50+SVM with the proposed Stacked AlexNet method.

Figure 10.11 compares overall parameters between existing CEN, ResNet-50+SVM and proposed Stacked AlexNet, where the X-axis gives the number of datasets, while the Y-axis gives overall values. The proposed Stacked AlexNet achieves better than existing methods.

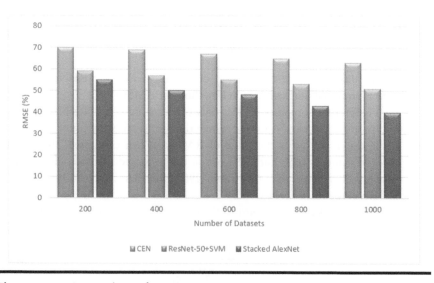

Figure 10.9   Comparison of RMSE.

Table 10.7   Analysis of RAE

Number of Datasets	CEN	ResNet-50+SVM	Stacked AlexNet
200	60	53	45
400	56	55	40
600	55	54	38
800	53	52	36
1,000	50	50	35

Table 10.8   Overall Comparative Analysis between Existing and Proposed Methods

Parameters	CEN	ResNet-50+SVM	Stacked AlexNet (Proposed)
Accuracy (%)	92	93	95
Precision (%)	90	91	93
Recall (%)	86	88	89
F1-Score (%)	81	82	85
RMSE (%)	63	51	40
RAE (%)	50	50	35

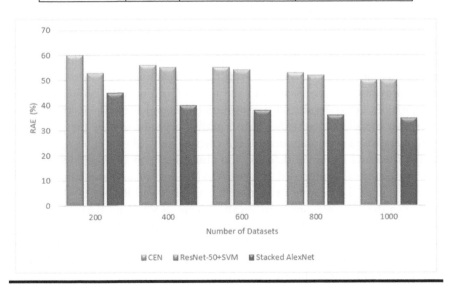

Figure 10.10   Comparison of RAE.

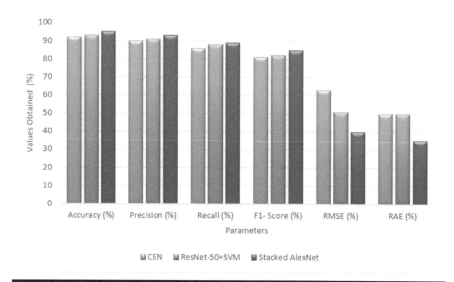

Figure 10.11 Overall comparative analysis.

10.10 Conclusion

The major threat to the supply of food across the world is plant disease. This research work illustrates the technological possibility of DL method depending on CNN to provide automated plant disease diagnosis by classifying the images. A public Plant Village dataset was used where the healthy and diseased leaf images are collected, and a deep convolutional neural network named as Stacked AlexNet is trained for classifying the species of crops. While comparing the proposed Stacked AlexNet with the conventional models, the proposed model provides robustness, reduces the number and quality requirements and also provides better results with convolutional neural network on the dataset. Thus, this model can assist the agriculturalist in production by preventing the plant disease and providing medical remedies quickly. Moreover, environmental complexities and issues are defeated and also achieve an accurate identification rate practically. This proposed Stacked AlexNet is evaluated and comparatively examined with the existing networks such as CEN and ResNet-50+SVM with respect to the accuracy, precision, recall, F-score, RMSE and RAE. As a result, the proposed Stacked AlexNet achieves 95% accuracy, 93% precision, 89% recall, 85% F1-score, 40% RMSE and 35% RAE. The future works concentrate on including game-theory process with multi-agent concept inside the AlexNet architecture to improve the overall accuracy.

References

Ali, H., Lali, M. I., Nawaz, M. Z., Sharif, M., & Saleem, B. A. (2017). Symptom based automated detection of citrus diseases using color histogram and textural descriptors. *Computers and Electronics in Agriculture, 138*, 92–104.

Behmann, J., Mahlein, A. K., Rumpf, T., Römer, C., & Plümer, L. (2015). A review of advanced machine learning methods for the detection of biotic stress in precision crop protection. *Precision Agriculture, 16*(3), 239–260.

Bharati, S., Podder, P., & Mondal, M. (2020). Artificial neural network based breast cancer screening: a comprehensive review. *arXiv preprint arXiv:2006.01767*.

Bharati, S., Podder, P., & Mondal, M. R. H. (2020). Hybrid deep learning for detecting lung diseases from X-ray images. *Informatics in Medicine Unlocked, 20*, 100391.

Bharati, S., Podder, P., Mondal, M., & Prasath, V. B. (2021). CO-ResNet: optimized ResNet model for COVID-19 diagnosis from X-ray images. *International Journal of Hybrid Intelligent Systems* (Preprint), *17*(1–2), 71–85.

Bharati, S., Podder, P., Mondal, M., & Prasath, V. B. (2021). Medical imaging with deep learning for COVID-19 diagnosis: a comprehensive review. *arXiv preprint arXiv:2107.09602*.

Brahimi, M., Arsenovic, M., Laraba, S., Sladojevic, S., Boukhalfa, K., & Moussaoui, A. (2018). Deep learning for plant diseases: detection and saliency map visualisation. In *Human and Machine Learning* (pp. 93–117). Springer, Cham.

Coulibaly, S., Kamsu-Foguem, B., Kamissoko, D., & Traore, D. (2019). Deep neural networks with transfer learning in millet crop images. *Computers in Industry, 108*, 115–120.

DeChant, C., Wiesner-Hanks, T., Chen, S., Stewart, E. L., Yosinski, J., Gore, M. A., …, & Lipson, H. (2017). Automated identification of northern leaf blight-infected maize plants from field imagery using deep learning. *Phytopathology, 107*(11), 1426–1432.

Ferentinos, K. P. (2018). Deep learning models for plant disease detection and diagnosis. *Computers and Electronics in Agriculture, 145*, 311–318.

Howard, A. G., Zhu, M., Chen, B., Kalenichenko, D., Wang, W., Weyand, T., …, & Adam, H. (2017). Mobilenets: efficient convolutional neural networks for mobile vision applications. *arXiv preprint arXiv:1704.04861*.

Kavitha, N. (2018). Plant leaf diseases detection using datamining – a survey. *IJRAR – International Journal of Research and Analytical Reviews (IJRAR), 5*(4), 233–237.

Khamparia, A., Bharati, S., Podder, P., Gupta, D., Khanna, A., Phung, T. K., & Thanh, D. N. (2021). Diagnosis of breast cancer based on modern mammography using hybrid transfer learning. *Multidimensional Systems and Signal Processing, 32*(2), 747–765.

Lee, S. H., Chan, C. S., & Remagnino, P. (2018). Multi-organ plant classification based on convolutional and recurrent neural networks. *IEEE Transactions on Image Processing, 27*(9), 4287–4301.

Liu, B., Ding, Z., Tian, L., He, D., Li, S., & Wang, H. (2020). Grape leaf disease identification using improved deep convolutional neural networks. *Frontiers in Plant Science, 11*, 1082.

Liu, H., Lee, S. H., & Chahl, J. S. (2017). A review of recent sensing technologies to detect invertebrates on crops. *Precision Agriculture, 18*(4), 635–666.

Lu, Y., Yi, S., Zeng, N., Liu, Y., & Zhang, Y. (2017). Identification of rice diseases using deep convolutional neural networks. *Neurocomputing, 267*, 378–384.

Mohanty, S. P., Hughes, D. P., & Salathé, M. (2016). Using deep learning for image-based plant disease detection. *Frontiers in Plant Science, 7,* 1419.

Ni, C., Wang, D., Vinson, R., Holmes, M., & Tao, Y. (2019). Automatic inspection machine for maize kernels based on deep convolutional neural networks. *Biosystems Engineering, 178,* 131–144.

Patil, J. K., & Kumar, R. (2017). Analysis of content based image retrieval for plant leaf diseases using color, shape and texture features. *Engineering in Agriculture, Environment and Food, 10*(2), 69–78.

Pertot, I., Kuflik, T., Gordon, I., Freeman, S., & Elad, Y. (2012). Identificator: a web-based tool for visual plant disease identification, a proof of concept with a case study on strawberry. *Computers and Electronics in Agriculture, 84,* 144–154.

Petrellis, N. (2018). A review of image processing techniques common in human and plant disease diagnosis. *Symmetry, 10*(7), 270.

Prasad, S., Peddoju, S. K., & Ghosh, D. (2016). Multi-resolution mobile vision system for plant leaf disease diagnosis. *Signal, Image and Video Processing, 10*(2), 379–388.

Rangarajan, A. K., Purushothaman, R., & Ramesh, A. (2018). Tomato crop disease classification using pre-trained deep learning algorithm. *Procedia Computer Science, 133,* 1040–1047.

Yang, N., Qian, Y., EL-Mesery, H. S., Zhang, R., Wang, A., & Tang, J. (2019). Rapid detection of rice disease using microscopy image identification based on the synergistic judgment of texture and shape features and decision tree–confusion matrix method. *Journal of the Science of Food and Agriculture, 99*(14), 6589–6600.

Zhang, Z., Liu, H., Meng, Z., & Chen, J. (2019). Deep learning-based automatic recognition network of agricultural machinery images. *Computers and Electronics in Agriculture, 166,* https://doi.org/10.1016/j.compag.2019.104978

Zhang, X., Qiao, Y., Meng, F., Fan, C., & Zhang, M. (2018). Identification of maize leaf diseases using improved deep convolutional neural networks. *IEEE Access, 6,* 30370–30377.

Zhang, S., You, Z., & Wu, X. (2019). Plant disease leaf image segmentation based on superpixel clustering and EM algorithm. *Neural Computing and Applications, 31*(2), 1225–1232.

Chapter 11

Classification of Coffee Leaf Diseases through Image Processing Techniques

Ali Hakan Işik and Ömer Can Eskicioglu

Department of Computer Engineering,
Burdur Mehmet Akif Ersoy University, Burdur, Türkiye

Contents

DOI: 10.1201/9781003311782-11

11.1 Introduction

Coffee is one of the most consumed beverages today. There are many different types of coffee. The quality of the coffee bean is one of the essential elements that is very important to its taste. Drinking coffee is among the common cultures of many different societies. The homeland of coffee is Asia and Africa. Coffee is the seed of a tree in the Rubiaceae family. These trees are 7–8 meters tall. Its flowers are white. They have their pleasant aroma.

Farmers harvest this plant two or three times a year. Coffee has a large trade volume around the world (Aroufai, 2020). It is extremely important that coffee trees are in a healthy production. The care of trees from diseases directly affects the harvest and quality of the product. In the study, the classification of leaf rust and leaf miner diseases that occur frequently in coffee trees has been made. Thus, the disease of coffee trees is detected and care can be provided according to the disease.

Rust disease on the coffee tree is one of the most important factors affecting coffee production. Symptoms of this disease are oily spots on the leaf surface that turn from orange to red and then brown with yellow edges. It is orange or yellow in the lower leaf and has a powdery structure on the leaf surface (Melo et al., 2006). The rusty leaves of the trees affected by this disease dry up and the tree becomes unable to produce a product. Often, the trees die within a few years.

Leaf miner disease of coffee trees is caused by the larvae of various moths, insects and flies. Harmful adults lay their larvae on the surface of the leaf. Later, the larvae enter the inner part of the leaf, causing tunneling.

In the literature, detailed research has been carried out on the diagnosis and detection of diseases in trees or leaves with deep learning. Similar studies have been investigated and examined. These studies are described below:

Türkoğlu and Hanbay (2018) study: A model based on Deep Convolutional Neural Networks is proposed for the diagnosis and detection of apricot diseases. In the convolutional layer, the window size was tested with five different filters and their performances were compared. The highest accuracy rate of 98.2% was obtained in the 9×9 window filter.

Özerdem and Acar (2011) study: Aim of this study was to determine the rust disease in lily flowers. A system that detects the disease status based on the change in leaves was designed using various GLCM-based classifiers. In the proposed system, K-Nearest Neighbor (KNN), Multilayer Perceptron (MLP) neural network and Least Squares Support Vector Machine (LS-SVM) were used as classifiers. As a result of the study, the highest accuracy rate of 88.9% was obtained.

Aslan (2021) study: Disease detection of peach trees was carried out using a Convolutional Neural Network. Classification of monilia laxa and sphaerolecanium prunastri diseases was performed using a pre-trained AlexNet model. Disease classification was done with 99.3% accuracy. It gives 1.44% higher performance than the studies in the literature.

Manso et al. (2019) study: It aimed to automatically determine the severity of leaf miner and leaf rust diseases encountered by farmers in Brazil with a smartphone. In order to determine the degree of the disease, background subtraction with a segmentation algorithm and background tests with HSR and YCbCr color scales are performed. In the classification part, artificial neural networks are used with an extreme learning algorithm. The results are promising and successful.

Hanbay (2018) study: Deep features obtained from Convolutional Neural Networks-based Vgg16, Vgg19 and AlexNet deep learning models were classified with KNN. The highest performance was found to be 94.8% using Vgg-16.

Jiang et al. (2019) study: Mosaic, Alternaria leaf spot, Gray spot, Rust and Brown spot are a type of apple leaf disease that is frequently seen in apples and affect the yield extremely. In this study, it is aimed to detect these diseases in apple leaves in real-time. A new detection model is proposed using the GoogleNet Inception structure and the Rainbow merging method. In a data set with 26,377 images, it was trained to detect five different diseases with the INAR-SSD model and showed 78.8% mAP detection performance.

Carneiro et al. (2021) study: It used a mobile application that can detect leaf mine and rust diseases in coffee leaves and measure the degree of disease. K-Means and Convolutional Neural Network are used with OpenCV. In the study, a less costly method was proposed with an average accuracy of 81.5%.

Jepkoech et al. (2021) study: A data set was created for the detection and diagnosis of coffee leaves. Images were taken from Kenya. There are five classes in the data set and it consists of 58,555 images. It is recommended to use deep learning and machine learning algorithms on this data set.

Ozguven and Adem (2019) study: It aimed to detect leaf spot disease in fields. Faster RCNN architecture has been proposed for the detection of leaf spots in sugar beet. The model was tested with 155 image data and 95.48% accuracy was achieved.

Esgario et al. (2020) study: It was aimed to use Convolutional Neural Networks to predict and describe the stress severity of coffee leaves caused by biotic agents. In the study, data augmentation methods were used to increase the accuracy value. With the ResNet50 model, biotic stress was classified with an accuracy of 95.24%. Disease severity estimation was found with 86.51% accuracy.

When the existing studies are examined, it is understood that there are studies on the detection and classification of diseases that occur on leaves or trees with deep learning methods. In this way, it is foreseen that the detected diseases will be treated appropriately. Studies in the literature are seen in Table 11.1; similar results were obtained with different methods. The results in our study and the results in the literature are compared. Our study gives much higher results than the examples in the existing literature. In our study, leaf rust and leaf mine diseases caused by the leaves of coffee trees were classified.

Table 11.1 Comparison of Literature Review

Author(s)	Method	Subject(s)	Results
Türkoğlu and Hanbay (2018)	Deep Convolutional Neural Networks	Apricot Diseases	The highest accuracy rate: 98.2%
Özerdem and Acar (2011)	KNN, MLP, LS-SVM	Rust Disease in Lily Flowers	The highest accuracy rate: 88.9%
Aslan (2021)	Pre-trained AlexNet	Disease Detection of Peach Trees	Accuracy: 99.3%
Hanbay (2018)	Vgg16, Vgg19, AlexNet + KNN	Apricot Diseases	The highest accuracy rate: 94.8%
Jiang et al. (2019)	GoogleNet Inception +Rainbow, INAR -SSD	Apple Leaf Disease	Detection Performance: 78.8% mAP
Carneiro et al. (2021)	OpenCV K-Means	Coffee Leaf Disease	Accuracy: 81.5%
Ozguven and Adem (2019)	Faster RCNN	Leaf Spot Disease	Accuracy: 95.48%
Esgario et al. (2020)	ResNet50	Stress Severity Of Coffee Leaves	Accuracy of Biotic Stress: 95.24% Accuracy of Disease severity estimation: 86.51%
Our Study	Xception, Resnet50, InceptionV3, VGG16, DenseNet121, DenseNet169, AlexNeT and MobileNeTv2	Coffee Leaf Disease	Xception: 100% Resnet50: 95.41% InceptionV3: 100% VGG16: 100% DenseNet121: 99.08% DenseNet169: 100% AlexNeT: 98.16% MobileNeTv2: 100%

11.2 Materials and Methods

In our study, a data set consisting of two classes and containing images of coffee leaves from Kaggle was used. In the data set used, there are images of leaf miners and leaf rust diseases. Histogram Equalization (HE), Contrast Limited

Adaptive Histogram Equalization (CLAHE), Gaussian Blur, Morphology Close, Morphology Gradient and RGB filtering were performed on these images. VGG-16, Xception, DenseNet121, DenseNet169, InceptionV3, ResNet50, AlexNet and MobileNetV2 deep learning models were used on the filtered images. It is aimed to obtain maximum performance values by working with 8, 16 and 32 batch size values and Adam, SGD, Nadam, Adadelta, Adamax and Adagrad optimization methods. The flowchart of our work is shown in Figure 11.1. According to this

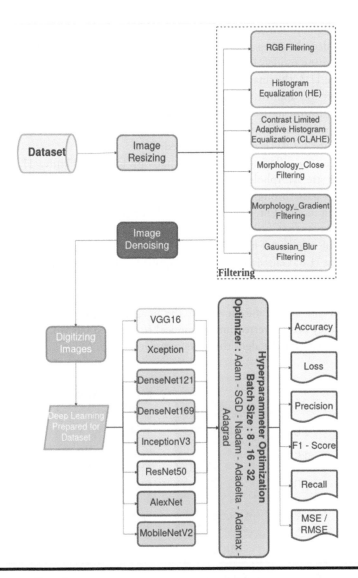

Figure 11.1   Flowchart.

diagram, images go through image preprocessing stages without entering deep learning architecture. After being translated into numerical expressions, it is given to deep learning architectures.

11.2.1 Data Set

There are 542 image data in the data set, 257 leaf mines and 285 leaf rust from two different classes. In Figure 11.2, there is a leaf image from each of the two classes in the data set. Two separate diseases are visible.

Images are adjusted to 224×224, 227×227 and 299×299 dimensions in accordance with deep learning models. Six different filtering processes were applied to the deep learning models in the study.

In Figure 11.3, the images of leaf metal and leaf rust were primarily resized and an RGB filter was applied.

Image optimization techniques are used to increase the performance of deep learning algorithms. Of these techniques, HE was applied in Figure 11.4. In Figure 11.5, the CLAHE method is applied.

There are two different types of Morphology filters in Figures 11.6 and 11.7. These filters are Morphology Close and Morphology Gradient. It is extremely important to pass through the filtering stages before the images are given to the deep learning model. Filtering is one of the basic elements that significantly affect model performance. Choosing the most suitable filter for solving the problem by increasing the number of filters is one of the goals in the preprocessing stage.

In Figure 11.8, Gaussian Blur filter is applied to the images in the data set.

In the image preprocessing part, the images were resized and different filters were applied. In the analysis, it was seen that the available data were sufficient and no need for data augmentation. Before the images are given to the deep learning algorithm, they are converted into numerical strings and labeled. Thus, the preparation of the data for the algorithm was completed.

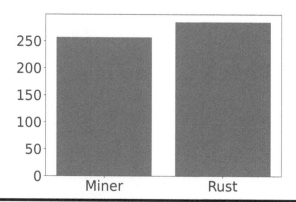

Figure 11.2   Comparison of data set classes.

Miner   Rust

Figure 11.3   RGB filtering.

Miner   Rust

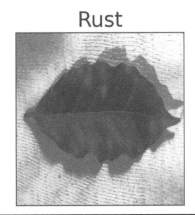

Figure 11.4   Applied Histogram Equalization.

Miner   Rust

Figure 11.5   Applied Contrast Limited Adaptive Histogram Equalization.

Miner

Rust

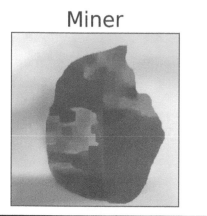
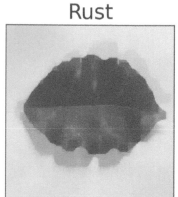

Figure 11.6   Morphology Close filtering.

Miner

Rust

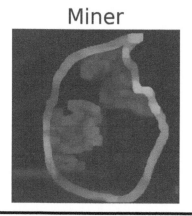
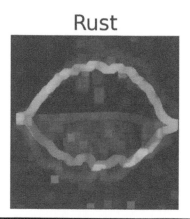

Figure 11.7   Morphology Gradient filtering.

Miner

Rust

Figure 11.8   Gaussian Blur filtering.

11.2.2 Deep Learning

It is aimed to find the model with the highest performance by using eight deep learning methods on the numerical data obtained after the preprocessing steps in our study. In our study, Vgg-16, Xception, InceptionV3, ResNet50, DenseNet121, DenseNet169, MobileNetV2 and AlexNet architectures were used.

VGG-16: The VggNet architecture is presented by Simonyan and Zisserman. VGG-16, one of the VGGNet architectures, is a deep learning algorithm developed for object detection, detection and identification (Simonyan & Zisserman, 2014). VGGNet is a broad network architecture with layers 11, 13, 16 and 19. The increase in layers in the VGG network significantly increases the processing capacity of the model (Ding et al., 2021). The increased depth in the VGG network has contributed to the learning of more complex features (Khamparia et al., 2021). The Vgg-16 architecture has one softmax, three full links, five pooling and thirteen convolution layers (Bharati et al., 2020). In our study, a 16-layer Vgg-16 architecture was used.

Xception: Xception is very similar to Inception architecture. The Xception architecture developed by Francois Chollet now consists of connections. It has 36 convolution layers and has 14 modules (Chollet, 2017). It has lower computational cost, thanks to its deeply separable architecture. The recommended image input is 299×299×3.

InceptionV3: It is a 42-layer deep neural network with 299×299×3 image inputs (Xia et al., 2017). It is more efficient than VGGNet architectures, but 2.5 times more computational than GoogleNet (Szegedy et al., 2016).

ResNet50: ResNet50 is a deep neural network consisting of 50 layers and 177 sublayers. There are many different architectures. The most commonly used architectures are ResNet18, ResNet50 and ResNet101. It ranked first with the lowest error rate (3.37%) in the ILSVRC competition held in 2015 (Bilal et al., 2021). Co-ResNet optimized over ResNet101 can be given as an example. This algorithm achieves higher performance values than existing ResNet architectures. Its optimization depends on the selection of hyperparameters suitable for the model (Aroufai, 2020; Bharati et al., 2021).

DenseNet: DenseNet is an efficient and high-performance deep neural network. DenseNet provides shortcuts between layers (Zhu & Newsam, 2018). Performance degradation with high parameter numbers is not a problem in this network. It is developed over the ResNet architecture. Each layer in the architecture receives information from all the previous layers (Huang et al., 2018).

MobileNet: When the problem level becomes more difficult and the number of available data increases, the cost of the study increases. The high number of parameters directly affects the speed of deep learning models. Researchers have proposed an efficient deep learning architecture with fewer parameters. In this architecture, instead of performing the standard convolutional operation in the feature extraction part, the deeply separable technique used in the Xception (Chollet, 2017) architecture is used. MobileNet is a more efficient deep learning model with fewer training parameters (Baydilli, 2021).

AlexNet: The AlexNet model was trained in ImageNet with 1.2 million images in the data set. ImageNet showed a high performance in the ILSVRC competition. Bu model genelde beş evrişimsel ve üç adet tam bağlantı katmanından oluşmaktadır (Bilal et al., 2021). It is quite similar to LeNet but is a larger and deeper model. It has a parameter calculation capacity of close to 60 million. It has 227×227×3 image inputs.

11.2.3 Performance Metrics

The confusion matrix is a performance measure for the classification process in deep learning and machine learning. It is a table with four different combinations of actual and estimated values. Table 11.2 contains the structure of the confusion matrix. Performance metrics are obtained from the relationship between the predictions classified by the algorithm and the actual values.

TP: True Positive (Actual: Yes & Predicted: Yes)
FP: False Positive (Actual: No & Predicted: Yes)
TN: True Negative (Actual: No & Predicted: No)
FN: False Negative (Actual: Yes & Predicted: No)

With the complexity matrix, we can explain the success performance of our classification model.

Accuracy: The ratio of true positive and true negative values to all values is called accuracy (Equation 11-1). It is the percentage of correct predictions.

$$Accuracy = \frac{TP + TN}{TP + TN + FP + FN} \tag{11.1}$$

Recall: The ratio of the sum of true positives, true positives and false negatives is called recall (Equation 11-2).

$$Recall = \frac{TP}{TP + FN} \tag{11.2}$$

Table 11.2   Confusion Matrix

	Predicted: No	*Predicted: Yes*
Actual: No	*True Negative*	*False Positive*
Actual: Yes	*False Negative*	*True Positive*

Precision: It gives the ratio of positive predicted values between true positive values (Equation 11-3).

$$Precision = \frac{TP}{TP + FP} \qquad (11.3)$$

F1-Score: The F1-score is a harmonic mean of sensitivity and precision. It is a measure of test accuracy (Equation 11-4).

$$F1 - Score = 2 * \frac{Precision * Recall}{Precision + Recall} \qquad (11.4)$$

Loss: It is the ratio of all the values that the classifier does not know correctly. Accuracy and Loss values are complementary to each other (Equation 11-5).

$$Error\ Rate = 1 - Accuracy \qquad (11.5)$$

Mean Squared Error (MSE): It is a regression loss function. It is the mean square loss per sample of all values found in the MSE data set. For each sample, the square loss is summed and averaged (Equation 11-6).

$$MSE = \frac{1}{N} \sum_{(x,y) \in D} \left(y - prediction(x)\right)^2 \qquad (11.6)$$

x: The feature used by the model to make predictions.
prediction(x): The value predicted by the x property.
y: The real value.
N: The number of samples.

11.3 Research Results

In our study, the diagnosis and classification of diseases of coffee leaves were made using deep learning techniques. In the study, deep learning models Vgg-16, Xception, InceptionV3, DenseNet121, DenseNet169, AlexNet, MobileNetv2 and ResNet50 were used. HE, CLAHE, Gaussian Blur, Morphology Close, Morphology Gradient and RGB filtering have been applied to each deep learning model. Our deep learning models have been tested with Adam, SGD, Nadam, Adadelta, Adamax and Adagrad optimization methods and the method that gives maximum accuracy has been selected. In addition to the changes in the hyperparameters, batch sizes 8, 16 and 32 have been tried in each optimization method and the performance has been recorded. Each training cycle was run 30 epochs. It is aimed to achieve maximum performance with eight deep learning models, six

Table 11.3   AlexNet Best Model Performance

Confusion Matrix		AlexNet Model Performance	
58	0	Accuracy: 98.1651%	MSE: 0.001983
2	49	Roc-Auc Score: 0.996619	MAE: 0.300157

different optimization methods and three different batch sizes in total. Each model was tested in 108 different variations and a total of 3,240 epoch training were carried out in sets of 30 epochs. A total of 25,920 epochs were trained on eight deep learning models, and the performances of the models were compared.

AlexNet deep learning model showed 98.16% accuracy rate by using Adagrad optimization method and Morphology Gradient filter together with 32 batch sizes. Table 11.3 shows the performance of the AlexNet deep learning model.

Figure 11.9 shows the graphs of Training-Validation Accuracy and loss values. The increase in accuracy and decrease in loss value during training means that the deep learning model learns and is expected.

DenseNet121 deep learning model showed 99.08% accuracy rate by using Adam optimization method and 8 batch sizes together with the CLAHE method. Table 11.4 shows DenseNet121's confusion matrix and performance metrics.

Figure 11.10 shows the Training-Validation graphs of DenseNet121 accuracy and loss values.

DenseNet169 deep learning model has 100.0% accuracy rate using the Adam optimization method and the CLAHE method together with 16 batch sizes. Table 11.5 shows DenseNet169's performance metrics and confusion matrix. DenseNet169 classifies 109 test data as free of error.

Figure 11.11 shows the Training-Validation graphics of the accuracy and loss values of the DenseNet169 deep learning model.

The Xception deep learning model has achieved 100.0% full performance by using Adamax optimization method and Morphology Gradient filter together with

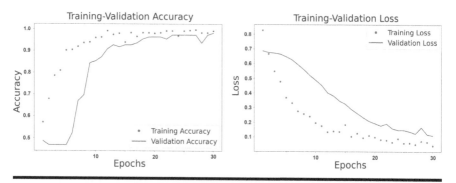

Figure 11.9   AlexNet Training-Validation Accuracy/Loss Graphics.

Table 11.4   DenseNet121 Best Model Performance

Confusion Matrix		DenseNet121 Model Performance	
47	1	Accuracy: 99.0825%	MSE: 0.010080
0	61	Roc-Auc Score: 0.997267	MAE: 0.014627

Table 11.5   DenseNet169 Best Model Performance

Confusion Matrix		DenseNet169 Model Performance	
51	0	Accuracy: 100%	MSE: 1.6767e-10
0	58	Roc-Auc Score: 1.0	MAE: 1.7788e-06

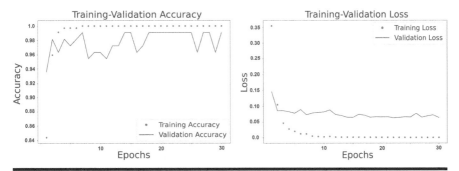

Figure 11.10   DenseNet121 Training-Validation Accuracy/Loss Graphics.

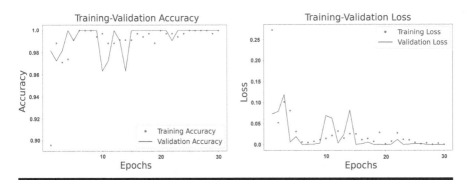

Figure 11.11   DenseNet169 Training-Validation Accuracy/Loss Graphics.

Table 11.6   Xception Best Model Performance

Confusion Matrix		Xception Model Performance	
50	0	Accuracy: 100%	MSE: 1.1850e-11
0	59	Roc-Auc Score: 1.0	MAE: 4.3295e-07

8 batch sizes. Table 11.6 shows the performance results of Xception deep learning architecture.

Figure 11.12 shows the Training-Validation graphs of the accuracy and loss values of the Xception deep learning model.

InceptionV3 deep learning model has achieved 100.0% full performance by using Nadam optimization method and Morphology Gradient filter with 16 batch sizes. The performance results of the InceptionV3 deep learning algorithm are shown in Table 11.7. The model provides full success.

Figure 11.13 shows the Training-Validation graphics of the accuracy and loss values of the InceptionV3 deep learning model.

By using the ResNet50 deep learning model, the Adam optimization method and the Morphology Close filter with 32 batch sizes, a 95.41% accuracy rate was achieved. ResNet50 has the lowest performance ratio of all results. Table 11.8 shows ResNet50's performance metrics and confusion matrix.

Figure 11.14 shows the Training-Validation graphics of the accuracy and loss values of the ResNet50 deep learning model.

The Vgg16 deep learning model was used with the Nadam optimization method and the CLAHE method together with the 16 batch sizes, resulting in 100.0% full accuracy. In Table 11.9, confusion matrix, performance and error metrics of VGG16 are given.

Figure 11.15 shows the Training-Validation graphics of the accuracy and loss values of the Vgg16 deep learning model.

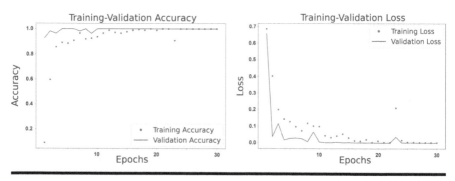

Figure 11.12   Xception Training-Validation Accuracy/Loss Graphics.

Table 11.7   InceptionV3 Best Model Performance

Confusion Matrix		*InceptionV3 Model Performance*	
59	0	Accuracy: 100%	MSE: 3.8726e-14
0	50	Roc-Auc Score: 1.0	MAE: 4.2485e-08

Table 11.8   ResNet50 Best Model Performance

Confusion Matrix		*ResNet50 Model Performance*	
49	2	Accuracy: 95.4128%	MSE: 0.0369606
3	55	Roc-Auc Score: 0.992562	MAE: 0.0518532

Table 11.9   Vgg16 Best Model Performance

Confusion Matrix		*Vgg16 Model Performance*	
48	0	Accuracy: 100.0%	MSE: 4.09423e-12
0	61	Roc-Auc Score: 1.0	MAE: 3.78303e-07

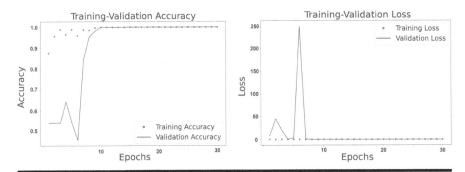

Figure 11.13   InceptionV3 Training-Validation Accuracy/Loss Graphics.

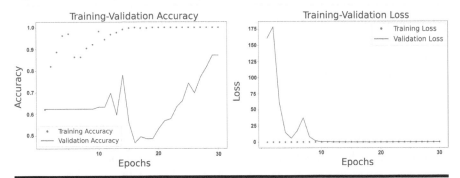

Figure 11.14   ResNet50 Training-Validation Accuracy/Loss Graphics.

Table 11.10   MobileNetv2 Best Model Performance

Confusion Matrix		MobileNetv2 Model Performance	
54	0	Accuracy: 100.0%	MSE: 0.001174
0	55	Roc-Auc Score: 1.0	MAE: 0.005918

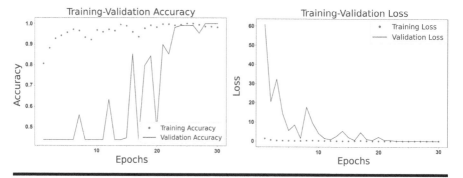

Figure 11.15   Vgg16 Training-Validation Accuracy/Loss Graphics.

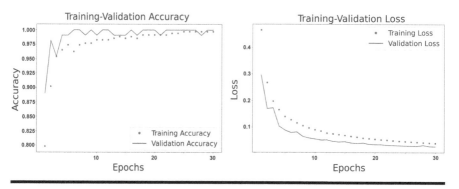

Figure 11.16   MobileNetv2 Training-Validation Accuracy/Loss Graphics.

By using MobileNetv2 deep learning model, the SGD optimization method and 8 batch sizes and HE method, 100.0% full accuracy was achieved. In Table 11.10, confusion matrix, error and performance metrics of MobileNetv2 are given.

Figure 11.16 shows the Training-Validation graphics of the accuracy and loss values of the MobileNetv2 deep learning model.

Figure 11.17 shows the performance comparison of eight models. Each model shows the desired success in the classification of diseases in coffee leaves. Deep learning solves this problem easily.

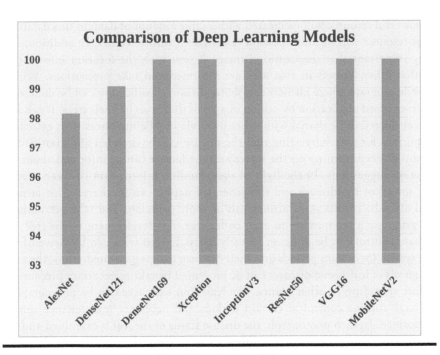

Figure 11.17 Comparison of deep learning models.

11.4 Discussion

In the study, the effect of different data preprocessing techniques on the performance results was examined in detail. In the study, it has been shown that deep learning techniques can classify with 100% accuracy when fed with sufficient data.

Deep learning algorithms show successful results in classifying the coffee leaves in our study. In addition, similar studies in the literature generally give acceptable results. In our study, we worked with AlexNet, DenseNet121, DenseNet169, Xception, InceptionV3, ResNet50, Vgg16 and MobileNetv2, and 100% success was achieved in DenseNet169, Xception, InceptionV3, Vgg16, MobileNetv2. AlexNet, ResNet50 and DenseNet121, classified with acceptably high accuracy. Deep learning methods are fed with data. It is in a structure that can be used as a data set for future studies. These data are very important for highly accurate and sensitive detection. Clean data is one of the indispensable parts of deep learning algorithms. In the literature, for the detection of plant diseases, disease diagnosis is made by deep learning using leaf data. It is recommended that this structure, which works from powerful computers, be efficient and of high-performance, and run on smartphones. It will be useful not only to label the image to be classified as a disease but also to create a general database.

A powerful resource will be created with a large amount of data on this database. This resource will be an important resource for future studies. In addition, it is very important that the captured image is sent with the location information so that other farmers in that area are informed and take precautions. With a mobile program where farmers can share, disease classification can be done with a server-based application by taking images of the leaves on their trees. It can also be considered to be shared with other users via mobile interfaces. It is extremely important for crop harvesting that the disease can be detected and classified by means of deep learning on the server and the farmer can be informed about the solution suggestions. In the light of these studies, information that can predict the spread of the disease and the general situation can be shared with farmers and officials. In this way, farmers can be more conscious and take precautions. By assigning a tag number to each coffee tree, the development of the tree and disease control can be done on a yearly basis. Tagged trees can be viewed from the system for certain periods and their 3D map can be generated. Thus, the early diagnosis of leaf-borne diseases can be prevented by taking necessary precautions before spreading to other plants. The leaves on each tree can be photographed through routine control at certain periods and necessary maintenance can be performed. In each photograph, the disease status of the leaf is examined and the tree is labeled according to the result examined. Thus, the care, disease diagnosis and detection of these trees, which have a high economic value, can be made.

11.5 Conclusion

In our study, the classification of rust and miner disease in coffee leaves was fulfilled through eight different deep learning methods. AlexNet, InceptionV3, Xception, Vgg16, DenseNet121, DenseNet169, MobileNetv2 and ResNet50 architectures are used in the study. InceptionV3, Xception, DenseNet169, Vgg16 and MobileNetv2 performed 100% performance. A total of six image filtering methods, including RGB, Histogram Equalization, Contrast Limited Adaptive Histogram Equalization, Morphology Close, Morphology Gradient and Gaussian Blur filters, were used before the deep learning algorithms. In our study, 8, 16 and 32 batch sizes and Adam, SGD, Nadam, Adadelta, Adamax and Adagrad optimization methods were used for each deep learning algorithm. Performance results were obtained with 108 different combinations of hyperparameters through each deep learning method. Thanks to the gridsearch, parameters provide the highest performance in the deep learning model. Throughout the study, Tesla K80 GPUs were used in Google Colaboratory environment. The deep learning algorithm in our study was tested in 864 different variations. The highest results obtained from the models were presented in the study. The designed deep learning algorithms provided the best results in classifying the disease state in coffee leaves.

References

Aroufai, İ. A. (2020). *Farkli Ülkelerde Yetiştirilen Kahve Çekirdeklerinin Antioksidan Özelliklerinin Ve Biyoalinabilirliklerinin Belirlenmesi Idriss Amit Aroufai Merve Sabuncu.* Bursa Uludağ Üniversitesi. http://acikerisim.uludag.edu.tr/jspui/handle/11452/11500

Aslan, M. (2021). Derin Öğrenme ile Şeftali Hastalıklarının Tespiti. *European Journal of Science and Technology, 23,* 540–546. https://doi.org/10.31590/ejosat.883787

Baydilli, Y. Y. (2021). Polen Taşıyan Bal Arılarının MobileNetV2 Mimarisi ile Sınıflandırılması. *European Journal of Science and Technology, 21,* 527–533. https://doi.org/10.31590/ejosat.836856

Bharati, S., Podder, P., & Mondal, M. R. H. (2020). Hybrid deep learning for detecting lung diseases from X-ray images. *Informatics in Medicine Unlocked, 20,* 100391. https://doi.org/10.1016/j.imu.2020.100391

Bharati, S., Podder, P., Mondal, M. R. H., & Prasath, V. B. S. (2021). CO-ResNet: optimized ResNet model for COVID-19 diagnosis from X-ray images. *International Journal of Hybrid Intelligent Systems, 17*(1–2), 71–85. https://doi.org/10.3233/HIS-210008

Bilal, M., Üniversitesi, E. H., Fakültesi, M., & Bölümü, M. (2021). Önceden eğitilmiş derin ağlar ile göğüs röntgeni görüntüleri kullanarak pnömoni siniflandirilmasi. *Konya Journal of Engineering Sciences, 1,* 2667–8055. https://doi.org/10.36306/konjes.794505

Carneiro, A. L. C., Silva, L. de B., & Faulin, M. S. A. R. (2021). *Artificial intelligence for detection and quantification of rust and leaf miner in coffee crop.* http://arxiv.org/abs/2103.11241

Chollet, F. (2017). Xception: Deep learning with depthwise separable convolutions. *Proceedings of the IEEE Conference on Computer Vision and Pattern Recognition,* pp. 1251–1258.

Ding, X., Zhang, X., Ma, N., Han, J., Ding, G., & Sun, J. (2021). Repvgg: Making vgg-style convnets great again. *Proceedings of the IEEE/CVF Conference on Computer Vision and Pattern Recognition,* pp. 13733–13742.

Esgario, J. G. M., Krohling, R. A., & Ventura, J. A. (2020). Deep learning for classification and severity estimation of coffee leaf biotic stress. *Computers and Electronics in Agriculture, 169,* 105162. https://doi.org/10.1016/j.compag.2019.105162

Hanbay, D. (2018). *Apricot disease identification based on attributes obtained from deep learning algorithms.* https://doi.org/10.1109/IDAP.2018.8620831

Huang, G., Liu, S., Van Der Maaten, L., & Weinberger, K. Q. (2018). Condensenet: An efficient densenet using learned group convolutions. *Proceedings of the IEEE Conference on Computer Vision and Pattern Recognition,* pp. 2752–2761.

Jepkoech, J., Mugo, D. M., Kenduiywo, B. K., & Too, E. C. (2021). Arabica coffee leaf images dataset for coffee leaf disease detection and classification. *Data in Brief, 36,* 107142. https://doi.org/10.1016/j.dib.2021.107142

Jiang, P., Chen, Y., Liu, B., He, D., & Liang, C. (2019). Real-time detection of apple leaf diseases using deep learning approach based on improved convolutional neural networks. *IEEE Access, 7,* 59069–59080. https://doi.org/10.1109/ACCESS.2019.2914929

Khamparia, A., Bharati, S., Podder, P., Gupta, D., Khanna, A., Phung, T. K., & Thanh, D. N. H. (2021). Diagnosis of breast cancer based on modern mammography using hybrid transfer learning. *Multidimensional Systems and Signal Processing 32*(2), 747–765. https://doi.org/10.1007/S11045-020-00756-7

Manso, G. L., Knidel, H., Krohling, R. A., & Ventura, J. A. (2019). *A smartphone application to detection and classification of coffee leaf miner and coffee leaf rust.* http://arxiv.org/abs/1904.00742

Melo, G. A., Shimizu, M. M., & Mazzafera, P. (2006). Polyphenoloxidase activity in coffee leaves and its role in resistance against the coffee leaf miner and coffee leaf rust. *Phytochemistry, 67*(3), 277–285. https://doi.org/10.1016/j.phytochem.2005.11.003

Türkoğlu, M., & Hanbay, D. (2018). Apricot disease identification based on attributes obtained from deep learning algorithms. In 2018 *International Conference on Artificial Intelligence and Data Processing* (IDAP), pp. 1–4. IEEE

Özerdem, M. S., & Acar, E. (2011). *The estimation of rust disease of daylily leaf images with GLCM based different classification methods, 2*(2), 95–105.

Ozguven, M. M., & Adem, K. (2019). Automatic detection and classification of leaf spot disease in sugar beet using deep learning algorithms. *Physica A: Statistical Mechanics and Its Applications, 535*, 122537. https://doi.org/10.1016/j.physa.2019.122537

Simonyan, K., & Zisserman, A. (2014). Very deep convolutional networks for large-scale image recognition. *arXiv preprint arXiv:1409.1556.*

Szegedy, C., Vanhoucke, V., Ioffe, S., Shlens, J., & Wojna, Z. (2016). Rethinking the inception architecture for computer vision. *Proceedings of the IEEE Conference on Computer Vision and Pattern Recognition*, pp. 2818–2826.

Xia, X., Xu, C., & Nan, B. (2017). Inception-v3 for flower classification. *2017 2nd International Conference on Image, Vision and Computing, ICIVC 2017*, pp. 783–787. https://doi.org/10.1109/ICIVC.2017.7984661

Zhu, Y., & Newsam, S. (2018). DenseNet for dense flow. *Proceedings of the International Conference on Image Processing, ICIP, 2017-September*, pp. 790–794. https://doi.org/10.1109/ICIP.2017.8296389

Chapter 12

The Use of Artificial Intelligence to Model Oil Extraction Yields from Seeds and Nuts

Chinedu M. Agu[1], Charles C. Orakwue[2], and Albert C. Agulanna[3]

[1]Chemical Engineering Department, Michael Okpara University of Agriculture, Umudike, Nigeria

[2]Chemical Engineering Department, Nnamdi Azikiwe University, Awka, Nigeria

[3]Materials and Energy Technology Department, Projects Development Institute (PRODA), Enugu, Nigeria

Contents

DOI: 10.1201/9781003311782-12

12.1 Introduction

The limitations in the availability of fossil fuels, as well as their non-biodegradability and environmental impact, have made it relevant to the search for alternative sources of energy (Murthy et al., 2020). Renewable energy sources such as solar energy, wind energy, and bioenergy (from biofuels) are considered the best alternatives due to their environmentally friendly nature. Biofuels such as biodiesel has a great potential in replacing fossil-derived fuels, including diesel and gasoline. Since one of the primary approaches to the production of biodiesel starts with the extraction of oils from seeds and nuts, it is necessary to optimize the oil extraction process. Seeds and nuts oil extraction is vital today because of the growing need to look for alternatives for conventional fossil-derived fuels. High availability of these seeds/nuts such as *Terminalia catappa (TC), Colocynthis vulgaris,* and *Irvingia gabonensis (IG),* and their complete biodegradability, encourages the use of vegetable oils. There are different methods of extracting oils from seeds and nuts. These methods include but are not limited to solvent extraction, mechanical press, and supercritical carbon. However, the commonly used extraction method is the solvent extraction method. The soxhlet extractor is the commonly used approach for solvent extraction. The importance of the extraction of vegetable oils from seeds has led to studies on its modeling and optimization (Agu, Menkiti, Ekwe, & Agulanna, 2020). Several approaches have been studied for the oil extraction process. These include kinetic modeling, thermodynamics, and optimization, which involve the application of mathematical, kinetic models and thermodynamic data. Another approach to modeling and optimization is the application of response surface methodology (RSM) and artificial neural networks (ANNs) tools (Garg & Jain, 2020).

Optimization is a requirement for boosting the production yield of biofuels (Samuel, Okwu, Amosun, Verma, & Afolalu, 2019; Samuel et al., 2020). ANN development dates back to five decades ago. However, its usefulness in several applications was found fifteen years ago, although its areas of application are rapidly growing (Sabzalian, Khashei, & Ghaderian, 2014). The fundamental working principle of ANN is based on artificially constructed neurons. These neurons are made of processing elements called perceptrons. Perceptrons represent learning algorithms that work in a similar way to the biological neuron. However, despite the functional resemblance of perceptrons to biological neurons, perceptrons require a series of nodes of numerical data to be passed through it rather than electrical signals. It is through the different input connections that data is entered into the neuron, each having predetermined weights. Then, the weighted input sum is utilized by the transfer function for determining the output value. Contrary to the conventional mathematical (kinetic) models used in neuro-computing techniques, ANNs processes are trained. Hence, the algorithm shows how the inputted data is used to obtain the output value with minimum error. Importantly, because the neural networks behave non-linearly during the training processes, the network models can extrapolate and interpolate, hence predicting the values outside and within the trained data range (Jensen, Karki, & Salehfar, 2004). The ANN limitation is seen in the failure of its black box in linking the input parameters with the response (Samuel et al., 2021).

12.2 Some Oil Seeds

TC tree is a tropical plant, which occurs naturally in the tropical regions, and originated in Meridional Asia, and is part of the family of Combretaceae (Agu et al., 2020). The tree is also reported to be broadly planted for ornamental purposes and it grows freely in dried and oxygen-filled sandy soils (Janporn et al., 2014). Globally, over 680,000 tons of TC seeds are produced annually. The plant predominantly grows in the Southeastern region of Nigeria (Janporn et al., 2014; Agu, Menkiti, Kadurumba, & Menkiti, 2015). TC kernels as non-food competing kernels contain both unsaturated and saturated fatty acids, minerals, amino acids (up to 25%), and lipids (up to 52%) (Janporn et al., 2014). The oil yield of the TC kernel is high (Meka, Nali, Songa, & Kolapalli, 2012; Monnet, Gbogeuri, Kouadio, Koffi, & Kouame, 2012; Agu, Menkiti, Nwabanne, & Onukwuli, 2019). The TC kernel has been reported to contain oil in a high amount: 50 wt% (Iha et al., 2014), 60 wt% (Weerawatanakorn, 2013), 60.45 wt% (Agu, 2014; Menkiti, Agu, & Udeigwe, 2015), and 63.65 wt% (Monnet et al., 2012). There have been several studies targeted on its use in the production of biodiesel (Iha et al., 2014), as well as in the production of transformer oil (Agu et al., 2019; Menkiti, Agu, Ejikeme, & Onyelucheya, 2017; Agu et al., 2015) from TC kernel oil.

Colocynthis vulgaris Shrad (CVS), which is also called melon, is commonly cultivated in the West African region of Africa, particularly during the rainy season, and used to thicken soups. The plant is part of the Cucurbitaceae family (Essien and Eduok, 2013). In the Southeastern part of Nigeria, CVS is commonly called "egusi" (Ogbonna and Obi, 2000). CVS and its seeds are widely utilized in producing jellies, juices, soups, salads, and sauces (Raj, Mohanty, & Bhargava, 2015; Essien and Eduok, 2013). Additionally, several countries in the Middle East and Africa extract oil from CVS seeds for frying and cooking purposes (Ekpa and Isaac, 2013). CVS is very rich in vegetable oil. The CVS seeds also contain dehydroporiferasterol, cholesterol, fatty acids, amino acid, and protein (Balakrishnan, Varughese,

& Subash, 2015). CVS seed is reported to contain approximately 35% protein and 50 wt% oil (Agu, Kadurumba, Orakwue, Mbamalu, & Agulanna, 2018).

IG, also recognized as "Ogbono" in the Southeastern region of Nigeria, belongs to Simaroubaceae family (Mgbemena, Ilechukwu, Okwunodolu, Chukwurah, & Lucky, 2019). It is a plant of economic value and its origin can be traced back to the tropical regions of Central and West Africa (Ekpe, Bassey, Udefa, & Essien, 2018). The *IG* tree is highly domesticated in West African regions (Ayeni and Ojokoh, 2019; Ogboru, Idibie, & Nwaokobia, 2019). The *IG* tree bears fruits seasonally and produces large numbers of edible fruit between April and July (Ekpe et al., 2018). For many years now, several types of research on *Irvingia gabonensis* kernel (IGK) were mainly focused on its medicinal and nutritional utilization. Also, its finely milled kernels are used as a thickener for traditional soups because of their high protein and fat content (Etta, Olisaeke, & Iboh, 2014; Zoué, Bedikou, Faulet, Gonnety, & Niamké, 2013). In local industrial utilization, the IG kernels are utilized to produce local soap because of their high oil content (Mateus-Reguengo, Barbosa-Pereira, & Rembangouet, 2020). IG oil content has been reported to be within the range of 60 wt% to 68.8 wt%, making it the desired product for industrial applications (Bello, Fade-Aluko, Anjorin, & Mogaji, 2011; Omeh, Ezeja, & Ugwudike, 2012; Agu, Menkiti, Ohale, &Ugonabo, 2021).

12.3 ANN and RSM

ANNs are the most common tool for artificial learning (Gueguim-Kana, Oloke, Lateef, & Adesiyan, 2012; Betiku, Okunsolawo, Ajala, & Odedele, 2015). It works on the principle of data processing, which is synonymous with the functionality of the human brain. Therefore, the ANNs comprise a cluster of interconnected neurons. ANN is based on the collection of biological mathematical techniques of statistical analysis, regression, and data learning by machine, with high complexity (Shanmuganathan, 2016). The application of ANN includes process modeling and optimization, data mining, language processing, image recognition, pattern matching, and signal processing (Okpalaeke, Ibrahim, Latinwo, & Betiku, 2020). Thus, the ANNs can be used for modeling, and also provide solutions to complex non-linear processes between a system (Nazghelichi, Aghbashlo, & Kianmehr, 2011; Ameer, Chun, & Kwon, 2017). Additionally, ANNs can function as tools to predict, control, and optimize processes (Esonye, Onukwuli, Ofoefule, & Ogah, 2019b; Fayyazi et al., 2015). The capability of ANNs to optimize processes has been observed in the production of methyl ester, transesterification, and esterification processes (Esonye, Onukwuli, & Ofoefule, 2019a; Ofoefule, Esonye, Onukwuli, Nwaeze, & Ume, 2019). In recent years, the ANNs tools have been employed in providing solutions to various biology, psychology, metrology, neurology, mathematics, medicine, science, and engineering problems (Betiku and Ajala, 2014). Nonetheless, for the extraction of oils, ANNs were applied for several types of research. During the evaluation of the SHC (specific heat capacity) and VI (viscosity index) for the production of oilseeds-based grease lubricant, Idoko, Oseni, and Tuleun, (2017) used ANNs. For the extraction of Argemone mexicana seeds oil prediction, ANN was used (Suryawanshi and Mohanty 2018). Similarly, for *Terminalia catappa L.* kernel oil prediction, ANN was also used (Agu et al, 2020).

Another statistical and mathematical tool employed to optimize processes involving responses is the RSM. RSM as a vital tool for optimization is applied in many engineering processes (Nazghelichi et al., 2011). A benefit of the RSM statistical approach is that it allows lesser experimental runs, yet provides passable outcomes (Onoji, Iyuke, Igbafe, & Daramola, 2017). Another benefit of the RSM statistical approach is that it can generate polynomial equations of second-order that have a relationship between the process (independent) parameters and the responses (dependent) parameters (Onoji et al., 2017). Several studies have reported the RSM application in seeds/nuts oil extraction yield predictions. For example, in the prediction of CVSS oil yield, RSM was applied and obtained an oil yield of 52.81 wt% (Kadurumba, Orakwue, & Agu 2018). Onoji et al. (2017) used RSM in oil yield extraction optimization for *Hevea brasiliensis* seed (HBS) oil and obtained 42.98 wt%. Similarly, RSM was applied in TCK oil prediction and obtained 60.45 wt% (Agu et al., 2015).

In other words, this chapter discusses seeds and nuts oil yield prediction by the application of ANN. *TC, Colocynthis vulgaris,* and *IG* are the seeds considered. The chapter explores seeds/nuts oil extraction, the method of extraction, and the oil yields. Furthermore, the process parameters and their effect on the process were also discussed. Additionally, the seeds/nuts oils physiochemical properties and gas chromatographic analysis were considered. More importantly, the chapter explores the reasons for using ANN as an Artificial Intelligence tool for this study. Finally, the efficacy of ANN and RSM was compared.

12.4 Extraction and Oil Yields of the Seeds Understudy

The process of extraction is influenced by several important factors and these factors are not dependent on the substance to be extracted. These influencing factors include pressure, temperature, extraction time, solvent, and the matrix properties of the material (including leaves, nuts, seeds, and plants) (Hernandez, Lobo, & Gonzalez, 2009). Seeds/nuts oil extraction can be carried out through various methods of extraction. These methods of extraction are classified as common (conventional) and novel/new (non-conventional) (Azmir et al., 2013; Reyes-Jurado, Franco-Vega, Ramirez-Corona, Palou, & Lopez Malo, 2014). The common methods of extraction are simultaneous distillation-extraction, solvent extraction, mechanical pressing, cold pressing (CP), steam distillation, and hydro-distillation (HD) methods (Reyes-Jurado et al., 2014). Conversely, the novel/new methods of extraction are ultrasound-assisted extraction (UAE) (Goula, 2013; Yolmeh, Najafi,

& Farhoosh, 2014) and supercritical fluid extraction (Zhao and Zhang, 2014). The most commonly used oil extraction method for seeds under study (TCK, CVSS, and IGS) is the solvent method (Kadurumba et al., 2018; Menkiti et al., 2017). Although this method is commonly used, it has several shortcomings, including the residual toxic solvent in the oil after extraction (Menkiti et al., 2017). Soxhlet extraction is a widely used solvent extraction method commonly used to extract oil from seeds and nuts. Soxhlet extraction is a popular technique, which is highly efficient than other common methods of extraction. However, the limitation of the soxhlet extraction is that it does not apply to thermo-liable compounds (Wang and Weller, 2006).

The component of the soxhlet extractor that is utilized for extracting valuable substances from the solutes (seeds, nuts, leaves, and plants) is the solvent. Here, the solutes are the *Terminalia catappa L.*, *CVS*, and *IGS*. Several solvents are utilized in the soxhlet extractor. The most common of these solvents is n-hexane, and its popularity is attributed to its high solubility and ease of recovery (Agu et al., 2021). Other notable solvents include chloroform, ethanol, petroleum ether, and benzene (Menkiti et al., 2015; Agu et al., 2021). The benefits of the extractor include the unrequired filtration after leaching, simplicity of its operation, cheap procurement cost, and the apparatus can maintain a relatively high temperature (Wang and Weller, 2006; Luque de Castro and Gracia-Ayuso, 1998). Nonetheless, just like every other apparatus and method of extraction, soxhlet extractor has few short-comings. These shortcomings include the inability to speed up the extraction process through agitation in the apparatus, a longer time of extraction, as well as the fact that it requires a large quantity of solvent (Wang and Weller, 2006).

The oil yields of *Terminalia catappa L.*, *CVS*, and *IGS* oils are dependent on several factors such as particle size, temperature, time, and solvent (Agu, Menkiti, Agulanna, & Nweke, 2018a). Several authors have reported the application different solvents using soxhlet extractor to extract oils from various seeds. Kadurumba et al. (2018) used n-hexane to extract *Colocynthis vulgaris* seed oil and obtained 53.86% yield. Agu et al. (2021) extracted *IG* seed oil through soxhlet extraction setup using hexane and recorded 68.8% (by weight) oil yield. Also, Menkiti, Agu, & Agu (2019) used hexane to extract *TC* oil and obtained 60.45% yield. Similarly, Agu et al. (2018a) extracted oil from the same substrate using n-hexane and petroleum ether and obtained oil yields of 60.45% and 56%, respectively. The high oil yields for these seeds indicate their potential industrial applications.

12.5 The Process Parameters Effect on Oil Yield

As earlier stated, the oil yields obtained from extraction *Terminalia catappa L.* kernel (TCK), *Colocynthis vulgaris Shrad* seed (CVSS), and IGS oils depend on particle size, temperature, as well as time. Figures 12.1, 12.2, and 12.3 show the particle size effect on oil yields from CVSS, IGS, and TCK, respectively. In the same way, Figures 12.4, 12.5, and 12.6 show the temperature effect on the oil extraction

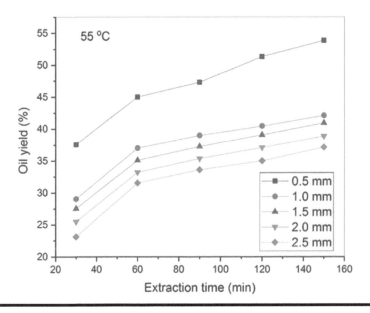

Figure 12.1   Particle size effect on CVSS oil yield.

Source: Kadurumba et al. (2018).

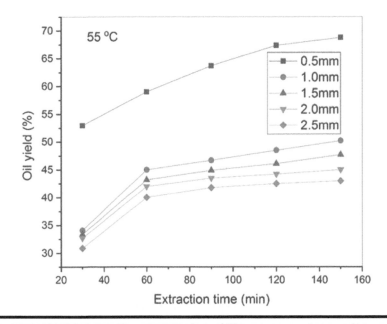

Figure 12.2   Particle size effect on IGS oil yield.

Source: Agu et al. (2021).

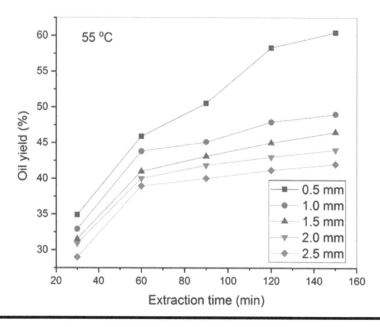

Figure 12.3   Particle size effect on TCK oil yield.

Source: Agu and Menkiti (2017).

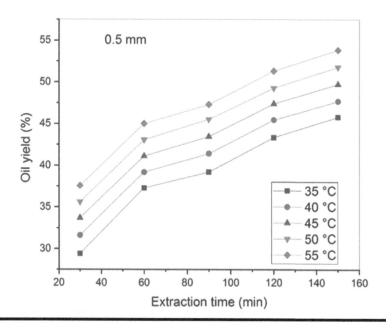

Figure 12.4   Temperature effect on CVSS oil yield.

Source: Kadurumba et al. (2018).

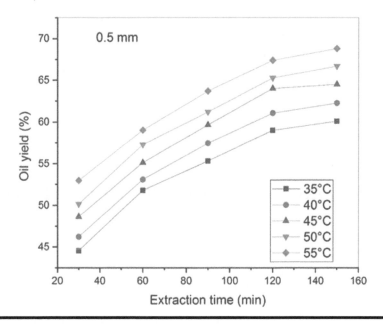

Figure 12.5 Temperature effect on IGS oil yield.

Source: Agu et al. (2021).

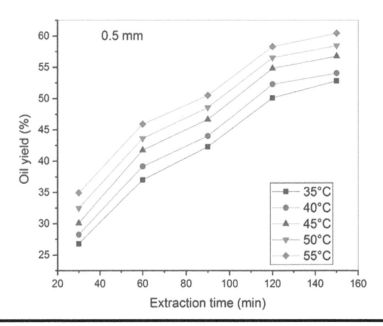

Figure 12.6 Temperature effect on TCK oil yield.

Source: Agu and Menkiti (2017).

yields from the aforementioned seeds, respectively. As reported by Agu et al. (2021), the oil yield of IGS oil increased as the temperature was increased. This indicates a direct proportionality of temperature with oil yield. Kadurumba et al. (2018) and Agu and Menkiti (2017) also reported the same observation for CVSS oil and TCK oil. Similarly, the IGS oil yield has a direct proportionality with extraction time, just as it is the case for TCK and CVSS. However, the oil yields for these three seeds have an indirect proportionality with particle size. As the particle sizes were reduced, the oil yields for the seeds increased and vice versa.

12.6 Fatty Acid Composition of the Seeds Understudy

The fatty acids compositions of the oils extracted from the seeds were determined through gas chromatography. As seen in Table 12.1, the *Terminalia catappa* kernels (TCK), CVSS, and IGS oils contain seven fatty acids each. The oil of these three seeds contains only four similar fatty acids, namely stearic acid, myristic acid, lauric acid, and linoleic acid. However, the TCK and IGS oils contain oleic acid and palmitic acid. Additionally, TCK oil contains linolenic acid, while CVSS oil contains palmitoleic acid, arachidic acid, and decanoic acid (also contained in IGS oil). The unsaturated fatty acid contents of TCK, CVSS, and IGS oils are

Table 12.1 Physiochemical Properties of TCK, CVSS, and IGS Oils

Fatty Acid	TCK oil (%)	CVSS oil (%)	IGS oil (%)
C10:0 (Decanoic acid)	–	7.64	1.11
C12 (Lauric acid)	0.94	8.8223	36.6
C14 (Myristic acid)	0.54	8.973	53.71
C16:0 (Palmitic acid)	36.01	–	5.23
C16:2 (Palmitoleic acid)	–	0.1253	–
C18 (Stearic acid)	6.4	18.514	0.8
C18:1 (Oleic acid)	33.25	–	1.82
C18:2 (Linoleic acid)	22.26	61.767	0.49
C18:3 (Linolenic acid)	0.59	–	–
C20 (Arachidic acid)	–	1.67774	–
Saturated fatty acids	43.89	37.9867	97.45
Unsaturated fatty acids	56.11	61.8923	2.3

Source: Agu et al. (2021); Kadurumba et al. (2018); Agu and Menkiti (2017).

56.11%, 61.8923%, and 2.3%, respectively. However, TCK, CVSS, and IGS oils contain 43.89%, 37.9867%, and 97.45% saturated acids, respectively. As shown in Table 12.1, the linoleic fatty acid content of the CVSS oil is 61.767%, making it the largest fatty acid in the oil. Essien and Eduok (2013) reported the same occurrence of linoleic acid (62.14%) for CVSS oil.

12.7 Physiochemical Properties of the Seeds Oils Studied

The oil physiochemical characteristics are usually reported after the oils have been extracted. In Table 12.2, the physiochemical properties of *Terminalia catappa L.* kernel (TCK), CVSS, and IGS oils are given. As shown in Table 12.2, the dielectric strength of TCK and IGS oils was 30.61kV and 25.83kV, respectively. The moisture contents of TCK oil (2.1) and IGS oil (3.75) are high compared to that of CVSS oil (0.78). High oil content is mostly attributed to moisture existence in the seeds before extraction. Low moisture content is attainable through effective drying of the seeds before extraction. The viscosity reported for TCK oil is 20.29 Cp. This is higher than those of IGS oil (19.37 Cp) and CVSS oil (7.64 Cp). However, the viscosities of the oils are enhanced through transesterification of the oils to meet

Table 12.2   Physiochemical Properties of TCK, CVSS, and IGS oils

Oil Property	TCK oil	CVSS oil	IGS oil	Standard method
Flash point (°C)	260	230	285	ASTM D93
Moisture content (%)	2.1	0.78	3.75	AOAC 926.12
Pour point (°C)	3	–	17	ASTM D97
Dielectric strength (kV)	30.61	–	25.83	IEC 60156
Iodine value (g/I$_2$/100g oil)	101.86	112.53	98.75	AOAC 993.20
Acidity (mg KOH/g oil)	4.3	1.66	5.18	AOAC 969.17
Viscosity (Cp)	20.29	7.64	19.37	ASTM D445
Specific gravity	0.870	0.817	0.900	ASTM D93
Color	Yellow	Yellow	–	ASTM D1209
Saponification value (mg KOH/g)	156.36	193.61	220.19	AOAC 920.16
Peroxide value (M/mol/kg)	3.01	6.82	12	AOAC 965.35

Source: Agu et al. (2021); Kadurumba et al. (2018); Agu and Menkiti (2017).

the designated standard for biodiesels. Also, the acid content of TCK oil, CVSS oil, and IGS oil are 4.3 mg KOH/g, 1.66 mg KOH/g, and 5.18 mg KOH/g, respectively (see Table 12.2). The oil sample acidity shows the quantity of the fatty acid contained in the oil. Therefore, the lower the acid value, the more stable the oil could be. Also, low acidity protects oils from peroxidation and rancidity (Aremu, Ibrahim, & Bamidele, 2015). Additionally, the suitability of oil for soaps and paints manufacturing, as well as its edibility is indicated by the acidity of the oil (Aremu et al., 2015). In Table 12.2, the saponification value for IGS oil is 220.19 mg KOH/g. The value is higher than the saponification value for CVSS oil and TCK oil, which were 193.61 mg KOH/g and 156.36 mg KOH/g, respectively. The saponification value measures the oxidative-prone nature of oil when stored. It also reveals the volatile nature of the oil. Oils with low saponification value may be unsuitable for the production of soaps, shampoo and oil-based ice cream. The peroxide value for the seed oil is 3.01 M/mol/kg (for TCK oil), 6.82 M/mol/kg (for CVSS oil), and 12 M/mol/kg (for IGS oil). The peroxide value indicates oil's lipid oxidative nature. Refined oils are reported to have lower peroxide values compared to unrefined ones (Aremu et al., 2015). Oils with high peroxide values are said to contain antioxidants in very low levels and have high rancidity. Nonetheless, the addition of certain antioxidants such as butyl hydroxyl anisole and propygadlate may lower the rancidity of oils (Kyari, 2008). The flashpoint of TCK oil is 260 °C. The value is higher than the flashpoint of CVSS oil (230 °C), but lower than the flashpoint of IGS oil (285 °C). The iodine value measures the unsaturation extent of oil. Iodine value is a characteristic for identifying oils extracted from the seed. As shown in Table 12.2, the iodine value of IGS oil is 98.75 g/I_2/100g oil, while those of TCK oil and CVSS oil were 101.86 g/I_2/100g oil and 112.53 g/I_2/100g oil, respectively.

12.8 Reasons for Using ANNs to Model Oil Extraction Yields of Seeds and Nuts

Optimization and modeling the process of oil extraction through solvent extraction is very important because it helps to maximize oil yield, reduce the cost of production, and save time. However, the conventional method of optimization and modeling consumes time and is burdensome. The conventional methods of modeling oil extraction processes through solvent extraction include kinetic models. ANN is a computational method that was manufactured on the premises of neurons present in the human system (the biological neural system). ANNs exhibit parallel processing and complex non-linear data handling ability, noisy data, coupled incomplete data (Perpetuo et al., 2012). Additionally, ANNs when trained have the capacity to fit and predict data. ANN simulation is employed in quantifying non-linear functions among the actual responses and connecting factors through iteratively training the obtained experimental data (Achanta, Kowaski, & Rhodes, 1995).

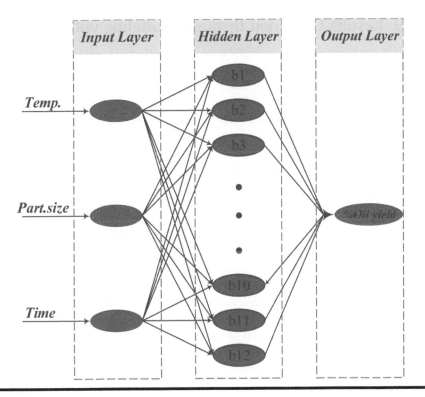

Figure 12.7   ANN architecture.

Source: Agu et al. (2020).

Thus, ANN is a superior technique for modeling non-linear datasets. As shown in Figure 12.7, the ANN architecture comprises a hidden layer, an output layer, which has one neuron, and an input layer, which has three neurons.

RSM is a tool that statistically describes how the independent parameters influence a process. It also describes parameters interaction. Recent studies have compared ANN and RSM to determine which tool gives the best optimization and modeling outcome. For example, Rajendra et al. (2009) carried out a comparison of the performance of RSM and ANN in predicting and optimizing biodiesel yield. The authors found out that ANN was a better predictive tool than RSM. Also, in the use of *Saccharomyces cerevisae* free cells and the influence of β-cyclodextrin on the production of benzene alcohol through the biological transformation of benzaldehyde, Adepoju and Olawale (2014) reportedly used RSM and ANN, with ANN giving more acceptable results. Additionally, in the prediction of TCK oil yield, Agu et al. (2020) used RSM and ANN. The authors reported that from the model-predicted results, ANN was effective and better due to its lower RMS and higher R^2 values.

12.9 Results Obtained through Modeling with ANNs

In ANN modeling, several topologies would be observed to know the hidden layer's optimum neuron number. For instance, where ANN and RSM were utilized in modeling TCK oil yield, the optimum number of neurons was varied between 10 and 15 (Agu et al., 2020). Additionally, root mean square error (RMS) and R^2 were used to measure ANN predictability of the network. In using RMS and R^2 for ANN predictability, the input layer, the optimum number of neurons, and the output layer must be selected where R^2 is the closest to 1.0, and the error values of the RMS are the lowest. Similarly, ANN and Adaptive Neuro-Fuzzy Inference System (ANFIS) were used for Huracrepitan seeds oil yield predictability by Nwosu-Obieogu, Aguele, and Chiemenem (2020). The authors confirmed that ANN gave the best prediction with an R^2 value of 0.999 and a mean square error (MSE) value of 5.6319E^{-13} (as the lowest MSE value). In the same way, Adepoju, Esu, Olu-Arotiowa, and Blessed (2019) used ANN and RSM for Butter Fruit seeds oil yield prediction. They reported that ANN gave a better prediction of the yield due to the R^2 value for ANN which was closest to 1. Recent studies used ANN and RSM models for predictions. Esonye, Onukwuli, Anadebe, Ezeugo, and Ogbodo (2021) reported higher Dyacrodes edulis seed oil of 2.12, 5.81, and 5.14% at more solute requirements of 10, 11.11, and 24%, faster rate of extraction of 0.62, 0.30, and 5.47%, and smaller particle sizes of 0.65, 0.26, and 1.10%, for M/C, ethanol, and n-hexane solvents, respectively, indicating better prediction compared to RSM. In another study, Okpalaeke, Ibrahim, Latinwo, and Betiku (2020) reported that the ANN model produced a 0.58% FFA optimum reduction at a 62.8 min reaction time, a dosage of 6 wt% of ferric sulfate, and a molar ratio of 18.51 of methanol/NSO as opposed to the 0.62% FFA optimum reduction at 75 min reaction time, a dosage of 5.03 wt% of ferric sulfate, and a molar ratio of 23.5 of methanol/NSO produced by RSM. This indicated that RSM was outperformed by ANN.

12.10 Criteria for Determining Better Predictive Tool between ANN and RSM

Several statistical tools which are used for the determination of the better predictive tool between ANN and RSM include but are not usually limited to the MSE, Coefficient of determination (R^2), RMS, coefficient of correlation (R), and absolute average deviation (AAD).

■ **Coefficient of determination (R^2)**
  R^2 is the sum of squares ratio, which is accounted for through regression to the deviation of the sum of squares around the mean for a model with a constant term. It can be determined using Equation (12.1). If R^2 for a model is closer

to 1.0, then the predictability of the model is high. This applies to both the kinetic (mathematical) models and the ANN and RSM models.

$$R^2 = 1 - \sum_{i=1}^{n} \left(\frac{\left(X_{i,cal} - X_{i,exp} \right)^2}{\left(X_{avg,exp} - X_{i,\ exp} \right)^2} \right) \tag{12.1}$$

■ **Coefficient of correlation (R)**
The coefficient of correlation represents the correlation between y and $\hat{y}$ as shown in Equation (12.2). The coefficient of correlation is commonly known as the multiple correlation coefficient. If R for a model is closer to 1.0, then the model suitably fits the process which it describes. This is applied to both the kinetic (mathematical) models, and in the ANN and RSM models.

$$R = \frac{\Sigma \left(\hat{y}_i - \bar{\hat{y}}_i \right) \left(y_i - \bar{y}_i \right)}{\left[\Sigma \left(y_i - \bar{\hat{y}}_i \right)^2 \right]^{\frac{1}{2}} \left[\Sigma \left(y_i - \bar{y}_i \right)^2 \right]^{\frac{1}{2}}} \tag{12.2}$$

■ **Root mean square (RMS)**
RMS refers to the square root of the mean square. The RMS is given in Equation (12.3). A model is classified as the best fit for a process if it has the lowest RMS value.

$$RMS = \sqrt{\frac{1}{N} \sum_{i=1}^{N} \left(\frac{X_{i,exp} - X_{i,cal}}{X_{i,exp}} \right)^2} \tag{12.3}$$

■ **Mean square error (MSE)**
MSE estimates or measures the average/mean of the squares of the errors. MSE is represented using Equation (12.4), with (y_i) and (f_i) as the actual and estimated values, respectively. The lower the MSE value of a model for a particular process, the better the model describes the process.

$$MSE = \frac{1}{N} \sum_{i=1}^{N} \left(f_i - y_i \right)^2 \tag{12.4}$$

■ **Absolute average deviation (AAD)**
The AAD defines the accuracy level of the prediction of a model and is given by Equation (12.5). AAD value is given in percentage. The lower the value of AAD for a model, the better the model describes the process.

$$AAD(\%) = \left(\frac{1}{N} \sum_{i-1}^{n} \left(\frac{y_{pred} - y_{exp}}{y_{exp}} \right) \right) \times 100 \tag{12.5}$$

12.11 Comparison of the Results from the ANN and RSM Models

It is important to compare the predictability of ANN and RSM models with the values obtained from experiments. Several researchers have used these numerical/statistical tools to determine the predictability of the ANN and RSM models. Agu et al. (2020) used RMS and R^2 to evaluate the predictability of ANN and RSM models. Figures 12.8 and 12.9 show that the ANN model has better fitting than the RSM model. The ANN values were closer to the experimentally derived data, compared to RSM values. Also, the R^2 values were the highest for ANN, while the RMS values were the lowest for ANN too, compared to the RSM (Agu et al., 2020). In comparing the ANN and RSM optimizing tools, Adepoju et al. (2019) reported that the R^2 values for ANN were 0.8712, while RSM was 0.8454. In another study, Akintunde, Ajala, and Betiku (2015) optimized the oil yield from

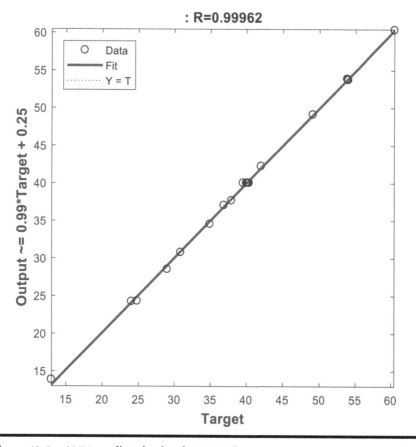

Figure 12.8   ANN predicted value for TCK oil.

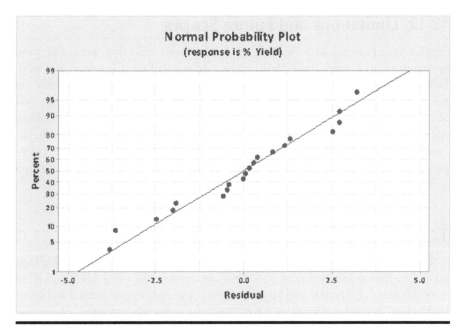

Figure 12.9   RSM predicted value for TCK oil extractions.

Source: Agu et al. (2020).

Bauhinia monandra seed using ANN and RSM. The authors used R, R^2, and AAD to evaluate the predictability of the optimization tools. ANN was the better optimization tool with the following values (AAD = 0.27%, R^2 = 0.9991, R = 0.9995), compared to that of RSM with these (AAD = 0.49%, R^2 = 0.9986, R = 0.9993) values. Additionally, Okpalaeke et al. (2020) applied ANN and RSM to mathematically model ferric sulfate-catalyzed esterification of neem seed oil. They reported that both models described the esterification process, with R^2 values of 0.9908 and 0.9656 for ANN and RSM, respectively. Also, the mean relative percent deviation (MRPD) of ANN (2.9%) was lower than 6.5% recorded for RSM. In another study, Kolakoti and Satish (2020) used RSM and ANN modeling tools to get the highest biodiesel yield from low-grade oil by a heterogeneous catalyst. When comparing the results, they observed that both models displayed reasonable performance in achieving optimum biodiesel yield. However, in determining the most efficient model, ANN showed the least MSE value of 0.08 and highest R-value of 0.9924, and R^2 value of 0.9848, an indication of its supremacy over RSM. In a more recent study, Esonye et al. (2021) modeled and optimized the extraction of Dyacrodes edulis seed oil by applying soft-computing tools like RSM and ANN, while ANN had better accuracy than RSM.

12.12 Limitations and Future Scopes

Studies have proved and presented ANN as superior modeling, prediction, and optimization tool, more than RSM for the extraction of oils from seeds and nuts. However, ANN has some limitations to its application. First, ANN is relied on precise information input to the system currently being studied, and on the method of training used. Therefore, a huge amount of data is required to ensure that the results are accurate. Therefore, further works are required to reduce the error in the model when additional inputs are required. Furthermore, ANN should be compared to other neural network tools such as recurrent neural networks (RNN), and convolutional neural networks (CNNs).

12.13 Conclusion

ANN was applied for oil yield predictions of the seeds/nuts, with special emphasis on *TC, Colocynthis vulgaris*, and *IGS*. Also, obtained results using ANN and RSM were compared. Extraction and oil yields from these seeds were presented and it was highlighted that solvent extraction was the commonest method for oil extraction. Also, these seeds contain a very reasonable amount of oil. Furthermore, the oils fatty acid composition and physicochemical characteristics of the aforementioned seeds oils considered were presented. The ANN models results indicate the high predictability of the oil yields from seeds and nuts. Thus, this chapter justifies the application of ANN in the predictability of the seeds and nuts oil yields. Moreover, it was affirmed that ANN gave a better fit, compared to RSM.

References

Achanta, A. S., Kowaski, J. G., & Rhodes, C. T. (1995). Artificial neural network: implication for pharmaceutical sciences. *Drug Development and Industrial Pharmacy*, 21, 119–155.

Adepoju, T. F., & Olawale, O. (2014). Transesterification of CASO with low amount of free fatty acids and its optimization. *Review of Energy Technologies and Policy Research*, 1, 20–27.

Adepoju, T. F., Esu, I. O., Olu-Arotiowa, O. A., & Blessed, E. (2019). Oil Extraction from butter fruit (*Dacryodes Edulis*) seeds and its optimization via response surface and artificial neural network. *Nigerian Journal of Technological Development*, 16(2), 56–62.

Agu, C. M., Menkiti, M. C., Agulanna, A. C., & Nweke, I. E. (2018a). Solvents comparative extraction performance for the synthesis of potential *Terminalia catappa* transformer oil. *Journal of Engineering and Applied Sciences*, 13 (2018), 25–39.

Agu, C. M. (2014). Production, "Characterization and Utilization Potential of Bioextracts as Transformer Oil" (Unpublished M.Eng. thesis). NnamdiAzikiwe University.

Agu, C. M., & Menkiti, M. C. (2017). Effects of natural antioxidants on the essential properties of modified Terminalia catappa L. kernel oil: a possible substitute for mineral oil transformer fluid. *Biofuels*, 11(6), 741–752.

Agu, C. M., Kadurumba, C. H., Orakwue, C. C., Mbamalu, M. P., & Agulanna, A. C. (2018). Optimisation of key process parameters for solvent extraction of oil from Colocynthis vulgaris Shrad seeds using response surface methodology. *Journal of the Chinese Advanced Materials Society*, 6(2), 169–185.

Agu, C. M., Menkiti, M. C., Ekwe, B. E., & Agulanna, A. C. (2020). Modeling and optimization of Terminalia catappa L. kernel oil extraction using response surface methodology and artificial neural network. *Artificial Intelligence in Agriculture*, 4, 1–11.

Agu, C. M., Menkiti, M. C., Nwabanne, J. T., & Onukwuli, O. D. (2019). Comparative assessment of chemically modified *Terminalia catappa* L. kernel oil samples – a promising ecofriendly transformer fluid. *Industrial Crops and Products*, 140, 111727. https://doi.org/10.1016/j.indcrop.2019.111727

Agu, C. M., Menkiti, M. C., Ohale, P. E., & Ugonabo, V. I. (2021). Extraction modeling, kinetics, and thermodynamics of solvent extraction of *Irvingia gabonensis* kernel oil, for possible industrial application. *Engineering Reports*, 3. https://doi.org/10.1002/eng2.12306

Agu, C., Menkiti, M., Kadurumba, C., & Menkiti, N. (2015). Process parameter optimization for transformer oil extraction from Terminalia catappa seed using response surface methodology. *Journal of the Chinese Advanced Materials Society*, 3(4), 328–344.

Akintunde, A. M., Ajala, S. O., & Betiku, E. (2015). Optimization of Bauhinia monandra seed oil extraction via artificial neural network and response surface methodology: a potential biofuel candidate. *Industrial Crops and Products*, 67, 387–394.

Ameer, K., Chun, B. S., & Kwon, J. H. (2017). Optimization of supercritical fluid extraction of steviol glycosides and total phenolic content from Stevia rebaudiana (Bertoni) leaves using response surface methodology and artificial neural network modeling. *Industrial Crops and Products*, 109, 672–685.

Aremu, M. O., Ibrahim, H. T., & Bamidele, O. (2015). Physicochemical characteristics of the oils extracted from some Nigerian plant foods – a review. *Chemical and Process Engineering Research*, 7, 36–52.

Ayeni, O. H., & Ojokoh, A. O. (2019). Effect of fermentation on the nutrient and anti-nutrient contents of African bush mango (*Irvingia gabonensis*) seeds. *Microbiology Research Journal International*, 27(6), 1–14.

Azmir, J., Zaidul, I. S. M., Rahman, M. M., Sharif, K. M., Mohamed, A., & Sahena, F. (2013). Techniques for extraction of bioactive compounds from plant materials: a review. *Journal of Food Engineering*, 117, 426–436.

Balakrishnan, N., Varughese, T. M., & Subash, P. (2015). A review on Citrullus lanatus thumb. *International Journal of Pharmaceutics Science Letters*, 5(3), 558–562.

Bello, E. I., Fade-Aluko, A. O., Anjorin, S. A., & Mogaji, T. S. (2011).Characterization and evaluation of African bush mango nut (Dika nut) (Irvingia gabonensis) oil biodiesel as alternative fuel for diesel engines. *Journal of Petroleum Technology and Alternative Fuels*, 2(9), 176–180.

Betiku, E., & Ajala, S. O. (2014). Modeling and optimization of Thevetia peruviana (yellow oleander) oil biodiesel synthesis via Musa paradisiacal (plantain) peels as heterogeneous base catalyst: a case of artificial neural network vs. response surface methodology. *Industrial Crops and Products*, 53, 314–322.

Betiku, E., Okunsolawo, S. S., Ajala, S. O., & Odedele, O. S. (2015). Performance evaluation of artificial neural network coupled with generic algorithm and response surface methodology in modeling and optimization of biodiesel production process parameters from shea tree (Vitellaria paradoxa) nut butter. *Renewable Energy*, 76, 408–417.

Ekpa, O. D., & Isaac, I. O. (2013). The fatty acid composition of melon (Colocynthis vulgaris Shrad) seed oil and its application in synthesis and evaluation of alkyd resins. *IOSR Journal of Applied Chemistry*, 4(4), 30–41.

Ekpe, O. O., Bassey, S. O., Udefa, A. L., & Essien, N. M. (2018). Physicochemical properties and fatty acid profile of Irvingia gabonensis (Kuwing) seed oil. *International Journal of Food Science and Nutrition*, 3(4), 153–156.

Esonye, C., Onukwuli, O. D., Anadebe, V. C., Ezeugo, J. N. O., & Ogbodo, N. J. (2021). Application of soft-computing techniques for statistical modeling and optimization of Dyacrodes edulis seed oil extraction using polar and non-polar solvents. *Heliyon*, 7, e06342.

Esonye, C., Onukwuli, O. D., & Ofoefule, A. U. (2019a). Optimization of methyl ester production from Prunus amygdalus seed oil using response surface methodology and artificial neural networks. *Renewable Energy*, 130, 61–72

Esonye, C., Onukwuli, O. D., Ofoefule, A. U., & Ogah, E. O. (2019b). Multi-input multi-output (MIMO) ANN and Nelder-Mead's simplex based modeling of engine performance and combustion emission characteristics of biodiesel-diesel blend in CI diesel engine. *Applied Thermal Engineering*, 151, 100–114.

Essien, E. A., & Eduok, U. M. (2013). Chemical analysis of Citrullus lanatus seed oil obtained from Southern Nigeria. *Organic Chemistry*, 54, 12700–12703.

Etta, H. E., Olisaeke, C. C., & Iboh, C. I. (2014). Effect of *Irvingia gabonensis* (Aubry-Lecomte ex O'Rorke) seeds on the liver and gonads of male albino rats. *Journal of Biology, Agriculture and Healthcare*, 4(1), 10–15.

Fayyazi, E., Ghobadian, B., Najafi, G., Hosseinzadeh, B., Mamat, R., & Hosseinzadeh, J. (2015). An ultrasound-assisted system for the optimization of biodiesel production from chicken fat oil using a genetic algorithm and response surface methodology. *Ultrasonics Sonochemistry* 26, 312–320.

Garg, A., & Jain, S. (2020). Process parameter optimization of biodiesel production from algal oil by response surface methodology and artificial neural networks. *Fuel*, 277, 118254. https://doi.org/10.1016/j.fuel.2020.118254

Goula, A. M. (2013). Ultrasound-assisted extraction of pomegranate seed oil — kinetic modeling. *Journal of Food Engineering*. 117, 492–498.

Gueguim-Kana, E. B., Oloke, J. K., Lateef, A., & Adesiyan, M. O. (2012). Modeling and optimization of biogas production on saw dust and other co-substrates using artificial neural network and genetic algorithm. *Renewable Energy*, 46, 276–281.

Hernandez, Y., Lobo, M. G., & Gonzalez, M. (2009). Factors affecting sample extraction in the liquid chromatographic determination of organic acids in papaya and pineapple. *Food Chemistry*, 114(2), 734–741.

Idoko, F. A., Oseni, M. I., & Tuleun, L. T. (2017). Artificial neural network prediction of viscosity index and specific heat capacity of grease lubricant produced from selected oil seeds and blends. *American Journal of Engineering Research (AJER)*, 6(3), 176–181.

Iha, O. K., Alves, F. C. S., Suarez, P. A. Z., Silva Cassia, R. P., Meneghetti, M. R., & Meneghetti, S. M. P. (2014). Potential application of Terminalia catappa L. and Carapa guianensis oils for biofuel production: physical-chemical properties of neat vegetable oils, their methyl-esters and bio-oils (hydrocarbons). *Industrial Crops and Products*, 52, 95–98.

Janporn, S., Ho, C., Chavasit, V., Pan, M., Chittrakorn, S., Ruttarattanamongkol, K., & Weerawatanakorn, M. (2014). Physicochemical properties of Terminalia catappa seed oil as a novel dietary lipid source. *Journal of Food and Drug Analysis*, 23(2), 1–9.

Jensen, R. R., Karki, S., & Salehfar, H. (2004). Artificial neural network based estimation of mercury speciation in combustion flue gases. *Fuel Processing Technology*, 85, 451–462.

Kadurumba, C. H., Orakwue, C. C., & Agu, C. M. (2018): Kinetics, thermodynamics and process parameter impact on solvent extraction of oil from Colocynthis vulgaris Shrad (melon) seeds. *Journal of the Chinese Advanced Materials Society*, 6(2), 186–206.

Kolakoti, A., & Satish, G. (2020). Biodiesel production from low-grade oil using heterogeneous catalyst: an optimisation and ANN modelling. *Australian Journal of Mechanical Engineering*, 1–13. https://doi.org/10.1080/14484846.2020.1842298

Kyari, M. Z. (2008). Extraction and characterisation of seed oils. *International Agrophysics*, 22, 139–142.

Luque de Castro, M. D., & Gracia-Ayuso, L. E. (1998). Soxhlet extraction of solid materials: An outdated technique with a promising innovative future. *Analytica Chimica Acta*, 369, 1–10

Mateus-Reguengo, L., Barbosa-Pereira L., & Rembangouet, W. (2020). Food applications of *Irvingia gabonensis* (Aubry-Lecomte ex. O'Rorke) Baill, the 'bush mango': a review. *Critical Reviews in Food Science and Nutrition*, 60, 2446–2459.

Meka, V. S., Nali, S. R., Songa, A. S., & Kolapalli, V. R. M. (2012). Characterization and in vitro drug release studies of a natural polysaccharide Terminalia catappa gum (Badam gum). *American Association of Pharmaceutical Scientists (AAPS) PharmSciTech*, 13(4), 1451–1464.

Menkiti, C. M., Agu, C. M., & Agu, I., E. (2019). Extraction kinetics and physicochemical studies of Terminalia catappa L Kernel oil utilization potential. *Iranian Journal of Chemistry & Chemical Engineering*, 38(3) 223–243.

Menkiti, M. C., Agu, C. M., & Udeigwe, T. K., (2015). Extraction of oil from *Terminalia catappa L.*: Process parameter impacts, kinetics, and thermodynamics. *Industrial Crops and Products*, 77, 713–723.

Menkiti, M. C., Agu, C. M., Ejikeme, P. M., & Onyelucheya, O. E. (2017). Chemically improved Terminalia catappa L. oil: a possible renewable substitute for conventional mineral transformer oil. *Journal of Environmental Chemical Engineering*, 5, 1107–1118.

Mgbemena, N. M., Ilechukwu, I., Okwunodolu, F. U., Chukwurah, J-V. O., & Lucky, I. B. (2019). Chemical composition, proximate and phytochemical analysis of Irvingia gabonensis and Irvingia wombolu peels, seed coat, leaves and seeds. *Ovidius University Annals of Chemistry*, 30(1), 65–69.

Monnet, Y. T., Gbogeuri, A., Kouadio, P., Koffi, B., & Kouame, L. P. (2012). Chemical characterization of seeds and seed oil from mature *Terminalia catappa* fruits harvested in Cote d'Ivoire. *International Journal of Biosciences*, 10, 110–124.

Murthy, S. K., Goyal, A., Rajasekar, N., Pareek, K., Nguyen, T. T., & Garg, A. (2020). Predictive modelling and surface analysis for optimization of production of biofuel as a renewable energy resource: Proposition of artificial neural network search. *Mathematical Problems in Engineering*, 2020, 4065964. https://doi.org/10.1155/2020/4065964

Nazghelichi, T., Aghbashlo, M., & Kianmehr, M. H. (2011). Optimization of an artificial neural network topology using coupled response surface methodology and genetic algorithm for fluidized bed drying. *Computers and Electronics in Agriculture*, 75, 84–91.

Nwosu-Obieogu, K.,Aguele, F., & Chiemenem, L. (2020). Soft computing prediction of oil extraction from Huracrepitan seeds. *Kemija u Industriji*. 69(11–12), 653–658.

Ofoefule, A. U., Esonye, C., Onukwulic, O. D., Nwaeze, E., & Ume, C. S. (2019). Modeling and optimization of African pear seed oil esterification and transesterification using artificial neural network and response surface methodology comparative analysis. *Industrial Crops and Products*, 140, 111707.

Ogbonna, P. E., & Obi, I. U. (2000). Effect of poultry manure and planting date on the growth and yield of egusi melon (Colocynthis citrullus T. L.) in the Nsukka Plains of South Eastern Nigeria, *Samaru Journal of Agricultural Research*, 16, 63–74.

Ogboru, R. O., Idibie, A. C., & Nwaokobia, K. (2019). Evaluation of proximate, ultimate and mineral composition of *Irvingia gabonensis* hook F. (Dika nut seed and shell). *American Journal of Biological Chemistry*, 7(2), 26–30.

Okpalaeke, K. E., Ibrahim, T. H., Latinwo, L. M., & Betiku, E. (2020). Mathematical modeling and optimization studies by artificial neural network, Genetic algorithm and response surface methodology: A case of ferric sulfate–catalyzed esterification of neem (Azadirachta indica) seed oil. *Frontiers in Energy Research*, 8, 614621. https://doi.org/10.3389/fenrg.2020.614621

Omeh, Y. S., Ezeja, M. I., & Ugwudike, P. O. (2012). The physiochemical properties and fatty acid profile of oil extracted from *Irvingia gabonensis* seeds. *International Journal of Biochemistry and Biotechnology*, 2(2), 273–275.

Onoji, S. E., Iyuke, S. E., Igbafe, A. I., & Daramola, M. O. (2017). Hevea brasiliensis (rubber seed) oil: modeling and optimization of extraction process parameters using response surface methodology and artificial neural network techniques. *Biofuels*, 10(6), 677–691.

Perpetuo, E. A., Silva, D. N., Avanzi, I. R., Gracioso, L. H., Baltazar, M. P. G., & Nascimento, C. A. O. (2012). Phenol biodegradation by a microbial consortium: application of artificial neural network (ANN) modelling. *Environmental Technology*, 33, 1739–1745.

Raj, A., Mohanty, B., & Bhargava, R. (2015). Modeling and response surface analysis of supercritical extraction of watermelon seed oil using carbon dioxide. *Separation and Purification Technology*, 141, 354–365.

Rajendra, M., Jena, P. C., & Raheman, H. (2009). Prediction of optimized pretreatment process parameters for biodiesel production using ANN and GA. *Fuel*, 88, 868–875.

Reyes-Jurado, F., Franco-Vega, A., Ramirez-Corona, N., Palou E., & Lopez Malo, A. (2014). Essential oils: antimicrobial activities, extraction methods, and their modeling. *Food Engineering Reviews*, 60(10), 1641–1650.

Sabzalian, M. R., Khashei, M., & Ghaderian, M. (2014). Artificial and Hybrid Fuzzy Linear Neural Network-Based Estimation of Seed Oil Content of Safflower. *Journal of the American Oil Chemists' Society*, 91, 2091–2099.

Samuel, O. D., Okwu, M. O., Amosun, S. T., Verma, T. N., & Afolalu, S. A. (2019). Production of fatty acid ethyl esters from rubber seed oil in hydrodynamic cavitation reactor: study of reaction parameters and some fuel properties. *Industrial Crops and Products* 141, 111658. https://doi.org/10.1016/j.indcrop.2019.111658

Samuel, O., Okwu, M., Oyejide, O., Taghinezhad, E., Afzal, A., & Kaveh, M. (2020). Optimizing biodiesel production from abundant waste oils through empirical method and grey wolf optimizer. *Fuel*. 281, 118701.

Samuel, O. D., Okwu, M. O., Tartibu, L. K., Giwa, S. O., Sharifpur, M., & Jagun, Z. O. O. (2021) Modelling of Nicotiana Tabacum L. oil biodiesel production: comparison of ANN and ANFIS. *Frontiers in Energy Research*, 8, 612165. https://doi.org/10.3389/fenrg.2020.612165

Shanmuganathan, S. (2016). Artificial neural network modelling, In *Studies in Computational Intelligence: An Introduction*. Eds. S. Shanmuganathan and S. Samarasinghe (Cham, Switzerland: Springer International Publishing), pp. 1–14.

Suryawanshi, B., & Mohanty, B. (2018). Application of an artificial neural network model for the supercritical fluid extraction of seed oil from Argemone mexicana (L.) seeds. *Industrial Crops & Products*, 123, 64–74.

Wang, L., & Weller, C. L. (2006). Recent advances in extraction of nutra-ceuticals from plant. *Trends in Food Science and Technology*, 17, 300–312

Weerawatanakorn, M. (2013). *Terminalia catappa seeds oil as a new dietary healthy oil source. The Annual Meeting of the International Society for Nutraceuticals and Functional Foods (ISNFF), Taipei, Taiwan.*

Yolmeh, M., Najafi, M. B. H., & Farhoosh, R. (2014). Optimization of ultrasound-assisted extraction of natural pigment from annatto seeds by response surface methodology (RSM). *Food Chemistry*, 155, 319–324.

Zhao, S., & Zhang, D. (2014). An experimental investigation into the solubility of Moringa oleifera oil in supercritical carbon dioxide. *Journal of Food Engineering*, 138, 1–10.

Zoué, L. T., Bedikou, M. E., Faulet, B. M., Gonnety, J. T., & Niamké, S. L. (2013). Characterisation of highly saturated Irvingia gabonensis seed kernel oil with unusual linolenic acid content. *Food Science and Technology International*, 19(1), 79–87.

Chapter 13

Applications of Artificial Intelligence in Pest Management

Muhammad Kashif Hanif[1], Shouket Zaman Khan[2], and Maria Bibi[1]

[1]Department of Computer Science, Government College University Faisalabad, Faisalabad, Pakistan

[2]Department of Entomology, University of Agriculture Faisalabad Sub-Campus Burewala-Vehari, Burewala-Vehari, Pakistan

Contents

DOI: 10.1201/9781003311782-13

277

13.1 Introduction

The world's population is expected to rise approximately 10 billion by the year 2050, which would further enhance the agricultural volume to meet the food security challenges by about 50% in comparison to 2013. The growth in food production would come chiefly from crop yield augmentation (80%), plant cropping intensity (10%) and remaining from the restricted expansion of land use. Dietary transitions to higher levels of fruits, vegetables and meat consumption relative to the cereals would be accelerated due to income augmentation in developing countries demanding corresponding paradigm shifts in agricultural production and mounting increasing pressure on natural resources. Currently, nearly 37.7% of the total earth surface is currently being cultivated for crop production. The crop yield growth rates have reduced to the extent which is not promising for future food security.

The share of the agriculture sector is declining in overall production and employment generation at varying speeds creating challenges across the countries while at the same time latest technological innovations and agricultural investments are improving productivity. Food losses and wastes privilege a substantial portion of agricultural products; minimizing them would reduce the need for increased agricultural outputs. However, the required acceleration in agricultural growth is being hindered owing to increased biodiversity loss, deprivation of natural resources and spread of quarantine and regulated non-quarantine pests and diseases of crop plants and domesticated animals, even some of these pests are developing resistance to antimicrobials (Manida, 2022).

Each organism struggles for its existence and better survival in nature by interacting with the components of the ecosystem (biotic and abiotic). Various types of associations are found between the insect pests and other components of nature, including plants, animals and humans. These associations can be conducive for the competition for food, shelter and space. Those insects are called insect pests which claim damage to human properties, cause injury to animals or plants, become the reason for epidemic or endemic outbreaks of diseases or any nuisance problem.

Pest management is a way/method to reduce pest population to a tolerable threshold. An acceptable and tolerable action threshold is an economically and ecologically justifiable pest population level at which application of pest control strategies will reduce the insect pest population to an extent below which extra application would not be cost-effective and justified (Arif et al., 2017). A regular pest monitoring program is a very basic step in an integrated pest management (IPM) program and decision-making irrespective of which control strategy is used. By conducting regular surveys and monitoring programs, an entomologist becomes able to accumulate the latest and up-to-date information about pest identification, pest hotspots and to evaluate the effectiveness of treatment. All the gathered information is very important for selecting and application of management strategies. Keeping in view the relationships of pest surveillance findings and ecological parameters, future pest predictions can be done (Arnaudov et al., 2012).

Despite different challenges, agriculture has a contributing role in the economy of developed as well as developing countries. Automation and technological innovations are emerging subjects and major concerns throughout the global regions. Tremendously increasing world population and its ever-growing food-based and employment demands are escalating as well. The conventional techniques which were practiced previously are not good enough now to meet emerging food security challenges. For fulfilling the increasing food requirements and generating more employment opportunities, newly introduced methods or innovations are being manipulated (Talaviya et al., 2020).

The major contributions of this chapter are as follows:

■ Discussed different innovative pest management strategies.
■ Described the role of artificial intelligence in pest management.
■ Explored the applications of different types of artificial intelligence in pest management.
■ Examined different challenges in pest management using artificial intelligence.

13.2 Innovative Pest Management Strategies

There are numerous innovative, efficient and cost-effective strategies in the field of entomology that are being used to manage insect pest problems in a comprehensive way. Some of these latest techniques are listed below:

1. An extensive database system has been established for making barcodes for important quarantine and agricultural pests which include data for more than 6,500 arthropod species, >65,000 sequences and >800 pictures. This database also contains associated information on biology, taxonomy and pest distribution along with host sequences, geo-localization and sampling information. This type of database is helpful in developing and implementing

IPM programs. These database systems will be helpful in developing pest forecasting models to predict pest population's fluctuations in time and space. This system might contain information to evaluate the relationship between pest outbreaks and environmental conditions. The proper functioning of predators and parasitoids in regulating pest populations can be evaluated by using this database. Different conventional and technological pest management tactics are depicted in Figure 13.1.

2. Species distribution models (SDMs), being a powerful technique in the branch of quantitative ecology, constitutes the extensively used modeling framework for precise risk assessment of various invasive species. Different tools are being used to develop SDMs, e.g. R-functions are utilized to determine geo-reference-based published incidences of invasive pest species. Among other tools, standard search engines are also manipulated to monitor invasive pest

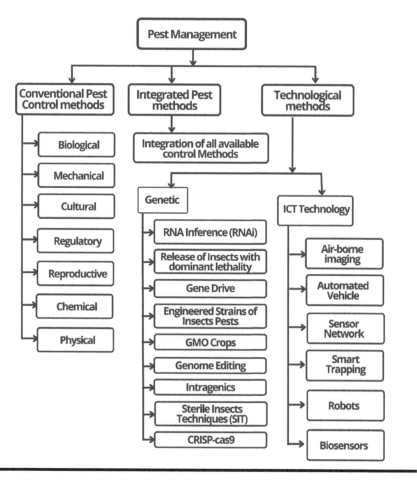

Figure 13.1   Conventional and technological pest management strategies.

species: Google Street View can be utilized to observe larger specimens, e.g. dead trees due to the attack of certain insect pests (Guisan et al., 2017).

3. Internet has become an ideal way of providing necessary data and analytical processing for IPM-based decision-making. Internet can help to run decision support systems that can be multi-source, multi-threaded and site-specific (Power & Kaparthi, 1998). Users can be part of the decision-making in these internet-based systems (Eastwood, 1998). Different websites that include geographical information system-based decision support systems, real-time weather information and interactive models are being developed quite commonly. Such systems integrate meteorological information (temperature, rainfall, etc.) with the insect pest phenology to formulate the pest forecasts and updates for extension specialists. These extension specialists then issue pest and diseases warnings for the farmers on the basis of weather data-driven forecast models (Bajwa et al., 2003).

4. Drone technology is very popular nowadays to monitor pest infestation and for precise applications of the natural enemies (bio-control agents) or pesticides on the identified hotspots of insect pests especially in those locations which are very difficult to reach. This drone technology minimizes the health-associated risk factors for applicators, saves time and permits pest control specialists to exterminate the pest problems precisely and efficiently (Iost Filho et al., 2020).

5. Thermal Imaging Technology is a very powerful means to detect and identify insect pest issues. Thermal detection tools which are capable to detect heat sources are manipulated in this technology. This technique is very effective to locate pest infestations, even in the concealed cracks and crevices in the walls or other similar locations (Ahmed et al., 2019).

13.3 Role of Artificial Intelligence in Smart Pest Management

There are various AI-based applications that are emerging continuously from the finance sector to agriculture but among these fields, there are some major domains of human life where AI is revolutionizing the world. The use of a system is based on intelligent algorithms in our daily life, making our lives much easier than past. The role of agriculture is significant in the world as we rely on it for our major requirements' fulfillment (Ghosh & Singh, 2020; Talaviya et al., 2020). Nowadays, the role of AI in agriculture for the development of automated agricultural systems is being a highly researched domain. Here, we will discuss how major domains of AI are playing their roles in smart agriculture and what types of challenges are being faced by researchers in the implementation of these automated systems. Table 13.1 shows the comparison of different automated and conventional pest management strategies.

Table 13.1   Comparison of Traditional and Artificial Intelligence-based Pest Management Techniques

Sr #	Traditional Pest Management Tactics	Artificial Intelligence Techniques in Pest Management
1	Labor-intensive and time-consuming IPM programs are manipulated for pest surveillance and forecasting. Such estimations do not even give 100% accuracy due to sudden fluctuations in environmental conditions and man-made pest estimates.	Growers are using AI to improve agricultural accuracy and efficiency by manipulating probabilistic models for making seasonal pest forecasting. Such forecasting can be visualized months before the start of growing season. This type of predictions helps to select most suitable crop variety, ideal location, time and optimize the use of farm resources.
2	Early detection of pest outbreaks rely only on visual observations by well-trained and pest experts, subsequently communication to concerned farmers and decision about management treatment take time.	AI oriented systems helps the farmers in early pest detection and send the relevant information through quickest methods of communication, e.g. SMS or Email. In this way, farmers can manage pest infestations in initial stages resulting in economic gains.
3	Manually individual reports are prepared after entering field pest scouting data into excel spread sheets and subsequently analyzing this data by using statistical software.	An automatically generated and typing-free digital reports describing the accurate identification, description of pest infestation and recommendations derived from AI algorithms.
4	During the pest scouting procedure, data-sharing or task-sharing is difficult with other coworkers.	During the pest scouting, location-oriented tasks are pooled with other associates to the treatment process more precise and convenient.
5	In an effective IPM program, the timing of pest infestation and treatment application is very important. When an invasive pest invades a new territory, most of the organizations are unprepared and helpless to timely manage the unknown and invasive pest.	AI-based systems continuously monitor worldwide pest distribution and issues the warnings/alerts that allow the users to take timely measures and the chances of getting surprises are minimized during the crop production duration.

(Continued)

Table 13.1 *(Continued)* **Comparison of Traditional and Artificial Intelligence-based Pest Management Techniques**

Sr #	Traditional Pest Management Tactics	Artificial Intelligence Techniques in Pest Management
6	IPM-based programs work by considering the various observations from plant protection inspectors. Different management resources are required to supervise the large-scale pest management operations.	AI-based IPM programs work by utilizing observations in real-time, assisting the communication process between the associates, AI-solutions minimizes management resources that are pre-requisite to brief plant protection inspectors, manage plant protection tasks, monitor the growth of pest outbreaks.
7	In IPM programs, well-trained experts are required to correctly identify the different insects and disease complexes in the crop and subsequently decide the economical treatment that makes sense.	AI digital solutions are quite easy to use, scalable for area-wide IPM programs and affordable.

Some of the recent applications of artificial intelligence in pest management are as follows.

■ Smart pest monitoring traps having sensor devices along with cameras have revolutionized pest prediction accuracy by daily image analysis and reducing human labor (Marković et al., 2021).

■ The hybrid AI-based model demonstrated the capability to accurately predict environmental conditions that become the reason for pest outbreaks in sugarcane. Thus, it serves as an early warning tool to timely adopt appropriate management strategy to reduce pest load (Figueredo et al., 2021).

■ To minimize the negative impacts of pesticides for applicators, consumers and the environment, AI-based smart machines are being developed to save the pesticide amount, reduce pesticide exposure and get excellent crop coverage at the same time (Facchinetti et al., 2021).

■ Optical remote sensors in association with machine learning have overwhelming utilization in the targeted application of pesticides to protect non-targeted beneficial arthropods (Kirkeby et al., 2021).

■ Autonomous robotic technology has optimized pest monitoring and prediction efficiency reduced the unnecessary applications of hazardous chemicals and crop monitoring is not a burden anymore (Shelake et al., 2021).

13.4 Branches of Artificial Intelligence

This section discusses the application of different types of artificial intelligence (AI) in pest management. The major branches of AI are described as follows:

1. Machine Learning
2. Neural Networks
3. Fuzzy Logic Expert Systems
4. Robotics
5. Evolutionary Computing

13.4.1 Machine Learning

Machine Learning (ML) is attributed as a major sub-domain of AI where machines are exhibiting the properties of self-learning, hence named as "Machine Learning." Applications of ML are ranging from finance to agriculture and ML models are being widely used for accomplishing data-driven tasks. ML approaches are enormously replacing conventional statistical approaches in the studies related to natural sciences (Thessen, 2016). In the domain of ML, instead of explicit coding for every line of an algorithm, models are trained on the given dataset to perform their tasks. ML methods have the potential to extract complex features from data thus more accurate model for prediction/classification can be developed in comparison with conventional methods (Olden et al., 2008). ML algorithms react to the given situation based on the learning; they experienced during their training on the datasets, unlike typical computer algorithms which strictly follow the programmed instructions for accomplishing their tasks (Durgabai & Bhargavi, 2018). Here, we will demonstrate the applications of ML models in pest management over conventional methods used for pest monitoring and control.

13.4.1.1 Random Forest

Random Forest (RF) is an ML approach introduced by Breiman (2000) which has the potential to model both classification and regression problems in an efficient manner. It is an ensemble learning approach, so an RF model is usually developed by assembling several decision trees (DTs) on its base like a typical "forest" (Kane et al, 2014). The RF model can extract features from complex data, be easy to implement, calculate test errors and run on larger datasets (Lind & Anderson, 2019).

Applications of RF in Pest Management

Pests' population monitoring is an important component of IPM; various researchers used the RF approach to the model certain phenomena. RF employed by (Carvajal et al., 2018; Lee et al., 2019; Skawsang et al., 2019; Balaban et al., 2019) to model dengue, Citrus flatid Planthopper (CFP), Black Planthopper (BPH), Sunn pest's nymphal stage population prediction, respectively.

13.4.1.2 Support Vector Machine

Support Vector Machine (SVM) is an ML approach that is being deployed by researchers in both regression and classification problems analyses (Yang et al., 2002). SVM-based statistical learning technique was developed by Vapnik in 1995. Different hyperparameters such as Kernel, C value and gamma are used for the development of SVM model. The generalization potency of SVM has been much more improved as compared to other conventional optimization techniques (Ramón et al., 2005).

Applications of SVM in Pest Management

The SVM approach was used to model population occurrence of mosquitoes, dengue, dendrolimus, superans and pantry beetle (Früh et al., 2018; Guo et al., 2017; Zhang et al., 2017).

13.4.1.3 Naïve Bayes

Naïve Bayes (NB) approach is an ML approach based on Bayes Theorem. It assumes that all input features are independent variables (existence of one variable does not affect the others) and these all-explanatory variables have a similar impact on the final outcome. NB learns the probabilistic associations between the explanatory and response variables through training data (Hill et al., 2014; Vembandasamy et al., 2015).

Applications of NB in Pest Management

1. NB technique used by Hill et al. (2014) to take appropriate decisions regarding pesticides application on kiwifruit based on pest monitoring.
2. Nandhini et al. (2016) used NB to classify turmeric leaf diseases, while Tripathy et al. (2012) deployed Gaussian NB to model groundnut pest population's fluctuations. Perez-Ariza et al. (2012) used Bayesian network for the prediction of coffee rust disease.

13.4.1.4 Decision Tree

DT is a data modeling approach for regression and classification problems analysis, and it is contributing to the ML domain as an important tool. DT comprises root nodes, internal nodes and leaf nodes. It uses numerous independent variables for building classification models or forecasting algorithms for an output variable (Song & Ying, 2015).

Applications of DT in Pest Management

DT was used for predicting population dynamics of *Prostephanus truncatus* and *Scirtothrips dorsalis* Hood, Olive fruit fly, respectively (Nyabako et al., 2020; Lin et al., 2015; del Sagrado & del Águila, 2007).

13.4.1.5 K-Nearest Neighbor

K-Nearest Neighbor (KNN) is another data modeling approach that had been used in the current scenario. It is used to classify unlabeled entities of dataset by assigning them the label of the class which is most familiar in characteristics to them (Zhang, 2016). KNN does not follow any learning stage because to classify any entity it uses a training split of the data every time. A training split of the data is known prior to the classification of unlabeled observation. The rule followed by KNN is that similar observations should have a same class label. To classify an unlabeled observation, the K parameter shows the number of similar known observations. KNN just uses the information in the training split of data instead of extracting any rule for classifying the unlabeled object (Medar & Rajpurohit, 2014).

Applications of KNN in Pest Management

For modeling the coffee pests and diseases (de Oliveria Aparecido et al., 2020) and predicting mosquitoes' abundance (Chen et al, 2019), the KNN approach is deployed.

Advantages of ML Approach over Conventional Methods for Pest Management

This section describes the advantages of ML approaches over conventionally used statistical approaches.

■ The datasets of natural sciences are recognized as non-linear and high-dimensional with complicated interactions and missing values but still, those methods are being used for their modeling which are linear and incapable to deal with complicated interactions, so the major advantage of ML methods is that they are capable to model high-dimensional and non-linear datasets (Haupt et al., 2008; Thessen, 2016, Olden et al., 2008).

■ ML approaches are highly customizable so that researchers can greatly adopt these methods to explore the solution of the given problem (Kampichler et al., 2010).

■ Through this data mining approach, we can analyze data and extract useful features, patterns and previously hidden information (Zorić, 2020).

13.4.2 Neural Networks

13.4.2.1 Artificial Neural Network

Another data modeling approach of ML is Artificial Neural Network (ANN) which is used to solve complex and non-linear problems. ANN comprises three types of layers, i.e. input, hidden and output layers. Each layer encompasses neurons/nodes. Nodes in ANN resemble neurons (basic functional unit of the brain) of the human brain where each node of a layer is linked to nodes at an adjacent layer through some connecting links (referred to as synapse of neuron structure). Every neuron in the input layer corresponds to one input variable, while every neuron in the output layer corresponds to an output variable. Nodes of hidden layers are connected to every node of the layer below and above them, but these are not connected with the nodes in the same layer. Each incoming connecting link has an associated weight, while every node has an offset value "bias." The outcome weights for the outgoing connecting links of hidden layers are determined by employing an activation function usually "non-linear" to the totaled weights of its incoming connecting links minus the neuron's bias value (Clark, 2020; Skawsang et al., 2019).

Application of ANN in Pest Management

1. There are several cases where researchers deployed ANN in pest management such as Yang et al. (2002) employed ANN to model paddy stem borer occurrence in rice fields.
2. Ruslan et al. (2019), Skawsang et al. (2019), and Yan et al. (2015) used ANN to build the prediction model for population abundance of Metisa plana, BPH, Melon thrips and diamondback moth.

13.4.2.2 Deep Neural Network

Deep Learning is a recent improvement in the domain of ML which is receiving much consideration in present days. Deep Neural Network (DNN) is attributed as an important tool of DL; it is an extension to ML approach ANN with dense and more layers as ANNs are shallow neural networks (Clark, 2020; Kamilaris & Prenafeta-Boldú, 2018). The most desirable characteristic of DL is that no manual feature extraction is required as it has the potential to automatically extract features from raw data (LeCun et al., 2015). ML community is effectively switching from ANN-based non-linear data modeling approach to DNN. Although DNN is an extension to ANN, their training algorithms are different as ANN deploys a costly algorithm "gradient descent," while DNN uses a restricted Boltzmann algorithm to overcome the problems of overfitting and cost (Hinton et al., 2006). Figure 13.2 depicts the architecture of a DNN, where neurons and connecting links collectively form a DNN architecture.

Applications of DNN in Pest Management

1. For managing the pests' attack in agriculture, DL approaches are enormously adopted by researchers as Qi et al. (2015) used an intelligent system based on DNN for better detection and classification of insect pests.
2. Rammer and Seidl (2019) modeled bark beetle outbreak through the DNN approach.
3. A DNN based on a faster R-CNN model was developed by Shen et al. (2018) to extract multi-scale feature maps of stored grained insects to classify them.

13.4.2.3 Convolutional Neural Network

Convolutional Neural Networks (CNNs) are an extension to DNN which are often used for pattern recognition in the image-based dataset. As DNN contains fully connected as well as deep layers along with fully connected layers, CNN also contains

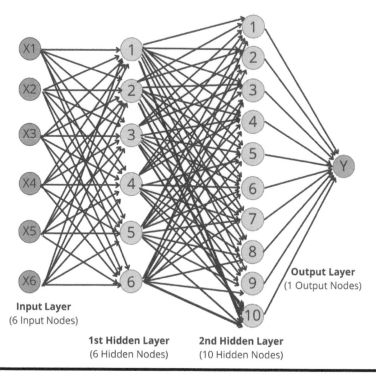

Input Layer
(6 Input Nodes)

1st Hidden Layer
(6 Hidden Nodes)

2nd Hidden Layer
(10 Hidden Nodes)

Output Layer
(1 Output Nodes)

Figure 13.2 Architecture of deep neural network.

various phases of pooling and filtering layers. These pooling and filtering layers can extract more intellectual patterns from given image-based dataset (LeCun et al., 2015; Rammer & Seidl, 2019). In the present era, CNNs are commonly considered the state-of-the-art solution in image recognition (Liang et al., 2019).

Applications of CNN in Pest Management

Pests and disease attacks can cause great harm to crops if appropriate measures are not taken to control them.

1. To classify citrus pests and disease, Xing et al. (2019) used the CNN approach constructed from the facet of parameter efficiency named Weakly DenseNet-16 and results reveal that it is a good lightweight network for pests and diseases classification, and can easily be used in mobile devices.
2. For the classification and detection of Asian Citrus Psyllid in citrus orchard, Partel et al. (2019) deployed an intelligent mechanism based on two CNNs. Soini et al. (2019) used computer vision and DL technique for the extraction of sub-images of citrus fruits from tree images and then a trained ML approach was employed for detection of Haunglonbing (HLB)-infected fruits.
3. For performing rice blast disease recognition, Liang et al. (2019) deployed the CNN approach.

13.4.2.4 Long Short-Term Memory

Long Short-Term Memory (LSTM) is a DL approach and a special type of RNN model that received significant consideration in the present decade. LSTM is attributed as a particular form of RNN developed by the establishment of gates mechanism into previously founded vanilla RNN to avoid the dilemma of vanishing gradient problem. In order to process data to obtain desired results, LSTM also has an end-to-end working mode as typical DL approaches. Unlike traditional ML techniques, complex feature selection and model testing are not crucial for LSTM. After model training, it revises network hyperparameters based on new data instead of building the model again. Researchers have also introduced an improved structure of LSTM to make the network more predictable and use lesser training time (Xiao et al., 2019).

Applications of LSTM in Pest Management

1. In order to detect and predict cotton diseases and pests, Xiao et al. (2019) used the RNN-LSTM approach in comparison to other ML approaches and certain models delivered top-best results. Chen et al. (2020) deployed bi-directional LSTM to model cotton pests and disease occurrence.
2. A hybrid DL approach (CNN- and RNN-based structures) was employed by Gangadevi and Jayakumar to detect the pest presence and the respective damages in the crop.

13.4.3 Robots and Robot Technology

Robotic technology has a concern with physical robots while the robots are programmable, embodied and autonomous or semi-autonomous machines that execute a series of actions without getting tired and in the agricultural field, the robots are concerned with following tasks from perception to action. AI has a crucial role in robotic technology in making robots intelligent. The process by which robots make intelligent decisions is often designated as "sense-plan-act" which means that robots first sense the environment with the help of a wide array of sensors, then plan what to do next on the basis of its perception, and programming knowledge and finally take action to execute different tasks in the real world (Bartneck et al., 2021). These man-designed machines make movements by themselves and these must have modeling, planning, sensing, actuation and control by programming. The robots perform their functions or repetitive tasks without any complaining although these machines require periodic and proper maintenance to avoid any malfunctioning. The sensors, effectors, actuators, controllers and common effectors (robots arms) are the five main parts in the majority of the robots (Ahmed et al., 2016). In order to develop a functional robotic system that is capable of executing real-world tasks, a huge variety of different programs, processes and systems must be precisely integrated. Agricultural robots are autonomous, mobile, decision-making and mechatronic devices that complete different crop production and protection-related tasks in fields under human supervision but without involving humans indirect labor and these machines have applications in different bio-sciences such as agriculture, agronomy, greenhouse, forestry, horticulture, including pest management, and currently numerous researchers across the globe are working hard to increase the scope of robotic applications in different fields of life and industry (Lowenberg-DeBoer et al., 2020).

Applications of Robotic Technology in Pest Management

1. Robotic technology is an emerging and efficient method of pesticide spraying in agriculture which has numerous benefits like reduced environmental impact by targeted applications (only hotspots areas), using fewer pesticides, more safety for farmers by reducing exposure to dangerous poisons and more sustainability for agriculture systems by reducing farm inputs. The reduced pesticide applications mean healthier and quality food products for consumers (Horrigan et al., 2002; Adamides, 2008).

2. The robots are also helpful in insect, pest, diseases and weeds identification. The robot takes specimens images by executing a fixed action and then detects whether they are designated insects or not. This recognition procedure of robot takes the total probability image by manipulating multi-template images and reverse mapping of histograms (Hu et al., 2018).

3. A "dog" robot having integration of controller area network (CAN) bus, laser system and a camera was developed for cotton crop as a field scout who visits the fields twice a week with a nominal cost of about 22 dollars/hectare and gets the information about the field problems such as the pest infestations are exceeding economic threshold levels or the disease symptoms on the plants demand pesticides application (Nagasaka et al., 2004).

13.4.4 Fuzzy Logic Expert System

Fuzzy logic (FL) is a method of computing which is based on "degrees of truth" rather than a simple "true or false" Boolean logic on which the modern computing system is based. FL is the reasoning process in which fuzzy rules are utilized to change the input into output. The FL rules consist of evidence and consequence and they are assumed to capture the reasoning of a human working in a situation with imprecision and uncertainty. The operators, who are unenthusiastic to use methods that they do not comprehend, use FL to make complex reservoir optimization models which are more appealing for them. They utilize optimization techniques, such as stochastic or deterministic dynamic programming (Malek et al., 2019). Boolean logic is dependent on probability theory, while FL is dependent on possibility theory (Thompson et al., 2012). FL stimulates human reasoning and imitates the process of how a person makes decisions by permitting a computer to behave like a human but less precisely and logically than traditional computers do

(Fellows, 2017). FL and fuzzy expert systems have a diversity of applications in different fields of life. Since the information used in monitoring the pest activity in the field is not perfect, the fuzzy expert system using FL is the best approach to cater to the uncertain and imprecise knowledge of pest monitoring and management activities. Various fuzzy expert systems have already been developed and utilized with the aim to provide IPM-based decision support (Siraj & Arbaiy, 2006).

Applications of Fuzzy Logic Expert System in Pest Management

1. Fuzzy expert system "FUzzy XPest" by using FL has been used to determine the type of pest in rice, damage caused by the pest and to forecast the pest activity (name of pest, size and damage to the plant) in the field that indicates the resultant damage caused by the pest (Siraj & Arbaiy, 2006).
2. A fuzzy expert system prototype has been developed by Pasqual and Mansfield (1998) with the purpose of insect pest identification and control of these pests.
3. A fuzzy expert simulation system "SMARTSOY" has been designed for pest management in soybean crops (Saini et al., 2002).
4. Karthik et al. (2020) developed the FL-based decision-making system to analyze the harmful impacts of different pesticides on human health.
5. Fuzzy expert models that help in weather predictions also support the farmers in taking right and timely decisions and precautionary measures to avoid the insect pests losses by adopting preventive measures (Sucharith et al., 2020).

13.4.5 *Evolutionary Computing*

Evolutionary Computing (EC) is a computer-based problem solving and exciting development in AI which gets inspiration from natural evolution and other biological-based systems. EC techniques are speculative algorithms modeled for the evolution of inherited characteristics from one generation to the next and include computational models of evolutionary processes. Evolutionary computation has different algorithm techniques like genetic algorithms, evolutionary programming, evolutionary strategies, estimation of distribution algorithms, differential evolution, artificial immune systems, particle swarm optimization, memetic algorithms and ant colony optimization. These evolutionary techniques proved successful in solving many complicated and difficult optimization problems (Eiben & Schoenauer, 2002; Dao, 2011; Wong, 2017). The working model of an automated pest management strategy is depicted in Figure 13.3.

Applications of Evolutionary Computing in Pest Management

1. An intelligent computational technique integrates the currently available phenological data which is associated with the pest and local meteorological conditions to make pest population predictions at different threshold levels. Beyond the economic threshold level of pests, appropriate action shall be executed automatically by the system.

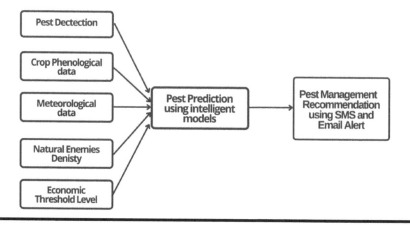

Figure 13.3   Working model of an automated pest management program.

2. The computation algorithms suggest appropriate recommendations for pesticide applications on the basis of phenological and weather data.
3. These intelligent computational-based algorithms help to diagnose diseases that are associated with insect pests.
4. Different computational algorithms can be manipulated to develop computationally intelligent IPM programs for different crops. Computationally intelligent IPM decision support minimizes the complexity of decision-making in pest management (Sangaiah et al., 2017).

13.5 Challenges of Artificial Intelligence in Pest Management

IPM has been tackling various important difficulties like the absence of simple but accurate pest sampling methods, pest surveillance and forecasting, correct identification, crop damage estimation, associated threshold levels and low-risk pest management strategies. The face of successful pest protection depends to a great extent on the adoption of different innovative and cognitive solutions. Some of these innovative applications are already available in the world market but large-scale research is still in process to explore and manipulate various applications to cope with the present and emerging entomological issues and the associated industry is still greatly deprived (Talaviya, et al., 2020).

1. When it comes to discussing convincing challenges that are being experienced by the farmers and manipulating independent decision-making and projecting solutions to solve them, the farming community is still at a budding stage. In order to explore the immense application scope of AI in the field of IPM, AI applications need to be more convincing and robust. Only

such manipulations can assist in real-time decision-making, dealing with frequent and abrupt changes in environmental conditions and utilizing applicable platforms/frameworks to collect background data in an efficient way.

2. Another important challenge is the inflated cost of various AI-based applications/systems that are currently available in the market for IPM-related issues. These applications/systems need to be more affordable and easily accessible to ensure that innovative technological and cognitive solutions reach the masses especially in under-developed and developing countries where most of the food losses occur owing to different pest-disease complexes and this exorbitant cost is the main bar in technology adoption and dissemination. The novel technology will be resourceful by helping farmers in IPM at a regular time period by reducing significant losses by pests. Most of the South-East Asian countries, including Pakistan, rely on monsoon rain spells for their successful crop cultivation. They are mostly dependent upon pest forecasting and predictions from the agriculture department during such environmental conditions. The AI-based applications will be helpful to predict meteorological conditions and resultant pest infestations in various agro-ecological zones. Accurate image recognition and pest forecasting with the use of AI technology will resolve most of the issues of the farmers (Talaviya, et al., 2020).

3. Another most prominent challenge in the application of AI technology in the pest management field is how the data is handled, which can be seen by different aspects such as data ownership, data sharing and cybersecurity-related issues. This is a difficult question that does not have a clear answer yet, either from the technical or from the legal point of view (Casten Carlberg & Jerhamre, 2021).

4. Most of the currently available datasets do not depict accurate and field-representative data because they are generally produced by a few people getting pest specimens or images in a limited time duration and from a limited area; as a result, performance precision can be compromised from such algorithms (Yuan et al., 2021). More practical datasets representing diverse field locations from diverse agro-ecological zones are the ideal one to improve performance (Su, 2020; Yuan et al., 2021).

5. Most of the farmer community is not familiar with the AI applications; as a result, they cannot fully comprehend the underlying principles responsible for working on different AL algorithms. In order to address such issues, user-friendly applications should be introduced (Li et al., 2020; Cravero & Sepúlveda, 2021). Since the farmers are getting more familiar with the smartphone, smartphone-specific applications should be designed to address this challenge (van Klompenburg et al., 2020; Yuan et al., 2021).

6. The major challenge faced by manipulation of ML approaches in field is the lack of programming skills in researchers, so these methods are resisted by them (Olden et al., 2008) and they preferably use typical statistical approaches which are easy and fast for calculation and result in easy to understand metrics such as p-value (Thessen, 2016).

7. An additional fence in the adoption of ML methods is the necessity for suitable amounts of training and testing data for the prescribed problem as the validity of the model's prediction is limited to the scope represented by data (Simonite, 2016). However, there are some methods available which are capable of modeling problems with small datasets but some approaches such as Bayesian network deliver less accurate results, while the conventional statistical methods are smart enough to use a lesser amount of data to build a valuable model.

8. The lack of interaction and cooperation between the natural science community and ML community is another factor, resisting ML methods adoption in real-world problems.

9. The limited number of tools and facilities to boost the applications of ML methods in real-world problems is another barrier in this regard which is now lesser to some extent.

10. Usually, students are equipped with the learning of statistical methods during their undergraduate and graduate studies, but ML is not taught as a mandatory course, so ML approaches have a lower implementation in the field as compared to conventional methods (Thessen, 2016).

13.6 Conclusion

With increasing human population pressure, the modern-day agriculture sector has versatile challenges to ensure food security and availability for everyone; there is a need to adopt the latest technological innovations in crop production and crop protection. AI is an emerging field that has the potential to revolutionize the agriculture sector, including pest management. Different fields of AI have numerous applications to improve pest monitoring, prediction and forecasting efficiency, and have optimized the use of pesticides having benefits for applicators, consumers, the environment and beneficial natural enemies. The drone technology and sensor devices provide the opportunity to classify and detect the diversity of arthropod fauna, and locate pest outbreaks and hotspot points in hard-to-reach areas of the field with minimum manipulation of human labor. The computation algorithms suggest appropriate recommendations for pesticide applications based on phonological and weather data. Computationally intelligent IPM decision support minimizes the complexity of decision-making in pest management.

References

Adamides, G., (2008). Agricultural robots in targeted spraying: a mini state-of-the-art review. *Journal of Field Robotics, 31*(6), 888–911.

Ahmed, A., Ibrahim, A., & Hussein, S. (2019). Detection of palm tree pests using thermal imaging: a review. *Machine Learning Paradigms: Theory and Application, 801*, 253–270.

Ahmed, H., Juraimi, A. S., & Hamdani, S. M. (2016). Introduction to robotics agriculture in pest control: a review. *Pertanika Journal of Scholarly Research Reviews, 2*(2), 80–93.

Arif, M. J., Gogi, M. D., Sufyan, M., Nawaz, A., & Sarfraz, R. M. (2017). Principles of insect pests management. In *Sustainable Insect Pest Management*. University of Agriculture, Faisalabad, Pakistan.

Arnaudov, V., Raykov, S., Davidova, R., Hristov, H., Vasilev, V., & Petkov, P. (2012). Monitoring of pest populations-an important element of integrated pest management of field crops. *Agricultural Science and Technology*, *4*(1), 77–80.

Bajwa, W. I., Coop, L., & Kogan, M. (2003). Integrated pest management (IPM) and Internet-based information delivery systems. *Neotropical Entomology*, *32*(3), 373–383.

Balaban, İ., Acun, F., Arpalı, O. Y., Murat, F., Babaroğlu, N. E., Akci, E., ..., & Temizer, S. (2019). Development of a forecasting and warning system on the ecological life-cycle of Sunn Pest. *arXiv preprint arXiv:1905.01640*.

Bartneck, C., Lütge, C., Wagner, A., & Welsh, S. (2021). *An Introduction to Ethics in Robotics and AI*. Springer Nature, Cham, p. 117. https://doi.org/10.1007/978-3-030-51110-4

Breiman, L. (2000). Randomizing outputs to increase prediction accuracy. *Machine Learning*, *40*(3), 229–242.

Carvajal, T. M., Viacrusis, K. M., Hernandez, L. F. T., Ho, H. T., Amalin, D. M., & Watanabe, K. (2018). Machine learning methods reveal the temporal pattern of dengue incidence using meteorological factors in metropolitan Manila, Philippines. *BMC Infectious Diseases*, *18*(1), 1–15.

Casten Carlberg, C. J., & Jerhamre, E. (2021). Artificial intelligence in agriculture: opportunities and challenges (Dissertation). Retrieved from http://urn.kb.se/resolve?urn=urn:nbn:se:uu:diva-443576

Chen, P., Xiao, Q., Zhang, J., Xie, C., & Wang, B. (2020). Occurrence prediction of cotton pests and diseases by bidirectional long short-term memory networks with climate and atmosphere circulation. *Computers and Electronics in Agriculture*, *176*, 105612. https://doi.org/10.1016/j.compag.2020.105612

Chen, S., Whiteman, A., Li, A., Rapp, T., Delmelle, E., Chen, G., & Dulin, M. (2019). An operational machine learning approach to predict mosquito abundance based on socioeconomic and landscape patterns. *Landscape Ecology*, *34*(6), 1295–1311.

Chen, Z., Wang, G., Li, M., Peng, Z., Ali, H., Xu, L., & Hou, Y. (2020). Development of single nucleotide polymorphism (SNP) markers for analysis of population structure and invasion pathway in the coconut Leaf beetle Brontispa longissima (Gestro) Using restriction site-associated DNA (RAD) Genotyping in Southern China. *Insects*, *11*(4), 230. https://doi.org/10.3390/insects11040230

Clark, R. D. (2020). Putting deep learning in perspective for pest management scientists. *Pest Management Science*, *76*(7), 2267–2275.

Cravero, A., & Sepúlveda, S. (2021). Use and adaptations of machine learning in big data—applications in real cases in agriculture. *Electronics*, *10*(5), 552. https://doi.org/10.3390/electronics10050552

Dao, T. T. (2011). Investigation on evolutionary computation techniques of a nonlinear system. *Modelling and Simulation in Engineering*, *2011*(35), 35. https://doi.org/10.1155/2011/496732

de Oliveira Aparecido, L. E., de Souza Rolim, G., De, J. R. D. S. C., Costa, C. T. S., & de Souza, P. S. (2020). Machine learning algorithms for forecasting the incidence of Coffea arabica pests and diseases. *International Journal of Biometeorology*, *64*(4), 671–688.

del Sagrado, J., & del Águila, I. M. (2007, November). Olive fly infestation prediction using machine learning techniques. In Conference of the Spanish Association for Artificial Intelligence (pp. 229–238). Springer, Berlin, Heidelberg.

Demirel, M., & Kumral, N. A. (2021). Artificial intelligence in integrated pest management. In *Artificial Intelligence and IoT-Based Technologies for Sustainable Farming and Smart Agriculture* (pp. 289–313). IGI Global. doi:10.4018/978-1-7998-1722-2.ch018

Durgabai, R. P. L., & Bhargavi, P. (2018). Pest management using machine learning algorithms: a review. *International Journal of Computer Science Engineering and Information Technology Research (IJCSEITR)*, *8*(1), 13–22.

Eastwood, B. R. (1998). Agricultural databases for decision support. *HortTechnology*, *8*(3), 320–324.

Eiben, A. E., & Schoenauer, M. (2002). Evolutionary computing. *Information Processing Letters*, *82*(1), 1–6.

Facchinetti, D., Santoro, S., Galli, L. E., Fontana, G., Fedeli, L., Parisi, S., ..., & Pessina, D. (2021). Reduction of pesticide use in fresh-cut salad production through Artificial intelligence. *Applied Sciences*, *11*(5), 1992. https://doi.org/10.3390/app11051992

Fellows, P. J. (2017). Properties of food and principles of processing. *Food Processing Technology*, Elsevier: Cambridge, UK, pp. 3–200.

Figueredo, L., Villa-Murillo, A., Colmenarez, Y., & Vásquez, C. (2021). A hybrid artificial intelligence model for Aeneolamia varia (Hemiptera: Cercopidae) populations in sugarcane crops. *Journal of Insect Science*, *21*(2), 11. https://doi.org/10.1093/jisesa/ieab017

Früh, L., Kampen, H., Kerkow, A., Schaub, G. A., Walther, D., & Wieland, R. (2018). Modelling the potential distribution of an invasive mosquito species: comparative evaluation of four machine learning methods and their combinations. *Ecological Modelling*, *388*, 136–144.

Ghosh, S., & Singh, A. (2020, May). The scope of artificial intelligence in mankind: a detailed review. In *Journal of Physics: Conference Series* (Vol. 1531, No. 1, p. 012045). IOP Publishing, Punjab, India.

Guisan, A., Thuiller, W., & Zimmermann, N. E. (2017). *Habitat Suitability and Distribution Models: With Applications in R*. Cambridge University Press, UK.

Guo, P., Liu, T., Zhang, Q., Wang, L., Xiao, J., Zhang, Q., ..., & Ma, W. (2017). Developing a dengue forecast model using machine learning: a case study in China. *PLoS Neglected Tropical Diseases*, *11*(10), e0005973.

Haupt, S. E., Pasini, A., & Marzban, C. (2008). *Artificial Intelligence Methods in the Environmental Sciences*. Springer Science & Business Media. https://doi.org/10.1007/978-1-4020-9119-3

Hill, M. G., Connolly, P. G., Reutemann, P., & Fletcher, D. (2014). The use of data mining to assist crop protection decisions on kiwifruit in New Zealand. *Computers and Electronics in Agriculture*, *108*, 250–257.

Hinton, G. E., Osindero, S., & Teh, Y. W. (2006). A fast learning algorithm for deep belief nets. *Neural Computation*, *18*(7), 1527–1554.

Horrigan, L., Lawrence, R. S., & Walker, P. (2002). How sustainable agriculture can address the environmental and human health harms of industrial agriculture. *Environmental Health Perspectives*, *110*(5), 445–456.

Hu, Z., Liu, B., & Zhao, Y. (2018). Agricultural robot for intelligent detection of pyralidae insects. In J. Zhou & B. Zhang (Eds.), *Agricultural Robots-Fundamentals and Applications*. IntechOpen. https://doi.org/10.5772/intechopen.79460

Iost Filho, F. H., Heldens, W. B., Kong, Z., & de Lange, E. S. (2020). Drones: innovative technology for use in precision pest management. *Journal of Economic Entomology*, *113*(1), 1–25.

Kamilaris, A., & Prenafeta-Boldú, F. X. (2018). Deep learning in agriculture: a survey. *Computers and Electronics in Agriculture, 147,* 70–90.

Kampichler, C., Wieland, R., Calmé, S., Weissenberger, H., Arriaga-Weiss, S. (2010) Classification in conservation biology: a comparison of five machine-learning methods. *Ecological Informatics, 5*(6): 441–450

Kane, M. J., Price, N., Scotch, M., & Rabinowitz, P. (2014). Comparison of ARIMA and Random Forest time series models for prediction of avian influenza H5N1 outbreaks. *BMC Bioinformatics, 15*(1), 1–9.

Karthik, S., Dash, S. K., & Punithavelan, N. (2020). A fuzzy decision-making system for the impact of pesticides applied in agricultural fields on human health. *International Journal of Fuzzy System Applications (IJFSA), 9*(3), 42–62.

Kathuria, S. (2020). Pest detection using artificial intelligence. *International Journal of Science and Research (IJSR), 9*(12): 1148–1152.

Kirkeby, C., Rydhmer, K., Cook, S. M., Strand, A., Torrance, M. T., Swain, J. L., …, & Græsbøll, K. (2021). Advances in automatic identification of flying insects using optical sensors and machine learning. *Scientific Reports, 11*(1), 1–8.

LeCun, Y., Bengio, Y., & Hinton, G. (2015). Deep learning. *Nature, 521*(7553), 436–444.

Lee, D. S., Bae, Y. S., Byun, B. K., Lee, S., Park, J. K., & Park, Y. S. (2019). Occurrence prediction of the citrus flatid planthopper (Metcalfa pruinosa (Say, 1830)) in South Korea using a random forest model. *Forests, 10*(7), 583. https://doi.org/10.3390/f10070583

Li, N., Ren, Z., Li, D., & Zeng, L. (2020). Automated techniques for monitoring the behaviour and welfare of broilers and laying hens: towards the goal of precision livestock farming. *Animal, 14*(3), 617–625.

Liang, Q., Xiang, S., Hu, Y., Coppola, G., Zhang, D., & Sun, W. (2019). PD2SE-Net: computer-assisted plant disease diagnosis and severity estimation network. *Computers and Electronics in Agriculture, 157,* 518–529.

Lin, C. N., Wei, M. Y., Chang, N. T., & Chuang, Y. Y. (2015). The occurrence of Scirtothrips dorsalis Hood in mango orchards and factors influencing its population dynamics in Taiwan. *Journal of Asia-Pacific Entomology, 18*(3), 361–367.

Lind, A. P., & Anderson, P. C. (2019). Predicting drug activity against cancer cells by random forest models based on minimal genomic information and chemical properties. *PloS One, 14*(7), e0219774.

Lowenberg-DeBoer, J., Huang, I. Y., Grigoriadis, V., & Blackmore, S. (2020). Economics of robots and automation in field crop production. *Precision Agriculture, 21*(2), 278–299.

Malek, S., Hui, C., Aziida, N., Cheen, S., Toh, S., & Milow, P. (2019). Ecosystem monitoring through predictive modeling. *Encyclopedia of Bioinformatics and Computational Biology, 3,* 1–8. https://doi.org/10.1016/B978-0-12-809633-8.20060-5

Manida, M. (2022). The Future of Food and Agriculture Trends and Challenges. Agriculture & Food E-Newsletter.

Marković, D., Vujičić, D., Tanasković, S., Đorđević, B., Randić, S., & Stamenković, Z. (2021). Prediction of pest insect appearance using sensors and machine learning. *Sensors,* 21(14), 4846. doi: 10.3390/s21144846

Medar, R. A., & Rajpurohit, V. S. (2014). A survey on data mining techniques for crop yield prediction. *International Journal of Advance Research in Computer Science and Management Studies, 2*(9), 59–64.

Nagasaka, Y., Zhang, Q., Grift, T. E., Knetani, Y., Umeda, N., & Kokuryu, T. (2004, December). Control system design for an autonomous field watching-dog robot. In *International Conference on Automation Technology for Off-road Equipment, ATOE 2004* (pp. 298–304).

Nandhini, M., Pream, V. S., & Vijaya, M. S. (2016). Identification and classification of leaf diseases in turmeric plants. *International Journal of Engineering Research and Applications*, 6(2), 48–54.

Nyabako, T., Mvumi, B. M., Stathers, T., Mlambo, S., & Mubayiwa, M. (2020). Predicting Prostephanus truncatus (Horn)(Coleoptera: Bostrichidae) populations and associated grain damage in smallholder farmers' maize stores: a machine learning approach. *Journal of Stored Products Research*, 87, 101592. https://doi.org/10.1016/j.jspr.2020.101592

Olden, J. D., Lawler, J. J., & Poff, N. L. (2008). Machine learning methods without tears: a primer for ecologists. *The Quarterly Review of Biology*, 83(2), 171–193.

Partel, V., Nunes, L., Stansly, P., & Ampatzidis, Y. (2019). Automated vision-based system for monitoring Asian citrus psyllid in orchards utilizing artificial intelligence. *Computers and Electronics in Agriculture*, 162, 328–336.

Pasqual, G.M., & Mansfield, J. (1998). Development of a prototype expert system for identification and control of insect pests. *Computer and Electronics in Agriculture*, 2, 263–276.

Perez-Ariza, C. B., Nicholson, A. E., & Flores, M. J. (2012, September). Prediction of coffee rust disease using bayesian networks. In *Proceedings of the Sixth European Workshop on Probabilistic Graphical Models* (pp. 259–266).

Power, D.J. & Kaparthi, S. (1998). The changing technological context of decision support systems. In *Context Sensitive Decision Support Systems*. Springer, Boston, MA, pp. 41–54.

Qi, Y., Cinar, G. T., Souza, V. M., Batista, G. E., Wang, Y., & Principe, J. C. (2015). Effective insect recognition using a stacked autoencoder with maximum correntropy criterion. *In 2015 International Joint Conference on Neural Networks (IJCNN)* (pp. 1–7). IEEE.

Rammer, W., & Seidl, R. (2019). Harnessing deep learning in ecology: an example predicting bark beetle outbreaks. *Frontiers in Plant Science*, 10, 1327. https://doi.org/10.3389/fpls.2019.01327

Ramón, M. M., Xu, N., & Christodoulou, C. G. (2005). Beamforming using support vector machines. *IEEE Antennas and Wireless Propagation Letters*, 4, 439–442.

Ruslan, S. A., Muharam, F. M., Zulkafli, Z., Omar, D., & Zambri, M. P. (2019). Using satellite-measured relative humidity for prediction of Metisa plana's population in oil palm plantations: a comparative assessment of regression and artificial neural network models. *PLoS One*, 14(10), e0223968.

Saini, H. S., Kamal, R., & Sharma, A. N. (2002). Web based fuzzy expert system for integrated pest management in soybean. *International Journal of Information Technology*, 8(1), 55–74.

Sangaiah, A. K., Abraham, A., Siarry, P., & Sheng, M. (2017). *Intelligent Decision Support Systems for Sustainable Computing: Paradigms and Applications* (Vol. 705). Springer. https://doi.org/10.1007/978-3-319-53153-3_1

Shelake, S., Sutar, S., Salunkher, A., Patil, S., Patil, R., Patil, V., & Tamboli, T. (2021). Design and implementation of artificial intelligence powered agriculture multipurpose robot. *International Journal of Research in Engineering, Science and Management*, 4(8), 165–167.

Shen, Y., Zhou, H., Li, J., Jian, F., & Jayas, D. S. (2018). Detection of stored-grain insects using deep learning. *Computers and Electronics in Agriculture*, 145, 319–325.

Simonite, T. (2016). Algorithms that learn with less data could expand AI's power. *MIT Technology Review, 601551.*

Siraj, F., & Arbaiy, N. (2006). Integrated pest management system using fuzzy expert system. In *Proceedings of Knowledge Management International Conference & Exhibition (KMICE),* Legend Hotel Kuala Lumpur, Malaysia. Universiti Utara Malaysia, Sintok (pp. 169–176).

Skawsang, S., Nagai, M., Tripathi, N. K., & Soni, P. (2019). Predicting rice pest population occurrence with satellite-derived crop phenology, ground meteorological observation, and machine learning: a case study for the Central Plain of Thailand. *Applied Sciences, 9*(22), 4846. https://doi.org/10.3390/app9224846

Soini, C. T., S., Fellah, & M. R. Abid, (2019, April). Citrus greening infection detection (cigid) by computer vision and deep learning. *In Proceedings of the 2019 3rd International Conference on Information System and Data Mining* (pp. 21–26). ACM.

Song, Y. Y., & Ying, L. U. (2015). Decision tree methods: applications for classification and prediction. *Shanghai Archives of Psychiatry, 27*(2), 130. doi: 10.11919/j.issn.1002-0829.215044

Su, W. H. (2020). Advanced machine learning in point spectroscopy, RGB-and hyperspectral-imaging for automatic discriminations of crops and weeds: a review. *Smart Cities, 3*(3), 767–792.

Sucharith, P., Suprith, K. P., Kasturi, U., & Ajina, A., (2020). Applications of fuzzy expert systems in farming. In *Fuzzy Expert Systems and Applications in Agricultural Diagnosis* (pp. 50–70). IGI Global. doi: 10.4018/978-1-5225-9175-7.ch004

Talaviya, T., Shah, D., Patel, N., Yagnik, H., & Shah, M. (2020). Implementation of artificial intelligence in agriculture for optimisation of irrigation and application of pesticides and herbicides. *Artificial Intelligence in Agriculture, 4,* 58–73. https://doi.org/10.1016/j.aiia.2020.04.002.

Thessen, A. (2016). Adoption of machine learning techniques in ecology and earth science. *One Ecosystem, 1,* e8621.

Thompson, J. A., Roecker, S., Grunwald, S., & Owens, P. R. (2012). *Digital soil mapping: Interactions with and applications for hydropedology.* Advances in Modeling, Mapping, and Coupling. doi: 10.1016/B978-0-12-386941-8.00021-6

Tripathy, A. K., Adinarayana, J., & Sudharsan, D. (2012). Data mining and wireless sensor network for groundnut pest thrips dynamics and predictions. *Journal of Emerging Trends in Computing and Information Sciences, 3*(6), 913–929.

van Klompenburg, T., Kassahun, A., & Catal, C., (2020). Crop yield prediction using machine learning: a systematic literature review. *Computers and Electronics in Agriculture, 177,* 105709. https://doi.org/10.1016/j.compag.2020.105709

Vembandasamy, K., Sasipriya, R., & Deepa, E. (2015). Heart diseases detection using Naive Bayes algorithm. *International Journal of Innovative Science, Engineering & Technology, 2*(9), 441–444.

Wong, K. C. (2017). Evolutionary algorithms: concepts, designs, and applications in bioinformatics. In *Nature-Inspired Computing: Concepts, Methodologies, Tools, and Applications* (pp. 111–137). IGI Global. doi: 10.4018/978-1-5225-0788-8.ch006

Xiao, Q., Li, W., Kai, Y., Chen, P., Zhang, J., & Wang, B. (2019). Occurrence prediction of pests and diseases in cotton on the basis of weather factors by long short term memory network. *BMC Bioinformatics, 20*(25), 1–15.

Xing, S., Lee, M., & Lee, K. K. (2019). Citrus pests and diseases recognition model using weakly dense connected convolution network. *Sensors, 19*(14), 3195. https://doi.org/10.3390/s19143195

Yan, Y., Feng, C. C., Wan, M. P. H., & Chang, K. T. T. (2015, October). Multiple regression and artificial neural network for the prediction of crop pest risks. In *International Conference on Information Systems for Crisis Response and Management in Mediterranean Countries* (pp. 73–84). Springer, Cham.

Yang, B. S., Kim, K., & Rao, R. B. (2002). Condition classification of reciprocating compressors using radial basis function neural network. *International Journal of COMADEM*, *5*(4), 12–20.

Yuan, Y., Chen, L., Wu, H., & Li, L. (2021). Advanced agricultural disease image recognition technologies: a review. *Information Processing in Agriculture*, *9*(1), 48–59. https://doi.org/10.1016/j.inpa.2021.01.003

Zhang, W., Jing, T., & Yan, S. (2017). Studies on prediction models of Dendrolimus superans occurrence area based on machine learning. *Journal of Beijing Forestry University*, *39*(1), 85–93.

Zhang, Z. (2016). Introduction to machine learning: k-nearest neighbors. *Annals of Translational Medicine*, *4*(11), 218. doi: 10.21037/atm.2016.03.37.

Zorić, A. B. (2020). Benefits of educational data mining. *Journal of International Business Research and Marketing*, *6*(1), 12–16.

Chapter 14

Applying Clustering Technique for Rainfall Received by Different Districts of Maharashtra State

Nitin Jaglal Untwal

Department of Management, Maharashtra Institute of Technology, Aurangabad, Maharashtra, India

Contents

DOI: 10.1201/9781003311782-14

14.1 Introduction

Maharashtra is situated in the north-central part of India. Arabian Sea is on the west side and Madhya Pradesh and Chhattisgarh share northern borders of Maharashtra. The southern border is shared by the states of Andhra Pradesh and Karnataka. The Sayadri ranges (Western Ghats) spread from north to south and it separates the coastal districts of Thane, Raigad, Ratnagiri, and Sindhudurg from other parts of Maharashtra. The average height of these Western Ghats is one kilometer and spread across 800 km. The Western Ghats are ridges that run across at right angle to monsoon winds creating an important climate divide. The Western Ghats and Konkan region get very heavy rainfall. The state receives rainfall during southwest monsoon winds (June to September). The lifeline and important rivers originate from Western Ghats and flow toward the east. The important rivers include Krishna, Bhima, and Godavari [1–5].

Rainfall is an important factor for the growth and development of the agriculture sector. Agriculture activities are mostly dependent on the amount of rainfall received during a particular period. Rainfall in a particular region can be estimated by way of developing a predictive model like Auto-Regressive Integrated Moving Average (ARIMA). Rainfall is having a very unstable character and hence understanding or identifying homogeneous rainfall regions is important as a part of regional climate studies. The identification of the region with the amount of rainfall received and categorizing or clustering it to form a group or clusters. These groups and clusters help the government to plan irrigation projects in order to fulfill the agriculture needs; hence, this study titled "Applying Clustering for Rainfall received by the different district of Maharashtra state" is conducted [6–9].

Machine learning includes unsupervised learning under which models are trained for unlabeled data sets and are allowed to act without any supervision. Unsupervised learning is applied to understand the meaningful patterns, a grouping inherent in data and extracting the generative features. Unsupervised learning is an algorithm that learns patterns from untagged data or unlabeled data.

Cluster analysis is used to determine similarities and dissimilarities in a given data set or objects. Data usually have some similarities which enable us to categorize or group them into clusters. The K-mean clustering is nonhierarchical. The reason for the popularity of K-mean clustering is its simplicity. K-mean clustering is a type of partitioning method having objects as data observations with nearest location and distance from each other. The nearest objects form mutually exclusive clusters. Each cluster is having its centroid which makes clusters distinctive.

Clustering is a technique of grouping the elements; it is an important method for classification and grouping. K-mean clustering is used to classify elements in different categories on the basis of the nearest distance from the mean. The main objective of K-mean clustering is creating a partition of n objects into k-clusters. Objects belonging to different clusters are considered on the basis of the closest average (mean).

It is represented by the following equation:

$$J = \sum_{j=1}^{k} \sum_{i=1}^{n} \left\| x_i^{(j)} - c_j \right\|^2 \tag{14.1}$$

where J = Objective function, k = Number of clusters, n = Number of cases, x = Number of cases i, and c_j = Centroid.

Drawbacks of K-mean clustering:

a. The early stage clusters affect the overall results.
b. When data set size is small, clustering is not accurate.
c. As we give variables the same weightage, we do not know which variable occupies more relevance in the clustering process.
d. The noise can reduce the accuracy of mean which further pulls the centroid away from its original position.

How to overcome the above drawbacks:

a. To increase the accuracy, data set should also be increased.
b. Use median to prevent outlier (noise).v

14.2 Research Methodology

Data source
Data taken for the study is from the Government of Maharashtra websites.
Period of study
The study period is commencing from 1901and ends in 2020. The data selected for analysis is monthly annual rainfall (Climatologically Normal) for Maharashtra district-wise.
Software used for Data Analysis
Python Programming.
Model applied
For the purpose of this study, we had applied K-mean clustering.
Limitations of the study
The study is restricted to only the Districts of Maharashtra state.
Future scope
A similar kind of cluster analysis can be done for Western India or Southern India.

Research is carried out in five steps:

■ Feature extraction and engineering
■ Data extraction
■ Standardizing and Scaling
■ Identification of Clusters
■ Cluster formation

14.3 Feature Engineering

It is an important element of machine learning pipeline. For the suitable representation of data, we need to craft the given raw data. The raw data need to be evaluated by applying domain knowledge, mathematical transformations, etc., to get good features. It also needs to process and wrangle for making it ready to be used for machine learning models or algorithms. It is very difficult to create a good machine learning model unless we have an in-depth idea about feature engineering. Feature engineering helps in model improvement by increasing the overall performance of the model.

Frames are introduced by Mervin Minsky as a data structure. Frames consist of a collection of slots and slot values. The slot contains information about the entities which are as follows:

a. Frame identification
b. Relationship with other frames
c. Descriptor of the requirement for frame
d. Procedural information
e. New instance information

14.4 Data Extraction

It is the process of fetching the data from an external source to a program and making it readable. The purpose of this study is to fetch raw data from the Government of Maharashtra (website) in the form of (Excel) file. The Excel file is named Maha.Excel and is fetched to Python program by using the code below (Figure 14.1).

Data is cleaned by removing the district column from the data frame by applying the python code below (Figure 14.2).

14.5 Standardizing and Scaling

The machine learning algorithm can work efficiently only when the input variables are standardized and scaled properly to a given range since the rainfall data had a huge variation which needs to be converted into scaling (Figure 14.3). When there is a good amount of variation in the data set, it needs to be converted to equal magnitude. The difference in magnitude can create difficulty since the K-mean algorithm is a distance-based algorithm. Scaling can be done by applying a standardizing method. Standardizing is the method where we bring down the standard deviation and mean of features to 1 and 0.

```
In [9]:  import pandas as pd

         data = pd.read_excel (r'C:\Users\nitin\Desktop\Maha.xlsx')
         print (data)
```

	DISTRICT	JAN	FEB	MAR	APR	MAY	JUN	JUL	AUG	SEP
0	AHMEDNAGAR	0.6	1.3	3.0	5.3	21.6	104.9	101.8	91.8	139.1
1	DHULE	2.5	1.0	3.2	1.6	10.3	117.5	168.9	131.4	105.7
2	JALGAON	3.3	2.4	4.3	1.4	7.5	132.1	191.0	195.6	123.1
3	KOLHAPUR	1.0	0.8	4.6	25.9	60.2	351.5	723.7	477.2	185.2
4	NASHIK	1.2	0.5	1.0	4.7	15.1	154.9	315.0	259.0	183.3
5	PUNE	0.6	0.1	1.6	7.6	27.4	156.9	312.9	225.1	166.1
6	SANGLI	1.7	0.8	4.3	22.6	54.0	119.0	150.6	107.2	131.3
7	SATARA	0.7	0.7	3.1	14.0	36.4	150.7	254.4	175.2	143.5
8	SOLAPUR	2.7	1.5	3.4	9.2	29.8	102.7	99.8	101.6	170.1
9	NANDURBAR	1.0	0.0	0.3	1.5	9.3	137.6	301.4	243.3	146.1
10	AURANGABAD	2.5	1.6	3.1	2.8	17.1	130.4	156.3	157.9	149.6
11	BEED	2.5	2.0	3.8	7.0	19.7	128.3	136.2	137.0	167.9
12	NANDED	4.9	4.5	8.4	8.8	15.9	155.2	247.1	242.6	171.5
13	OSMANABAD	3.4	2.6	3.9	7.5	26.3	132.1	154.2	154.2	182.9
14	PARBHANI	5.8	2.9	7.9	7.5	14.4	154.6	215.3	219.9	167.4
15	LATUR	4.4	3.6	7.8	11.5	21.1	144.8	217.9	220.4	169.4
16	JALNA	3.2	2.0	4.5	2.7	17.5	139.3	165.0	159.9	142.2
17	HINGOLI	5.0	4.8	7.2	6.1	13.4	185.2	243.3	255.7	164.9
18	AKOLA	8.6	5.3	8.8	4.4	9.7	142.9	226.3	204.3	128.8
19	AMRAVATI	10.1	6.3	7.8	3.7	6.4	137.2	254.2	243.8	151.4
20	BHANDARA	15.9	13.2	17.7	10.2	11.4	168.0	376.4	391.2	201.6
21	BULDHANA	4.6	3.0	6.1	2.9	8.0	139.7	191.5	195.3	120.1
22	CHANDRAPUR	11.4	8.9	14.6	10.8	11.6	180.6	374.0	374.1	203.1
23	NAGPUR	13.7	10.9	15.9	9.7	11.0	158.0	308.9	280.6	176.4
24	YAVATMAL	8.6	4.6	11.0	7.7	11.9	173.6	267.1	262.8	151.5
25	WARDHA	11.2	9.2	13.1	8.5	15.9	169.7	273.6	273.2	163.8
26	GADCHIROLI	9.6	7.6	14.0	12.2	17.0	209.2	454.0	441.4	198.4
27	WASHIM	9.0	5.7	7.5	4.9	8.3	173.0	245.4	250.4	156.8
28	GONDIA	15.2	11.2	16.3	9.1	8.4	174.1	418.1	424.3	212.3

Figure 14.1   Data fetching in Python Environment for clustering.

```
In [10]:  # Remove DISTRICT columns
          data.drop(['DISTRICT'], axis=1, inplace=True)
          data.shape

Out[10]:  (29, 12)
```

Figure 14.2   Data cleaning by dropping DISTRICT column from data frame.

```
In [12]:  # standardizing the data
          from sklearn.preprocessing import StandardScaler
          scaler = StandardScaler()
          data_scaled = scaler.fit_transform(data)

          # statistics of scaled data
          pd.DataFrame(data_scaled).describe()
```

Figure 14.3   Descriptive statistics for scaled data.

Applying the python code as follows:

	0	1	2	3	4	5	6	7	8	9	10	11
count	2.90E+01	2.90E+01	2.90E+01	2.90E+01	2.90E+01	2.90E+01	2.90E+01	2.90E+01	2.90E+01	2.90E+01	2.90E+01	2.90E+01
mean	3.22E-16	-2.68E-16	-1.38E-16	1.44E-16	2.41E-16	-2.49E-17	-2.45E-16	1.23E-16	-2.07E-16	-7.66E-17	-3.37E-16	-6.97E-16
std	1.02E+00	1.02E+00	1.02E+00	1.02E+00	1.02E+00	1.02E+00	1.02E+00	1.02E+00	1.02E+00	1.02E+00	1.02E+00	1.02E+00
min	-1.12E+00	-1.14E+00	-1.42E+00	-1.19E+00	-9.52E-01	-1.21E+00	-1.29E+00	-1.47E+00	-2.14E+00	-1.67E+00	-1.51E+00	-2.00E+00
25%	-6.99E-01	-7.78E-01	-7.82E-01	-6.48E-01	-6.45E-01	-5.43E-01	-7.35E-01	-7.82E-01	-6.82E-01	-5.93E-01	-7.44E-01	-6.59E-01
50%	-2.82E-01	-3.34E-01	-2.23E-01	-8.90E-02	-2.68E-01	-1.20E-01	-1.19E-01	-1.28E-01	1.45E-01	-2.17E-01	-2.91E-01	-1.87E-01
75%	7.27E-01	4.43E-01	3.35E-01	3.08E-01	2.04E-01	3.11E-01	3.93E-01	2.51E-01	5.89E-01	5.56E-01	7.03E-01	5.40E-01
max	2.24E+00	2.52E+00	2.18E+00	3.23E+00	3.28E+00	4.44E+00	3.73E+00	2.40E+00	1.98E+00	2.91E+00	2.06E+00	2.86E+00

14.6 Identification of Clusters by the Elbow Method

The Elbow method is used to find out clusters in a given data set. In this method, we plot the explained variation as a function of clusters. The elbow of the curves defines the number of clusters. This indicates that the definite number of clusters further adds more clusters and does not give much better modeling data.

There are various tools to measure explained variation. Explained variation measures the ratio to which a given model accounts for dispersion. Variation is measured by variance. Increasing the number of clusters improves the fit (explained variation) as more parameters (clusters) are used but this is overfitting and the elbow method removes this constraint. In clustering identification, the number of K identification is a difficult task. The optimum number of K can be defined by applying the Elbow method.

Inertia is the measure of how well defined are the clusters in a data set by applying K-mean. It is calculated by measuring the distance between the data points and their centroid, calculating the square of the distance and further adding these squares across one cluster. An optimum model is one having lower inertia and less number of clusters.

Inertia is calculated as follows:

$$Inertia\ (k) = \sum\nolimits_{\{i \backslash in\ C\_k\}} \left(y\_{\{ik\}} - \mu\_k\right)^{\wedge}2 \qquad (14.2)$$

where μ_k = mean of a cluster, k and C_k = set of indices of genes attributed to cluster k.

Now, we will carry out the process of cluster identification by creating an Elbow plot and further by calculating inertia.

Before identifying the clusters numbers, we assume that three clusters exist, but after applying the Elbow technique, we get to know the exact number of clusters existing in a given data set (Figure 14.4). Further, we will calculate the inertia. Inertia is the sum of square error for each cluster, hence lowering the denser inertia of the clusters. In our case, the inertia is 5, by applying the Python code below:

14.7 Cluster Formation

As we apply the python code below (Figure 14.5), we get the results for clusters 1–5 for different districts of Maharashtra according to their characteristics and features.

```
In [17]:  # fitting multiple k-means algorithms and storing the values in an empty list
          SSE = []
          for cluster in range(1,20):
              kmeans = KMeans(n_jobs = -1, n_clusters = 3 , init='k-means++')
              kmeans.fit(data_scaled)
              SSE.append(kmeans.inertia_)

          # converting the results into a dataframe and plotting them
          frame = pd.DataFrame({'Cluster':range(1,20), 'SSE':SSE})
          plt.figure(figsize=(12,6))
          plt.plot(frame['Cluster'], frame['SSE'], marker='o')
          plt.xlabel('Number of clusters')
          plt.ylabel('Inertia')
```

```
Out[17]:  Text(0, 0.5, 'Inertia')
```

Figure 14.4   Number of cluster formation for scaled data.

```
In [18]:  # k means using 5 clusters and k-means++ initialization
          kmeans = KMeans(n_jobs = -1, n_clusters = 5, init='k-means++')
          kmeans.fit(data_scaled)
          pred = kmeans.predict(data_scaled)

          C:\Users\nitin\anaconda3\lib\site-packages\sklearn\cluster\_kmeans.py:938: Futu
          reWarning: 'n_jobs' was deprecated in version 0.23 and will be removed in 0.25.
          warnings.warn("'"'n_jobs' was deprecated in version 0.23 and will be"

In [19]:  frame = pd.DataFrame(data_scaled)
          frame['cluster'] = pred
          frame['cluster'].value_counts()

In [44]:  pd.set_option("display.max_rows", None, "display.max_columns", None)

          print(frame['cluster'])
          0     4
          1     4
          2     4
          3     3
          4     1
          5     1
          6     1
          7     1
          8     1
          9     4
          10    4
          11    1
          12    0
          13    1
          14    0
          15    1
          16    4
          17    0
          18    0
          19    0
          20    2
          21    4
          22    2
          23    2
          24    0
          25    2
          26    2
          27    0
          28    2
          Name: cluster, dtype: int32
```

Figure 14.5   Cluster formation results with classification for scaled data.

14.8 Results and Analysis

We categorized the data selected for analysis as monthly annual rainfall (Climatologically Normal) for Maharashtra district-wise into five clusters as follows:

Cluster one – High Rainfall

In cluster one, the highest average rainfall is observed in Nashik district with 85.5 mm climatologically average (refer Table 14.1). The highest monthly rainfall of 315 mm is also registered in Nashik district. The second-highest average rainfall is observed in Pune district with 84.64 mm and 312 mm for the period under the study. The average monthly rainfall for Satara district and Latur district is 74.04 mm and 75.83 mm. The lowest average rainfall was registered in Solapur district with 53.87 mm.

Cluster one represents a category of districts having high rainfall in Maharashtra. The reason for high rainfall is the geographical position of these districts which is near to the Western Ghats. The Western Ghats have most of the rainfall from the southwest monsoon.

Cluster two – Moderate Rainfall

In cluster two, the Gadchiroli district has the highest average rainfall of 120.81 mm (refer Table 14.2). The highest average monthly rainfall for cluster two is recorded as 454 mm. All districts under cluster two have a very good average monthly rainfall; at the same time, the average highest monthly rainfall is above 300 mm except Wardha. The district grouped in cluster two has high rainfall in the months of July and August. The monsoon delivers a good amount of rainfall. The cluster two districts have a significant forest area under its geographical coverage which also contributes to good monsoon.

Table 14.1 Average Minimum and Maximum Rainfall for Cluster One

Code	District	Average	Min	Max
4	NASHIK	85.8	0.5	315
5	PUNE	84.64167	0.1	312.9
6	SANGLI	60.88333	0.8	150.6
7	SATARA	76.04167	0.7	254.4
8	SOLAPUR	53.875	1.5	170.1
11	BEED	59.03333	2	167.9
13	OSMANABAD	64.94167	2.6	182.9
15	LATUR	75.83333	3.6	220.4

Table 14.2   Average Minimum and Maximum Rainfall for Cluster Two

Code	District	Average	Min	Max
28	GONDIA	114.225	8.4	424.3
26	GADCHIROLI	120.8167	6.4	454
25	WARDHA	85.58333	8.5	273.6
22	CHANDRAPUR	106	7.9	374.1
23	NAGPUR	89.03333	9.7	308.9
20	BHANDARA	107.725	10.2	391.2

Another reason which contributes to high rainfall is the southwest monsoon which originates in Bay of Bengal and progressively moves inland and mostly affects central India and Vidharbha region.

Cluster three – High Moderate Rainfall

Kolhapur receives a good and consistent rainfall from June to September; at the same time, it receives good rainfall in the months of October and December (refer Table 14.3).

Cluster four – Average Rainfall

The monsoon system developed in the Arabian Sea is hogged by Kokan, Nashik, and Pune giving only scanty rainfall to these districts (refer Table 14.4). The region sandwich between Vidarbha and Konkan has the worst rainfall. The district under cluster four has a fluctuation in rainfall patterns since 1901. The monsoon in the cluster four district is uncertain and poor. The cluster four district mostly has a dry spell. The average monthly rainfall ranges from 47.76 mm low with Ahmednagar district and Dhule with 50.6 mm which shows poor rainfall in the region. The cluster four district receives a low rainfall from both the monsoon winds.

Cluster five – Below-average Rainfall

The worst and the lowest rainfall affected district is included in cluster five (refer Table 14.5). The southwest monsoon worst affected part is accompanied by cluster five. The dry spell of the southwest monsoon is the most responsible factor for below-average rainfall.

Table 14.3   Average Minimum and Maximum rainfall for Cluster Three

Code	District	Average	Min	Max
3	KOLHAPUR	166.0667	0.8	723.7

Table 14.4 Average Minimum and Maximum Rainfall for Cluster Four

Code	District	Average	Min	Max
0	AHMEDNAGAR	47.76667	0.6	139.1
1	DHULE	50.6	1	168.9
2	JALGAON	60.90833	1.4	195.6
9	NANDURBAR	74.225	0	301.4
10	AURANGABAD	59.68333	1.6	157.9
16	JALNA	60.80833	2	165
21	BULDHANA	62.24167	2.9	195.3

Table 14.5 Average Minimum and Maximum rainfall for Cluster Five

Code	District	Average	Min	Max
12	NANDED	80.09167	4.5	247.1
14	PARBHANI	74.75	2.9	219.9
17	HINGOLI	81.61667	4.8	255.7
18	AKOLA	67.95	4.4	226.3
19	AMRAVATI	74.78333	3.7	254.2
24	YAVATMAL	81.9	4.6	267.1
27	WASHIM	78.40833	4.9	250.4

14.9 Conclusion

The districts in Maharashtra state are categorized on the basis of rainfall received as climatology average monthly rainfall for twelve months (1901–2020). The number of cluster categories to be five which will help to formulate policy toward agriculture. The cluster analysis also helps in identifying regional imbalance in rainfall. Cluster one represents a category of districts having high rainfall in Maharashtra. The reason for high rainfall is the geographical position of these districts which is near to the Western Ghats. The district grouped in cluster two has high rainfall in the month of July and August. The monsoon delivers a good amount of rainfall. The cluster two districts have a significant forest area under its geographical coverage which also contributes to good monsoon. The monsoon system developed in the Arabian Sea is hogged by Kokan, Nashik, and Pune giving only scanty rainfall to these districts. The region sandwich between Vidarbha and Konkan has the worst rainfall. The district under cluster four has a fluctuation in rainfall patterns since 1901. The monsoon in the cluster four district is uncertain and poor. The cluster four district mostly has a dry spell. The average monthly rainfall ranges from 47.76 mm low with Ahmednagar district and Dhule with 50.6 mm which shows poor rainfall in the region. The worst and the lowest rainfall affected district is included in cluster five. The southwest monsoon worst affected part is accompanied by cluster five. The dry spell of the southwest monsoon is the most responsible factor for below-average rainfall.

References

1. J.C. Bezdek, *Pattern Recognition with Fuzzy Objective Function Algorithms*, Plenum Press, New York, (1981).
2. Y.D. Chen, G. Huang, Q. Shao, and C.-y. Xu, *Regional analysis of low flow using l-moments for Dongjiang Basin, South China*, Hydrolog. Sci. J. 51 (2006), 1051–1064. doi: 10.1623/hysj.51.6.1051
3. F. Dikbas, M. Firat, A.C. Koc, and M. Gungor, *Classification of precipitation series using fuzzy cluster method*, Int. J. Climatol. 32 (2012), 1596–1603. doi: 10.1002/joc.2350
4. J.C. Dunn, *A fuzzy relative of the isodata process and its use in detecting compact well separated clusters*, J. Cyber. 3 (1974), 32–57. doi: 10.1080/01969727308546046
5. M.K. Goyal and V. Gupta, *Identification of homogeneous rainfall regimes in Northeast Region of India using fuzzy cluster analysis*, Water Resour. Manag. 28 (2014), 4491–4511. doi: 10.1007/s11269-014-0699-7
6. J.A. Greenwood, J.M. Landwehr, N.C. Matalas, and J.R. Wallis, *Probability weighted moments: Definition and relation to parameters of several distributions expressable in inverse form*, Water. Resour. Res. 15 (1979), 1049–1054. doi: 10.1029/WR015i005p01049
7. L. Gao, D. Liu, G. Feng Luo, G. Jie Song, and F. Min. *First-arrival picking through fuzzy c-means and robust locally weighted regression*. Acta Geophys. 47 (2021), 1623–1636.
8. M. Tükel, E. Tunçbilek, A. Komerska, G. Aydın Keskin, and M. Arıcı. *Reclassification of climatic zones for building thermal regulations based on thermoeconomic analysis: A case study of Turkey*. Energy Buildings 246 (2021), 111121. https://doi.org/10.1016/j.enbuild.2021.111121
9. N.B. Guttman, *The use of L-moments in the determination of regional precipitation climates*. J. Clim. 6 (1993), 2309–2325. doi: 10.1175/1520-0442(1993)006<2309:TUOLMI>2.0.CO;2

Chapter 15

Predicting Rainfall for Aurangabad Division of Maharashtra by Applying Auto-Regressive Moving Average Model (ARIMA) Using Python Programming

Nitin Jaglal Untwal

Department of Management, Maharashtra Institute of Technology, Aurangabad, Maharashtra, India

Contents

DOI: 10.1201/9781003311782-15

313

15.1 Introduction

Marathawada Division or Aurangabad Division is located at the center of Maharashtra state. It has eight districts under its territorial jurisdiction. The Marathawada region was formed by the Nizam of Hyderabad state. It shares borders with Andhra Pradesh and Karnataka. It lies east of Khandesh and west of Vidharba [1, 2]. The Marathawada region receives rainfall from southwest monsoon winds. The agriculture sector in this region is dependent on Monsoon rainfall. The Monsoon is uncertain in nature for the Marathawada region since sometimes it is having floods, sometimes having draughts. The Monsoon is uncertain in nature since dry spells hamper the rainfall. The rainy season starts in June and ends up in September. The rainfall is uncertain as the Monsoon is poor; hence due to uncertainty in the climatic condition, the agriculture sector had to suffer [3–5]. As stated above about the problem of inconsistent rainfall, researchers had decided to investigate by conducting the study titled "Predicting rainfall for Aurangabad Division of Maharashtra by applying Auto-Regressive Moving Average Model (ARIMA) using Python programming [6–11]. Time series analysis using the ARIMA model is an emerging area in predictive analytics. It had attracted researchers because of its utility and accuracy. The main objective of the ARIMA model is to study the past observation based on which the future model is generated to forecast a given variable. The success of the ARIMA model depends on appropriate model identification and evaluation.

It is important to understand under what circumstances the ARIMA model is applied.

- No dependent variable is available.
- Good sufficient past data is available.
- Autocorrelation.
  Every predictive model requires an independent variable. It is also important to correlate with the independent and dependent variables to proceed with creating an ARIMA model. In some cases, we do not have a separate independent variable having a linear relationship with the dependent variable; in such a condition, we need to consider the ARIMA model since it considers the past values of the variable to forecast its future value.
- Good sufficient past data is available
  For developing an ARIMA model, we always required good structured and complete past data. The data should be sufficient to apply the ARIMA model. The data should have consistency regarding time intervals (Monthly, Quarterly, Year-wise).
- Autocorrelation
  The data must be autocorrelated. The past values of variables should have a linear relationship. Autocorrelation is the first and the most important test before applying the ARIMA model.

15.2 ARIMA Model

Predicting the future value of a variable in the area of finance, science, economics, and weather forecasting, the important factor is to select the optimal model which can predict accurate forecasts depending on historical data. The ARIMA model is considered to be the most reliable model in such a situation. The ARIMA model was proposed by Box and Jenkins in 1970. The model had wide areas of application in forecasting and showed tremendous potential to generate a short-term forecast [6–15].

The ARIMA model analyzes the forecast of equally spaced univariate time series. An ARIMA (AR) stands for Auto-Regressive which states that there exists a relationship between the past values and the future values, (I) stands for Integrated, and (MV) stands for Moving Average [16–25].

It is represented by the following equation:

$$yt = \Phi 0 + \Phi 1 \; yt - 1 + \Phi 2 \; yt - 2 + \cdots + \Phi p \; yt - p$$
$$+ \varepsilon t - \theta 1 \; \varepsilon \; t - 1 - \theta 2 \; \varepsilon \; t - 2 - \cdots - \theta q \; \varepsilon \; t - q \tag{15.1}$$

where actual values of the data are denoted as yt; coefficients are denoted as Φi and θj. The random errors are denoted by εi and the degrees of Auto-Regressive and Moving Averages are represented by integer's p and q.

The ARIMA model is a mixture of two equations. Auto-Regressive is the equation based on past lags and Moving Average is the equation based on error.

15.3 Research Methodology

Data source
Data taken for the study is from the State Government website.
Period of study
The study period is commencing in 1901and ends in 2015. The interval for data selected for analysis is yearly annual rainfall for Marathawada (now Aurangabad Division).
Software used for Data Analysis
Python Programming.
Model applied
For the purpose of this study, we had applied the ARIMA model.
Limitation of the study
The study is restricted to the Marathawada region only.
Future scope of the study
In the future, the study can be extended by adding the overall region of Maharashtra state.

Methodology

For creating a predictive rainfall model, we had selected and applied the ARIMA model. The research is carried out in three steps. First, we need to check the Autocorrelation further; we need to evaluate different ARIMA models and select the appropriate model. The best fit model is selected after comparing the AIC score of different ARIMA models.

Research is carried out in three steps:

- Model Identification
- Model Evaluation
- Parameter Estimation

15.4 Model Identification

In ARIMA model identification, we need to first check the Autocorrelation at different Lag1, Lag2, Lag3, Lag4, Lag5, etc. Further, we need to ensure the test of stationary. In stationary, the time series mean, variance, and Autocorrelation are constant.

Autocorrelation refers to the relationship between successive values of the same variable. Now here, we will be checking the Autocorrelation in our time series data by using Python programming. Checking the Autocorrelation at different lags (Figures 15.1–15.5) shows an Autocorrelation plot for Lag = 1 to Lag = 5 for Marathawada.

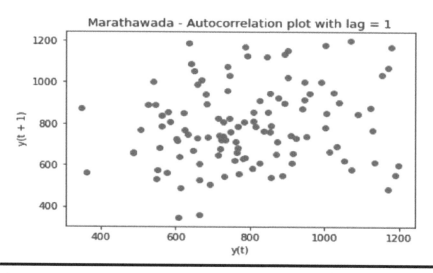

Figure 15.1   Autocorrelation plot with Lag = 1 for Marathawada.

The above plot in Figure 15.1 shows a very weak degree of Autocorrelation for Lag = 1; hence, we further check the Autocorrelation for Lag =2.

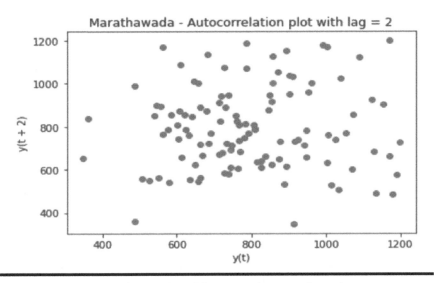

Figure 15.2   Autocorrelation plot with Lag = 2 for Marathawada.

The above plot in Figure 15.2 shows a very weak degree of Autocorrelation for Lag = 2; hence, we further check the Autocorrelation for Lag = 3.

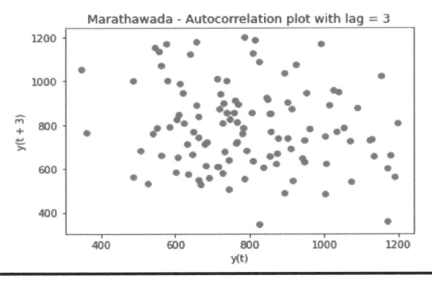

Figure 15.3   Autocorrelation plot with Lag = 3 for Marathawada.

The above plot in Figure 15.3 shows a very weak degree of Autocorrelation for Lag = 3; hence, we further check the Autocorrelation for Lag = 4.

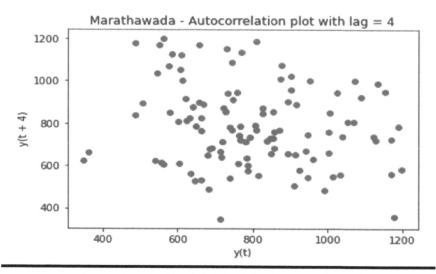

Figure 15.4   Autocorrelation plot with Lag = 4 for Marathawada.

The above plot in Figure 15.4 shows a very poor degree of Autocorrelation for Lag = 4; hence, we further check the Autocorrelation for Lag = 5.

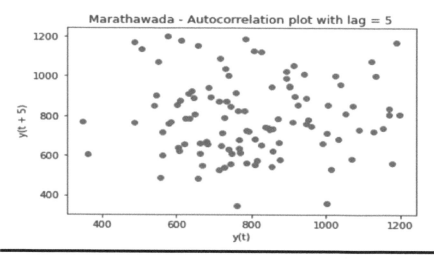

Figure 15.5   Autocorrelation plot with Lag = 5 for Marathawada.

The above plot in Figure 15.5 shows a very weak degree of Autocorrelation for Lag = 5. The above plot Lag1 to Lag5 depicts almost no Autocorrelation (Figures 15.1–15.5 show the Autocorrelation plot for Lag = 1 to Lag = 5 for Marathawada). The test of stationery can be further assessed by rolling mean and rolling standard deviation.

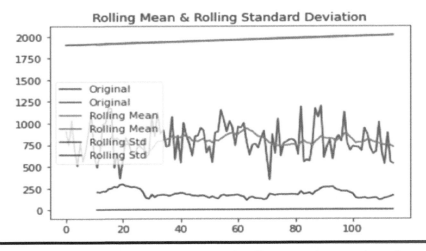

Figure 15.6 **Rolling Standard Deviation and Rolling Mean for Marathawada.**

The time series is not stationary since the rolling standard deviation and rolling mean increase with time. Figure 15.6 shows Rolling Standard Deviation and Rolling Mean for Marathawada. The data is not stationary; we need to first convert data into stationary. It requires log transformation to stabilize the variance. To apply log transformation, we need to make the difference (d). How many times we take difference as reflected indifference (d) and it is better to start with a minimum difference of *d=1*.

As one of the best methods of identifying the best ARIMA model here, we are considering the more reliable method of Akaike Information Criterion (AIC) for ARIMA model evaluation.

15.5 Model Evaluation

For model evaluation, we need to calculate the AIC for various models. It determines the order of an ARIMA model.

It is represented as follows:

$$AIC = -2 \, Log \, (L) + 2 \left(p + q + k + 1 \right) \dots \dots \qquad (15\text{-}2)$$

where L is the Likelihood of the data, $K = 1$ If $c \neq 0$ and $K = 0$ if $c = 0$.

We have tested seven ARIMA models. Below (Figures 15.7–15.14) are the details of different ARIMA models as python programming output. The ARIMA model (1,1,1) have an AIC of 2588.73.

27/04/2022, 14:23   marathawada testeted original

```
 ARIMA Model Results
==============================================================================
Dep. Variable:                   D.y   No. Observations:              194
Model:                 ARIMA(1, 1, 1)   Log Likelihood            -1290.365
Method:                       css-mle   S.D. of innovations          184.905
Date:               Tue, 08 Jun 2021   AIC                         2588.730
Time:                        11:54:01   BIC                         2601.802
Sample:                             1   HQIC                        2594.023

==============================================================================
                 coef    std err          z      P>|z|      [0.025      0.975]
------------------------------------------------------------------------------
const         -0.0677      0.289     -0.235      0.815      -0.633       0.498
ar.L1.D.y      0.1877      0.071      2.640      0.008       0.048       0.327
ma.L1.D.y     -0.9999      0.014    -69.201      0.000      -1.028      -0.972
                                  Roots
==============================================================================
                 Real           Imaginary           Modulus         Frequency
------------------------------------------------------------------------------
AR.1            5.3282           +0.0000j            5.3282            0.0000
MA.1            1.0001           +0.0000j            1.0001            0.0000
```

Figure 15.7   Results for ARIMA (1,1,1) model.

The ARIMA model (1,0,1) has an AIC of 2596.14 with significant p-values.

27/04/2022, 14:26   marathawada testeted original

```
 ARMA Model Results
==============================================================================
Dep. Variable:                     y   No. Observations:              195
Model:                    ARMA(1, 1)   Log Likelihood            -1294.073
Method:                       css-mle   S.D. of innovations          184.426
Date:               Tue, 08 Jun 2021   AIC                         2596.146
Time:                        11:56:11   BIC                         2609.238
Sample:                             0   HQIC                        2601.447

==============================================================================
                 coef    std err          z      P>|z|      [0.025      0.975]
------------------------------------------------------------------------------
const        793.2267     16.274     48.742      0.000     761.330     825.123
ar.L1.y        0.2279      0.218      1.044      0.297      -0.200       0.656
ma.L1.y       -0.0474      0.216     -0.220      0.826      -0.470       0.375
                                  Roots
==============================================================================
                 Real           Imaginary           Modulus         Frequency
------------------------------------------------------------------------------
AR.1            4.3884           +0.0000j            4.3884            0.0000
MA.1           21.0938           +0.0000j           21.0938            0.0000
```

Figure 15.8   Results for ARIMA (1,0,1) model.

The ARIMA model (1,0,0) has an AIC of 2594.19 with significant p-values.

27/04/2022, 14:27 marathawada testeted original

```
ARMA Model Results
==============================================================================
Dep. Variable:                      y   No. Observations:                  195
Model:                     ARMA(1, 0)   Log Likelihood               -1294.097
Method:                       css-mle   S.D. of innovations            184.448
Date:                Tue, 08 Jun 2021   AIC                           2594.193
Time:                        11:56:34   BIC                           2604.012
Sample:                             0   HQIC                          2598.169

==============================================================================
                 coef    std err          z      P>|z|      [0.025      0.975]
------------------------------------------------------------------------------
const        793.2507     16.120     49.209      0.000     761.656     824.845
ar.L1.y        0.1815      0.071      2.569      0.010       0.043       0.320
                                    Roots
=============================================================================
                  Real          Imaginary           Modulus         Frequency
-----------------------------------------------------------------------------
AR.1            5.5088           +0.0000j            5.5088            0.0000
-----------------------------------------------------------------------------
```

Figure 15.9 Results for ARIMA (1,0,0) model.

The ARIMA model (2.1,1) results – the ARIMA model (2,1,1) have an AIC of 2590.51.

27/04/2022, 14:29 marathawada testeted original

```
ARIMA Model Results
==============================================================================
Dep. Variable:                    D.y   No. Observations:                  194
Model:                 ARIMA(2, 1, 1)   Log Likelihood               -1290.255
Method:                       css-mle   S.D. of innovations            184.832
Date:                Tue, 08 Jun 2021   AIC                           2590.510
Time:                        11:57:08   BIC                           2606.850
Sample:                             1   HQIC                          2597.126

==============================================================================
                 coef    std err          z      P>|z|      [0.025      0.975]
------------------------------------------------------------------------------
const         -0.0715      0.299     -0.239      0.811      -0.657       0.514
ar.L1.D.y      0.1820      0.072      2.524      0.012       0.041       0.323
ar.L2.D.y      0.0339      0.072      0.469      0.639      -0.108       0.176
ma.L1.D.y     -0.9999      0.014    -69.784      0.000      -1.028      -0.972
                                    Roots
=============================================================================
                  Real          Imaginary           Modulus         Frequency
-----------------------------------------------------------------------------
AR.1            3.3740           +0.0000j            3.3740            0.0000
AR.2           -8.7396           +0.0000j            8.7396            0.5000
MA.1            1.0001           +0.0000j            1.0001            0.0000
-----------------------------------------------------------------------------
```

Figure 15.10 Results for ARIMA (2,1,1) model.

The ARIMA model (2.0,1) results – the ARIMA model (2,0,1) have an AIC of 2596.91.

```
27/04/2022, 14:30                                            marathawada testeted original

ARMA Model Results
==============================================================================
Dep. Variable:                      y   No. Observations:                  195
Model:                     ARMA(2, 1)   Log Likelihood               -1293.457
Method:                       css-mle   S.D. of innovations            183.837
Date:                Tue, 08 Jun 2021   AIC                           2596.914
Time:                        11:57:52   BIC                           2613.279
Sample:                             0   HQIC                          2603.540

==============================================================================
                 coef    std err          z      P>|z|      [0.025      0.975]
------------------------------------------------------------------------------
const        793.0335     16.960     46.760      0.000     759.793     826.274
ar.L1.y       -0.2744      0.301     -0.913      0.361      -0.864       0.315
ar.L2.y        0.1536      0.083      1.859      0.063      -0.008       0.316
ma.L1.y        0.4462      0.296      1.506      0.132      -0.135       1.027
                                    Roots
=============================================================================
                  Real          Imaginary           Modulus         Frequency
-----------------------------------------------------------------------------
AR.1           -1.8103           +0.0000j            1.8103            0.5000
AR.2            3.5968           +0.0000j            3.5968            0.0000
MA.1           -2.2410           +0.0000j            2.2410            0.5000
-----------------------------------------------------------------------------
```

Figure 15.11 Results for ARIMA (2,0,1) model.

The ARIMA model (2.1,0) results – the ARIMA model (2,1,0) have an AIC of 2642.61.

```
27/04/2022, 14:32                                            marathawada testeted original

ARIMA Model Results
==============================================================================
Dep. Variable:                    D.y   No. Observations:                  194
Model:                 ARIMA(2, 1, 0)   Log Likelihood               -1317.307
Method:                       css-mle   S.D. of innovations            215.014
Date:                Tue, 08 Jun 2021   AIC                           2642.615
Time:                        11:58:15   BIC                           2655.686
Sample:                             1   HQIC                          2647.908

==============================================================================
                 coef    std err          z      P>|z|      [0.025      0.975]
------------------------------------------------------------------------------
const         -1.5743      9.597     -0.164      0.870     -20.384      17.235
ar.L1.D.y     -0.4815      0.071     -6.772      0.000      -0.621      -0.342
ar.L2.D.y     -0.1310      0.072     -1.831      0.067      -0.271       0.009
                                    Roots
=============================================================================
                  Real          Imaginary           Modulus         Frequency
-----------------------------------------------------------------------------
AR.1           -1.8381           -2.0632j            2.7633           -0.3658
AR.2           -1.8381           +2.0632j            2.7633            0.3658
```

Figure 15.12 Results for ARIMA (2,1,0) model.

The ARIMA model (2.0,0) results – the ARIMA model (2,0,0) have an AIC of 2596.03.

27/04/2022, 14:33 marathawada testeted original

```
ARMA Model Results
==============================================================================
Dep. Variable:                      y   No. Observations:                  195
Model:                     ARMA(2, 0)   Log Likelihood               -1294.019
Method:                       css-mle   S.D. of innovations            184.374
Date:                Tue, 08 Jun 2021   AIC                           2596.038
Time:                        12:01:43   BIC                           2609.130
Sample:                             0   HQIC                          2601.339

==============================================================================
                 coef    std err          z      P>|z|      [0.025      0.975]
------------------------------------------------------------------------------
const        793.1707     16.583     47.831      0.000     760.669     825.672
ar.L1.y        0.1766      0.072      2.462      0.014       0.036       0.317
ar.L2.y        0.0283      0.072      0.394      0.693      -0.113       0.169
                                    Roots
=============================================================================
                  Real          Imaginary           Modulus         Frequency
-----------------------------------------------------------------------------
AR.1            3.5923           +0.0000j            3.5923            0.0000
AR.2           -9.8228           +0.0000j            9.8228            0.5000
-----------------------------------------------------------------------------
```

Figure 15.13 Results for ARIMA (2,0,0) model.

27/04/2022, 14:35 marathawada testeted original

```
ARIMA Model Results
==============================================================================
Dep. Variable:                    D.y   No. Observations:                  194
Model:                 ARIMA(1, 1, 1)   Log Likelihood               -1290.365
Method:                       css-mle   S.D. of innovations            184.905
Date:                Tue, 08 Jun 2021   AIC                           2588.730
Time:                        11:54:01   BIC                           2601.802
Sample:                             1   HQIC                          2594.023

==============================================================================
                 coef    std err          z      P>|z|      [0.025      0.975]
------------------------------------------------------------------------------
const         -0.0677      0.289     -0.235      0.815      -0.633       0.498
ar.L1.D.y      0.1877      0.071      2.640      0.008       0.048       0.327
ma.L1.D.y     -0.9999      0.014    -69.201      0.000      -1.028      -0.972
                                    Roots
=============================================================================
                  Real          Imaginary           Modulus         Frequency
-----------------------------------------------------------------------------
AR.1            5.3282           +0.0000j            5.3282            0.0000
MA.1            1.0001           +0.0000j            1.0001            0.0000
-----------------------------------------------------------------------------
```

Figure 15.14 Results for ARIMA (1,1,1) model.

Table 15.1   Different ARIMA Model with Akaike Information Criterion (AIC)

Sl. No.	ARIMA Model	AIC	BIC	Likelihood
1	(1,1,1)	2588	2601	-1290
2	(1,0,1)	2596	2609	-1294
3	(1,0,0)	2594	2604	-1294
4	(2,1,1)	2590	2606	-1290
5	(2,0,1)	2596	2613	-1293
6	(2,1,0)	2642	2655	-1317
7	(2,0,0)	2596	2609	-1294

15.6 Parameter Estimation

The AIC score is used to compare models (refer Figures 15.7–15.14). The model with a lower score is considered to be the best fit. The next step is to compare the AIC, BIC, and likelihood scores of different ARIMA models. The best ARIMA model is the lowest with AIC, BIC, and likelihood scores are selected as the best. The ARIMA model (1,1,1) has registered the lowest AIC, BIC, and likelihood scores with significant p-values. Table 15.1 describes various ARIMA model with AIC. In Table 15.1, we can find the value of AIC, BIC, and likelihood.

15.7 Conclusion

After trial and testing with different ARIMA models, the ARIMA model (1,1,1) is found to be fit for predicting the annual rainfall of Marathawada with significant p-values. We have selected the best ARIMA model depending on the AIC. The model is ranked to select the best ARIMA model. The AIC, BIC, and likelihood scores of different ARIMA models are then compared. The best ARIMA model is the lowest with AIC, BIC, and likelihood scores are selected as the best. The ARIMA model (1,1,1) has registered the lowest AIC, BIC, and likelihood scores with significant p-values.

References

1. Box, G., and G. Jenkins. 1976. *Time Series Analysis Forecasting and Control*. 31, 238–242. Holden-Day, Inc., San Francisco, CA.
2. Chen, L., J. Peng, Z. Liu, and R. Zhao. 2017. "Pricing and Effort Decisions for a Supply Chain with Uncertain Information." *International Journal of Production Research* 55 (1): 264–284.

3. Chen, L., J. Peng, C. Rao, and I. Rosyida. 2018. "Cycle Index of Uncertain Random Graph." *Journal of Intelligent and Fuzzy Systems* 34 (24): 1–11.
4. Deng, Z., J. Ma, and H. Du. 2002. "Two-Segment Least Square Method for Parameter Estimation of ARMA Model." *Science Technology and Engineering* 2 (5): 3–5.
5. Diamond, P. 1988. "Fuzzy Least Squares." *Information Sciences* 46 (3): 141–157.
6. Ding, F., D. Meng, J. Dai, Q. Li, A. Alsaedi, and T. Hayat. 2018. "Least-Squares Based Iterative Parameter Estimation Algorithm for Stochastic Dynamical Systems with ARMA Noise Using the Model Equivalence." *International Journal of Control, Automation and Systems* 16 (3): 630–639.
7. Feng, J., and Y. Lan. 2019. "Regulating a Firm with Bilateral Unknown Demands." *Journal of Data, Information and Management* 1 (4): 117–128.
8. Fu, H., and Z. Wang. 2004. "Determination Method of Parameter Function of Generalized Time-Varying ARMA Model." *Mechanical Strength* 26 (6): 636–641.
9. Wold, H. 1938. *A study in the analysis of stationary time series* (Doctoral dissertation). Almqvist & Wiksell.
10. Khodabandeh, M., and A. M. Shahri. 2014. "Uncertainty Evaluation for a Dezert-Smarandache Theory-Based Localization Problem." *International Journal of General Systems* 43 (6): 610–632.
11. Li, J. 1994. "Application of ARMA Time Series Model in Modal Parameter Identification." *Journal of Mechanical Engineering of Drainage and Irrigation* 4 (1): 54–57.
12. Li, Y., and Y. Liu. 2019. "A Risk-Averse Multi-item Inventory Problem with Uncertain Demand." *Journal of Data, Information and Management* 1 (4): 77–90.
13. Lio, W., and B. Liu. 2018a. "Residual and Confidence Interval for Uncertain Regression Model with Imprecise Observations." *Journal of Intelligent and Fuzzy Systems* 35 (2): 2573–2583.
14. Lio, W., and B. Liu. 2018b. "Uncertain Data Envelopment Analysis with Imprecisely Observed Inputs and Outputs." *Fuzzy Optimization and Decision Making* 17 (3): 357–373.
15. Liu, B. 2007. *Uncertainty Theory.* 2nd ed. Berlin: Springer-Verlag.
16. Liu, B. 2009. "Some Research Problems in Uncertainty Theory." *Journal of Uncertain Systems* 3 (1): 3–10.
17. Liu, B. 2010. *Uncertainty Theory: A Branch of Mathematics for Modeling Human Uncertainty.* Berlin: Springer-Verlag.
18. Sheng, Y., and S. Kar. 2015. "Some Results of Moments of Uncertain Variable through Inverse Uncertainty Distribution." *Fuzzy Optimization and Decision Making* 14 (1): 57–76.
19. Tanaka, H., S. Uejima, and K. Asai. 1982. "Linear Regression Analysis with Fuzzy Model." *IEEE Transactions on Systems, Man, and Cybernetics* 12 (6): 903–907.
20. Walker, G. 1931. "On Periodicity in Series of Related Terms." *Proceedings of the Royal Society of London* 131 (818): 518–532.
21. Yang, X., and B. Liu. 2019. "Uncertain Time Series Analysis with Imprecise Observations." *Fuzzy Optimization and Decision Making* 18 (3): 263–278.
22. Yao, K. 2018. "Uncertain Statistical Inference Models with Imprecise Observations." *IEEE Transactions on Fuzzy Systems* 26 (2): 409–415.

23. Yao, K., and B. Liu. 2018. "Uncertain Regression Analysis: An Approach for Imprecise Observations." *Soft Computing* 22 (17): 5579–5582.
24. Yule, G. 1927. "On a Method of Investigating Periodicities in Disturbed Series, with Special Reference to Wolfer's Sunspot Numbers." *Philosophical Transactions of the Royal Society of London* 226 (226): 267–298.
25. Zhai, J., and M. Bai. 2017. "Mean-Variance Model for Portfolio Optimization with Background Risk Based on Uncertainty Theory." *International Journal of General Systems* 12 (22): 294–312.

Index

Note: Locators in *italics* represent figures and **bold** indicate tables in the text.